Criticism and Literary Theory 1890 to the Present

Chris Baldick

Longman

London and New York

Longman Group Limited,
Longman House, Burnt Mill,
Harlow, Essex CM20 2JE, England
and Associated Companies throughout the world.

*Published in the United States of America
by Longman Publishing, New York*

© Longman Group Limited 1996

First published 1996

ISBN 0 582 033810 CSD
ISBN 0 582 033837 PPR

British Library Cataloguing in Publication Data

A catalogue record for this book is
available from the British Library

Library of Congress Cataloging-in-Publication Data
Baldick, Chris.
    Criticism and literary theory 1890 to the present / Chris Baldick.
      p. cm. -- (Longman literature in English series)
    Includes bibliographical references and index.
    ISBN 0–582–03381–0 (csd). -- ISBN 0–582–03383–7 (ppr)
    1. Criticism. I. Title. II. Series.
PN81.B294 1996
801'.95'0904--dc20   95–40515
                                                      CIP

Set by 20 in 9½ on 11pt Bembo
Produced by Longman Singapore Publishers (Pte) Ltd
Printed in Singapore

To Maudie

Contents

Editors' Preface

The multi-volume Longman Literature in English Series provides students of literature with a critical introduction to the major genres in their historical and cultural context. Each volume gives a coherent account of a clearly defined area, and the series, when complete, will offer a practical and comprehensive guide to literature written in English from Anglo-Saxon times to the present. The aim of the series as a whole is to show that the most valuable and stimulating approach to the study of literature is that based upon an awareness of the relations between literary forms and their historical contexts. Thus the areas covered by most of the separate volumes are defined by period and genre. Each volume offers new and informed ways of reading literary works, and provides guidance for further reading in an extensive reference section.

In recent years, the nature of English studies has been questioned in a number of increasingly radical ways. The very terms employed to define a series of this kind – period, genre, history, context, canon – have become the focus of extensive critical debate, which has necessarily influenced in varying degrees the successive volumes published since 1985. But however fierce the debate, it rages around the traditional terms and concepts.

As well as studies on all periods of English and American literature, the series includes books on criticism and literary theory and on the intellectual and cultural context. A comprehensive series of this kind must of course include other literatures written in English, and therefore a group of volumes deals with Irish and Scottish literature, and the literatures of India, Africa, the Caribbean, Australia and Canada. The forty-seven volumes of the series cover the following areas: Pre-Renaissance English Literature, English Poetry, English Drama, English Fiction, English Prose, Criticism and Literary Theory, Intellectual and Cultural Context, American Literature, Other Literatures in English.

David Carroll
Michael Wheeler

Longman Literature in English Series

General Editors: David Carroll and Michael Wheeler
Lancaster University

Pre-Renaissance English Literature

* ★ English Literature before Chaucer *Michael Swanton*
* English Literature in the Age of Chaucer
* ★ English Medieval Romance *W. R. J. Barron*

English Poetry

* ★ English Poetry of the Sixteenth Century *Gary Waller*
* ★ English Poetry of the Seventeenth Century *George Parfitt (Second Edition)*
* English Poetry of the Eighteenth Century, 1700–1789
* ★ English Poetry of the Romantic Period, 1789–1830 *J. R. Watson (Second Edition)*
* ★ English Poetry of the Victorian Period, 1830–1890 *Bernard Richards*
* English Poetry of the Early Modern Period, 1890–1940
* ★ English Poetry since 1940 *Neil Corcoran*

English Drama

* English Drama before Shakespeare
* ★ English Drama: Shakespeare to the Restoration, 1590–1660 *Alexander Leggatt*
* ★ English Drama: Restoration and Eighteenth Century, 1660–1789 *Richard W. Bevis*
* English Drama: Romantic and Victorian, 1789–1890
* English Drama of the Early and Modern Period, 1890–1940
* English Drama since 1940

English Fiction

* ★ English Fiction of the Eighteenth Century, 1700–1789 *Clive T. Probyn*
* ★ English Fiction of the Romantic Period, 1789–1830 *Gary Kelly*
* ★ English Fiction of the Victorian Period, 1830–1890 *Michael Wheeler (Second Edition)*
* ★ English Fiction of the Early Modern Period, 1890–1940 *Douglas Hewitt*
* English Fiction since 1940

English Prose

* ★ English Prose of the Seventeenth Century, 1590–1700 *Roger Pooley*
  English Prose of the Eighteenth Century
  English Prose of the Nineteenth Century

Criticism and Literary Theory

  Criticism and Literary Theory from Sidney to Johnson
  Criticism and Literary Theory from Wordsworth to Arnold
* ★ Criticism and Literary Theory, 1890 to the Present *Chris Baldick*

The Intellectual and Cultural Context

  The Sixteenth Century
* ★ The Seventeenth Century, 1603–1700 *Graham Parry*
* ★ The Eighteenth Century, 1700–1789 *James Sambrook (Second Edition)*
  The Romantic Period, 1789–1830
* ★ The Victorian Period, 1830–1890 *Robin Gilmour*
  The Twentieth Century: 1890 to the Present

American Literature

  American Literature before 1880
* ★ American Poetry of the Twentieth Century *Richard Gray*
* ★ American Drama of the Twentieth Century *Gerald M. Berkowitz*
* ★ American Fiction 1865–1940 *Brian Lee*
* ★ American Fiction since 1940 *Tony Hilfer*
* ★ Twentieth-Century America *Douglas Tallack*

Other Literatures

  Irish Literature since 1800
  Scottish Literature since 1700
  Australian Literature
* ★ Indian Literature in English *William Walsh*
  African Literature in English: East and West
  Southern African Literature in English
  Caribbean Literature in English
* ★ Canadian Literature in English *W. J. Keith*

★ *Already published*

Acknowledgements

We are grateful to the following for permission to reproduce copyright material.

Faber & Faber Ltd/Harcourt Brace & Co for extracts from *Selected Essays* by T S Eliot, copyright 1950 by Harcourt Brace Jovanovich Inc. renewed 1978 by Esme Valerie Eliot and an extract from *Selected Prose of T S Eliot* ed. Frank Kermode (Faber & Faber, 1975), copyright © 1975 by Valerie Eliot; Methuen & Co Ltd for extracts from *Sacred Wood* by T S Eliot (7th ed. 1950).

Author's Preface

This book aims to provide students of literature with a critical introduction to the major developments in literary criticism and literary theory in English since the 1890s. This is an exceptionally crowded field of enquiry, to which no volume of this size could do justice without some degree of simplifying compression. So I have not attempted, as several previous studies have done, to engage in prolonged consideration of a few major or representative critics. As I explain further in the Introduction, I have concentrated not so much on the major figures in themselves as on the principal critical debates and problems as they have presented themselves to successive generations, and the schools or alliances that have developed around those debates. The account I offer here, then, is not a succession of studies in the thought of individual critics – although some brief presentation of individual positions must play its part – but an introduction to the changing 'agenda', as I call it, of critical discussion in the English-speaking world. The advantages of such an approach are, first, that it embraces a wider spectrum of critical writing than simply the work of the 'major' critics, and, second, that it brings the views of different critics into relation with one another, showing each position as a partial response to others within a continually unfolding series of dialogues. Readers who wish to pursue further their interests in particular critics will find in the reference section at the back of this book a sequence of biographical and bibliographical notes on fifty significant critics, with recommendations for further reading on each of them.

The structure of this book follows a chronological design involving a somewhat arbitrary division of the period into four phases: from 1890 until the end of the Great War; from 1918 until the end of the Second World War; from 1945 until the revolutionary turmoil of 1968; and from 1968 until the early 1990s. In one sense, then, the book is a short and selective history of criticism and literary theory in English in the century from 1890. One chapter is devoted to each of the four phases, but within each chapter chronology gives way to a topical subdivision. At the start of each chapter there is an attempt to define the distinctive 'agenda' of problems and tasks with which critics of that time were confronted, or which they set for themselves. This is followed by two or three sections on the main lines of development and debate in the period, and then by special sections devoted to Shakespeare criticism, criticism of the novel, and changing conceptions of the literary canon; a final section takes a wider view of general trends in criticism such as the social and national contexts of critical writing and publication. It should, then, be possible for a reader who is particularly interested in following the development of Shakespeare criticism, or of theories of the novel, to hop through the relevant specialist sections, although of course these sections will make more sense in the context of the larger developments mapped in the first half of each chapter.

I hope that the chronological divisions of this history will not prove too distracting, and that they will not be taken as hard boundaries. All such divisions are arbitrary to some degree, but I trust that the chapters themselves will justify the scheme by showing each of the four phases to have its own special concerns. If this book had been devoted principally to the careers of the major critics, then there would indeed be an awkward artificiality in breaking, say, the work of F. R. Leavis or of Cleanth Brooks across the line defined by the year 1945. But since its actual focus is upon the successive debates, movements, and schools within the critical arena, the highlighting, however artificial, of generational divisions should still serve a useful purpose.

It might seem an even more glaring artificiality in this book's scope to find that unlike so many recent accounts of modern literary theory, it confines its attention to critical work written in English. Most introductory works in this field are in effect – and for good reason – brief guides to aspects of recent French and German philosophy, psychology, and anthropology, with some additional attention to older Russian and Swiss linguistics. They are usually introductions to particular schools of *thought*, whereas this book attempts to offer an introduction to a substantial body of *writing* in English, in other words to a special genre of literature – criticism – that fully deserves its own volumes in this Longman Literature in English Series. The parameters of the series offer an occasion upon which it is appropriate to isolate the Anglophone traditions of critical writing in the twentieth century, and to examine them for themselves. This is, to be sure, a good deal easier when dealing with criticism in the first two-thirds of the century, when the English-speaking critical world was relatively self-enclosed, than it is for the flourishing of literary theory after the late 1960s, when that world seemed suddenly to have made Paris its capital. I hope that in my last chapter, in which this potential problem could be expected to present itself, I have not in fact underestimated the important influences of continental European thought; my aim has merely been to place these influences (which have not been starved of attention) 'offstage' for the purpose of this exposition. So long as this device is not mistaken for some sinister chauvinist 'marginalization', it may serve harmlessly enough to clarify the object of our enquiry.

If there is anything really scandalous in the design of this work, it lies in the apportioning of almost equal space to the four chronological phases. This is, quite deliberately, an affront to the vanities of the present generation, which, in each age, imagines that its current preoccupations are uniquely worthy of discussion, the concerns of the previous age having been definitively exposed as benighted illusion. Since the 1970s, this kind of thinking has been encouraged on a wide scale, and the critical writing of previous decades has, to the standard retrospect, been allowed to shrink into a single bogey of Error. Arrogances of this sort are usually condemned to being regarded, in their turn, by the next generation as blindspots or 'provincialisms' of the intellect; and if this book can correct them in a small way by drawing attention to the variety and vitality of criticism in earlier decades, it will have served a useful end.

Having declared some of the limits of this work, I should remind the reader that it is designed also to point beyond them by indicating other books that treat its subject, and aspects of it, in greater detail and from different standpoints. The appendices include general bibliographies of works on modern criticism, and special bibliographies of works of individual critics. Also provided in the appendices is a chronology of critical works, in parallel with chronologies of historical events and of other literary publications. A special feature of this chronology is that it includes notable critical journals as well as books of criticism and literary theory.

I would like to thank the University of Lancaster for granting a term's sabbatical leave during the preparation of this book; the staffs of the Cambridge University Library and the Lancaster University Library; my former colleagues Alison Easton, Keith Hanley, Tony Pinkney, Richard Wilson, and Scott Wilson, and others at Lancaster who discussed this project with me; the series editors, David Carroll and Michael Wheeler, for their encouragement and patience; John Simons and Ian Patterson for their generous gifts of critical memorabilia, and above all Maud Ellmann for reading and improving all the earlier drafts.

CB
Cambridge, April 1995

Chapter 1
Introduction

In the century after 1890, literary criticism and theory underwent remarkable transformations. A pursuit engaged in by a few dozen gentlemen-amateurs and journalists in a handful of metropolitan centres converted itself into a profession comprising a corps of thousands within the worldwide academic and publishing industries, linked by countless specialist journals and international conferences. Its vocabulary and concepts, once generally available to the educated readership of public journals, refined themselves into specialist technical and theoretical terminologies with their own dictionaries and glossaries. Its dialogue with that educated readership, with whom in Victorian times it shared a range of common assumptions, standards, and tastes, became a more persistently antagonistic or 'adversarial' campaign on behalf of disconcerting modernist literary experiments: formerly delegated to assess past and present literary work by the standards of consensual public taste, it assumed for itself the new duty of scrutinizing that public taste itself by the standards of a disaffected intellectual and artistic minority. Yoking the ideals of literary modernism to the professional codes and routines of the universities, it entered – between the 1920s and the 1960s – a 'heroic' phase of innovation and expansion, claiming at times to have become the very centre of modern culture and supreme guardian of its values. Even as it subsided into a phase of self-consuming scepticism in the 1970s, it claimed to have undermined the rival disciplines of history, philosophy, and psychology by collapsing them into its own domain of 'fictions' or 'texts', and to have placed itself on an equal footing with the creative literature that it had once humbly served. This story of literary criticism's expanding ambitions and achieved cultural prominence forms a significant – and at times sensational – chapter in the history of intellectual life in the modern English-speaking world.

The following chapters will attempt to give a more detailed version of this story and its subsidiary episodes. As a necessary preliminary, though, it will be worth clearing the ground with some consideration of certain general problems involved in making sense of this story: problems of definition that repeatedly haunt any attempt to decide what 'criticism' is, at any given time, and what its limits may be; problems of determining the nature of 'progress' (or decline) in the history of criticism; and problems of identifying and connecting the protagonists – critics, schools of criticism, journals, institutions, ideologies – of that history. This introductory chapter will first address these questions, partly in order to emphasize the complexity of the historian's task in this field, and therefore the degree to which this book's account of modern criticism remains open to revision and challenge. It will then go on to offer an outline of the major developments in criticism and literary theory in the century as a whole, within the framework of which the reader can better grasp the stages and episodes traced in the four chronological chapters that follow.

Nothing is more likely to introduce fundamental confusions into the discussion of criticism and its history than the common assumption that 'criticism' is and has been a single and continuous activity. We use the term as a convenient catch-all label for a varied field of different, often competing activities and discussions, usually forgetting both this diversity and the historical variations within it. Such habits are abetted by some standard histories of criticism, like W. K. Wimsatt's and Cleanth Brooks's *Literary Criticism: A Short History* (1957), which explicitly assert that criticism throughout the ages has been a continuous debate around the same perennial problems, and by university courses in the history of criticism, which, since the late nineteenth century, have commonly thrown together philosophical writings on poetic fictions in general (Aristotle, Plato, Kant) with biographical prefaces to the works of particular authors (Johnson, Arnold), defences of poetry's moral standing (Sidney, Shelley), debates on the relative stature of ancient and modern authors (Dryden, Eliot), psychologies of the imagination (Burke, Coleridge, Keats), general diagnoses of cultural malaise (Arnold, Eliot, Leavis), analyses of individual works (Bradley, Empson), and manifestos of poetic practice (Horace, Wordsworth), erasing the boundaries between the various discourses – neighbouring, sometimes overlapping, but still distinct – within which these authors and their audiences were writing and reading. The temptation to overlook the specific *occasions* which both generate and distinguish these various kinds of writing is matched by the habit of regarding the history of criticism as a sequence of interchangeable *ideas* without reference to the social and cultural position of the 'critic'. There is an important difference between the incidental writings of an ancient Greek philosopher on poetics, or a sixteenth-century courtier on rhetoric, and the works of a 'man of letters' operating in the modern literary marketplace that was opened up only in the eighteenth century, just as there will be generic differences among the writings of the same 'man of letters' according to the occasion: a review, a literary biography, an editorial preface, a treatise on poetics, a manifesto, a parody, a public lecture, an anthology, and a dedicatory epistle. If we begin to acknowledge this variety, we can recognize too the impossibility of settling any definition of 'criticism' in pure form. The term covers too many kinds of discussion, each of them linked with other activities and discourses – philosophy, journalism, politics, linguistics, biography, psychology, gossip, pedagogy, ritual commemoration, aesthetics, dramaturgy, bibliography, ethics, history, censorship, and advertising. Criticism, then, is a hybrid or bastard discourse, or an arena of intermingling and jostling discourses, with no convincing pedigree that could entitle it to sovereignty over a single and integral domain.

If criticism thrives upon its own impurities, this does not mean that the dream of purity has not from time to time possessed it. The idea of a literary criticism liberated from all 'external' influences and pursuing a single, self-defined goal may be, as I would argue, an illusion; but it has nonetheless made its mark upon the history of modern criticism, in successive campaigns to rescue critical discourse from the thrall of other powerful discourses. The efforts of nineteenth-century Aestheticism to detach criticism from the categories of morality comprise one major instance, and another is the determination of the American 'New Critics' in the middle of the twentieth century to release critical analysis from the domination of historical and linguistic scholarship. Other critics in this period have sought either to disqualify certain kinds of critical discussion as foreign intrusions from rival discourses, or to renounce the entire confused legacy of past critics so as to found criticism anew on 'scientific' principles. That these campaigns should all eventually fail is hardly surprising; but that they should have been launched at all says something significant about literary criticism in the modern age. Much of the history of literary criticism since Matthew Arnold's essays of the 1860s is a record of attempts to claim the title of 'criticism' for one set of activities – comparative judgement, or interpretation, or structural analysis, or political critique – while debarring the others. A full account of any twentieth-century critics or critical schools should include not only the specific kinds of critical discourse in which they engaged, but also the kinds that they neglected or repudiated.

The specification of discourses which I am desiderating for an ideal account of criticism would need to be applied both to general distinctions such as that between philosophical and journalistic discourses and their respective audiences, and to more detailed contrasts between critical writings in different genres. As I have suggested above, our understanding of criticism, as a form of literature has not yet benefited from any adequate analysis, or even enumeration, of its sub-genres; but it should be clear to anybody who reads those antique texts that have belatedly been categorized as 'criticism', that certain genres have died out since the eighteenth century, while others have taken their place. The verse epistle containing advice to younger authors may still be practised by way of homage to Horace and Pope, but if so, it has had no importance as criticism. Playwrights no longer open their performances with defensive prologues, as Dryden did, although some – like Bernard Shaw and Edward Bond – have used the opportunity of the printed edition to publish a political essay. The dedication to a noble patron was once – in Dryden's day, again – a significant genre, or at least occasion, of critical writing, but it has died along with the patronage system. In place of these forms there developed new genres of criticism for the public marketplace of literature in the eighteenth century: the book review, and the semi-biographical preface to the works of an author. Samuel Johnson's *Lives of the Poets* were at first designed for the latter purpose. In the Romantic age, the public lecture-series on literary topics assumed a certain prominence in the critical practice of Coleridge and Hazlitt, but the privileged genre was the aggressive-defensive preface of the literary innovator, Wordsworth's Prefaces of 1800 and 1802 to *Lyrical Ballads* being the classic example. Victorian readers could sample a different kind of criticism again, in the longer general literary and biographical articles of such purveyors of 'the higher journalism' as the *Cornhill*, the *Westminster* or the *Fortnightly*. In the later decades of the nineteenth century, they also witnessed the more frequent publication of book-length life-and-works studies of individual authors, most of them by 'men of letters', some by university professors, all ultimately descended from Johnson's *Lives*. The scholarly journal, in which one might read an article on punctuation or phonetics in relation to some literary work, was also born in this period.

The twentieth century cannot claim to have invented any significant new genre of criticism apart from the radio talk (really a version of the public lecture) and the paperback blurb (for which there are some precedents in Victorian advertising), but it established for itself new systems and hierarchies of inherited critical genres. Especially favoured was the 'essay in criticism', which in the middle of the century tended to mean – as it had not in the Victorian age – an interpretative essay on a particular work. The critical essay, in this particular text-centred version, was the standard form of training and assessment in the university literature course, and it was the basis for related forms such as the public lecture, the editorial preface, the article in a learned journal, and the extended book review or 'review article', although each of these forms required a different tone and particular conventions of its own. Most books of criticism in this period are not extended expositions of a single argument or investigation, but collections of essays originally written for different occasions and subsequently gathered within the same covers in the hope that they share some common theme or intellectual disposition. T. S. Eliot's *The Sacred Wood* (1920), a landmark in modern criticism, is just such a collection of old reviews and incidental essays. The same critic's hugely influential essay 'The Metaphysical Poets' (1921) in *Homage to John Dryden* (1924) was originally a review of Herbert Grierson's scholarly anthology of *Metaphysical Lyrics and Poems of the Seventeenth Century*, and indeed it borrows many of its ideas from Grierson's own introduction to that work. This has not prevented the essay from being read as a manifesto. Ezra Pound's book *Make It New* (1934), whose title is frequently cited as the major slogan of modernism itself is, ironically, a retrospective gathering of essays and reviews which were not at all new: most of them were fifteen years old when the book appeared. To take later examples, F. R. Leavis's *The Common Pursuit* (1952) collects several essays written upon various occasions over a period of twenty years, and Lionel Trilling's *The Liberal Imagination* (1950), is a miscellany of reviews, essays, lectures, and prefaces from the previous ten years, most of them revised since their original versions: five of its chapters were originally delivered as conference papers or lectures and then published in journals; four were originally editorial introductions to other books, of which three were for popular reprints of classic American novels; most of the others were review articles when they first appeared in one of half-a-dozen periodicals to which Trilling contributed in the 1940s. The subjects discussed range from Tacitus to the recent Kinsey Report (1948) on male sexuality, but Trilling claims in the preface that they have, nonetheless, a certain unity.

Other notable books of literary criticism are published versions of lectures and similar talks. The famous instances are A. C. Bradley's *Shakespearean Tragedy* (1904) and E. M. Forster's *Aspects of the Novel* (1927), but once could add several others including T. S. Eliot's *The Use of Poetry and the Use of Criticism* (1933), Frank Kermode's *The Sense of an Ending* (1967), and Raymond Williams's *The English Novel from Dickens to Lawrence* (1970). The distinguishing requirements of this genre are that the lecture should be digestible by the relevant audience in its spoken form, without reference to footnotes (although these will appear in the published text), and that it should be sufficiently varied and entertaining rather than densely involved, as a scholarly article might be. An unusual product of the lecture-hall is I. A. Richards's *Practical Criticism* (1929), which incorporates numerous samples of his students' written exercises. The lecture series will usually involve numerous contrasts and comparisons between the works of different writers, and sometimes the construction of some sort of tradition or lineage. This makes it an exercise very different from the genre of the prefatory essay to a reprinted 'classic', which is necessarily focused upon the contexts and special historical importance of one novel or selection of verse. In their different ways, then, the lecture and the essay are the constituent forms from which books of literary criticism are built. Surprisingly few important works of criticism are extended book-length treatments of single subjects, and most of these are either examples of the genre of critical biography (or similar single-author study) or revised versions of doctoral theses – like Jonathan Culler's *Structuralist Poetics* (1975) – or both, as in the case of Lionel Trilling's *Matthew Arnold* (1939). Several major critics, T. S. Eliot and

Virginia Woolf among them, never wrote such extended critical mono-
graphs, confining themselves entirely to lectures and essays.

The differentiation of critical genres rests ultimately upon the diversity
of possible *audiences* for criticism. Here, the dominant fact of twentieth-
century criticism is the divergence between, on the one hand, the public
marketplace of literary consumption in which the book-review and the
literary biography have favoured places, and, on the other, the enclosed
space of the university, where the published lecture-series, the theoretical
textbook, and the scholarly article are the more respected forms. The
presumed audience of the 'public' critic will be the ideal 'common reader'
who is interested in books and their authors but unwilling to spend time
on technical and theoretical minutiae; for the academic critic, the
imagined readership is a 'captive' audience of students or fellow-scholars
who are in some way obliged to keep abreast of specialist terminologies
and arcane debates. These are by no means mutually sealed realms:
academics have very often written reviews for public journals, while non-
academic criticism has its place in the university library, and the important
modern genre of introductory essays to paperback 'classic' novels represents the best of both worlds, designed for both kinds of readership. For
instance, J. Hillis Miller's introduction to the Penguin edition of Dickens's
Bleak House is probably the only example of 'deconstructionist' literary
analysis to have reached a large readership outside the academies. However, these are exceptions that tend to prove the rule of accelerating
incompatibility between the languages and conventions of the 'public'
and the academic varieties of criticism and literary theory. The mutual
distrust and incomprehension that has commonly prevailed between these
two worlds gives rise to the caricatures of the commercialized hack-
journalist who advertises his friends' worthless books in the columns of
a philistine newspaper, and the academic pedant who can parrot all the
technical formulae without being able to respond to the power of literature or to recognize the difference between a good and a bad book.
Among the many regrettable effects of this division has been the nursing
of nostalgic illusions about a supposed Golden Age before it appeared,
whether in the period of the great Victorian periodicals or in the earlier
age of Johnson. Students of eighteenth-century satire, however, will
recognize the hack and the scholastic pedant as stock types from that
period. The conflict itself, with its accompanying stereotypes, is as old as
the institutions of bookselling and reviewing. As Terry Eagleton argues
in *The Function of Criticism* (1984), criticism has constantly been dogged
since the eighteenth century by a chronic contradiction 'between an
inchoate amateurism and a socially marginal professionalism',[1] giving rise
to a different version of the same tension in successive periods. What
changes dramatically in the twentieth century is the scale and power of the
publishing market on the one side, and the academic institutionalization of
literature on the other. These twin developments tend to stifle the last

remaining hopes for that ideal combination of truly critical independence with public engagement and dialogue. Those few critics who manage to sustain such a combination and to straddle the two worlds – the case of Edmund Wilson is the one most often mentioned – assume an almost mythic status in critical lore.

In a curious way, the rival institutional camps of modern criticism – the publishers' market and the academy – mirror each other's dynamics. Both camps have contributed to a critical culture of short-lived fashions and spectacular contests, of the rapid exhaustion and supersession of successive intellectual sources, as new products are rushed out to displace the old. The market's constant thirst for eye-catching novelties and gimmicks is matched by the universities' competitive straining for research 'output', which compels its scholars into new fields and theoretical manoeuvres as the old ones reach saturation 'coverage'. Once all the major authors have been edited and analysed by the professors, then the minor authors, and then the completely unheard-of, must be put through the mill in turn, and new theoretical models developed so that the next generation can start again on the major authors in a different language; and so on *ad infinitum*, at least in principle. The same ruthless laws of the market that give rise to the plugging of books on television chat-shows and the staging of artificial controversies in the book pages of the newspapers work their way also through the academic institutions, generating a cut-throat intellectual bazaar of contending critical 'schools' whose only point of agreement is that the critical methods of twenty years ago are too shop-soiled to be put on sale at all. Commercial and academic cultures conspire, then, to keep up a dizzying pace of innovation in an activity that had, until the twentieth century, assumed its essential concepts to be unchanged since the time of Aristotle. In this they are abetted by the literary doctrines of modernism, which insist upon the need continually to 'make it new', before one's fresh language becomes stale and clichéd in public currency.

These overwhelming influences have helped to put in place a certain model of 'progress' in criticism and literary theory, one in which the market-driven notions of obsolescence and supersession are dominant. It is assumed that, as a new critical method, theory, or even style is developed, it must *displace* its predecessor (even though there will remain other rivals in the same ring), as a newly proved scientific theorem may drive the disproven hypotheses from the field. The impulses behind such assumptions are not only economic; they are also psychological. One important element in literary history is, as Harold Bloom has argued in *The Anxiety of Influence* (1973) and later works, the psychic conflict between literary 'parents' and their successors, who are obliged either to obey or to rebel through their own works. As with poets in Bloom's scheme, so with critics: the successful new critic must find a way symbolically to assassinate the last incumbent. The title of Eliot's *The Sacred Wood*, indeed, alludes to anthropological accounts of a priesthood of which each occupant is killed by his successor. Thus the Victorian critical 'father', Matthew Arnold, is displaced, through symbolic execution, by Eliot, who is in turn displaced by, say, Northrop Frye, who then awaits ritual dismemberment by Harold Bloom or some other ambitious younger rival. This model of Oedipal conflict between individual critics does make a certain credible sense of the more spectacular intellectual contests in criticism, albeit at the risk of indulging a masculine cult of heroic self-projection; but its mythology of single (and mortal) combat also radically oversimplifies the true multiplicity and complexity of debate in the critical arena, where the clashing of ignorant armies by night usually drowns out the one-to-one heroics of the solitary gladiators.

Like the economic metaphor of the new product that drives its competitor from the market, the image of the parricidal priest tends to ring out the old and ring in the new all too suddenly, encouraging us to believe that any older form of criticism is, once challenged by a newer rival, simply either bankrupted or buried. A sober inspection of the actual state of affairs in critical discussion at any given time will, however, have first to acknowledge the simultaneous currency of several incongruous styles, methods, and schools of thought, some of them old enough to be 'discredited' to all except their practitioners, some of them too new and unfamiliar to be digested by many outside the circle of the latest vanguard. Although we may wish to assign such rivals to different orders of time, as the 'past' and the 'future' of criticism, these 'residual' and 'emergent' movements (to borrow Raymond Williams's terms) actually occupy, and contend over, the same moment. To take a 'snapshot' of any brief period in modern criticism is usually to reveal the uncomfortable co-existence of surviving intellectual antiques and shiny new discoveries. Displacement, of the kind that is often assumed to take place, is hardly ever to be noticed, at least until long after it should have happened. This may well be because literary criticism, although it can resemble both a marketplace and a priesthood, has never arrived at the status of a *science*, and thus cannot disprove and then immediately discard its older versions. There are, admittedly, areas of literary theory in which progress of a scientific kind can be registered: the technical analysis of narrative structures and conventions has undoubtedly advanced from the makeshift distinctions used by Henry James and Percy Lubbock in the early years of the twentieth century to the far more sophisticated analytic apparatus developed by the French theorist Gérard Genette some fifty years later. Yet the more controversially evaluative, comparative, and judicial functions of criticism can show no advance of this kind; if there is 'progress' in this sphere, it is not of the scientific but of the political kind, in which hitherto unrepresented interest-groups and constituencies assert their values alongside and against (but never finally in place of) the rest. New arrivals in the critical arena, then, should not, without strong evidence, be assumed to have superseded their older competitors. They should rather be seen as superimposing their methods and doctrines upon an already existing and continuing critical practice. If we need a new metaphor for this less decisive process of succession, it may as well be the geological image of sedimented mineral deposits, one lying athwart and atop the other without actually erasing it.

These considerations are aired here partly in justification of the structure of this book's exposition, which departs consciously from the normal procedures of histories of criticism and literary theory. Too often, these histories or surveys encourage the illusion of orderly succession and supersession by treating one critic or critical school after another as if in ascending order of virtue or enlightenment. In some cases this is merely an inadvertent side-effect of a decision, respectable enough in itself, to consider in detail each major critic or critical movement in turn rather than to show them in direct relation to one another. No historical narrative, after all, can really represent the simultaneous activity of several participants without pausing to describe them independently and in some sort of succession, and of course this book falls under just the same constraints. There are, however, some basic choices to be made about the design of such a history, and the reader should be aware of the different versions in which it can be presented. The traditional method, adopted in René Wellek's monumental eight-volume *History of Modern Criticism 1750–1950* (1955–92) and in various shorter accounts, is to choose a small number of leading or representative critics from each period and then to subject the writings of each one in turn to more or less extended and more or less isolated scrutiny. There are clearly some advantages to such an approach, particularly for the reader who is content to detach the leading critics from their contexts. Its disadvantages are those of the 'great man' school of history, in which major developments are supposed to issue from the heads or hearts of a few talented or determined individuals, and partly those of the 'history of ideas' tradition, in which the influence of social, cultural, and institutional factors is often neglected. In reaction against the idealism of this approach, some historians have lately borrowed the principles of the French social theorists Michel Foucault and Pierre Bourdieu and concentrated instead on the history of modern criticism as a purely *institutional* process comprising the reproduction of particular techniques and disciplines of knowledge through the educational system. This approach is certainly more aware of the real contexts of critical discussion and writing, but it risks dismissing out of hand the relatively independent role of *ideas*, which it wants to discount on principle; and it renders invisible the important traditions of criticism outside the academies.

My own approach represents an attempt to respect the importance both of ideas and of institutions, while devoting more attention to the mixed arena of debate than to the detailed examination of a few outstanding critics. The aim – which cannot, I should warn, be fulfilled in all parts of the book – is to bring to the foreground the 'agenda' of critical discussion in each of four chronological phases, and to subordinate to this the treatment of individual critics, whose works may be reviewed separately under different headings of the agenda itself. The second half of each chapter includes sections on specific items of critical debate – Shakespeare, the novel, the canon of great literature – and here especially the major critics are noticed, if at all, only in so far as they address these questions, while minor or secondary figures appear more prominently on the same principle. The purpose of these arrangements is not that of 'levelling' the distinctions between major and minor critics, some of which of course remain debatable: where any critic is of substantial importance relative to others, this is indicated without undue embarrassment. The point is rather to emphasize that the 'great' critics work in dialogue with a range of other voices, not in lonely eminence.

It will be worth setting out here in summary form a few of the major developments in criticism and literary theory since 1890, before moving on in the following chapters to examine their evolution through the four chronological phases. This preliminary survey of the salient features can be arranged under three heads: the dominant *ideas* in this century of critical discussion; the fundamental shift in criticism's *institutional* location and centre of gravity; and the question of criticism's social and cultural *functions*. As we shall see, these turn out to be interlinked, but there is some convenience in separating them temporarily for the sake of analysis.

If we needed to sum up the single most influential, and troublesome, intellectual tendency in Anglophone criticism since the 1890s in one word, it would be 'formalism'. This is not so much a coherent critical or artistic 'movement' (although it has at times taken on organized forms, in critical schools, journals, and manifestos), nor a widely endorsed slogan (the term was used originally in a purely pejorative sense), as a recurrent theoretical principle in critical debate. Formalism arises from the attempts of disaffected artists and their champions to elude the demands placed upon them to express mortal truths or to reflect accepted versions of reality through their art. It refuses to abide by the belief that a work of art should have a particular kind of 'content', whether factually truthful, morally wholesome, spiritually uplifting, or politically orthodox. A work of literature, says the formalist, may have any subject-matter, or even none at all, for it cannot be valued according to what it is deemed to 'contain', as of it were merely a vehicle delivering a more or less important cargo. What is both distinctive and valuable about a work of literature is that it has a form – a beginning, a middle, an end, an internal structure of repetitions and parallels – that separates it from the relative formlessness of the rest of reality, thus beckoning us out of our habitual world into the freshly created and autonomous 'world' of the art-work. It is precisely this distance from the normal world that should be cherished in a work of art, not any approximation of the work to reality or to a prescribed ideal. Formalism is a recurrent negation of what it assumes to be the dominant public expectations regarding literature and its meanings. It repeatedly rebukes a philistine public for seeking a 'content', a 'message', even a 'meaning' in literary works, and mocks the *naïveté* and passivity underlying such demands.

There are precedents for the formalist position in some of the critical writings of Coleridge and other leaders of the Romantic movement in the early nineteenth century; but its fully developed version, at least in the English-speaking world, belongs to the period after about 1890. Formalism feeds upon dissatisfaction with the 'realist' principle in the arts, which had become deeply established in the second half of the nineteenth century. The rise of formalism in English-speaking criticism accompanies and indeed justifies the emergence of the kinds of artistic experiment that we place under the general label of 'modernism', in joint rebellion against the inherited Victorian norms. Critical theorists and poetic practitioners agreed that the new 'mass' reading public – believed to be complacent and gullible – had to be jolted out of its unimaginative torpor by new kinds of literary shock-tactics in order to awaken its powers of perception and sensitivity. Formalism endorses the new techniques and strategies of modernist writers by identifying cliché, custom, and the habitual 'stock response' of the narrow mind as the greatest dangers – greater, certainly, than any alleged indecency or ugliness in the subject-matter of plays or novels. It argues that readers need to be unsettled and challenged by unfamiliar forms of narrative and language, not reassured with easily digestible 'meanings'. In a modernist work such as T. S. Eliot's poem 'The Waste Land' or Virginia Woolf's novel *The Waves*, the formal disjunctions *are* the meaning, which one will miss if one goes looking for a moral message. For the formalist, the test of a genuine work of literature is the degree to which it *resists* giving up a meaning of the kind that could be summarized in terms other than those presented by the work itself. Formalism, then, might be defined as the theory of which the modernist movements provide the practice. This would indicate the strong historical relationship between the two, but it would underestimate the scope of the claims made by formalist criticism, which imply in principle that all artistic works – not just the more recent modernist examples – illustrate the same theory. It might then be preferable to say that formalism universalizes as theory the implications of modernist practice.

The formalist idea has asserted itself in Anglophone criticism in various different shapes: Oscar Wilde's repudiation of 'morality' as a criterion for the judgement of books is one early instance, while a somewhat different case is the adaptation since the 1960s of the principles ('defamiliarization' and others) of the Russian formalists. In between these examples stands the major tradition of Anglo-American critical argument from T. S. Eliot in the 1920s to W. K. Wimsatt in the 1950s, usually referred to as the 'New Criticism'. The aim of this powerful formalist tradition was to emphasize the specifically *literary* nature of the texts it examined, differentiating them from ordinary non-literary communications; its usual method was to detach the poem or other literary work from its biographical or historical occasions, and thus to see it not as the 'expression' of an author's personality or of the spirit of the age, but as an object of analysis *in itself*, with observable properties of its own: structural devices of apposition or enjambment, for instance, or rhythmic patterns, or uses of symbolism, or rhetorical features ranging from onomatopoeia to irony. The practitioner of the New Criticism would not, however, merely produce a list of such metrical or figurative devices found in a work, but would attempt to show how their total combined effect is a unique complex of sounds and meanings, richer than any abstracted summary or paraphrase of its 'message'. The New Criticism dominant in the second quarter of the twentieth century then gave way to a second wave of formalist criticism in the 1970s, which sometimes claimed that literary works were not 'about' anything other than their own fictional status, and sometimes (in its attempted political versions) that certain formal features such as the use of omniscient third-person narrative voice were inherently conservative, regardless of the work's 'content', while other literary devices were just as automatically 'subversive'. These newer formalisms are often more sophisticated than the New Criticism, especially in their awareness of the difficulties of distinguishing literary from non-literary languages; but they share the same hostility to realism and its allegedly 'naïve' assumptions about language, and the same endorsement of modernist formal disruption as the antidote to mental torpor and ideological complacency.

While formalism, in one shape or another, has occupied the high ground of criticism and theory throughout this period, it has always been besieged by opposing schools which accuse it of abstracting literary works too drastically from their social, cultural, or historical contexts. The New Criticism, for example, eventually fell into disfavour as it repeatedly discovered the same 'universal' literary properties (irony, ambiguity, paradox) in works of widely different kinds from diverse historical periods; and a similar charge was levelled at its successor, the school of 'deconstruction'. The detractors of formalism – a mixed array, again, including both Marxists and romantic conservatives – were determined to retain the notion of a literary work's 'content', and to show that it referred not just to itself but to a known world. Reacting against the arid formal analysis of texts, they often produced little more than 'content analysis': that is, the discussion of themes and topics in literary works (Conrad's view of women, say), in abstraction from all formal questions of fiction, structure, figurative language, and literary convention. It was then easy enough for the formalist critic to show how inadequate such approaches were, in that they failed to distinguish literary works from other kinds of document. The victory of formalism over its opponents, which was sealed by the end of the 1930s, was partly a matter of arrogating the very term 'literary criticism' to the formalists' own practice of intensive verbal analysis; other ways of commenting upon literary works were just not literary – being 'merely' moral, philosophical, sociological, psychological, and so forth – or just not criticism, but history or biography or linguistics or bibliography. The rise of formalism was represented by its protagonists as a battle on behalf of literary criticism, with its focus on the 'internal' properties of literary works themselves, against the stranglehold of literary history, with its interest in 'external' factors and broad tendencies. Literary history could be dismissed as the equivalent of Victorian butterfly-collecting: a meaningless accumulation of samples, arbitrary labels, dry facts, and speculative 'influences'. Criticism, on the other hand, put us into direct contact with poems, plays, and prose fictions; it led to a knowledge *of* literature rather than merely a knowledge *about* it. The heroic phase of modern Anglo-American criticism, from the 1920s to the 1960s, was marked by the subordination of literary-historical and literary-biographical study to the ascendant discourses of critical analysis and evaluation. In terms of method, this entailed a new practice of 'close reading', attending to the specific formal features of texts rather than to the general world-views of their authors. Nothing distinguishes twentieth-century literary criticism more sharply from that of previous ages than this close attention to textual detail.

The institutional context and basis of literary criticism and theory in the period after 1890 is characterized above all by the spectacular development of professional academic criticism. It is commonly accepted that critics can be divided into three kinds, although one individual may occupy two or even three of these roles successively or simultaneously. There is first the poet-critic, who is usually concerned to justify his or her own artistic practice against rivals or against hostile reception. The roll-call of notable critics in the English language is dominated by this type: Sir Philip Sidney, John Dryden, Alexander Pope, William Wordsworth, S. T. Coleridge, Percy Bysshe Shelley, Edgar A. Poe, Matthew Arnold, Walt Whitman, Henry James, T. S. Eliot, Ezra Pound, D. H. Lawrence, Allen Tate. The second kind is the 'man of letters' – a reviewer, editor, or periodical essayist who may also be a practitioner of the same art, but whose first responsibility is to the reading public, or to that section of it addressed by a specific journal. Samuel Johnson is the first great type here, followed by William Hazlitt, Thomas De Quincey, Thomas Carlyle, Ralph Waldo Emerson, John Stuart Mill, G. H. Lewes, George Eliot, R. H. Hutton, Matthew Arnold (again), Leslie Stephen, William Dean Howells, Paul Elmer More, T. S. Eliot (again), John Middleton Murry, Virginia Woolf, Edmund Wilson. The third kind is the academic critic, tied professionally to a university or similar institution. This type originates in the Scottish universities of the late eighteenth century, when courses in 'Rhetoric and Belles-Lettres' were established; but it makes no serious impression upon criticism until the latter part of the Victorian period. The first prestigious literary academics were Edward Dowden, Professor of English at Trinity College, Dublin from 1867, who wrote biographical studies of Shakespeare, Shelley, and Browning, and founded the Arden edition of Shakespeare, and David Masson, Professor of Rhetoric and English Literature at the University of Edinburgh from 1865, and author of a seven-volume life of Milton. Their more influential successors include George Saintsbury, A. C. Bradley, Irving Babbitt, I. A. Richards, F. R. Leavis, G. Wilson Knight, Cleanth Brooks, Northrop Frye, Frank Kermode, and Harold Bloom, to pick only a few names from a now extensive list. There are intermediate types, who are both public journalists and professional teachers (Lionel Trilling is a notable case), and numerous examples of academic critics who have also published unremembered poems or novels. On the whole, though, these rough-and-ready distinctions stand up well enough. If we apply them to the critical scene in the twentieth century, we find that the first two kinds of critic – the poet-critic and the periodical reviewer – survive only precariously in this period, overwhelmed by the growing ranks of academics. After Eliot, Woolf, and Lawrence, hardly any leading critic in the twentieth century has also been a leader in poetry or in fiction.

The academic 'professionalization' of criticism and literary theory has had substantial consequences going well beyond the numbers of salaried critics. A parallel publishing market has arisen, especially in the United States, which has no need to respond to public demands for relevance or intelligibility: subsidized university presses disseminate books to other university libraries, and have them reviewed by subsidized university journals. The habits of the teacher, as distinct from the public reviewer, have tilted criticism heavily in the direction of 'explication' and similar reproducible routines, and have generated countless explanatory introductions to difficult and not-so-difficult writers. Professional standards of 'rigour', emanating from the scientific departments of the campuses, have put pressure upon literary academics to devise appropriately demanding programmes of linguistic, bibliographical, or theoretical study to compensate for the suspiciously pleasurable pursuit of poetry-appreciation. For similar reasons, academic criticism has favoured the study of especially 'difficult' texts, or those requiring prior training or some kind – from *Beowulf* to the *Cantos* of Ezra Pound. It has reconstructed the canon of literature upon the principle that the truly literary work is one requiring from its readers a certain labour of interpretation. In this, its preferences coincide with those of modernist criticism, in such a way as to produce an alliance that has been fateful for the idea of literature in the twentieth century. After a period of confrontation with the entrenched interests of linguistic and historical scholarship in the first part of the century, the eventually victorious advocates of 'pure' (that is, largely formalist) criticism in the universities established a new practice of literary study based upon the principles of T. S. Eliot and other modernist writers, and went on to champion the cause of modernist innovation, speedily consecrating its major works as 'set texts' in the classroom. The alliance was consolidated in the 1930s and 1940s, when the critical allies of modernism obtained academic positions that would become far more influential with the post-war expansion of the university systems – in the 1950s in the United States, and more modestly in the 1960s in Britain.

The enormous shift in criticism's centre of gravity towards the campus library accompanied, and to some extent caused, a decline in the critical authority of public journals, and in the viability of the 'little magazines' in which modernist artists exhibited their experiments, their manifestors, and their quarrels. Whereas these kinds of publication concentrated the attention of the public critic and the poet-critic on problems of current literary practice, the academic critic had no necessary interest in the contemporary scene, and could just as easily proceed in entire ignorance of it. Criticism thus drifted apart from the activity of literary production, turning either in the specialist direction to the intensive interpretation of established works from previous ages, or in the generalist direction to the elaboration of comprehensive theoretical models of literary meaning or value – which in turn developed their own specialisms. While the public critic would in principle address the whole range of literary, historical, and cultural questions raised by the latest books, the academic critic could become an 'expert', dealing perhaps only with one author, and contributing to such specialist periodicals as the *Blake Newsletter* or *Milton Studies*. The degree of professional expansion and specialization attained at the end of the century can be gauged by consulting any recent directory of the Modern Language Association of America, the professional body for teachers of literature. Its 1992 directory, for instance, records a membership of more than 32,000, affiliated to 110 specialist divisions or discussion groups; nearly a third of the membership – 10,500 – attended its 1991 convention in San Francisco. The safest place to go if one wants to avoid professional teachers of literature would seem to be South Dakota, which had only 31 MLA members in that year, compared with 3,778 in California.[2]

No introductory history of modern criticism could account satisfactorily for the remarkable changes in criticism's nature and status without examining its changing function or 'mission' in the world. And the key to an understanding of this question lies in the work of Matthew Arnold, the English poet and critic. Arnold does not directly belong to the period covered by this book (he died in 1888), but he certainly dominates much of its literary criticism from beyond the grave. Most of the twentieth century (and more obviously the latter part of the nineteenth) could safely be said to belong to the 'Arnoldian age' in English-language criticism. Before proceeding to events after 1890, we need to take this

preliminary step back in order to take our bearings. This can be done
without exploring in any great detail Arnold's particular literary judgements or arguments, because the relevant problems are the larger ones of
literature as a whole and of its value.

Writing in the context of increasing social complexity and diminishing
religious belief, Arnold made the astonishing claim that literature (or
'poetry', as he usually put it) would soon take the place of religion as
our principal means of understanding our lives and of consoling us for
its sorrows. As he asserted in his essay 'The Study of Poetry' (1880),

> The future of poetry is immense, because in poetry, where it is
> worthy of its high destinies, our race, as time goes on, will find an
> ever surer and surer stay. There is not a creed which is not shaken,
> not an accredited dogma which is not shown to be
> questionable, not a received tradition which does not threaten to
> dissolve. Our religion has materialised itself in the fact, in the
> supposed fact; it has attached its emotion to the fact, and now
> the fact is failing it. But for poetry the idea is everything; the
> rest is a world of illusion, of divine illusion . . . The strongest part
> of our religion today is its unconscious poetry.

Since poetry does not rely upon the veracity of its statements, it cannot
be refuted as the dogma of a church may be, as Arnold sees. He continues:

> More and more mankind will discover that we have to turn to
> poetry to interpret life for us, to console us, to sustain us.
> Without poetry, our science will appear incomplete; and most of
> what now passes with us for religion and philosophy will be
> replaced by poetry.[3]

Arnold draws here on his Romantic predecessors, Wordsworth and Shelley, in claiming that poetry is the organizing 'soul' to which fact, science,
and reasoning are the corruptible body. As an intangible essence, poetry
is immune from the kind of destruction recently visited upon the 'facts'
of the Bible or upon the Church of England's articles of belief, as Arnold
pithily indicates: 'Compare the stability of Shakespeare with the stability of
the Thirty-nine Articles!'[4] Shakespeare, of course, cannot be 'disproved',
because his work does not consist – except accidentally – of facts or
doctrines, and yet he, or Wordsworth, or Tennyson, may give us rather
more spiritual sustenance than the vicar's last sermon. Poetry can take
the dry 'facts' of science or of religious doctrine, and saturate them with
life-giving value, humanizing an inhuman world.

The corollary of Arnold's high claim for poetry is that criticism has a
much weightier responsibility to determine which works truly fulfil the
destiny of literature to interpret and sustain. For Arnold, 'criticism' is not

so much the activity of literary analysis and interpretation of specific works as an attitude of disinterested enquiry and intellectual flexibility, applied to all manner of cultural and political questions in such a way as to allow the 'best ideas' to circulate, regardless of their immediate practical benefit. It corresponds to the freedom of the intellectual from 'provincial' loyalties to class, creed, or country, seeking only what is best in itself. Arnold's mocking resistance to the self-satisfaction of the 'philistine' Victorian middle-class has become a model for the detachment of the literary intellectual in the English-speaking world from utilitarian and practical goals. His most important legacy to modern *literary* criticism is the idea of literature as the new human 'centre' of modern culture, taking the place of dogmatic religion. This brings with it the assumption that literary criticism can replace theology as the queen of the sciences, at the summit of humanistic learning, that critics can constitute a new priesthood, guarding the sacred flame of humane 'values' against the threats of materialism, and even that the flexible literary habits of mind learned through the encounter with poems and fictions can substitute for the disciplines of meditation and prayer. It would be misleading to pretend that most – or even many – modern critics have explicitly subscribed to such ideas. In fact, the most influential of them – T. S. Eliot – was, even before his conversion to the Church of England, strongly suspicious of their secular and Romantic tendency. Nonetheless, as a kind of myth of literature's (and thus of criticism's) purpose and destiny, the Arnoldian prophecy of a literary substitute for religion helped to sustain the high ideals and missionary fervour of criticism's heroic phase, from the 1920s to the 1960s, especially in Britain. In the works of I. A. Richards, for example, the founder of the 'Cambridge School' of English Studies, we find the idea (taken from Shelley) that the arts 'are our storehouse of recorded values',[5] and that without them we could not make sense of our varied experiences. Like Arnold, Richards believed that values needed to be safeguarded from the corrosions to which factual beliefs were exposed in the modern world, and that literature was a vitally important means of navigating through the rough seas of modern scepticism, in that it gave us values detached from positive beliefs. Writing in the aftermath of the Great War of 1914–18, he foresaw a period of unprecedented confusion resulting from the increasing dissemination – through cinema and radio, now, as well as print – of raw information, which needed to be ordered, to be given value and meaning in a world whose older moral traditions were collapsing. 'If this should happen,' he wrote, 'a mental chaos such as man has never experienced may be expected. We shall then be thrown back, as Matthew Arnold foresaw, upon poetry. It is capable of saving us; it is a perfectly possible means of overcoming chaos.'[6] For Richards, and for his followers, the 'New Critics', the reading of poetry, and of similarly symbolic prose works, was a kind of secular sacrament that could heal the psychological wounds of the modern world; criticism, as a training in the achievement of such mental poise, was nothing less than a path to salvation.

In different terms, other important critics in the first half of the twentieth century presented literature and the informed reading of literature as a redemption of the fallen modern world. W. B. Yeats, T. S. Eliot, and F. R. Leavis all draw upon traditional religious cosmologies to present a history of Western Man's spiritual disintegration since the scientific revolution of the seventeenth century, at the same time offering the metaphoric richness of literary language as the reintegration of the residuary fragments. What had been lost in real history could be recovered through critical reconstitution of the literary tradition. Again, the critic became the priest through whose knowledge of the traditional texts one could recover a lost wholeness. Most vociferously in the work of F. R. Leavis and his followers, but also in the more muted tones of other schools, literary criticism in its heroic phase assumed a 'central' position in its culture as keeper of living human values, regarding all other intellectual pursuits and disciplines as merely fragmentary specialisms. And during this phase, it was for the most part taken at its own valuation: the leading critics were respected as oracles, often more highly than philosophers or historians, and their works were discussed extensively in the more expensive magazines and newspapers. Toward the end of this phase, the British poet and critic A. Alvarez acknowledged this peculiar recent status of literary criticism, while also recognizing its imminent end:

> As the seventeenth century read sermons more or less for pleasure, so the twentieth has devoted itself religiously to critical essays. I am afraid that the bulk of them will eventually prove as unreadable as the sermons.[7]

The analogy here with another once-favoured genre of improving prose literature is a telling one, but Alvarez's prediction seems partly misconceived. Literary criticism has indeed already forfeited its assumed cultural centrality, and the critical essays of a previous generation (including not a few copies of his own book, *The Shaping Spirit*, from which the above quotation comes) are indeed gathering dust in second-hand bookshops along with the theological tracts. But it is not that older works of criticism are unreadable; more that the motive for reading them, once quite strong, has tended to weaken along with the expectation that one could find in current criticism a clue or signpost by which to find one's way in the complexities of modern culture. The best critical writing, past and present, of course still does satisfy that expectation, and Alvarez's prognosis applies only to the mediocre bulk. As the following chapters ought to demonstrate, that still leaves a substantial critical literature from which we can gather continuing rewards.

Notes

1. Terry Eagleton, *The Function of Criticism: From* The Spectator *to Post-Structuralism* (1984), p. 69.
2. PMLA 107 (1992), pp. 720–9, 759.
3. Matthew Arnold, *English Literature and Irish Politics* ed. R. H. Super (Ann Arbor, MI, 1973), pp. 161–2.
4. Arnold, *English Literature*, p. 63.
5. I. A. Richards, *Principles of Literary Criticism* (1924), p. 22.
6. I. A. Richards, *Science and Poetry* (1926), p. 83.
7. A. Alvarez, *The Shaping Spirit: Studies in Modern English and American Poets* (1958; revised 1963), pp. 102–3.

Chapter 2
Descents from Decadence: 1890–1918

The Critical Agenda

The chief items on the agenda of literary-critical discussion in the period between 1890 and 1918 can be summarized briefly under three heads. First, there is the intellectual digestion and critical assessment of important and disturbingly 'modern' cultural forces, movements, and figures, chiefly from continental Europe. Second is the problem of defending the liberty and integrity of literary art against an increasingly inhospitable philistine world and its puritanical moralism; this resistance being bound up with the vexed question of the relationship of art to morality. In the third place we can identify a search for some settlement, whether by conquest or by compromise, between the competing claims to critical authority of scholarly and scientific objectivism on the one side, and aesthetic or 'impressionistic' subjectivism on the other; that is to say between a professional Knowledge of literature and an amateur Taste for it.

The first of these items assumes a special prominence because the English-speaking world itself appeared to be going through no major cultural efflorescence of its own since the deaths of the principal Victorian writers. Accordingly, it seemed to be a time to import and absorb the more exciting productions of Russia, Norway, Germany, and above all France; a time to pause for critical reflection too upon the legacies left by some late nineteenth-century authors in English: on the eccentricities of Browning and Meredith, on the fictional realism of James and Howells, or on the formal and moral fluidities of Walt Whitman. The greater, more controversial heroes and villains, however, were the foreign writers, with Ibsen, Tolstoy, Zola, and the French Symbolist poets at their head, Nietzsche and Wagner hovering somewhere behind them. All of these figures – except for the excessively shocking Zola – found their enthusiastic champions in the Anglo-Saxon world, although in Britain at least these champions tended, notably, not to be Anglo-Saxons themselves. The Ibsenite party was led with energetic brilliance from London by Bernard Shaw (in *The Quintessence of Ibsenism* (1891)) and with sweet reasonableness from New York by William Dean Howells. Its yet unnoticed Dublin representative, who contributed an admiring essay to the *Fortnightly Review* in 1900, was a young student signing himself James A. Joyce. Tolstoy found a standard-bearer in Howells, who placed the Russian novelist at the head of an international pantheon of realists, including James, Twain, Flaubert, Hardy, Galdos, Verga, and even – with cautious reservations – Zola. An eclectic miscellany of modern European thought and art – including that of Ibsen, Tolstoy, and Nietzsche – was put before the public by Havelock Ellis (later renowned as a sexologist) in his *The New Spirit* (1890), and by James G. Huneker in his enthusiastic articles for New York magazines. The work of the French Symbolists was partly summarized for import by George Moore in *Impressions and Opinions* (1891), and expounded with far greater effect by Arthur Symons in *The Symbolist Movement in Literature* (1900). This last book became a landmark in modern poetry, notable for the stimulus it provided to Yeats and Eliot, although its ambitions are confined to sketching pen-portraits of Rimbaud, Verlaine, Mallarmé, Huysmans, and their associates, with brief elucidations of their esoteric anti-materialist doctrines. The limitations of Symons's work are not his alone: they are to be found in most examples of this genre of critical advocacy, in which the disciple typically eschews critical analysis of the master's writings in favour of expounding the new gospel and defending it against public miscomprehensions. Shaw's book on Ibsen is confessedly a presentation of the dramatist's 'message', and thus, for all its provocative zest, falls into what is at this period a large category of works devoted to summarizing the creeds of various authors treated as teachers and prophets. Browning was a prominent victim of this approach, in such forgotten studies as *The Message of Robert Browning* by A. Austin Foster and *Browning's Teaching on Faith, Life and Love* by W. Arthur Hind (both 1912). Among the more interesting examples of the type is J. A. Symonds's *Walt Whitman: A Study* (1893), which is really an extended funeral oration to the poet whose new democratic religion had saved Symonds himself from despair and enabled him to live with his homosexuality.

It was this kind of connection between writers of the then modern movement and the spectre of aberrant sexuality, especially after the conviction of Oscar Wilde on indecency charges in 1895, that brought serious literary critics right up against the formidable obstacle of Anglo-Saxon prudery, an ever-vigilant antagonist armed with real powers of legal restraint. This was a period in which such dirty books as Hardy's *Jude the Obscure* (1895), Dreiser's *Sister Carrie* (1900), Lawrence's *The Rainbow* (1915), and Joyce's *A Portrait of the Artist as a Young Man* (1916) encountered censorship and suppression, and almost any French novel was to be suspected of filthy intentions. Whether they were writing of natives like Whitman, Swinburne, and Hardy, or of foreigners like Ibsen, Verlaine, and Zola, literary critics found themselves repeatedly obliged to rebut furious accusations of indecency. There was a larger cultural incompatibility here, as Howells pointed out, between the French novel-reading public composed of sophisticated adults, and the British and American publics, which were accustomed to 'family reading' fit to be heard by modest girls.[1] In that sense, it was evident to the more enlightened critics of the time that European literary culture was mature enough to see human life whole, while the world of Anglo-Saxon letters was still bound within an artificial childhood. It should not be thought that their advocacy of allegedly indecent authors like Ibsen was an 'innocent' pastime. On the contrary, these critics were following Matthew Arnold's example in consciously ranging themselves against the restrictions of Anglo-Saxon culture, and with varying degrees of boldness or exasperation were seeking to break down its philistine obsession with moral conduct to the exclusion of all else.

The crux of the problem was the assumed link between literature and morality. Under the Victorian dispensation, the God-fearing middle classes learned to expect from their writers imaginative work characterized by an elevated selection of subject matter and a positive and ennobling moral tone, if not by an optimistic and piously moral conclusion. The arrival of new kinds of writing in the last decades of the century – fictional and dramatic realism in particular – was genuinely baffling in its apparent degradation of art's once noble purposes: it seemed gratuitously nasty in its irreligious treatment of human destiny, and agnostic even about the difference between right and wrong behaviour. The literary critic was called upon to explain this state of affairs; for there were rival 'authorities' willing to account for it in their own terms: the Hungarian pseudo-scientist Max Nordau offered the explanation that the more controversial modern artists were indeed clinically degenerate, in his widely-discussed book *Degeneration* (1895), before the furious polemics of Howells and Shaw dismissed him as a dishonest and self-contradictory quack. Some critics hedged defensively, hastening to distinguish their own heroes' acceptable kind of realism from the genuine nastiness of the French novel. Thus Symonds detached Whitman's healthy treatment of sex from the prurience of Zola's fiction; while the young American writer Hamlin Garland absolved Ibsen of any connection with 'sterile French sexualism', further predicting in his manifesto *Crumbling Idols* (1894), that the American realism of the future would 'not deal with crime and abnormities [*sic*], nor with deceased persons. It will deal, I believe, with the wholesome love of honest men for honest women, with the heroism of labor, the comradeship of men . . .'.[2] This may sound uncannily like something from Stalin's Russia, but it arises confusedly in fact from distinctively American traditions of cleanly optimism. The more wholehearted and militant opponents of puritan moralism, however, were making no excuses or apologies. The demand that art conform itself to moral standards was for them a sheer impertinence. This conviction is expressed by leading critics of several otherwise distinct schools: it unites in common cause the Ibsenite realists with the anti-realist Decadents, the anti-academic modernist rebels with at least some of the academic conservatives.

For the Decadent group, the direct challenge to moralism was flung down by Oscar Wilde in his Preface to *The Picture of Dorian Gray* (1891) where he asserted flatly that 'There is no such thing as a moral or an immoral book. Books are well written, or badly written. That is all.'[3] After Wilde's downfall, Arthur Symons took up the campaign, declaring roundly: 'I contend on behalf of the liberty of art, and I deny that morals have any right of jurisdiction over it. Art may be served by morality; it can never be its servant.'[4] The realists had already launched their own offensive with Shaw's *Quintessence of Ibsenism*, which argues that artists have a duty to subvert the public's thoughtless conformity to conventional moral codes. Shaw later went further in proclaiming that 'it is necessary for the welfare of society that genius should be privileged to utter sedition, to blaspheme, to outrage good taste, to corrupt the youthful mind, and, generally, to scandalize one's uncles.'[5] In more moderate tones W. D. Howells responded to moralizing attacks on Hardy's *Jude the Obscure* by expressing his belief that 'anything which treats faithfully of life cannot be immoral, no matter how far it ventures.' For Howells, in fact, the truthfulness of a literary work *is* its morality.[6] Similar arguments in defence of realist fiction still had to be made again by H. L. Mencken in his *Book of Prefaces* (1917), which rails against the stupidities of censorship in America. Among the new wave of modernist critics in London by this time it was taken for granted that moral considerations were fatal to art: Ford Madox Hueffer paid tribute to Howells and Henry James for releasing the novel from its old moralizing traditions, while Ezra Pound claimed, like Howells, that true art, however 'immoral' it looked, was virtuous because of its truthfulness. Even among the normally more cautious academic community, there were significant literary professors influenced by Pater and Wilde who braved the same issues: Walter Raleigh at Oxford went out of his way in his book *Shakespeare* (1907) to rebuke puritanical critics of *Measure for Measure*, while at Columbia University Professor J. E. Spingarn insisted in 1911 that since the artist is devoted purely to expression, 'obviously morals can play no part in the judgment which criticism may form of his work.'[7] The new consensus against moralizing judgement of literary works, and against overt moral didacticism in art, was, then, a broad one. And for those who did not wish to repudiate entirely the moral significance of literature, there was a compromise position available – essentially a version of Howells's and Pound's realist view: that the moral quality of a literary work was inseparable from the full complexity of its sincere or truthful apprehension of life, and thus not a detachable element that could be translated into the simplicities of moral codes. It was in such terms that Henry James presented the problem in his 1908 Preface to *The Portrait of a Lady*, and that A. C. Bradley attempted to resolve it in his Oxford Lecture of 1904 on Shelley.

The third principal item on the agenda of criticism in this period – the very possibility of arriving at objective critical standards – will be considered at more length in the next section of this chapter. It will be worth sketching a preliminary map of the discussion and its contexts at this stage, though. What we find here is a choice of two contrary directions in which the discussion of literature can tend: towards reliance upon personal taste and subjectively recorded impressions, or towards reliance upon accumulated knowledge. Each direction is perceived in this period as leading to an 'extreme' position imperilling balanced critical judgement – of dilettantism in the cultivation of personal taste, or of pedantry in the accumulation of facts. In these terms the extension lecturer John Churton Collins warned readers of the *Saturday Review* in 1894 that unless the English universities organized the study of literature on a sound basis, criticism would slide into these two complementary vices: 'there an extreme of flaccid dilettantism, here an extreme of philological pedantry.'[18] George Saintsbury, a periodical essayist turned professor, likewise deplored in his *History of Nineteenth Century Literature* (1896) the tendency of critics to divide between the scholarly types who had no real sense of literature and the literary types who had no real sense of scholarship. A few years later, Irving Babbit, Professor of French at Harvard University, was to make just the same complaint about the state of literary study in America, clearly identifying dilettantism and pedantry as twin evils in his book *Literature and the American College* (1908). It is worth noticing that all of these diagnoses come from university men: a fact which indicates that the opposed tendencies in the discussion of literature had come into their sharpest collision within the academic institutions themselves. Here the battle had been joined between the practitioners of philology (that is, linguistic study of etymology, sound-changes, and grammatical problems) and those who championed the study of literature 'as literature' rather than as linguistic data. Where literature was studied and taught in universities at the end of the nineteenth century, it was almost always under the respectably 'scientific' regime of philologists, mostly trained in German universities, who ensured that the classification of historical and linguistic facts, usually about the literature of the Middle Ages, took precedence over the study or appreciation of modern literature – this being dismissed as a lightweight matter of private opinion and chatter beyond the scope of serious scholarship. The task before their opponents, the advocates of 'humane' literary teaching, was, then, to construct a credible discipline of legitimate academic study, a mode of criticism that was neither idly subjective nor aridly factual.[9] In this attempt to establish a study of literature for literature's sake, momentous in its consequences for the course of twentieth-century criticism, they needed to draw upon the ideas of the art-for-art's-sake school of

Walter Pater and Oscar Wilde while studiously repudiating any taint of its notorious vices. This was not to be a simple manoeuvre.

Aesthetes and Academics

The inauguration of the modern, post-Arnoldian age of criticism in the English-speaking world can be dated conveniently from 1890, when the London magazine *The Nineteenth Century* published a dazzlingly paradoxical dialogue by Oscar Wilde entitled 'The True Function and Value of Criticism'. Revised and republished alongside the earlier 'The Decay of Lying' in Wilde's book *Intentions* (1891) as 'The Critic as Artist', this irreverent essay pulled the very foundations from under the most important Victorian assumptions about the relationship of criticism to literature. The simplest way of identifying the kind of challenge it presented is to focus on its deliberate subversion of Matthew Arnold's formulation of criticism's task. In 'The Function of Criticism at the Present Time' (1864), Arnold had called for English intellectual life in all spheres to raise itself above short-term practical polemics and to join the more disinterested effort of French and German writers 'to see the object as in itself it really is', free from immediate partisan considerations and personal crotchets.[10] By 'criticism' Arnold meant the understanding and assessment of social, political, and religious questions as well as of the arts, but his demand for disinterested objectivity held good for literary criticism too. Walter Pater, however, insinuated a fatal qualification to the formula in the Preface to his book *The Renaissance* (1873), where he wrote in ostensible agreement with Arnold that

> 'To see the object as in itself it really is,' has been justly said to be the aim of all true criticism whatever; and in aesthetic criticism the first step towards seeing one's object as it really is, is to know one's own impression as it really is, to discriminate it, to realise it distinctly.[11]

Pater's refocusing of the critical task from the object to the observer made all the difference between a doctrine of impersonal objectivity – for which no convincing credentials had ever really been produced – and a new practice of personal aesthetic impressionism. Pater's apparently minor revision of Arnold's formula, then, was potentially an invitation to open the floodgates of subjective caprice in criticism. Wilde drew the logical and absurd conclusion: that 'the primary aim of the critic is to see the object as in itself it really is not'.[12] Instead of humbly explicating the intentions of the artist, the critic should now weave a new work of art from his own impressions, thus making criticism itself a new form of artistic endeavour, more challenging and more creative in its freedoms than the work of the artists themselves. If the newly liberated impressionistic critic can be said to be interpreting a primary work of art at all, it is only in the sense that an actor interprets his part in a drama: turning it into a unique performance of his own according to his personal temperament and style.

Wilde's startling paradoxes on the status of criticism were matched in his companion-piece 'The Decay of Lying' by even more outrageous heresies on the status of art. Again cast in the form of a dialogue between languid cigarette-smoking dilettanti, this piece turns on its head the relation of art to nature, proposing that it is life that imitates art, not the other way round: fogs and sunsets are an invention of the impressionist painters, while nineteenth-century civilization is largely an invention of the novelist Balzac.

This dialogue involves an outright assault not just on realist assumptions of art's reproduction of external nature, but on the parallel assumption of most anti-realist romantics – the belief that art expresses the internal promptings of sincere feeling. In both directions, Wilde severs the sacred ties that bind the work of art to the world around it, proclaiming the absolute independence of an art that never expresses anything but itself. It is not any supposed correspondence to internal or external truths that produces art, but the artifice of convention and style; and the attempt, either realist or romantic, to return to life or nature can only produce bad art. Just as Wilde releases criticism from its obligations to the work of art in 'The Critic as Artist', so in 'The Decay of Lying' he frees the work of art from any requirement to imitate or represent anything outside its own self-contained artifice.

These semi-fictionalized heresies bring to a culminating intransigence many previous romantic assertions of the autonomy of art. Wilde had to some extent moved beyond the pure aestheticism of 1880s, and had arrived at a sense in which art could be understood to serve life; but this involved the final paradox, that it was the uselessness of art that made it useful: by raising itself above life, art thereby challenged us to live up to its higher standards of beauty and perfection. Wilde's critical dialogues are provocations rather than dogmatic theses, and his theory of art is also essentially a theory of provocation, valuing the arts for their ability to disconcert and affront. The other Irish dramatist and controversialist who set about the conquest of London in the 1890s – Bernard Shaw – arrived at similar general conclusions by a different route: in his splendid polemical article 'A Degenerate's View of Nordau' (1895, later re-titled *The Sanity of Art*), Shaw defended the value of the arts by arguing that they extend our senses in the direction of a higher beauty, thus making us dissatisfied with the injustice, meanness and ugliness of our world and inciting us to demand better of it.

For most of the Decadent critics of the 1890s, the example of Pater and of the French Symbolist writers led to conclusions less drastic than Wilde's, but more fruitful in their later consequences for literary criticism. The most important critics to emerge from this movement were Arthur Symons, editor of the short-lived decadent journal *The Savoy* in 1896, and his friend and collaborator W. B. Yeats. Between them they evolved in the late 1890s a fairly consistent view of poetry as a form of ecstatic escape from the concerns of a materialistic world into the higher truths of the spirit. So far this was an orthodox idealist Romantic attitude, with a predictable hostility to realist fiction, although it took the idea of the artist's seclusion from society to new lengths. Where Symons and Yeats departed from at least the Victorian mainstream of their Romantic inheritance, though, was in sharply opposing poetry against rhetoric, poetry being essentially symbolic in its invocation of emotions and spirituality, rhetoric being discursive or descriptive in its repetition of conventional ideas. In this they were adopting the principles of their masters: of Pater, who had suggested that literature and the other arts could aspire to the condition of music in aesthetic purity, and of Paul Verlaine, who had called upon poets to suppress the rhetorical element in their work (indeed, to wring its neck, as he put it). Verlaine's dictum is quoted approvingly in Symons's *The Symbolist Movement in Literature*, a work that arose partly from discussions with Yeats, and that commends the French poets' mystical retreat into a closed world of artistic perfection. For these critics, the literature of the nineteenth century had been contaminated by rhetoric, which implied an impure attachment to external concerns and to the vulgarizing awareness of an audience to be pleased. Rhetoric meant the world of the newspapers (regarded by both men as a sort of cultural plague), of distracting self-assertion, and of propaganda, the noisy world from which the artist must retreat in order to cultivate the impersonal life of the spirit and its symbols. Yeats later adapted his critical position to accommodate an appreciation of the bodily life, of personality, and even of oratory (truly impassioned speech, as distinct from the falsity of rhetoric), but in his early essays he holds the uncompromising symbolist line against contamination of the poet by 'externalities'. An essay of 1902 on Edmund Spenser advises that 'The poet, if he would not carry burdens that are not his and obey the orders of servile lips, must sit apart in contemplative indolence playing with fragile things.' Yeats's earlier review of Symons's book similarly called for

> a casting out of descriptions of nature for the sake of nature, of the moral law for the sake of the moral law, a casting out of all anecdotes and of that brooding over scientific opinion that so

often extinguished the central flame in Tennyson, and of that
vehemence that would make us do or not do certain things . . . [13]

In his conscious repudiation of these aspects of literary Victorianism,
Yeats was to provide, as we shall see, a highly influential example to the
younger modernist critics. The literary principle that was carried away
from the break-up of the Decadent movement was above all the suspicion
of moralizing and rhetorical traditions. Symons, in his last important
work, *The Romantic Movement in English Poetry* (1909) still maintained
that there was an eternal battle between rhetoric and poetry; and Yeats,
writing in 1917, gave us the memorable aphorism 'We make out of the
quarrel with others, rhetoric, but of the quarrel with ourselves, poetry.'[14]

There were other possible uses to be made of Pater's critical heresies,
that did not have to end up in the flagrant paradoxes of Wilde or in
what was sometimes regarded as the 'sterile' purism of the Decadent and
Symbolist positions. Symons himself identified Pater's most important
achievement as the liberation of criticism from moral dogmatism and
from rigid criteria of judgement; in short, flexibility and sympathy. Rather
than just licensing a withdrawal from the artist's work into the critic's
personal impressions, the undogmatic Paterian approach could bring about
a more intimately involved appreciation of the artist's aims and temperament, looking more attentively for the work's qualities than for its failures
to match a preconceived standard such as Arnold's 'high seriousness'.
After Pater's subversion of the critic's claim to objectivity, the attempt to
sustain fixed standards of judgement was widely discredited, and the need
for sympathetic flexibility widely accepted in its stead, even in the least
decadent of circles. Howells, for example, a democratic realist hostile to
the aristocratic tone of English aestheticism, came to the same kind of
conclusion in 1902:

> Criticism no longer assumes to ascertain an author's place in
> literature. It is very well satisfied if it can say something suggestive
> concerning the nature and quality of his work, and it tries to say
> this with as little of the old air of finality as it can manage to
> hide its poverty in.[15]

This sort of humility is in one sense of course the diametric opposite of
Wilde's model of the critic as independent artist, but it is the more
orthodox stance even among Pater's immediate disciples. One of these,
the prolific literary historian George Saintsbury, presented the arrival
of the undogmatic spirit as the great liberating breakthrough in modern
criticism, in his three-volume *History of Criticism and Literary Taste in
Europe* (1900–04; the appearance of 'Taste' in the title is significant). The
new gospel, finally recognized after centuries of dogmatism, is that criticism must adjust itself to literature, not the other way round, that we

must judge a work by its own merits, not by a preconceived standard. The establishment of this principle he credits principally to Coleridge, but Pater's application of it is warmly supported, including its hedonistic relishing of ecstatic moments of response. While Saintsbury upheld the Paterian method as Professor of Rhetoric and English Literature at the University of Edinburgh, Walter Raleigh, who held chairs in English literature successively at Glasgow and Oxford, likewise resisted the fixed standard in the name of sympathetic appreciation. His 1912 essay on Matthew Arnold (collected in *Some Authors* (1923)) accuses the Victorian critic of rigid classicism and of lack of real sympathy for English literature in general and for the Romantics in particular. Raleigh's earlier *Wordsworth* (1903) openly rejects such 'judicial' fault-finding approaches in favour of a Paterian sympathetic identification with his subject, setting out to read Wordsworth as the poet himself would have wished to be read. His insufferably pretentious early work *Style* (1897) had gone even further in the rejection of explicit standards, upholding instead the spontaneity of instinctive good taste. In the United States, too, J. E. Spingarn summarized the position of modern criticism in 1911 by announcing that the impressionists and anti-impressionists alike now shared a common Romantic assumption that their critical task was to elucidate what an author was trying to express and then judge how well that aim had been achieved, rather than measure the work against a neoclassical standard such as the true imitation of nature or of classical models. Accordingly, all the inherited baggage of mechanical concepts like rules, genres, style, rhetoric, technique, themes, moral judgements, social contexts, and literary history itself should be discarded in favour of a direct intuitive encounter with the imaginative source of the artist's expression.[16]

Spingarn's 'expressionist' rejection of all critical categories and concepts harmonizes with the attitudes of the English Paterians – with Saintsbury's dismissal of critical theory and with Raleigh's contempt for judicial standards. There was an evident danger that such positions would lead to the mere exhibition of personal taste, and indeed to the extinction of criticism itself. For according to the logic of pure Aestheticism as cultivated by Wilde in the 1880s, the refined appreciation of aesthetic sensations did not in itself require the existence of literary or artistic works at all, but could be derived just as well from the presence of a lily or of a rosy-cheeked boy.[17] In principle, then, the independent qualities of a literary work could be ignored in favour of the aesthete's generalized enthusiasm for beauty. An extreme example of this problem was picked up by John Churton Collins in reviewing the *Retrospective Reviews* (1893) of the minor aesthete Richard Le Gallienne, who had written 'What matters it that one does not remember or even has never read great writers? Our one concern is to possess an organization open to great and refined impressions.'[18] Where it had become a licence for ignorance, as here, the free play of taste clearly required some stabilizing control and correction.

The problem with the impressionist position was identified clearly by W. C. Brownell, a New York publisher's editor, in his short book *Criticism* (1914), where he complained that all the impressionist can say ultimately is 'I have true taste', whereas criticism that is to be of any value for its readers must also be able to justify its decisions in some rational form. Meanwhile for academic critics especially, the establishment of sound knowledge as a counterweight against the freewheeling of impressionism had become a professional obligation.

A revealing passage in J. A. Symonds's *Walt Whitman* helps to give us a sense of the importance of this issue for the very grounding of the critic's own authority. In the midst of rhapsodizing about Whitman's universal qualities as a poet (his works 'embody the essence of realities in living words which palpitate and burn for ever,' and so forth), Symonds pauses to remark

> I do not think it needful to quote examples. Those who demur and doubt may address themselves to an impartial study of his writings. It is enough for me, trained in Greek and Latin classics, in the literatures of Italy and France and Germany and England, who have spent my life in continuous addiction to literature, and who am the devotee of what is powerful and beautiful in style – it is enough for me to pledge my reputation as a critic upon what I have asserted.[19]

Symonds comes dangerously close here to asking us to accept his word as a gentleman of taste, but in fact the weight of his credentials falls upon his knowledge: he is a gentleman with a library, and his taste has been trained. The academic followers of Pater also needed, at least officially, to introduce this element of qualification to their delectations of literature. George Saintsbury, for example, acquired a doubtful reputation as a 'wine-tasting' critic, partly because he was indeed an authority on fine wines, but also because he asserted that aesthetic theory had no more connection with poetic criticism than the geology of the vineyard had with wine-tasting.[20] And in his many works of literary history he does often give the impression that he is ransacking the cellars of European literature in search of piquant flavours. But in his occasional peevish self-justifications he claims to be pursuing the historical and comparative method rather than mere tasting, and he insists that sure critical taste and judgement can be founded only upon the critic's extensive reading in as many literatures and periods as possible.

Taste tempered by Knowledge was the formula trusted by those academic critics who had, with Pater, abandoned the rigidity of objective standards. As an educational objective, this ideal of informed taste, avoiding both the aridity of mere factual knowledge and the arbitrary passivity of mere appreciation, was propounded at the University of Cambridge by the first active Professor of English Literature there, Sir Arthur Quiller-Couch, in his lectures of 1913–14. The ideal graduate from his courses, he hoped, would 'be remarkable less for something he can take out of his wallet and exhibit for knowledge, than for *being* something, and that "something" a man of unmistakeable intellectual breeding, whose trained judgement we can trust to choose the better and reject the worse.'[21] The most convincing exponent, though, of the responsible correction of taste by knowledge was A. C. Bradley, Professor of English at Glasgow, and subsequently Professor of Poetry at Oxford. Bradley's celebrated *Shakespearean Tragedy* (1904) adopts a recognizably Paterian ideal of sympathetic understanding of the works from within, eschewing the application of external standards, and its starting-point is less the text in itself than our overall impression of its effect upon us; but this impression has always to be responsible to the actual evidence of the text, just as any interpretation of a play must attempt to account for all of its facts. Bradley tempers the impressions of aesthetic appreciation, then, with a scientific respect for evidence. It is worth noting also that the knowledge that he calls upon is a knowledge of the chosen text in its entirety, not – as with Saintsbury – a general accumulated knowledge of literature as a whole, nor a specialist knowledge of language, history, or theatre.

Bradley has another claim to importance as a mediator between aestheticism and academic criticism. His inaugural lecture as Oxford Professor of Poetry in 1901, boldly entitled 'Poetry for Poetry's Sake', borrows the arguments of the aesthetes and symbolists in order to isolate the proper object of the academic critic's attention as poetry itself, as distinct from the ulterior ends by which it may be judged. Poetry is for Bradley an end in itself with its own intrinsic value, which is not to be confused with any social, moral, or religious value that it may also happen to have or to lack. Poetry is neither a part of the outer world, nor a copy of it, but an autonomous world of its own, whose special laws the critic must respect in order to appreciate it. In particular the critic should beware of importing into this sovereign sphere of the imagination the inadmissible laws of the outer world, whether of morality or of knowledge. Bradley distinguishes himself from the aesthetes only in disclaiming the notion that art is the supreme goal of human life, and in disputing the concept of pure form isolated from expression. Adopting the Paterian principle of the indivisibility of form and content in poetry, he dismisses on the one side the formalist heresy of form detached from substance, and the more common error of conceiving a substance prior to form. Poetic value resides in the poem as a whole, which contains neither of these abstractions. Bradley uses an argument that was forty years later to become central to the doctrine of the New Critics: that one cannot change the words of a poem without changing the meaning, so a prose paraphrase will always fail to embody the poem's 'content'; the poem simply 'means itself'.[22]

Within its academic context, Bradley's endorsement of the autonomy of poetry was more than just a prestigious echo of Aestheticism; it had a further value, alongside similar defences of 'literature itself' from extrinsic concerns, in defining a distinct object of inquiry for the academic discipline of literary study, qualifying it for independence from neighbouring disciplines such as philosophy, history, and philology. Troublesome as they might be in some of their extreme versions and in their morally disreputable associations, the principles of Pater, Wilde, and Symons could, if sifted carefully, be adapted to secure the foundations of a truly independent field of academic inquiry.

As organized under the title of 'English', though, this new discipline had still to emancipate itself from the grip of the philologists. For this reason we hear a good deal from professors of literature in this period about the utter irrelevance of merely linguistic facts to the true understanding of literary works. John Churton Collins conducted a ferocious public campaign against philology's stranglehold on English Studies. The least insulting thing he could say about it was that it was a science, and should therefore keep clear of subjects belonging to the humanities. On more intellectual grounds, W. J. Courthope took issue with the philologists' insistence that English literature has its roots in Anglo-Saxon poetry. On the contrary, he argued in his *History of English Poetry* (1895–1910) and elsewhere, it began only with Chaucer. This of course implied a radical disconnection between the philologists' field of the history of language on the one side, and the autonomous history of literature on the other – a divorce celebrated enthusiastically by Quiller-Couch at Cambridge. Quiller-Couch again insisted that Chaucer was the true father of English literature, which was descended from Roman, not Saxon sources. The notion that *Beowulf* was the founding work of the English tradition was, he told his students a few months before the outbreak of the Great War, 'a falsehood grafted upon our text-books by Teutonic and Teutonising professors'.[23]

These were, at least on the surface, arguments about literary history – a neighbouring discipline of inquiry which by its nature had contributed to the relaxation of objective standards in criticism itself. For the literary historian, the understanding of works from earlier periods requires the suspension of inappropriate modern critical expectations, just as modern works cannot be held to the standards of previous ages. Literary history then, in its dissolution of 'eternal' criteria, could be called upon as an ally of the Paterian sympathetic approach in supporting the appreciation of literary works according to their own standards rather than by the measure of codes imported from other contexts. Apart from Saintsbury, who combines the two traditions in his work, serious literary historians of this period held aloof from aesthetic impressionism, regarding the 'personal sympathy' of Pater's followers as a poor basis for historical understanding; but they concurred all the same in the abandonment of the old *a priori* standard of judicial criticism as an obstruction to their neutrally scientific investigations and reconstructions of literary 'evolution'. Impressed by the scientific aims and prestige of modern French literary history as practised by Hippolyte Taine and Ferdinand Brunetière, some of the leading British and American literary historians adopted the principle of 'inductive' investigation, working up from the observable facts rather than down from abstract rules and principles. In such terms Richard G. Moulton, Professor of Literary Theory and Interpretation at Chicago, had called for a science of literary study in his *Shakespeare as a Dramatic Artist* (1888), and later codified its principles in his textbook *The Modern Study of Literature* (1915). For Moulton, judicial criticism was a legitimate activity, but its arbitrary expressions of taste and opinion were best left to the reviewers so that the scientific scholars could get on with studying the laws of literary development. Moulton's scientific formulation of the task of literary interpretation – that it should seek to account for all the evidence of the text – provided the rule followed by Bradley in his work in Shakespeare. Leslie Stephen in his *English Literature and Society in the Eighteenth Century* (1904) similarly sets aside judicial canons the better to trace in partly Darwinian terms the ways in which the various species of literature are determined by the larger organism of society. He sees it as the historian's duty to explain why works of the past appealed to people of their time, whether or not we value them now: their value should be understood as being relative to the conditions for which they were fitted.

To the more conservative upholders of stable critical standards, it seemed that criticism was being undermined by a new relativism sponsored by an unprincipled alliance of whimsical aesthetes and neutral scientists. From their different camps both groups had destabilized the order of literary values in their open abstention from judgement – the one by making it relative to the capricious impressions of personal taste and sympathy, the other by making it relative to the prevailing historical conditions. There were temporary advantages to both groups in this conjunction of opposites against inherited dogmatisms, and there were even – as we have seen in Bradley's case – credible forms of reconciliation between the sympathetic and the scientific approaches. But the alliance was to prove an unstable one, with distrust on both sides. Before long, literary history would come to appear as a pedantic impediment to the liberties of criticism just as its sister-science philology had been, and would be thrown off and reconstructed on a critical rather than a scientifically neutral basis. Already in this pre-war period we find protests from Symons, Raleigh, Spingarn, and others in the impressionist camp, against the bogus scientific 'laws' of literary evolution derived from Brunetière, against the mechanical confusion of the contextual conditions of literature with its freely creative essence; essentially against the tyranny of irrelevant Knowledge over Taste.

So far as we have been considering only the solvent tendencies of post-Paterian criticism and literary history and their corroding effects upon the objectivity of critical standards. But these developments were not universally welcomed, and it is important to review also the rearguard actions of those critics who hoped to reconstitute a more stable foundation for critical judgement after the model of Matthew Arnold. A significant school of Arnoldian classicists made itself heard in the first years of the twentieth century, particularly in the United States. To this group belong the Harvard philosopher George Santayana, his colleague Irving Babbitt, with Paul Elmer More, assistant editor and then editor of the New York weekly *The Nation*, and – from the very different background of English Toryism – the literary historian W. J. Courthope. These critics react not only against the recent sapping effects of literary relativism but more generally and ambitiously against the longer tradition of Romantic lawlessness in the culture of the nineteenth century.

Santayana, a Spaniard by birth, was to quit the uncongenial Puritan climate of New England for permanent residence in Europe in 1912. But while still at Harvard he surveyed, with a condescension even more Olympian than Arnold's, the barbarism – as he saw it – of modern liberal and Protestant (that is, Romantic) literature in *Interpretations of Poetry and Religion* (1900), and measured it against the higher wisdom of Lucretius and Dante in *Three Philosophical Poets* (1910). In his general reflections upon poetry, Santayana demands more from it than just sensuous power; it must re-interpret our experience and our destiny for us in the light of higher ideals and a comprehensive vision. By these standards, even Shakespeare is found wanting in imaginative completeness and philosophical coherence, while the further disintegration of western culture into the Romantic cult of passionate intensity is worse still in denying us any sane universal grasp of reality. In his most substantial critical essay, 'The Poetry of Barbarism' (1900), Santayana takes the egotistical eccentricities of Browning and Whitman as examples of this final lapse from classical sanity into a blind vehemence of aimless imaginative passion. Whitman is charged with abandoning reason in formless primitivism, and Browning censured for celebrating passionate experience for its own sake, without reference to ideals or general concepts. Both poets present us only with chaotic impressions of a self-satisfied vitality, failing to rise above the undisciplined profusion of their sensations. Great art, however, must embody rational ideals and aspirations, with formal discipline: 'Clarification of ideas and disentanglement of values are as essential to aesthetic activity as to intelligence. A failure of reason is a failure of art and taste.'[24] Santayana places little personal blame on these poets, whose charm and power he acknowledges; rather, their insufficiency is attributed finally to the fundamental incoherence of western culture since antiquity, divided as it is between its two sources of classical civilization and Christian religion. In the end, no poet after Homer can hope to be as coherent as Santayana would demand. Accordingly, he has eventually to unbend forgivingly to the virtues of the moderns. By 1913, he even relaxes Arnold's own standards by paying tribute to the pure spirituality of Shelley, despite his deluded revolutionism.

Santayana's literary criticism is to some extent incidental to his larger body of work in philosophy and general aesthetics. His colleague Irving Babbitt, taking his cue partly from Santayana's strictures, developed a more sustained critique of nineteenth-century literature and criticism, in a sequence of anti-Romantic works. *Literature and the American College* (1908) denounces the twin evils of pedantry and dilettantism in modern literary study, seeing them as complementary departures from the humanist conception of balanced wisdom. They are the academic manifestation of the rise of 'naturalism', by which Babbitt means the cult of nature in either its sentimental (i.e. Romantic) or its scientific form. The sources of these cultural ills are traced in *The New Laokoon* (1910), and the principles of a humanist response to them explored in *The Masters of Modern French Criticism* (1912). The weightiest arguments are those developed in *The New Laokoon*, where Babbitt grants the necessity of the Romantic revolt against an excessively artificial neo-classical taste, but bemoans the fact that in casting off mechanical formalism Rousseau and his followers abandoned form, restraint, and discipline along with it, running away with one half-truth or irrational imagination in reaction against another half-truth of unimaginative reason. The humanist law of measure and balance, Babbitt argues, calls instead for a reconciliation of the two, an imaginative reason of the kind achieved by the greatest poets. Rousseau's followers, though, have pitted the senses and the imagination against the reason, basking in a sensual reverie disguised as mystical idealism, so that whereas in great art we have the intellectualizing of sensation, in the works of the Romantics we find the sensualizing of the intellect. Because 'naturalism' abandons the human law of self-restraint in favour of the natural law of unlimited self-expansion, a humanist revival is needed to combat both its scientific and its Romantic excesses.

Babbitt is at his sharpest when showing how the apparently antagonistic split halves of nineteenth-century culture – Romantic fancy and scientific fact – are related through the common cult of natural expansion, and how they have since arrived at an implicit accommodation: having surrendered the notions of reason, law, and classification to the scientists, the Romantic rebels now find that their art is in practice reduced to 'catering to those who wish relaxation from analysis – to the tired scientist, and the fagged philologist and the weary man of business'.[25] But it is also at this point that he is most panicky and self-contradictory. Scientific vigour and Romantic reverie are presented here in gendered terms as the 'masculine' and 'feminine' sides of modern culture, but Babbitt, in all other contexts an advocate of balance and reconciliation, seeks now to correct only 'that predominance of the feminine over the masculine virtues that has been the main cause of the corruption of literature and the arts during the past century'.[26] Uncomfortable, like many other professors of literature, about the 'sissy' reputation of literary study, he reacts with a call for the re-masculinizing of culture, at least in the sense that the dreamy indistinctness of the Romantics' conception of the world must be combated by a renewed emphasis on the value of the rational category, the intellectual distinction: 'The revival of this firm and masculine distinction,' Babbitt declares, 'can alone save us from the confusions that have crept into modern life and literature.'[27]

Concluding his survey of major critics in *The Masters of Modern French Criticism*, Babbitt attempted to salvage the idea of critical standards from the twin relativisms of the scientific and impressionist schools. Conceding that the critic could no longer pluck a fixed yardstick from the air or from Aristotle, he insisted that some standard more reliable than personal caprice or temporary popularity must be upheld. The best restraint upon our merely personal judgement would be the collective wisdom, not of humanity as a whole (as Brunetière had once proposed), but of the perceptive minority. Under this flexible discipline, the humanist critic would be selective yet sympathetic, invoking neither a purely external law nor a purely subjective prejudice but a standard responsive both to individual insight and to the needs of a larger cultural order.

The literary criticism of Paul Elmer More, later yoked with Babbitt's under the slogan of the 'new humanism', is of a more applied nature. Where Babbitt takes criticism into the realm of the History of Ideas, More as a periodical essayist and reviewer assesses particular writers' reputations as biographies and collected editions happen to arrive on his desk at *The Nation*. The governing themes and anxieties of his *Shelburne Essays* (11 vols, 1904–21), are, however similar: the unrestraint of nineteenth-century literature and the need for the recognition of higher laws to check the relativism of modern thought. Like Santayana, More sees Browning as a false prophet of blindly vehement passion, who failed to raise us to the contemplation of man's higher nature; but he is harsher than Santayana on Shelley's undisciplined emotionalism, and on the unbalanced emphasis and vulgarity of Dickens. In a general survey of Victorian literature he regrets that most modern writers from Tennyson to Swinburne and Whitman have been mere 'singers of the flux', falsely worshipping the 'idol of Mutability';[28] they have neglected that vital principle of permanence in human destiny which the poets of the seventeenth century recognized. The Romantic abandonment to the changing stream of nature, in disregard of the spirit of permanence, leads to social anarchy and an enfeebled literature, demonstrated in the failure of modern writers to produce great tragedies. More's evident alarm at the swirling flux of the modern temperament goes even deeper than Babbitt's, and calls forth a stronger craving for some fixed transcendental principle. Despite recognizing in Matthew Arnold's criticism a tendency to invoke dead precepts of the past, he holds fast to that element of Arnold's work which shows purposeful moral valuation, against Pater's insidious invitation to hedonistic surrender. More even denies Pater the status of critic at all, since he obliterated the independent reality of other artists in his own consistent mood of weary impotence. As with Babbitt, the proper humanist response to the effete fluidities of the impressionist school is to mount a 'virile' reaction against the prevailing philosophy of the flux.

These American humanists found the force of their resistance fatally inhibited by the nebulous character of their ideals, which come down to intelligence and self-control, pitted against the repugnant throbbings of sensuality. Unable to agree on how much modern fluidity could safely be contained, they were also unwilling to endorse external authorities to stem it, falling back instead on abstract models of balance and upon the cloudy Emersonian notion of the 'inner check'. No such scruples bothered their inferior English counterpart W. J. Courthope, a civil servant, sturdy Imperialist, and sometime literary editor of the *National Review*, an organ of strict Conservative principle. For Courthope the stabilizing force to be set against modern cultural wilfulness was unquestionably that of Nation and Empire. Through the six volumes of his *History of English Poetry* he attempts to follow the evolving expression of the English national life through its poets, who disclose the spiritual sources of their country's majestic history. Where a more sophisticated literary historian like Leslie Stephen could identify the bases of literary movements in their links with specific social groups, Courthope can see only the undifferentiated spirit of the nation as a whole unfolding itself in literature. The argument of his *History* maintains consistently that the great poets have harmonized the opposed tendencies of the national spirit just as the English Constitution itself perfectly balances the claims of Liberty and Authority. Courthope's extraordinary lectures as Professor of Poetry at Oxford have since been forgotten without trace (he was unfortunate in having Bradley as his successor), but they provoked some murmurs of approval in their day, and in their published form as *Life in Poetry, Law in Taste* (1901) they are worth revisiting for the model they provide of high Imperialist, ultra-classicist critical principle. Courthope appears here as a defender of the 'law' of organic national life and of 'universal' literary principles derived from Aristotle, against the relativisms of Pater and Saintsbury and the *laissez-faire* principle of unregulated personal taste. Even Arnold is too lax for him, and is scolded for his decadent individualist abstention from the currents of national life. Modern literature's excess of individualism (in Browning, again) must be corrected by a renewed sense of the universal; the poet must individualize universal truths, not universalize his individual eccentricities. Decadence and pessimism can be overcome by renewing the connection of literature to the active life of the nation, as Rudyard Kipling imperfectly apprehends in his sense of manly discipline and imperial order. Both the effete tastes of the aesthetes and the coarsened tastes of the vulgar can be corrected by the reassertion of an acknowledged critical standard, derived from the practice of the classic (i.e. representatively national) writers. Courthope sees it as 'the object of all patriotic endeavour to strengthen the established principle of authority in matters of taste, and to widen its base so as to meet the needs of our imperial society.'[29]

By performing the part of King Canute against the onrushing tide of decadent relativism, the critical partisans of Arnoldian classicism inevitably invite their measure of ridicule. But (with the exception of Courthope) it would be misleading to dismiss them as unthinking reactionaries. Reactionaries they certainly were – their rhetoric of balance notwithstanding – but the critical distance they put between themselves and the Romantic tradition did produce genuine illuminations of the problems of nineteenth-century literature, of a kind that enabled T. S. Eliot and others in the next generation to set new bearings.

Modernism Nascent

A special development towards the end of this phase of criticism is the emergence of a movement that we would now recognize as 'modernist' in its principles. Although the full unfolding of this major critical trend belongs to the years after 1918, some of its distinctive features are already apparent from about 1910, in the work of an advance-guard comprising Ford Madox Hueffer (later known as Ford Madox Ford), Ezra Pound, and W. B. Yeats.

Along with Henry James, Yeats provided the early modernist critics with a vital example of a late-Victorian and now twentieth-century literary artist dedicated to freeing his craft from the encumbrances of Victorian conventions. The purified directness of his poetry had prompted Symons in 1900 to praise its impersonality and to single out as its truly modern feature Yeats's realization that verse should have the simplicity of good prose. This same idea of poetry living up to prose standards later became a much-repeated doctrine of Ezra Pound's, although he was to attribute it to Hueffer rather than to Symons or Yeats. Similarly Yeats's poems are praised by Pound for casting off the old baggage of rhetoric; but in this case, as in some others, Yeats was, in addition to being a model of the new artistic practice, an active critical proponent, as we have seen, of its declared principles, consciously recreating the very standards by which he was to be appreciated. Beyond his immediate campaign against rhetoric, Yeats also initiated an important modernist tradition of simplified literary history – with important consequences in its developments by

Pound and Eliot. Not content just to avoid or object to the over-rhetorical excesses of nineteenth-century poetry, he sought to account for their origins in some earlier cultural calamity. His essay of 1902 on Spenser places that poet's career at the crucial point at which the old gaiety of Merry England was about to be obliterated by bourgeois puritanism and the prostitution of poets to the aims of the State. Two years later in his little magazine *Samhain* he contrasted the vitality of language and experience in the Middle Ages with the vacuous rhetorical commonplaces of the modern age: 'It is the change that followed the Renaissance, and was completed by newspaper government and the scientific movement, that has brought upon us all these phrases and generalizations, made by minds that would grasp what they have never seen.'[30] Drawing here upon the Victorian medievalism of John Ruskin and William Morris, Yeats casually wraps up a few centuries of cultural history into a simple lapsarian tale of 'dissociation', as it would later be called, and directs the attention of his modernist followers to the dating of the great anti-poetical Fall.

Ford Madox Hueffer acted as a significant intermediary between the generations of Yeats and of Pound. In 1909, Yeats was 44 years old, Pound 24, while the 36-year-old Hueffer was conducting his brief but exciting editorship of the *English Review*, which he had founded at the end of the previous year. A collaborator with Conrad and a disciple of James, the well-connected Hueffer managed to combine in his journal the talents of the older writers – James, Conrad, Wells, Yeats – with those of newly established Edwardians like Forster, Chesterton and Bennett, and at the same time discover and encourage important new talents including those of D. H. Lawrence, F. S. Flint, Wyndham Lewis, and Ezra Pound. His own critical writings are few, but they are timely in their support for fresh methods and in their impatience with England's insular Victorian heritage. He defended the fiction of Conrad and James as the most important modern work, contrasting its impersonal and selective methods of 'impressionism' with the clumsier descriptive approach of the naturalists and with the intrusive commentaries of the Victorians. In poetry, he expressed his boredom with the tradition of Tennyson and Swinburne, and with the hackneyed ruralism of English verse, looking forward to a new school of poets who would embrace contemporary urban life. He also offered his younger followers a new model of the critical essay, which he made far more informal and direct in its unadorned assertions, sometimes irritatingly chatty in tone. Most of all he enjoyed the sight of young troublemakers like Pound and Lewis aggressively casting off the Victorian traditions. One of his *English Review* essays, defending the duty of the critic to upset conventionally accepted valuations, offered the following hypothetical case:

Now, supposing that a critic should arise to say that *Paradise Lost* is a dull and pompous work, and that the figure of Milton, by obscuring the less well-known seventeenth-century poets, has shut our eyes to a whole world of lyrical beauty for which all the epics and all the prose writing of Milton can never make amends, all men with their accepted ideas on a literary hierarchy will exclaim against the impertinence or the very atheism of the critic.[31]

That critic did indeed 'arise', under Hueffer's own encouragement, and his name was Ezra Pound.

The American poet-critic had arrived in London in 1908, and immediately set about making himself the indispensable organizer and propagandist of the new literary generation, circulating his provocative views through a succession of little magazines on both sides of the Atlantic: Hueffer's *English Review*, A. R. Orage's *The New Age*, and Harriet Shaw Weaver's *The Egoist* in London, Harriet Monroe's *Poetry* in Chicago, and Margaret Anderson's *Little Review* in New York. By 1915, he could summarize the heresies for which he had already become notorious:

I am known to hold theories which some people think new, and which several people know to be hostile to much that hitherto had been accepted as 'classic' in English poetry: that is to say, I reverence Dante and Villon and Catullus; for Milton and Victorianism and for the softness of the 'nineties I have different degrees of antipathy or even contempt.[32]

Pound's enthusiasms were for the very old and the very new. By the year 1918 he had published a book-length revaluation of medieval European literature – *The Spirit of Romance* (1910) – and shorter critical endorsements not just of Yeats and D. H. Lawrence but of the newer arrivals James Joyce and T. S. Eliot. His chief heresies were in effect bolder developments of ideas suggested earlier by Yeats, with whom Pound spent three winters from 1913 acting as the elder poet's secretary. Fulfilling Hueffer's prophecy, Pound adopted an implacable anti-Miltonism, that was to unsettle for the next three decades the reputation of a poet usually placed second only to Shakespeare in the English pantheon. Pound wished to demote him to a rank slightly below that of Drummond of Hawthornden. 'Milton is the worst sort of poison,' he wrote, and 'a thoroughgoing decadent in the worst sense of the term.' This 'most unpleasant of English poets' had blighted the course of English poetry with his stilted Latinisms and the hollow noise of his bombast; as for his ideas, they only showed 'his asinine bigotry, his beastly hebraism, the coarseness of his mentality'.[33]

There was, fortunately, more to this than name-calling. The critical assassination of Milton was in one sense the belated revenge of the

Symbolist school against its old enemy, English Puritanism, achieved by striking at its most sacred poet. Certainly larger cultural antagonisms were involved, and Milton was accused as merely the most prominent villain in a general poetic delinquency, the general pattern of which follows Yeats's sketch of the great Fall into moralizing rhetoric. In Pound's version, the Renaissance corrupted its linguistic energies through the over-cultivation of rhetoric, so that from the time of Shakespeare until the rediscovery of poetry as a musical art by Swinburne in the 1860s, English poetry was a degraded instrument in the hands of puritan doctrinaires and moralizing preachers like Whitman, Tennyson, and Wordsworth ('a silly old sheep', despite his gift for natural imagery[34]). Few nineteenth-century writers escape this whipping: Browning and Swinburne are spared in England, Flaubert and Turgenev in Europe, but the century as a whole is condemned for blurry sentimentalism, for emotional slither, for stupidity and softness. Pound's hostility to Victorian literature is not to be mistaken for a generalized assault on the past, of the kind announced by the Italian Futurists. On the contrary, Pound seeks to show that the post-Miltonic line of poets represented a departure from the true traditions of poetry to which he urges a return – the classical and medieval tradition from Homer through Chaucer and Dante to Shakespeare. To do this he has to go back to its earlier phases and draw a new map of European literature.

Pound's forays into literary history show him to be a new kind of medievalist, indeed a new kind of literary historian. Contemptuously abandoning the safe routines of the academic philologists and the 'scientific' historians, he embarked on a militantly *critical* account of the poetry of the past, measuring it all against his own contemporary Imagist standards for verse: directness of treatment, avoidance of rhetorical ornament, precision and intelligence. Periods, influences, contexts, conventionally accepted reputations, and the other scholarly evasions could afford no protection against the searching critical questions of today: whose work is really still worth reading now? What is needed, Pound believes, is 'a literary scholarship which will weigh Theocritus and Yeats with one balance, and which will judge dull dead men as inexorably as dull writers of today, and will, with equity, give praise to beauty before referring to an almanack.'[35] Established historical scholarship and the philological study of literature have failed by treating all facts as if they had equal value. The German philological tradition is especially obnoxious in setting up scholarly 'authorities' on specialist subjects divorced from vital human values. In his wartime essay 'Provincialism the Enemy' (1917), Pound rails against 'the whole method of this German and American higher education,' which is 'evil because it holds up an ideal of "scholarship", not an ideal of humanity.'[36] Invoking the humanist watchword of discrimination, Pound presses instead the claim of a new revaluation of literary traditions, one that rejects all provincialisms and specialisms. The provincialism of national canons will be set aside in the search for excellence in world literature, just as the provincialism of time – the conventional attachment to the tastes of the preceding generation – must be resisted by rediscovering forgotten works of excellence. For Pound, the study of literature is not an accumulation of dead knowledge but a form of hero-worship, in which authentic heroes – Catullus, Arnaut Daniel, Villon, Dante, Flaubert, James – have to be restored in place of the over-praised usurpers like Virgil (the Milton of his age), Petrarch, Ariosto, Tasso, Milton, or Tennyson. Pound approaches criticism with the aim, odd as it might seem, of a popularizer, determined to make available the very best of the world's poetic riches. The style of his critical writings has a blunt informality and an opinionated urgency, while their structure is often characterized by the loose disconnection of interim drafts. They seem to be the rough notes of an anthologist rather than the polished deliberations of a critic. Indeed *The Spirit of Romance*, like some of his essays, is a sort of annotated anthology of translations, and his 1918 essay on Henry James breaks down into the form of an extended reading list.

While revaluing the past, Pound was also assessing his contemporaries by new critical standards. Holding to Yeats's principle, he praised the poetry of Eliot for its rejection of rhetoric. Verse should, he held, attain the directness of good prose, and so should shun the ornamental descriptions and the syntactical inversions of the Miltonic tradition. The more positive qualities he demanded were those of intelligence, 'hardness', and precision, the last being the most essential to the poet's function. In reaction against the 'soft' vagueness of the 1890s, Pound cultivated a steely scientistic conception of the poet, who is likened both to a pure mathematician in aloofness from practical motives and to various kinds of recording instrument in exactness of sensitivity. The poet provides us with our most reliable 'data' for measuring new ethical or emotional conditions. Indeed, 'the poet is a sort of steam-gauge, voltameter, a set of pipes for thermometric and barometric divination.'[37] This ostentatiously technological vocabulary is used partly to disguise the fact that Pound is reviving the old Romantic model of the heroic artist-as-prophet. He recalls, for instance, Flaubert's claim that the disaster of the Franco–Prussian war could have been avoided if people had understood his novel *L'Education sentimentale*, and quotes letters of Henry James with the purpose of showing that the American novelist had foreseen the inevitable conflict between Germany and the English-speaking world. It is in this context of prophetic divination that he makes his much-quoted assertion that 'Artists are the antennae of the race'.[38]

It is a curious feature of Pound's critical writing that his demands for a new precision are often couched in lamentably imprecise terms, as when he predicts that the poetry of the twentieth century 'will move against poppy-cock'.[39] All the same, the importance of his work is inescapable. Far from being a mere continuation of Yeatsian Symbolism, it manages to synthesize the positions of Symbolist, realist, and humanist critics: it praises Lawrence, Joyce, and Eliot for their 'realism', and conceives of poetry as a true record of perception; and it follows the humanists not just in anti-philological polemic but in the demand for intelligence, against the vague emotionalism of the nineteenth century. It rarely gives us any measured analyses of individual works, but in the international scope of its interests, in the combative informality of its style, and above all in its implacable assertion of the primacy of critical valuation over neutral history, it places Pound at the head of the modernist revolution in literary criticism as in poetry.

Shakespeare the Omniscient

The Victorian critical and theatrical traditions in England had, with the backing of the great Romantic Shakespeareans Coleridge and Hazlitt, elevated the figure of Shakespeare to the status of 'oceanic' Genius, even a kind of national divinity. He was also the great literary enigma, concealing his own personality behind his creations like a hidden god. The implications of this status for criticism were severely distracting: when the critics were not pouring out awestruck Bardolatrous effusions to the sublimity of the National Poet, they were trying to unlock the 'riddle' of the sonnets, or of Hamlet's madness. A coded warning about the dangers of peeping behind the surface of art into its secret depths had been issued by Oscar Wilde in his teasing narrative 'The Portrait of Mr W. H.', published (in its less explicit shorter version) in *Blackwood's Edinburgh Magazine* in 1889. In this story an effete young man claims to discover the truth about the sonnets and their dedicatee, and wins his friends around to the explanation that Shakespeare was in love with a beautiful boy actor named Will Hughes; but when his corroborating evidence is exposed as a forgery, he commits suicide. After composing this tale, Wilde threatened his friend Robert Ross with a sequel discussing the question 'whether the commentators on *Hamlet* are mad or only pretending to be.'[40]

The flood of cranky Shakespeareana nonetheless continued unabated in this period. Solutions to the riddle of the sonnets included *Shakespeare's Sweetheart* (1907) by Sarah H. Sterling and *Shakespeare Self-Revealed in His Sonnets* (1904) by 'J.M.'. The wisdom of the Bard on all aspects of human – and indeed vegetable – life was illustrated in such works as D. H. Madden's *The Diary of Master William Silence: A Study of Shakespeare and of Elizabethan Sport* (1897), William L. Rushton's *Shakespeare's Legal Maxims* (1907), August Goll's *Criminal Types in Shakespeare* (1909), and in *Shake-*

speare's Garden (1903) – a complete account of plants in Shakespeare by the aptly-named J. Harvey Bloom. Meanwhile on the schismatic fringes of the literary church, the disputes intensified between the 'Stratfordians' (who believed in the one and indivisible Bardhead of William Shakespeare himself) and the anti-Stratfordian advocates of Lord Bacon or of some sinister committee as the true author, as in Harold Johnson's *Did the Jesuits Write Shakespeare?* (1910). In reaction against the plentiful excesses of this strange English cult, Bernard Shaw kept up a mischievous debunking campaign, exposing Shakespeare's dramatic blunders and maintaining that *As You Like It* was the most ridiculous play ever to have been staged.

Some sort of critical sanity was urgently needed amid this chaos. It was offered most persuasively by A. C. Bradley in a number of his lectures, of which the most important are collected in his *Shakespearean Tragedy* (1904). In its subsequent fortunes, this is the single most successful critical work of the Edwardian period, having been reprinted repeatedly for the benefit of successive generations of students. Its modern reputation is as a work representative of its earnest time, safely traditional but perhaps excessively concerned with the minutiae of character – an imbalance challenged only by the insights of younger critics in the 1930s. In fact Bradley's book involves several departures from nineteenth-century orthodoxy, and the dangers of its motive-hunting characterology were clearly identified (by John Churton Collins and Walter Raleigh, among others) as soon as it was published. The impression of reassuring stability which *Shakespearean Tragedy* afford us derives partly from the limits of its subject (it avoids the quicksands of the 'problem plays' and has nothing to say on Shakespeare's poetic language), partly from its magisterial weighing of evidence, and partly from Bradley's philosophical demand for an all-embracing equilibrium. A Hegelian philosopher by training, Bradley draws silently upon Hegel's theory of tragedy, with its conflicts of ethical principle, but brings it down to the apparently more palpable level of individual character, so that the tragic conflict becomes a matter of internal spiritual imbalance or over-emphasis. Proceeding from the general rule that character is destiny, he can set out to establish the meaning of each play by judicious assessment of all the 'clues' offered by the leading character's actions and speeches. The book invites some comparison with Conan Doyle's contemporaneous Sherlock Holmes stories, as we are led to the solution that accounts for all the evidence through the elimination of unsatisfactory partial hypotheses. It is a detective process into which we as lay readers are flatteringly invited, as Bradley asks us to check critical hypotheses against our own unspecialized knowledge of human psychology. Before long, we know his methods, and can retrace the steps of his deductions.

Bradley's confidence in the comprehensive sanity of his approach emboldens him to reject some of the most authoritative pronouncements on Shakespeare, notably those of Coleridge. To begin with, he disregards

Coleridge's valuation by removing *Antony and Cleopatra* from the highest rank of Shakespearean tragedy, and thus (along with seven other tragic plays) from his book, which is concerned only with the 'pure' tragedy of *Hamlet, Macbeth, Othello,* and *King Lear.* In the analysis of Iago's character too, he overrules Coleridge's famous diagnosis of 'motiveless malignity' in favour of conscious, in fact semi-artistic, egoism. More ambitiously still, he disputes the shared view of Schlegel, Coleridge, and Dowden on the cause of Hamlet's delay, refusing to attribute it to an excess of the reflective faculty, and advancing his own explanation in terms of the prince's melancholy. Establishing his independent authority as a balanced arbiter of interpretations, Bradley can also address the larger question of Shakespeare's tragic conception of the world. To the relief of readers who have been troubled by the novels of Thomas Hardy, he can show that Shakespeare's view is no pessimistic fatalism; but then neither does it present a fundamentally benign order of things temporarily invaded by evil, since evil is part of the original order. Bradley has to conclude that Shakespeare abstains from giving us theological solutions, and that his tragedies in general – and *King Lear* in particular – confront us instead with the painful mystery of human greatness and its waste.

As if to compensate for his inability to provide the solution to the whole riddle – or even to the problem of Hamlet's behaviour towards Ophelia, over which he worries for many pages before admitting defeat – Bradley undertakes to answer a host of minor queries in appendices with titles like 'Where was Hamlet at the time of his father's death?' and 'Did Emilia suspect Iago?'. These diversions have been widely regretted and mocked, but in fact most of them show a clear awareness of the limits of relevant speculation. For example, the notorious question 'How many children had Lady Macbeth?' is in fact dismissed as a red herring in Bradley's note on the Macbeth progeny: 'It may be that Macbeth had many children or that he had none. We cannot say, and it does not concern the play.'[41] Likewise Bradley chides those earlier commentators who had convinced themselves that they knew the colour of Lady Macbeth's eyes or hair: 'They know much more than Shakespeare, who tells us absolutely nothing on these subjects.'[42] He is, however, open to the reproach of confusing self-contained fictions with real life when he lapses, in the main chapters, into discussing the childhood of Cordelia or the demeanour of Hamlet before his father's death. Despite defending the marvellous improbabilities of Shakespeare's plays against those who would condemn them by the inappropriate standards of a realistic novel, Bradley himself evidently wants to rewrite these plays as Victorian novels, with the characters' motives explained and all the loose ends of the plots neatly tied up.

These tendencies in Bradley may be more or less irritating or perhaps charming to some readers, but they are symptoms of larger presuppositions. One of the founding premises of *Shakespearean Tragedy*, pitted against Romantic myths of the Bard as an unconscious child of Nature, is that Shakespeare was a conscious artist. This was a necessary reassertion, and Bradley does not mean by it that Shakespeare was always in perfect control of his materials: there are defects of construction in *King Lear*, and notorious inconsistencies of psychology in *Hamlet*. He does mean, though, that Shakespeare must always have been in full command of his intentions, and that these can therefore be reconstructed by the critic. So, discussing the great riddles of Iago's and Hamlet's motives for their actions, Bradley concedes that the characters themselves may not be able to read their own enigmas, 'But Shakespeare knew the answer, and if these characters are great creations and not blunders we ought to be able to find it too.'[43] Bradley's detective or cryptographic quest for consistency, in characters and other aspects of the plays, is founded on this unreliable supposition, which is unable to admit anything intermediate between a blunder and a willed design, and which adopts a religious conception of Shakespeare's infallible knowledge of all human souls, even his own. In another Oxford lecture, on Shelley (1904), Bradley conceded that poets do not express a pre-existing view of life but discover one through their work. But in *Shakespearean Tragedy* he repressed this element of the uncontrollable and the unconscious (in the Romantic or Freudian senses), and thus found himself rather at sea in such a work as *King Lear*. His book is certainly notable for the extent to which it undertakes close interpretative scrutiny of selected passages – a surprisingly rare critical procedure before the 1920s – but its larger aim, like that of the biographical hobbyists, is to look not *at* Shakespeare's works so much as *through* them, to their omniscient progenitor.

Bradley's leading competitor was a disappointment. Walter Raleigh's *Shakespeare* (1907) should, as the keystone volume in the prestigious *English Men of Letters* series, have been a more distinguished work than it turned out to be. Raleigh makes some sharp responses to Bradley's character-based approach, but otherwise gives us little more than a routine celebration of the National Poet's many-splendoured breadth of mind, with his work constructed reassuringly into the shape of a maturing life: the buoyancy of the early comedies and histories, the agonized internal turmoil of the 'dark' comedies and mature tragedies, the restful serenity of the late romances (a pattern established by Edward Dowden's *Shakespere* (1875)). Against Bradley, who had argued rather absurdly that the late romances end happily because they are dominated by non-tragic characters, Raleigh can discover in himself an unaccustomed Aristotelian streak, replying that we must proceed the other way round, from plot to character: thus Cordelia is a function of the dramatic story and her imagined childhood is of no possible relevance, while Hamlet's character is not a principal cause of his situation. Raleigh goes further: 'A play is not a collection of the biographies of those who appear in it. It is a grouping of certain facts and events around a single centre, so that they may be seen at a glance.'[44] Here the Oxford Professor forgets his Aristotle and stumbles inadvertently upon a 'spatial' conception of Shakespeare's plays that was to become the basis of the new critical school of the 1930s, but he makes nothing of it. In fact his objection to character-study is founded on an 'intentionalist' principle shared with Bradley himself, the difference being that the story is taken to have been primary in Shakespeare's own mind, the study of character therefore distracting us from access to that creative source. And, even more urgently than Bradley, it is a direct contact with the playwright's omniscient mind that Raleigh seeks, for its unparalleled knowledge of the 'eternal truths of human nature'.[45]

Like Bradley again, Raleigh is convinced that Shakespeare discloses his mind to the attentive reader in the plays and the sonnets (he dismisses the view that these poems were more conventional than personally confessional, as Churton Collins and others held). In his earlier work, *Wordsworth* (1903), Raleigh had treated *The Prelude* as a reliable autobiography rather than as a poem, and had automatically identified the speaker in poems like 'Anecdote for Fathers' with the poet himself. Similarly in *Shakespeare* he peers through the writings to the man behind them. So in reading Shakespeare 'we are overwhelmed by the sense that we are in the presence of a living man,' and at the awful conclusions of his tragedies we have at least 'the comfort of the sure knowledge that Shakespeare is with us'.[46] The living man Shakespeare is, however, not as other men are: he is broader in spirit, more universal than the one-sidedness of lesser beings. He is, indeed the biggest and most potent creator of them all, and his divinity, so far removed from the effeteness of Wilde's fantasized pederast, asserts itself in sublimely Priapic or phallic majesty, especially 'when he collects his might and stands dilated, his imagination aflame, the thick-coming thoughts and fancies shaping themselves, under the stress of the central will, into a thing of life . . .'[47]

It is perhaps not surprising that American critics have for the most part tactfully absented themselves from the Shakespearean rites. We have noted already, though, that George Santayana, enjoying the critical aloofness of a Spanish-American high classicist, lamented in general terms the philosophical incoherence of the Stratford poet in his *Interpretations of Poetry and Religion* (1900). Eight years later his elegant essay on *Hamlet* took this objection further, admiring the complexity of the prince's characterization but remarking that Hamlet and his author are both blind to ultimate issues. Shakespeare is generally more impressive in weaving the texture of his works than in building their structure, just as Hamlet embroiders philosophical problems without grasping their totality. Santayana reads the prince as a type of the perplexed modern romantic mind, and specifically as a kind of soulful northern barbarian, earnestly idealistic but lost amid the complexities of a culture whose roots lie in the more corrupt and sceptical Mediterranean world. In thus specifying the cultural matrix of Hamlet's confusion, Santayana denies that the play represents any 'universal' destiny; rather it shows us a particular kind of unripeness, which he implies is the immaturity of Protestantism itself. Rather than treat the play as a clear window into the mind of its author, Santayana more honestly takes it to be a mirror for its readers, 'in which our incoherent souls see their own image'.[48]

The Novel and Realism

Critical discussion of 'The Novel' as a literary genre dignified with serious aesthetic properties of its own, as distinct from incidental assessment of individual novels and novelists, can be dated from a few years before our period. It was not that the middle of the nineteenth century was without its conscientious reviewers of novels; only that the leading critics like Arnold had little to say on this form, and those who did write on it seldom reflected in general terms on its particular formal problems as a literary art. This situation had been transformed in the early 1880s by a transatlantic controversy about the new American realism of Henry James and W. D. Howells. It was these two novelists, in fact, who had started the debate in their critical articles. Howells's eulogistic essay 'Henry James, Jr' (1882) in New York's *Century Magazine* had been received in the British press as a national insult, because of its suggestion that the work of James represented a finer art than that of Dickens and Thackeray, especially in its artistic impartiality and in its 'analytic' development of character. James's own essay 'The Art of Fiction' (1884) modestly avoided any comment on that controversial comparison, but it called all the same for a more convincing realistic representation of life from novelists, at the same time announcing that it was time for a considered theory of the novel as an art. James's essay in effect inaugurated in the Anglo-American world the modern theory of fiction, while Howells's tribute helped to shape its first debates by arranging the critics into antagonistic camps.

As it appeared from Britain, Howells was holding up his compatriot as a better novelist than the British writers of the last generation, chiefly on the strength of James's concentration on psychological character-analysis at the expense of external action or plot. There arose in opposition to the threat of the American realists a campaign which carried along with it at various times over the next twenty years such British critics as George Saintsbury, Edmund Gosse, J. A. Symonds, Andrew Lang, Arthur Symons, and W. E. Henley, together with the popular novelists R. L. Stevenson, Rider Haggard, and Hall Caine. The reaction was a confused alliance, directed largely against straw figures. It included both a hard core of Tory critics carrying the cavalier banner of 'Romance' against the democratic roundhead Howells, and a looser array of objectors who questioned the concept of realistic representation on more abstract aesthetic grounds. The motives for resistance varied from distaste for excessive psychological analysis in fiction and fear of contamination by European pessimisms and sexualisms, to the defence of art in general against slavish copying of the external world. The Tory Romancers – Saintsbury, Henley, and Lang – hoped to resist what they saw as the American emphasis on manners and motives by calling for a return to 'poetic' action and adventure in fiction. Their heroes were Scott and Stevenson, their villains not just the Americans but such overly analytic or psychological English novelists as George Eliot and George Meredith. At times they seem to suggest that the future of the novel lay with *Kidnapped* or *King Solomon's Mines* rather than with *The Portrait of a Lady* or *Middlemarch*. Their position is summarized by George Saintsbury in the expanded version of his essay 'The Present State of the English Novel' (1892), where he declares realism to be already exhausted, giving way to the higher poetry of action and incident. His advice to the novelist is 'Disrealize everything, and never forget that whatever art is, it is not nature.'[49] Fortunately, he remarks, there is still too much healthy beefiness in the English character for it to succumb to the sterile pessimism of the Russian novel. Saintsbury went on to write appreciations of such romancers as Harrison Ainsworth and Bulwer Lytton in *The Historical Novel* (1895), and in his later book *The English Novel* (1913) he nominated Scott as one of the four great novelists in English, with Fielding, Austen, and Thackeray.

Some of the other British opponents of realism were in fact closer to the position of James than they probably realized. Arthur Symons, for instance, expressed similar admiration for the French novelists Balzac and Flaubert, and impatience with the clumsy joviality of the English novel. His real objection was to the schematic and charmless realism of the Zola school, which he condemned on strictly aesthetic rather than moral grounds as a submission to exteriority and materialism. Following the defection of Huysmans from Zola's group in the direction of mysticism, he hoped (with other 1890s critics) that the novel would now explore the spiritual and subconscious depths rather than the social surface of life. Edmund Gosse, in his essay 'The Limits of Realism in Fiction' (1890), also looked forward to some new mood of mystery in the novel, the realist school having inevitably come to grief in dealing with the fundamental aesthetic problem of reflecting life's breadth in the small mirror of art. Gosse was a more attentive student of realist fiction than most British critics, refusing to be panicked into treating it as a moral disease; and in fact he paid tribute to the twin schools of Zola and James for having swept away the absurdities of earlier conventions:

Whatever comes next, we cannot return, in serious novels, to the
inanities and impossibilities of the old 'well-made' plot, to
the children changed at nurse, to the madonna heroine and the
god-like hero, to the impossible virtues and melodramatic vices.
In future, even those who sneer at realism and misrepresent it
most wilfully, will be obliged to put in their effects in ways more
in accord with veritable experience.[50]

Two years later, in 'The Tyranny of the Novel', Gosse came round to
calling for a new realism, expressing impatience with the concentration
of almost all novels on the courtship of hero and heroine. There were
great expanses of human life – especially of working life – lying unexplored, and so far only Zola had set out to chart them. An early prophet
of the 'death of the novel', Gosse warned that the demand for novels
could collapse as it had in the 1820s if some new subject-matter were
not found.

The last eccentric gasp of the British anti-realist school (or of this
phase of its existence) is to be found in the flamboyant critical writings
of G. K. Chesterton, and especially in his *Charles Dickens* (1906). The
aim of this lively and argumentative book was to revive Dickens's reputation from the disapproving shadow of realist standards. Dickens is
adopted as a heroic romancer who produces mythologies rather than
novels, and whose *David Copperfield* stands as a great refutation of the
realists, proving that life really *is* exaggerated and incredible. It is clear
that Chesterton's real enthusiasm is for the early works of his hero,
particularly for their exuberant optimism, which contrasts so sharply with
the pessimism of the modern age; and he regrets Dickens's decline into
realism in his later novels as a betrayal of his true genius. The absurd
extreme of Chesterton's anti-realism is reached in his refusal even to
discuss novels themselves:

> Dickens's work is not to be reckoned in novels at all. Dickens's
> work is to be reckoned always by characters, sometimes by
> groups, oftener by episodes, but never by novels . . . Strictly, there
> is no such novel as *Nicholas Nickleby*. There is no such novel as
> *Our Mutual Friend*. They are simply lengths cut from the flowing
> and mixed substance called Dickens . . . [51]

This outright denial of form is a desperate measure by which Chesterton
can shield Dickens from the standard against which he had been found
wanting by the American realists, that of 'the art of the novel'.

Turning to Howells and James themselves, we find a balanced and
undogmatic assessment of the aesthetic problems of realism, with which
the British critics rarely credited them. Far from believing in any simple
reflection of life, they take from the first the problems of artistic selection,

composition, and arrangement to be central to their craft. Neither upholds any naïvely 'photographic' conception of the novelist's representation of life; indeed, even Zola had denied this, to deaf ears. For Howells, realism is essentially a commitment to truth-telling, a refraining from the temptation to tidy up the complications and asymmetries of events into an easy formula or thesis. His many magazine reviews and essays repeatedly defend his realist heroes against the charge of moral indifference, often sharply returning the accusation upon the romantic tradition: thus Zola and other realists have shown crime and violence to be sordidly unattractive, whereas the purveyors of historical romances have glamorized them shamelessly. The realist shows the impartiality or impersonality befitting an anatomist of human affairs, whereas the inartistic novelist intrusively comments and moralises upon events, Thackeray being the most prominent sinner in this regard. Against Thackeray's 'confidential' manner of addressing the reader directly in judgement of his characters, Howells asserts that the business of the novelist 'is to put certain characters before you, with as little of the author apparent as possible.'[52] Howells's other leading principle was the priority of character over plot. This point was again directed partly at the inferior sort of popular historical romance, with its succession of improbable disasters undergone by woodenly formulaic characters. But it stands as an accusation too against the British tradition of Fielding, Scott, Thackeray, and Dickens. For Howells, the predominance of plot was a sign of primitive technique in fiction, from which the modern novel must emancipate itself. Among the English novelists before George Eliot, he singles out Jane Austen as the most modern: she shows an ability rare in English fiction, that of subordinating the excitements of incident to the development of character. By the end of the century, Howells had come to admit that the realist crusade had in fact been too 'romantic' all along in its idealistic hopes (notably in the case of Zola, a poet in spite of himself), and had met defeat at the hands of a public which preferred the sugared falsehood to the bitter truth. Still, there remained Tolstoy and a few other truth-tellers whose work still called for public defence and praise.

Henry James's critical writing is a good deal less combative. It includes some grumbling against the obtuse moralism and prudery of Anglo-Saxon culture, but in general it exhibits a series of self-regarding, even self-caressing meditations upon the problem of shaping the endless complications of life into the composed form of the novelist's art. The most significant of his critical works after 1890 are his essays on the major French novelists – of which the best are his assessments of Flaubert and Balzac (both 1902) – and his celebrated Prefaces to the New York Edition of his own novels (1907–17). James retains a conception of the novelist as hero, and his own heroes are Flaubert, Turgenev, George Eliot, and Henry James, not necessarily in that order. Balzac and Zola are flawed heroes pitting themselves against impossibly encyclopaedic ambitions and finally breaking under their burdens. Flaubert is praised as the novelist's novelist, but James cannot agree with Howells's view of Tolstoy's supremacy: the author of *War and Peace* appears alongside Dumas and Thackeray in James's famous indictment of the nineteenth-century novel in his Preface to *The Tragic Muse*. Here he complains against the works of these authors that they are pictures without adequate composition; they may have life in them, 'but what do such large loose baggy monsters, with their queer elements of the accidental and the arbitrary, artistically *mean?*'[53] James's own ideal, on the other hand, is clearly the Flaubertian discipline of artistic economy, which can incorporate the variousness of life while organizing it around a coherent 'centre' of interest.

The challenge before the novelist, which means, in his Prefaces, before James himself as he recollects the germination and development of his various works, is then to work up from the confusions and potentially endless ramifications of his material an 'organic form' in which all the elements are interrelated so as to satisfy the requirements both of realistic representation and of artistic composition. His reminiscences about the mysterious quickening of his novels into this form of life do throw out a few unconnected observations about his own preferred methods – the advantages of the dramatic or 'scenic' method of presentation over the descriptive, the use of one character's consciousness of events as the centre of the novel – but these are not offered as a doctrine or a system, as they would come to be in the manuals of James's disciples. As an authority on the technique of fiction, the Henry James of the Prefaces is largely an invention of Percy Lubbock and others who attempted to remove his stray observations from their context and to codify them. The direct legacy of his critical essays is more a matter of attitude and style: a seriousness of approach to matters of form and craft in the construction of novels, and in critical writing an appearance of heroic striving for that elusive formulation of art's secret which is somehow always just too subtle for even the most elaborate syntax finally to capture. The critical prose of F. R. Leavis would later fall fatally under the spell of the master-conjuror's strenuous teasings. In the short term, though, it was James's standing as the dedicated artist that counted for most.

Ford Madox Hueffer's short book *Henry James* (1913) announces without hesitation that James is the greatest of living writers, an artist of international rank who has raised the novel in English at last to the status of an art worthy of comparison with European fiction. Hueffer dismisses 'the botched and amateurish productions of the schools of Scott, Dickens, Thackeray, Reade, Dumas, and George Eliot,'[54] complaining of their buttonholing or sermonizing intrusiveness. It is notable that Hueffer praises James and Conrad, here and in other critical essays, in terms not of realism but of 'impressionism', thereby stressing their art of selective presentation. By this time James and Conrad were being held up (by Hueffer, Pound, Mencken, and James himself) as examples of an art superior to that of the more insular English realists Wells and Bennett, who were found to have failed in digesting their material into composed forms. Pound, for instance, in essays of 1918 on James and on Joyce's *Portrait*, praises these two novelists as more sensitive and comprehensive than the Wells–Bennett school. Virginia Woolf, who would later pass influential judgement upon the same Edwardian realist tradition, had by this time written numerous anonymous reviews for the *Times Literary Supplement*, in which her strongest admiration had been expressed for Tolstoy, Dostoevsky, Charlotte Brontë, Hardy, and Conrad. Of the majority of Victorian novelists she complains in Jamesian terms that they did not know how to leave anything out of their works. But for James himself she shows a notably qualified enthusiasm, objecting in an early review of *The Golden Bowl* (1905) to his excessively detailed analyses and to his wearying effort 'to get everything said that there is to say.'[55] She is in effect invoking a yet more exacting standard of artistic economy which would place even 'the Master' among the baggy monsters he had fought.

Even though there were still those in this period, like Arthur Symons and Irving Babbitt, who doubted whether the shapelessness of the novel could ever really be disciplined to the highest standards of art, a larger body of critics followed James in treating it with the seriousness applied to drama and painting, and in asking more of it than it had generally yet given in formal accomplishment. Novelists regarded as 'difficult', like Meredith and James, or 'philosophical' like Eliot and Hardy, called forth full-length critical studies devoted to their works. And there were even a few works on technical construction, such as Joseph Warren Beach's *The Method of Henry James* (1918) and Clayton Hamilton's *Materials and Methods of Fiction* (1909), which has a chapter on 'point of view' citing James's *What Maisie Knew*. These, however, were relatively isolated symptoms of a growing attention to form, which appeared against a background of a still habitual concentration on favourite characters and authors. Chesterton's outright refusal to discuss novels rather than the undifferentiated substance of the author's mentality is only the most extreme instance of the general trend. The most marketable kind of work on novels is indicated by Howells's lavishly illustrated two-volume work *Heroines of Fiction* (1901), a coffee-table book which debates the relative charms of several favourite characters. If we turn to a more sober and respectable critical study such as Leslie Stephen's *George Eliot* (1902) in the *English Men of Letters* series, we can see a similar bias in weaker form.

Stephen's book is intelligent and sympathetic, and in many respects still a useful introduction to Eliot's life and work. It proposes an interesting theoretical compromise (rather like Hueffer's) between realist and impressionist conceptions of novelistic truthfulness. By no means hagiographic, it judges *Romola* quite severely and faults the imbalances of the other novels by turns. But its dominant concern is really to define

the temperament and powers of observation shown by George Eliot, and
to weigh the extent to which her various characters convince and attract
the reader. Thus the later novels are said to suffer from their author's
withdrawal from direct observation of life, and many of the leading male
characters (Stephen Guest, Will Ladislaw, Felix Holt, Daniel Deronda)
are criticized as weakly-drawn dummies or unworthy heroes. It remains,
for all that, one of the better works on fiction in a phase of criticism as
yet untouched by Jamesian theory.

Canons for Everyman

Although in various ways the Symbolists, Arnoldian classicists, and early
modernists were holding out for a clear distinction between the highest
literary achievements and the merely notable, the three decades after
Arnold's death in 1888 are not marked by the maintenance of any
strictly closed canon of excellence. The dissolution of 'objective' standards
brought about by the catholic curiosity both of impressionist dilettantes
and of scholarly literary historians allowed considerable room for the
shifting of reputations, for the rediscovery of lost writers, and for
the cherishing of medieval antiquities regardless of poetic worth. In any
case, no critic of wide authority had yet appeared to fix the valuations
of the novel, nor of American literature in any genre; and apart from the
superiority of Shakespeare little interest was shown in the relative standing
of other dramatists. The only canon that had acquired some stability was
that of English poetry (usually taken at this time to include Scottish
poets). Edmund Gosse helpfully provided readers of the New York magazine *Forum* in 1889 with a list of the fifteen greatest poets in this tradition,
in order to show that America had not yet produced an indisputable rival
to them. His list comprises Chaucer, Spenser, Shakespeare, Milton,
Dryden, Pope, Gray, Burns, Wordsworth, Coleridge, Byron, Shelley,
Keats, Tennyson, and Browning. In a further article replying to respon-
dents, he justified his exclusion of Marlowe and Scott, and mentioned
Herrick and Elizabeth Barrett Browning as possible outsiders.

   The English poetic pantheon as presented by Gosse was not a settled
matter for his contemporaries. Even Milton, as we have seen, was open
to assault from Pound, who wished to reinstate Chaucer as England's
second poet; and other names were at least conjured with. Christina
Rossetti, for instance, was spoken of in the highest terms by Symons,
Saintsbury, and Hueffer: Saintsbury called her one of the world's great
religious poets, and Hueffer went further by claiming that she was 'far
and away the greatest master of words and moods that any art has

produced'.[56] William Blake was a favourite of the aesthetes of the 1890s: Symons in 1907 published a whole book on him, as Swinburne had before him; and Saintsbury expressed some admiration, although more for the *Poetical Sketches* than for the *Songs* or the prophecies. Well before the major rehabilitation in the 1920s, John Donne was being studied by some of the decadent poets, and Saintsbury in his widely-used textbook *A Short History of English Literature* (1898) praised him as the most gifted writer of his age apart from Shakespeare – to the horror of Churton Collins, who protested on behalf of Milton and Jonson. An interesting feature of this period's poetic pantheon, at least by contrast with later reversals, is the almost universal veneration in which Shelley is held, even at the most politically conservative end of the spectrum occupied by Courthope, Saintsbury, and Raleigh. These and other critics – including the normally unswerving Santayana – turn against what they see as Arnold's cruel treatment of him. The name of Hopkins does not appear in discussions of modern poetry for the simple reason that his works were not published until 1918; and similarly Emily Dickinson, unpublished until 1890 (when her poems were greeted with enthusiasm by Howells), took some time to become more widely appreciated. Longfellow, Emerson, Poe, and Whitman, however, were all evidently well known and granted some importance even among the most insular of British critical circles. Poets of quite minor achievement were treated with respect in the literary histories: Arthur Symons in his *The Romantic Movement in English Poetry* (1909) gives some measure of attention to no fewer than eighty-seven poets, many of them scarcely heard of since then.

In prose fiction and drama, reputations were even less fixed. There is one curious case here, that of Herman Melville, whose works had disappeared almost entirely from sight, going unmentioned in several accounts of American prose writers. Otherwise it is notable that critics of this period tend to assume in their readers a knowledge of characters in Scott, Thackeray, and Meredith that could not be called upon so confidently in later periods. Jane Austen survived well, being immune to the cold blast of realism that damaged other reputations; but the Brontë sisters tended to be overshadowed by the partisans of Dickens and Thackeray. The realist critics were more interested in maintaining an international pantheon of novelists (with either Flaubert or Tolstoy at its summit) than in the cruder line of British authors, and they left it to Saintsbury to attempt the establishment of orders of merit: as we have noted, he placed Fielding, Scott, Austen, and Thackeray in the highest places, but in the turmoil of controversy at this time he carried no special authority. Given the miserable state of nineteenth-century dramas in English, the glories of the dramatic tradition were less often spoken of, Shakespeare of course excepted. One special category was singled out by some critics as requiring vigilant exclusion from the canon, this being Restoration comedy. Leslie Stephen abandoned the historian's impartiality to remark that this kind of drama 'must have been written by blackguards for blackguards', while the wholesome American realist Hamlin Garland attested that the plays of Wycherley and his contemporaries 'sicken us with the odor of the filth through which their writers reeled the night before.'[57] But even these expressions of disgust reveal that critics and their readers were familiar with the works in question; Stephen indeed shows that he is also aware of the plays of Aphra Behn.

This was a period of rapidly expanding mass education and mass literacy, the age also of the 'yellow press' in Britain and of 'muckracking' journalism in the United States. Fresh millions of readers had been created, and were able to acquire reading-matter cheaply, but they did not know by habitual association where to find the best books. An important response to this situation was the promotion by several publishers of 'classic' works in cheap pocket editions (in hard covers, as the age of the paperback was yet to come), in series with uplifting titles like the Temple Classics or the Muses' Library. The most substantial of these series were launched in the first years of the new century: The World's Classics in 1901 from the Oxford University Press, and the more ambitious Everyman's Library in 1906 from J. M. Dent under the editorship of Ernest Rhys. Accompanying these projects came various attempts to list the essential works of English literature that every well-read person should know. Two grammarians, H. Marmaduke Hewitt and George Beach, offered an extensive list ranked in four grades of importance in their *Manual of Our Mother Tongue* (1894). Their canon is fairly eccentric in its exclusion of Austen, Arnold, Browning, and Tennyson and its strong emphasis on works of theology and Scottish philosophy. Shakespeare is placed in a top category of his own, while the next rank includes historical works by Hallam, Carlyle, and Macaulay and other prose writings by Bacon, Bunyan, Newton, Addison, Johnson, Adam Smith, Jeremy Bentham, and J. S. Mill (but not Ruskin or Darwin, who appear nowhere on the list). Among the poets, Spenser, Milton, Dryden, Pope, Gray, Goldsmith, Burns, Wordsworth, and Byron are given places in this rank, but not Sidney, Jonson, Coleridge, Shelley, or Keats (Marlowe, Donne, Marvell, Herrick, and Blake are not listed even in lower ranks). Few novels are permitted this high position, but they include the entire sequence of Scott's Waverley novels, with *Robinson Crusoe*, Eliot's *Adam Bede*, and two works by Thackeray; Fielding, Dickens, Hawthorne, and Charlotte Brontë are allowed lower rankings.

A more important and more credibly representative effort along the same lines was Arnold Bennett's book *Literary Taste: How to Form It; with detailed instructions for collecting a complete library of English Literature* (1909). This was a self-help manual aimed at those who felt guilty about not reading the classics. It begins with some rousing encouragement (the purpose of literary study is not to pass away one's leisure hours but in fact to become alive to the world and to understand it), and some soothing advice to the intimidated (a book is just a man talking to you), but it also has some stern warnings to make: 'If you differ with a classic, it is you who are wrong, and not the book.'[58] Bennett's choice of Charles Lamb's 'Dream Children' as a sample to illustrate the nature of a classic is unfortunate, but the substance of the book is really the list of works (almost all from Everyman and other reprint series) recommended as first-rate. The entire home library of classics in 337 volumes costs less than £27, which is offered as a fair price for the ability to know what you are talking about in literature.

Bennett's selections differ from those of Hewitt and Beach in shifting the emphasis from theology and the eighteenth-century Scottish Enlightenment to the more liberal and scientific tradition of the nineteenth century: a majority of the recommended works are from the period since 1790, and they include controversial books by Paine, Wollstonecraft, Darwin, Rossetti, Pater, and Morris. Bennett does not expect us to read more than five of the Waverley novels, but he does include the full eighteen-volume Everyman set of Dickens and the complete novels of Austen, along with an abridged edition of Richardson's *Clarissa*. Fielding, Sterne, and Thackeray are represented, within a much broader array of novelists from Fanny Burney and Maria Edgeworth to Elizabeth Gaskell and Wilkie Collins. A number of poets, including Donne, Herrick, Blake, Tennyson, Browning, and Arnold, are restored to the canon, with a liberal selection of dramatists including Marlowe, Beaumont and Fletcher, Ford, Massinger, Webster, Wycherley, and Congreve. Bennett's canon, then, is more modern-looking than that of Hewitt and Beach in its catholic inclusion of poets, playwrights, and novelists: on the whole, only Americans and sinners (Rochester, Swinburne, Wilde) are notably excluded. Where it most significantly agrees with its predecessors is in the unquestioned assumption that 'Literature' includes all manner of non-fictional prose writings by scientists, travellers, economists, philosophers, critics, theologians, biographers, and historians. Hewitt and Beach may have preferred the claims of Paley's *Evidences of Christianity* and Dugald Stewart's *Moral Philosophy*, while Bennett regarded Malthus's *Essay on Population* and Ruskin's *Stones of Venice* as essential reading, but they concurred in the belief that literature meant good books of all kinds, not just good 'imaginative' or fictional books. This assumption, that works like Boswell's *Life of Johnson* or Gibbon's *Decline and Fall* and even Newton's *Principia* were just as much part of English Literature as Milton (all three are on Bennett's list), was the common sense not only of Ernest Rhys's Everyman series but of academic literary historians too. George Saintsbury's *History of Nineteenth Century Literature* (1896), for instance, has chapters not just on the poets, dramatists, and novelists, but on scientific, theological, historical, philosophical, and critical writing, and on journalism and periodicals. By contrast with the impending academic and modernist reductions of the literary canon to poems, novels, and plays, this generic inclusiveness is by far the most important feature of the canonical formation in the period before 1918.

Men of Letters and Great Loins

We have reviewed some of the issues foremost in the critical debates of this quarter-century, ranging from the moral status of modern writing to the possibility of maintaining objective critical standards; but there remain several significant trends which stand out more clearly in retrospect than they did to the participants themselves. To the ear of a literary critic of a later generation, the most important peculiarity of this period is a dog that does not bark: a resounding silence, that is to say, in one of the departments of criticism later taken to be its central function. Interpretation and analysis, so prominent in later periods as to be synonymous with criticism itself, appear to have been of little interest to critics at this time. The conduct of critical writing is instead founded upon the assumption that the critic's task is to define an impression of an author's sensibility or characteristic temperament, or to pick out a work's leading moods and character-portraits, not to delve into detailed questions of style, structure, or meaning. In a more general sense, of course, there was 'interpretation' of the kind that summarizes the true intentions of a controversial author like Ibsen or Whitman, and defends them against misunderstandings. And in the cases of some notoriously obscure writers like Browning and Meredith there were specialist guidebooks offering keys to the hidden meaning, just as there were those who set out to solve the famous enigmas of Shakepeare's sonnets or of his *Hamlet*. These examples, though, are the cranky exceptions that prove the rule. Only Bradley, to some extent provoked to resist these precedents while also falling victim to their cryptographic habits, conducts a modern-looking critical investigation into meanings, with detailed interpretation of passages. Otherwise it is widely taken for granted that it is not the critic's aim to intrude upon the inner secrets of literary works, but rather to weave around them a well-composed fabric of appreciation and comparative valuation. As for meanings, it is assumed that the reader has taken those already, without need for further interrogation. This bias against analysis may be attributed to the continuing strength of Romantic hero-worship in literary affairs, an inheritance which deflected the critic's attention towards the qualities of authors and away from the properties of their works.

The literary criticism written according to these assumptions is certainly incurious and even inattentive, but it maintains at least a high standard of composition, the critical essay being still at this time a genre of *belles-lettres*. Not just in its outstanding stylists – Wilde, Shaw, Yeats, Santayana, Chesterton – but among the majority of critics there is an evident desire to keep the standards of their writing up to those of a genuine prose art. This convention of 'fine writing' brings with it the inevitable excesses of vacuous elegance among the minor aesthetes, of digressive elaboration in the works of Saintsbury, and of preening preciousness in Walter Raleigh, but on the whole the criticism of this period is, by comparison with that of the later interpretative age, strikingly well written.

Two observations also need to be made about the leading personnel of literary criticism. An obvious development, well noted at the time, was the new prominence of academic critics. David Nichol Smith, for example, in a published lecture at Oxford, 'The Functions of Criticism' (1909), remarked that in contrast with the Victorian age of the independent 'man of letters' and periodical essayist, the leading critics of his day were now academics: he named Bradley, Raleigh, Saintsbury, the medievalist scholar W. P. Ker, and Courthope (who in fact was not an academic by profession). In one sense Smith spoke too soon, not foreseeing the impact of the modernist 'little magazines' and of poets and novelists outside the universities in the next two decades; but in broad outline he was picking up a trend of evident importance. A second significant development is still not adequately remarked, this being the emergence and the distinctive perspicacity of Irish and American critics in a scene hitherto dominated by English and Scottish interests. The advantages of cultural distance from the conventions of the British middle class are obvious enough in the work of the Irish critics Wilde, Shaw, and Yeats; but the more portentous breakthrough was the rise of the American critic. W. D. Howells, who had already done battle with the London journals, turned the tables on their condescension towards American letters by observing in a *Harper's Monthly* article in 1891 that it was the English who were now the true provincials in world literature: while American writers were responding to modern international movements from all parts of Europe, English authors were turning their backs upon this wider world to cultivate a narrowly national literature. Howells was speaking mainly of fiction and drama, but his comments are borne out in the comparative study of this period's criticism as well. The interests of British (and especially of English) criticism can be seen to have been deformed by a kind of ancestor-worshipping imperative, noticeable not only in Courthope's search for the national spirit in English poetry and in the academic over-emphasis on Anglo-Saxon 'origins', but also in the cult of the Bard and in the widespread fear that the novel would suffer foreign contamination. The American critics, released from the inhibiting grip of these preoccupations, show on the other hand the benefit of a wider international scope. The work of Howells, James, Santayana, Babbitt, and Pound has this more comprehensive range of comparison, arising from unashamed literary affiliation to continental European traditions. Academic literary study in the United States, too, showed a parallel development in the growth of Comparative Literature, a discipline unknown in Britain but fostered by Babbitt, Spingarn, Moulton, and other professors in America by way of resistance to the narrowness of their English departments. It was not that the centre of criticism in the Anglophone world had yet shifted across the Atlantic (the migrations of Wilde, Yeats, Shaw, James, Pound, Santayana, and Eliot tell their own tale: that the old literary centre still held); it was more that the American critics had given clear evidence of a greater range and freshness of insight by comparison with what Pound mocked as 'the British school of criticism for the preservation of orderly and innocuous persons.'[59]

It is hardly possible in our own age of gender-awareness in criticism to re-read the critics of the 1890s and the early twentieth century without being struck by the overwhelmingly masculine emphasis that prevails among them. In the first place, women were hardly visible as critics at this time: Virginia Woolf's early reviews were almost all anonymous, and apart from her work there is little to note except the erratic opinions of Alice Meynell, the participation of several women poets and editors in the modernist little magazines, and some sophisticated essays on fiction by the outstanding art historian and fantasy-writer 'Vernon Lee' (Violet Paget). For the most part, the world of criticism, especially in London, gives off the unmistakable whiff of the gentleman's club. Some of Hueffer's essays in fact openly presume that their readers are ensconced in their clubs; and many of the literary journals of the time sported clubland titles like *The Athenaeum, Belgravia, Pall Mall Magazine*, and *The Savoy*. We have noted already how Raleigh approached Shakespeare criticism as a kind of phallic cult, how Courthope countered the effeteness of the Decadents with an appeal for Imperialist manliness, and how Babbitt resisted the supposed predominance of criticism's indiscriminate 'feminine' sympathy by reasserting the need for masculine judgement. A clue to the nature of these anxieties can be found in one of Babbitt's formulations: 'It is of course well, and indeed indispensable, that the critic should cultivate the feminine virtues, but on condition, as Tennyson has put it, that he be man-woman and not woman-man.'[60] The devastating impact of Wilde's disgrace is felt here and throughout the critical culture of the period, threatening the critic's status with the taint of unmanliness. The posthumously published correspondence of Walter Raleigh shows him to have been deeply disturbed by these doubts, to the point of despising all critics as eunuchs; he eventually abandoned this effeminate occupation with some relief in favour of writing a history of the Royal Air Force. A more masculine kind of literature was demanded also by Saintsbury and the other advocates of 'Romance', whose ideal for the novel came close to the active heroic code of the boys' adventure story. Sir Arthur Quiller-Couch carried this ideal into his Cambridge lectures, pointedly addressing only his male auditors even though his audience was made up mainly of female students. His challenge to the young men of 1914 was to prove that they were men enough to match the great English heroes from Sir Philip Sidney to Scott of the Antarctic, and he advised them to use 'straight' active verbs rather than passive constructions, to distinguish their masculine expression from the prose style of a neuter. Having listed the true manly authors, 'Q' issued his final exhortation:

> Mention of these great masculine 'objective' writers brings me to my last word: which is, 'Steep yourselves in *them*: habitually bring all to the test of *them*: for while you cannot escape the fate of all style, which is to be personal, the more of catholic manhood you inherit from those great loins, the more you will assuredly beget.'[61]

We are led back again to the phallic source of literary power, in anxious reaction against the perceived effeminacy of literary study. Even the more modern spirits, less inclined to revere great English loins, are touched by similar concerns: Henry James worries in his essay 'The Future of the Novel' (1899) about the debasing effects of the predominantly female readership of fiction, and remarks in his Flaubert essay that women have no sense of artistic form. Ezra Pound's insistence on a new 'hardness' in literature to correct the 'softness' of the 1890s is a vaguer reformulation of the same worry.

It would be easy for the modern reader to take a simple attitude of condescension towards the critics of this period, and to dismiss them as antediluvian, or benighted in pre-theoretical and pre-analytic ignorance. A direct re-examination of their work, however, tends to illustrate the presumptuous folly of believing that all literary wisdom dates from 1920 or 1967. Even if one does adopt this essentially self-congratulatory standard, then surprising anticipations not just of the New Criticism (in Bradley) and myth criticism (in Yeats), but of Russian Formalist, structuralist and post-structuralist concepts (in Pound, in Santayana, and in Raleigh, of all people) can be found scattered in their writings, and there is even an early version of feminist critique (of the 'images-of-women' variety) in some of Shaw's work. The difference is not one of willingness to theorize (the major debates on realism and critical impressionism were in fact openly theoretical) but a question of the prevailing priorities in the agenda and the assumed duties of the critic. The literary critics of the 1890–1918 period simply had different battles to fight. The critic's most pressing duty is not, after all, analysis, but (in Sidney's terms) the defence of poetry: that is, the protection of literary imagination and creativity from the interference and sheer intolerance of myopic moralists and censorious puritans. Given the continuing pressures of puritanical conformism and provincialism in British and American culture, and the danger that the English-speaking countries would effectively insulate themselves against the wider modern world of art and thought, the critics of this period had a hard task before them; but their most confident leaders, from Wilde, Howells, Yeats, and Shaw to Hueffer and Pound, discharged it with some success and with lastingly attractive panache.

Notes

1. Edwin H. Cady (ed.), *W. D. Howells as Critic* (1973), pp. 149–50; from 'The Editor's Study', *Harper's Monthly*, June 1889.
2. Hamlin Garland, *Crumbling Idols* (New York, 1894), p. 71; p. 25.
3. Richard Ellmann (ed.), *The Artist as Critic: Critical Writings of Oscar Wilde* (New York, 1969), p. 235.
4. Arthur Symons, *Studies in Prose and Verse* (1904), p. 284; from Preface to 2nd edition of *London Nights* (1896).
5. Bernard Shaw, *Major Critical Essays* (1931), p. 317; from Preface to *The Sanity of Art* (1908).
6. Cady (ed.), *Howells as Critic*, p. 274; from 'My Favourite Novelist and His Best Book', *Munsey's*, April 1897.
7. J. E. Spingarn, *The New Criticism: A Lecture* (New York, 1911), p. 27.
8. John Churton Collins, *Ephemera Critica; or Plain Truths About Current Literature* (1901), p. 92.
9. For the American debates on this problem, see Gerald Graff and Michael Warner (eds), *The Origins of Literary Studies in America: A Documentary Anthology* (New York, 1989).
10. Matthew Arnold, *Lectures and Essays in Criticism*, ed. R. H. Super (Ann Arbor, MI, 1962), p. 258.
11. Walter Pater, *The Renaissance: Studies in Art and Poetry*, ed. Adam Phillips (Oxford, 1986), p. xxix.
12. Ellmann (ed.), *Artist as Critic*, p. 369; from 'The Critic as Artist'.
13. W. B. Yeats, *Selected Criticism and Prose*, ed. A. Norman Jeffares (1980), p. 118 (from 'Edmund Spenser'); pp. 51–2 (from 'The Symbolism of Poetry', 1900).
14. Yeats, *Selected Criticism*, p. 170; from 'Anima Hominis', 1917.
15. Cady (ed.), *Howells as Critic*, pp. 392–3; from 'Emile Zola', *North American Review*, November 1902.
16. Spingarn, *The New Criticism*.
17. See Ian Small, *Conditions for Criticism* (Oxford, 1991) for an account of this problem and its consequences.
18. Richard Le Gallienne, *Retrospective Reviews* (1893); cited in Collins, *Ephemera Critica*, p. 154.
19. J. A. Symonds, *Walt Whitman: A Study* (1893), p. 153.
20. George Saintsbury, *A History of Criticism and Literary Taste in Europe, Volume III: Modern Criticism* (1904), p. 169.
21. Sir Arthur Quiller-Couch, *On the Art of Writing* (Cambridge, 1916), p. 12.
22. A. C. Bradley, *Oxford Lectures on Poetry* (1909), p. 24. On Bradley's specification of literary studies' 'object', see Josephine M. Guy and Ian Small, *Politics and Value in English Studies* (Cambridge, 1993), pp. 162–4.
23. Quiller-Couch, *Art of Writing*, p. 162.

24. George Santayana, *Selected Critical Writings* ed. Norman Henfrey (2 vols, Cambridge, 1968), p. 112.
25. Irving Babbitt, *The New Laokoon: An Essay on the Confusion of the Arts* (Boston, MA, 1910), p. 207.
26. Babbitt, *New Laokoon*, p. 249.
27. Babbitt, *New Laokoon*, pp. 244–5.
28. Paul Elmer More, *Shelburne Essays: Seventh Series* (New York, 1910), p. 260; p. 263; from 'Victorian Literature'.
29. W. J. Courthope, *Life in Poetry, Law in Taste* (1901), p. 29.
30. Yeats, *Selected Criticism*, pp. 136–7; from 'First Principles', *Samhain*, 1904.
31. Ford Madox Hueffer, *The Critical Attitude* (1911), p. 12.
32. Ezra Pound, *Literary Essays of Ezra Pound*, ed. T. S. Eliot (1954), p. 362; from Preface to *Poetical Works of Lionel Johnson*, 1915.
33. Pound *Literary Essays*, p. 216 (from 'The Renaissance', *Poetry*, 1914); p. 238 (from 'Elizabethan Classicists', *The Egoist*, November 1917).
34. Pound, *Literary Essays*, p. 277; from 'The Rev. G. Crabbe, LL.B', *The Future*, 1917.
35. Ezra Pound, *The Spirit of Romance* (1910), p. 8.
36. Ezra Pound, *Selected Prose 1909–1965* ed. William Cookson (New York, 1973), p. 191.
37. Pound *Selected Prose*, p. 115; from 'Patria Mia', 1913.
38. Pound, *Literary Essays*, p. 297; from 'Henry James', *Little Review*, 1918.
39. Pound, *Literary Essays*, p. 12; from 'Credo', *The Poetry Review*, February 1912, reprinted from Ezra Pound, *Pavannes and Divisions* (1918).
40. Cited by Richard Ellmann, *Oscar Wilde* (1987), p. 282.
41. A. C. Bradley, *Shakespearean Tragedy: Lectures on 'Hamlet', 'Othello', 'King Lear', 'Macbeth'* (1904; Harmondsworth, 1991), p. 462 ('Note EE').
42. Bradley, *Shakespearean Tragedy*, p. 347n.
43. Bradley, *Shakespearean Tragedy*, p. 208.
44. Walter Raleigh, *Shakespeare* (1907), p. 199.
45. Raleigh, *Shakespeare*, p. 193.
46. Raleigh, *Shakespeare*, p. 13.
47. Raleigh, *Shakespeare*, p. 7.
48. Santayana, *Selected Critical Writings*, p. 145.
49. George Saintsbury, *Miscellaneous Essays* (1892), p. 409.
50. Edmund Gosse, *Questions at Issue* (1893), pp. 152–3. Gosse's essay 'The Tyranny of the Novel' is collected in the same volume.
51. G. K. Chesterton, *Charles Dickens* (1906; 8th edn, 1913), p. 66.
52. Cady (ed.), *Howells as Critic*, p. 270; from 'My Favorite Novelist and His Best Book', 1897.
53. Henry James, *The Critical Muse: Selected Literary Criticism* ed. Roger Gard (Harmondsworth, 1987), p. 515.
54. Ford Madox Hueffer, *Henry James: A Critical Study* (1913), p. 79.
55. Virginia Woolf, *The Essays of Virginia Woolf, Volume I: 1904–1912* ed. Andrew McNeillie (1986), p. 23; from the *Guardian*, 1905.
56. Frank McShane (ed.), *Critical Writings of Ford Madox Ford* (Lincoln, NE, 1964), p. 148; from 'Impressionism – Some Speculations', *Poetry*, 1913.
57. Leslie Stephen, *English Literature and Society in the Eighteenth Century* (1904), p. 35; Garland, *Crumbling Idols*, p. 40.
58. Arnold Bennett, *Literary Taste: How to Form It* (1909), p. 33.
59. Pound, *Selected Prose*, p. 421; from 'Remy de Gourmont', *Fortnightly Review*, 1915.
60. Irving Babbitt, *The Masters of Modern French Criticism* (Boston, MA, 1912), p. 339.
61. Quiller-Couch, *Art of Writing*, pp. 247–8.

Chapter 3
The Modernist Revolution: 1918–1945

T. S. Eliot and the Critical Agenda

The interval between the two world wars was in literary criticism a period of revolution. In this it resembles the first decades of the nineteenth century, when the critical principles of the Romantic movement overwhelmed an older code of polite decorum. Both revolutions were accelerated by all-engulfing warfare and political upheaval in Europe, and both were launched by poets clearing a public space for their own innovations in verse; but whereas the earlier revolution seemed to have behind it the inexorable groundswell of insurgence, the later triumph of modernist criticism gave the appearance of being a sudden putsch. More calculating, even conspiratorial, in its deliberate subversion, the modernist faction of literary criticism emerged at the end of the Great War from the underworld of Ezra Pound's coteries and little magazines with a decisive new leader, cunningly disguised as a London bank clerk. This was the poet and sometime extension-lecturer T. S. Eliot, an American expatriate who had become literary editor of the *Egoist* magazine in 1917, working alongside Pound and his associates. Eliot issued two small books of essays in the post-war years – *The Sacred Wood* (1920) and *Homage to John Dryden* (1924) – in which he took the initiative in drawing up a new agenda for literary criticism over the next four decades. In almost every significant critical debate until his death in 1965, it was the terms established by Eliot that governed the discussion, whether or not he was himself a direct participant; and any important new venture in critical work would take its bearings from his early writings. Thus we will find in this chapter's review of the salient developments in this period and its principal controversies that Eliot's writ runs widely: the battle between partisans of 'classicism' and 'romanticism' in the 1920s issues directly from his early provocations; the new procedures of critical 'close reading' developed on both sides of the Atlantic are conducted by repeated reference to his principles and example, as are the related rebellions of literary criticism against historical and linguistic scholarship in the universities; most attempts to define criticism's contemporary role in society are cast in terms of his diagnosis of cultural disintegration; the drastic reconstruction of Shakespeare criticism around metaphor rather than character receives his unexpected sponsorship; and the rewriting of the English poetic canon follows his initial draft almost to the letter. Only in the criticism of the novel and in the drawing-up of the American canon is his influence anything less than regnant.

It is likewise from Eliot that one must begin in sketching the main lines of influence that link the most important schools of criticism active in this period. In the simplest terms, a genealogy of the modernist advance-guard in literary criticism after the Great War would need to draw two thick lines from Eliot's early writings, one of them leading through the work of I. A. Richards of Cambridge University and on to the younger Cambridge critics around F. R. Leavis and his journal *Scrutiny*, the other to the 'Fugitive' group of poets and critics based in Tennessee, and thus on to the wider American grouping later known as the New Critics. There are various minor branches and some crossed lines that can be identified in more detail later in this chapter and in the next, but the principal fact about the long arm of Eliot is that the two most formidable critical schools in the phase from the Depression through to the Cold War – the New Critics in the United States and the *Scrutiny* circle in Britain – both traced their intellectual descent directly to Eliot, and quoted him incessantly.

The significance of Eliot's revolution in criticism will have to be developed in piecemeal fashion through the several subdivisions of this chapter, because it manifests itself across so many otherwise distinct spheres of critical discussion. For now, it may be sufficient to characterize his position as one of reaction, in terms of 'impersonality' and of classical 'order', against a Romantic and Victorian inheritance that was assumed to have exaggerated the importance of free personal self-expression in literature. Far more is involved, though, in this reaction than a shift of fashions for one kind of poem or play rather than another. As we shall see, Eliot brought into collision within literary-critical valuation the larger forces of contending historical, cultural, religious and political traditions; and moreover he did so at an advantageous moment when the dominant cultural habits of the nineteenth century stood starkly discredited by the disaster of the Great War, especially in the eyes of a younger generation looking for new directions. An apparently inconsequential preference for the work of certain seventeenth-century poets over most of the major nineteenth-century poets in fact dragged along behind it an extensive conservative condemnation of Western liberalism, Protestantism, Romanticism, democratic humanitarianism, individualism, and their various conceptions of 'progress'; in short, the central values of nineteenth-century art and thought, along with those of previous centuries.

Eliot's criticism reverberates, then, with the values of a cultural politics.

More immediately, it also carries specific implications for the practice of literary criticism itself, which can be understood most clearly again by reference to Eliot's doctrine of impersonality in literature. In his most influential essay, 'Tradition and the Individual Talent', Eliot declared that 'the poet has, not a personality to express, but a particular medium'; and accordingly he insisted that 'Honest criticism and sensitive appreciation is directed not upon the poet but upon the poetry.'[1] Eliot here and in other writings distinguished sharply between the subjectivity of the living personality and the objectivity of the artist's independent creation, suggesting that critics had for the most part been looking impertinently in the wrong place: falsely assuming that literature was the more or less simple expression of personality, they had discussed the biography, the temperament, or the private opinions of writers, while neglecting the free-standing public entity that is the work of art itself. This – at least by extrapolation from Eliot's incidental suggestions – was the principal challenge posed to criticism by the new objective or impersonal conception of literature. The modernist revolution in criticism was very largely a matter of revising fundamental assumptions of this kind and of evolving a new language and new procedures for the examination of literary works as autonomous objects of inquiry, no longer to be confused with the lives or 'philosophies' of their authors. Biographical criticism was by no means eradicated in this period. Indeed in one form it gained a new lease of life from the diffusion of Freudian ideas in Anglophone intellectual life at this time, just as historical and sociological criticism was revived by the currency of Marxism in the 1930s. But these approaches encountered strong suspicion directed at their 'external' or distracting tendencies. The new programme of re-focusing attention from author to text was carried through most thoroughly by the New Critics in America, who catalogued a whole series of misplaced critical assumptions as errors, as 'fallacies', and, in the pontifical jargon cultivated by Eliot himself, even as 'heresies'. Among these truancies of criticism were counted a number of confusions between the work itself and its historical or social context, its doctrinal argument or philosophy, its effects upon readers, and its supposed expression of authorial personality. To discuss any of these matters was not necessarily illegitimate or sinful, but it was beside the real critical point and was not really a consideration of the work in its achieved and public form. As it took hold in the universities, this kind of argument strengthened the campaign against the academic study of literary history, undertaken on behalf of a purified form of literary criticism and especially of intensive 'close reading' or detailed analysis of poems.

The new schools of close scrutiny had something more to seek out in their chosen texts than fine phrases or technical problems of metre. Rather than conceive of the literary work (typically the lyric poem) as an expression of ideas to which ornamental sounds have been added, they insisted on taking it as an organically integrated whole, in which style and meaning, technique and sense were inseparable. They sought out the formal coherence of the work and its internal tensions, particularly as concentrated in the central figure of metaphor, where the abstract and the concrete were wedded. This was both a method and at the same time a criterion of value, in that the poem in which content and form were not indissolubly fused was a failure, just as the critical habit that treated content and form in abstraction from one another was a heresy. Two inheritances were being repudiated at once: a body of critical assumptions – largely Victorian – in which literature was taken to be the utterance of noble philosophical truths wrapped in melodious sounds, and at the same time the questionable or even corrupt literary tradition – largely but not exclusively Romantic and Victorian – upon which those assumptions had sustained themselves, and in which preaching and melody did seem to have been unconvincingly allied. The new procedures of close reading were not, then, a neutral body of critical techniques so much as investigations into the soundness of the old canon, which had to be tested rigorously for its degree of organic integrity. Here again, the guiding hint was provided by Eliot, who valued the poetry of Donne for its fusion of thought and feeling into an integrated 'sensibility' (a key term of the period), while casting doubt on the success of later poets in harmonizing the intellect and the senses: from Milton to Swinburne, English poetry, he suggested, had fallen victim to a 'dissociation of sensibility' in which poets thought and felt alternately rather than simultaneously.[2] From this suggestion, a new programme of critical inquiry offered itself, especially to the critics of the *Scrutiny* group, and a radically revised canon of English poetry emerged in which the Metaphysical poetry of Donne's school was elevated to a new central position while the work of Milton, Shelley, and Tennyson suffered severe relegation.

The project of 'close reading' received a further impetus from the extraordinary challenges posed by new modernist forms of poetry and prose in this period. The problems faced by critics before the war in making sense of the international realist developments associated with Ibsen and Zola were as nothing to those presented to post-war criticism in the shape of Pound, Cummings, Proust, Stein, Joyce, Woolf, and of course Eliot himself. Formal and linguistic experimentation of these unfamiliar varieties called for new kinds of attention to be paid to contemporary writing, and provided years of work for critics – or at least for interpreters – willing to unravel and explicate the notorious difficulties of the new writing. Works of defensive exposition devoted to individual masters now had to spend less time on summarizing the 'message' and more on unpicking the detailed allusions and formal complexities of their works, as in Stuart Gilbert's *James Joyce's Ulysses* (1930) and F. O. Matthiessen's *The Achievement of T. S. Eliot* (1935). A bewildered reading public demanded some explanation of the logic of these new developments, and

received answers in several general critical defences of the modernist
insurgence: Laura Riding's and Robert Graves's *A Survey of Modernist
Poetry* (1927), F. R. Leavis's *New Bearings in English Poetry* (1932), and
Cleanth Brooks's *Modern Poetry and the Tradition* (1939) were the most
important apologies for the new writing, while Edmund Wilson's *Axel's
Castle* (1931) provided a more historical and critically independent
account. In addition to these demands, critics had also to assimilate, or
at least take the measure of, major intellectual systems which were
impinging upon literary controversy: psychoanalysis, anthropology, and
Marxism. For most of Eliot's followers, this meant resisting the intrusive
'external' claims of these systems in the name of literary criticism's independence as a discrete practice; but for others who resisted Eliot's strict
quarantining of art, these systems offered exciting kinds of connection
between literature and other realms of meaning. Some of these early
applications of Freud and Marx to literature were certainly marred by the
heretical abstraction of 'content' from verbal form; but at least in the New
York circles around Edmund Wilson they were absorbed into a more
sensitive critical approach.

Defending and accounting for the difficulty of modernist writing was
a task that often brought with it a larger agenda of cultural critique, in
which the critic held the ills of contemporary civilization responsible for
the obscure ruses of its artists. Eliot himself suggested that the modern
artist needed to be allusive and difficult because twentieth-century society
was so complex and various, and he tended to link the artist's problems
with the disintegration of social cohesion. Just as the revision of the
poetic canon involved an indictment of modern civilization as mechan-
ically devoted to progress, so for Eliot and his followers on both sides of
the Atlantic the defence of poetry in a hostile age involved the critique
of contemporary social and political evils, from a sourly conservative
perspective. The American critics who formed the early core of the New
Criticism pitted a reactionary agrarianism against the modern industrial-
democratic society that had crushed the finer sensibility of the old South
under its utilitarian juggernaut, while in Britain the *Scrutiny* critics
bewailed the cultural debasement or 'levelling-down' inflicted on literary
awareness by mass education and the cinema. Several important critics in
this period incorporated political and social indignation into their literary
work in a manner recalling that of the Victorian prophets Carlyle, Arnold,
and Ruskin – and with the same kinds of target. They began by scorning
the pre-war optimistic social meliorism of Shaw and Wells, and moved
on in the 'red' 1930s to resist the cultural politics of an often crudely
euphoric literary Left. In both cases, the conservative critics voiced an
embittered protest against the ideals of historical Progress.

Literary understanding for Eliot and his followers implied a renunci-
ation of the nineteenth-century dream of historical evolution or advance,
in favour of a 'timeless' apprehension of Tradition and Myth. Historical

progress had been a disaster, but the virtue of art was that it admitted us into an ahistorical order in which such 'progress' had no meaning. At the end of this period, the American literary scholar Joseph Frank looked back over the work of such modernist writers as Ezra Pound, Djuna Barnes, Marcel Proust, James Joyce and T. S. Eliot in his article 'Spatial Form in Modern Literature' (1945), noting how they had all resisted and erased the concept of history by adopting a 'spatial' method instead of temporal one, relying on an aesthetic logic of juxtaposition rather than of development.[3] As in the creative wing of modernism, so in the critical: the new literary ideals of critical discourse typically adopted the spatial configurations of visual art in place of the temporal sequences of music as their model, and in a fundamental metaphoric shift the eye took over from the ear. Nothing is more symptomatic of revolution in literary-critical discourse than such a replacement of one group of key metaphors by another, since this discourse is more deeply reliant on its metaphors than poetry itself is. The Romantic revolution, as M. H. Abrams demonstrated in his book *The Mirror and the Lamp* (1953), substituted the metaphor of the lamp (illuminating expression) for that of the mirror (imitative reflection) in its new conception of the writer's function. The critics of the modernist period attempted, although with less resounding success, a similar reversal. The vorticist writer and artist Wyndham Lewis devoted a long and rambling book, *Time and Western Man* (1928), to the evils of time-bound thought in the modern world. The Jungian psychologist Maud Bodkin published a much-noticed work on recurring 'timeless' motifs and themes in world literature, *Archetypal Patterns in Poetry* (1934). Several theorists of the novel scorned the importance of chronological plot or development in favour of 'patterns' and 'themes'. As poetic imagery came to occupy a central place in the discussion of the poet's 'vision', so the most purely melodious or sonorous English poets – Milton, Shelley, Tennyson, Swinburne – suffered a sharp crash in their reputations. The accustomed habits of Shakespeare criticism too collapsed under the onslaught of a new school of interpretation led by G. Wilson Knight, in which the development of plot and character was replaced by 'patterns' of imagery. The modernist critical revolution brought about in these fields a consistent shift in the basic terms of discussion.

'Classical' and 'Romantic' Positions

Eliot announced his new principles in what were clearly anti-Romantic terms. *The Sacred Wood* begins with an endorsement of Matthew Arnold's severe verdict upon the English Romantics, and, on the way to formulating its 'depersonalization' of literature, it continues with a long sequence of damning remarks on the damage done by the Romantic cults of personality and genius, including the paradox that while 'there may be a good deal to be said for Romanticism in life, there is no place for it in letters.'[4] Several of the essays that appeared in the book had originally been commissioned for the *Athenaeum* by its then editor, John Middleton Murry, an admirer and personal associate of D. H. Lawrence. Murry himself wrote a review of *The Sacred Wood*: while regretting Eliot's disdainful and superior tone, he recognized this new declaration of literary objectivity as an important contribution to criticism, but at the same time he insisted that a good case could be made, on some other occasion, for the legitimacy of Murry's own preferred mode of biographical and psychological criticism.[5] An inevitable clash of principles between the personal and the impersonal was announced here, and could not be long postponed: Murry and Eliot were almost the same age, and stood at the beginning of the 1920s as obvious rivals. As the decade progressed, they found themselves in charge of literary journals representing opposed 'classical' and 'romantic' schools, firing off regular broadsides against each other. Eliot founded the *Criterion* in 1922, and in the following year Murry, whose wife Katherine Mansfield had just died, set up the *Adelphi* in her memory and in the service of D. H. Lawrence's prophetic message to the world. A long-running battle between the Romanticism of the *Adelphi* and the new classicism of the *Criterion* began almost immediately. Before examining this contest, however, we should set Eliot's anti-Romantic campaign in its intellectual context.

There were two kinds of anti-Romanticism current at the end of the War, both of which Eliot absorbed and superseded. The first was represented in Irving Babbitt's fourth book, *Rousseau and Romanticism* (1919), which was his most extended indictment of nineteenth-century culture. Babbitt portrayed the literary consequences of Rousseau's sentimental primitivism as a catalogue of moral and artistic failings: egotism, self-indulgence, immaturity, indolence, escapism, irresponsibility, and the restless cultivation of intensity and spontaneous instinct for their own sakes: abandoning the necessary inner struggle between good and evil, the Romantics had lost themselves on 'a sort of endless pilgrimage in the void'.[6] As the clinching evidence in his argument, Babbit produced the spectacle of the Great War, 'the crowning stupidity of the ages',[7] which showed where the Romantic unleashing of natural instinct from moral control had led the Western world. Babbitt's 'humanist' denunciation of the Romantic vagrancy is magnificently controlled, and marshals a wealth of damning biographical detail against its victims; but for the younger modernist writers even this was insufficient. A second, more aggressive variety of anti-Romantic criticism is found in the work of the English Imagist poet T. E. Hulme, who had been killed in the War in 1917, leaving behind him some earlier articles and notebooks. These were to be published in 1924 as *Speculations*, although Eliot had seen most of them before 1917. Hulme's most important essays, 'Humanism and the Religious Attitude' and 'Romanticism and Classicism' trace the sins of Rousseauism much further back to the individualism of the Renaissance, indeed to the very 'humanism' to which Babbitt was still clinging. Where Babbitt trusted half-heartedly in the restraining effect of religious authorities to whose dogmas he could not submit, Hulme insisted that dogma – especially that of Original Sin – had to be upheld as absolute truth in the face of the humanist and Romantic belief in the self-perfecting infinite capacity of Man. Babbitt's half-measures could not stop the Romantic rot, which depended on the fallacy of innate human goodness; to contain the 'spilt religion' of Romanticism[8] there needed to be revived the conception of humanity as limited and therefore requiring the secure controls of dogmatic discipline and order. This was anti-Romanticism with the gloves off, abandoning Babbitt's gentility for a counter-attack in the splenetic manner of Pound: 'I object even to the best of the romantics. I object still more to the receptive attitude. I object to the sloppiness which doesn't consider that a poem is a poem unless it is moaning or whining about something or other.'[9] In reaction against the damp, vague, soft emotionalism of Romantic poetry, Hulme predicted that 'we are in for a classical revival', and that 'a period of dry, hard, classical verse is coming.'[10] The virtue of true poetry, after all, was not in vague abstractions gesturing at infinity, but in its precision: the fresh poetic image could make us see the physical world anew.

Two roughly congruent varieties of anti-Romanticism, then – those of humanist restraint and of Imagist impatience – had been outlined before *The Sacred Wood*. Each, though, was deficient for Eliot's purposes. Babbitt's version, like that of Paul More, was a kind of abstract moral condemnation, which did not stoop from its general injunctions of ethical self-control to show in any detail what was wrong with Romanticism as a specifically literary practice or how to get beyond it. On the other side, the Imagist protest of Pound and Hulme could name the more irritating mannerisms of Romantic poetry, but could get little further than throwing violent insults and adopting a 'hard' attitude against emotionalism. To call Wordsworth a silly old sheep, as Pound had done, was scarcely an adequate basis for a new poetics; and on the whole, Pound's criticism after the war rarely rises above this level of irascible outburst. Eliot's successful assumption of the leading role in anti-Romantic criticism had much to do with his adoption of a measured, superior tone appropriate to the more respectable London journals. It also derived from his more precise focus on literary problems of feeling and language.

The basis of Eliot's supersession of Romantic principles was not any simple rejection of emotion and personality but the formulation of a more satisfactory relation between them and the work of art, in which the private emotion should be completely digested or objectified in the public form. An initially vague or formless feeling could become, through its transmutation into art, a precise emotion. Quoted out of context, his famous declaration that 'Poetry is not a turning loose of emotion, but an escape from emotion; it is not the expression of personality, but an escape from personality'[11] may look like an evasive denial of human feeling, but in fact the escape, which is a transfer of the feeling into the impersonal work of art, is conceived as an intensification of the feeling in such a form that it can be reproduced successfully in the reader. This becomes clear in Eliot's formulation of his theory of the 'objective correlative' in his essay 'Hamlet and His Problems':

> The only way of expressing emotion in the work of art is by finding an 'objective correlative'; in other words, a set of objects, a situation, a chain of events which shall be the formula of that particular emotion; such that when the external facts, which must terminate in sensory experience, are given, the emotion is immediately evoked.[12]

Without such a focus in the concretely available literary image, the emotion – however sublime or powerful in itself – will remain vague or chaotic, and so will go ungrasped by the reader. Thus in one essay, Eliot complains of Swinburne's poetry that the emotions are not focused upon their objects nor intensified, but merely diffused among vague verbal associations. There needs to be a shared 'objective' point of reference, whether this be a clearly imagined dramatic situation or a concrete symbol, between author and reader, if the originating feeling is to reach beyond its merely private significance and become independently valuable. The case of William Blake, whom Eliot discusses in another essay, shows the same problem at the level of mythology: in his extreme Protestant disaffection from accepted religious ideas, Blake in his longer poems fell back upon a merely private mythology, whereas Dante had been able to assume a philosophy and a mythology in common with his readers.

It was possible for a Romantic critic like J. M. Murry to accept the doctrine of impersonality in this sense as an inevitable requirement of successful poetic communication. What was more difficult to accept was the apparent conjuring trick by which Eliot seemed to make the author's personality vanish entirely into the work of art. Eliot's assertion that 'the more perfect the artist, the more completely separate in him will be the man who suffers and the mind which creates'[13] threatened a divorce between realms of experience and of writing, of life and literature, which Murry was not prepared to see sundered. For him, the suffering hero and the creative artist, whether Keats, Dostoevsky, or Lawrence, were the same thing, and the essence of literature was spiritual trial and struggle leading to self-discovery. In Eliot's clear separation of the art-object from its author he rightly detected the influence of a French aestheticist tendency descending from Flaubert, upon whom Murry published two dismissive essays in 1922, mocking his adoption of the religion of Art as a retreat from Life into an ivory tower. To the aesthetic perfectionism of Flaubert and Henry James, Murry greatly preferred the energies of Russian fiction, in Tolstoy, Dostoevsky, and Chekhov, which he valued in terms of their vital or soulful capacity for inner exploration. On a similar basis he began to pit the native strengths of English literature against the limited French traditions of classicism, in his 1923 essay 'On Fear; and On Romanticism', which declared that English writers inherit 'a sense that in the last resort they must depend upon the inner voice' and that 'the writer achieves impersonality through personality'.[14] It was this article in the *Adelphi* that provoked the battle waged over the next four years with the *Criterion*.

Unlike Hulme, Eliot had not in *The Sacred Wood* declared himself a partisan of any 'classical' revival, although his anti-Romantic tendency was obvious enough. Murry's direct endorsement in nationalistic terms of the Romantic principle and of the 'inner voice', though, brought him into the open at last as a defender of classical positions. Eliot's reply was 'The Function of Criticism' (1923), an essay in which he summarizes the essential difference between Classicism and Romanticism as 'the difference between the complete and the fragmentary, the adult and the immature, the orderly and the chaotic.'[15] As for the inner voice, which Murry had conceived as the true path of spiritual enlightenment in opposition to Church authorities, Eliot condemned it as an excuse for lawless abandonment of literary principle, and in a bizarre image associated it with the behaviour of football enthusiasts on a train to Swansea. The classical principle required an allegiance to something outside of ourselves, beyond the inner promptings of our vanity or lust: a government, a Church, and in literary-critical affairs 'the common pursuit of true judgment' rather than personal prejudice.[16] In another essay the same year, Eliot applied his classicist principle to the question of contemporary literature, in reviewing Joyce's *Ulysses*. He agreed with Richard Aldington, his former colleague on the *Egoist*, that a new classicism was desirable, but he refused to follow Aldington's condemnation of Joyce's book as 'chaotic': on the contrary, it had achieved by its use of Homeric myth the discovery of an essential new method 'of controlling, of ordering, of giving a shape and a significance to the immense panorama of futility and anarchy which is contemporary history.'[17] Classicism could not be achieved by a mummified reproduction of outdated forms, but only by ordering in such a way the actual materials of contemporary life. Eliot's is certainly a 'classicism' remote from that of Johnson or even of Arnold; in fact it looks uncannily like a pseudonym for his own variant of modernism.

The year 1923 was not the best moment to declare oneself a classicist;

for in the same year Professor Herbert Grierson of the University of Edinburgh (the same scholar whose anthology of metaphysical poetry had inspired Eliot's own famous remarks on Donne and the dissociation of sensibility) gave a public lecture at Cambridge entitled 'Classical and Romantic', in which he cast grave doubt on the possibility of reviving classical literary principles in modern conditions. From his historical review of this vexed antithesis, he concluded that although the 'romantic' mood is always with us, as an impulse to break down accepted conventions, the 'classical' requires a settled and self-confident society with widely shared assumptions to sustain it. In the absence of such cultural foundations, the 'classicist' longing for Greek balance, as in Goethe and Arnold, amounted to nothing more than another version of romantic nostalgia, and could not be regarded as 'classical' in the full sense.[18] Eliot's project was of course far from being a mere nostalgic Hellenism, but it had before it the same obstacle of cultural disorder, which could not be overcome by an artistic effort of will. His opponents were quick to point out both that Eliot's work appeared to flout all norms of classically serene balance and that in any case a new classicism was impossible in the modern age.

Murry's most powerful riposte to Eliot, in the essay 'The "Classical" Revival' (1926) employs both these arguments: 'The Waste Land' (which is too intellectualized a poem to survive beyond the decade) violates all the classical principles of order, decorum, and clarity which Eliot has been preaching in his criticism, and shows Eliot to be in fact 'an unregenerate and incomplete romantic' rather than a classicist, because 'to envy classicism is not to be a classicist; it is to be, most unenviably, a romantic'.[19] Eliot will have to choose, Murry writes, between his classical principles, which should logically lead him into the Catholic church, and his romantic practice, which should take him on the path followed by Shakespeare and Keats: that of free spiritual self-exploration. Eliot in fact chose to join the Church of England a few months later, thus confirming Murry's clear conviction that the true difference between them was religious. Murry's romanticism, like that of Lawrence, was overtly Protestant, and his refusal to credit the possibility of a serious modern classicism was founded on the belief that the 'classical' religious certainties enjoyed by Dante and Chaucer were irrecoverable: modern English literature was born (in Shakespeare) from the rejection of Catholicism and from the new individualist quest for truth through self-discovery. As he argued more thoroughly in an earlier response to Eliot, 'Romanticism and the Tradition' (1924), Romanticism has been since the Renaissance the inescapable condition of literature, which, growing from the same roof as religion and increasingly replacing its organized dogmatic forms, has itself become 'the great religious adventure of the human soul'.[20] While Eliot was trying to distinguish between literature and religion, Murry was proclaiming their common identity. He shared with Eliot a belief that the ego must submit to something larger than its limited self, but for him this must not be some 'external' authority so much as a deeper self in touch with the divine. Accordingly, impersonality could be found only through the self-exploration of personality, order only through the flux. In terms of literary principles, this meant that 'We cannot apprehend a work of literature except as a manifestation of the rhythm of the soul of the man who created it.'[21] The great titans of literature, like Shakespeare and Dostoevsky, displayed something more important than Eliot's narrowly conceived aesthetic perfection: they had individuality, life, and profundity of soul, which was the essential requirement, literature being the record of the soul's struggle to find truth, life, and harmony.

In these grand terms, Murry defended his critical concentration upon personality or individual self-development against what he feared was a restrictive aesthetic purism in Eliot's doctrine. His early lecture published as 'The Nature of Poetry' presents the task of the critic as that of achieving a direct personal encounter with the dark mystery of the artist's rhythm of life, an intuitive apprehension of his mystic secret, a 'wrestling with the ineffable',[22] this last phrase being an apt description of Murry's work at its most romantic. At the same time he repudiated simple impressionism and insisted that the critic must arrive at principles and judgements that would distinguish the greatest works from the rest. Outside the debate with Eliot, indeed, he expressed some agreement with those 'classical' critics who maintained a connection between literary and moral value, from Aristotle to Babbitt. But his real interest was in biographical and psychological study of writers in their processes of spiritual voyaging: his early book on Dostoevsky (1916), and his later *Keats and Shakespeare* (1925), like his account of Lawrence in *Son of Woman* (1931), are essentially spiritual biographies far removed from the critical analysis he practises in *The Problem of Style* (1922) and in some of his early essays.

The romantic tendency in this period's criticism is marked by its attachment to the spiritual or psychological 'depths' of literary creation, whereas the classicist tendency calls for attention to the visible surface. The investigation of depths could lead the critic into the new possibilities of psychoanalysis, as in the case of Herbert Read, a late convert from Hulmean and Eliotic classicism who discovered romantic principles chiefly through his interest in Freud and Adler. Read had edited Hulme's *Speculations* in 1924, but in the Thirties he was defending the creative sources of Romantic inspiration against classical rigidity in *Form in Modern Poetry* (1932), and writing sympathetic studies of Romantic poets in *Wordsworth* (1930) and *In Defence of Shelley* (1936), using a clumsy form of psychoanalytic diagnosis. Shelley, for instance, could not help using vague imagery because he suffered from narcissism and latent homosexuality – disorders which enhance the value of his work in its visionary perception of oneness. This defence of Shelley was mounted in direct opposition to what Read saw as Eliot's irrational prejudice against the Romantic poet.

But Read had already repudiated Eliot in *Form in Modern Poetry* by insisting that the critic must not stop at an examination of the work of art in itself, but must be concerned also with the writer's state of mind. He earned himself the distinction of being quoted in Eliot's *After Strange Gods* (1934) as an advanced example of the modern heretic.

The true heresiarch of modern Romanticism was Murry's hero D. H. Lawrence, whose writings on other authors are again concerned more with spiritual depths than with the formal aspects of literary works. The only full-length critical book he published in his lifetime, *Studies in Classic American Literature* (1923), is scarcely concerned with novels at all, but is a sequence of violent prose-poems on the condition of the American soul and its inner torments. Like the psychoanalysts, Lawrence has a strong sense of the contradiction between the overt meaning of a work and its deeper significance; but his investigation of these depths is subject to scarcely any control or direction. His fascinating wartime essay entitled 'Study of Thomas Hardy', published posthumously in *Phoenix* (1936), takes us on a general tour of the universe before briefly touching on some of Hardy's characters, as in this discussion of Phillotson in *Jude the Obscure*:

> Why was Phillotson like a newt? What is it, in our life or in our feeling, to which a newt corresponds? Is it that life has the two sides, of growth and of decay, symbolised most acutely in our bodies by the semen and the excreta? Is is that the newt, the reptile, belong to the putrescent activity of life; the bird, the fish to the growth activity? Is it that the newt and the reptile are suggested to us through those sensations connected with excretion? And was Phillotson more or less connected with the decay activity of life? Was it his function to reorganise the life-excreta of the ages? At any rate, one can honour him, for he was true to himself.[23]

Lawrence can be honoured for better critical writing than this, as we shall see below, but he often illustrates spectacularly the decay-activity to which Romantic criticism is especially vulnerable.

Although Eliot's principles predominated among the most important critics of this period, his attempt to establish them as a new 'classicism' failed. By 1933 he had given up that battle, preferring the conflict between 'orthodoxy' and 'heresy'. Even Wyndham Lewis, a 'hard' anti-Romantic of the Hulme persuasion, admitted in *Men Without Art* (1934) that would-be classicists were condemned to some form of Romantic personal assertion by their necessary opposition to the prevailing social values, so that sadly 'We are all romantics today.'[24] As the battle between Eliot and Murry exhausted itself, there emerged a curious sort of consensus between their positions, which had been potentially available all along.

Both critics identify Milton as a destructive influence on English verse, both place a high value on the integrating force of the complex metaphor, both see poetry as in intuitive language more alive than abstract philosophizing, and both insist on the artistic process as a surrender of the ego. Eliot, as critics of a later generation came to see, harbours a strong residue of unacknowledged Romantic thinking in his own criticism, which the slogans of classicism tended to mask at the time. His early essay 'Andrew Marvell' (1921), for instance, defends the poetic qualities of 'wit' repudiated by the Romantics, but in doing so it leans heavily on Coleridge's description of the reconciling activity of the imagination. In his later book *The Use of Poetry and the Use of Criticism* (1933), Eliot discovered a strong admiration for Keats, and especially for his letters, which happened also to be the sacred texts favoured by Murry. The two critics joined in valuing Keats while rejecting as inferior the work of Shelley: Eliot for his incoherence, Murry for his devotion to abstract thought. In so far as it affected literature rather than religious politics, Eliot's 'classicism' really involved the strong rejection of one kind of Romanticism, found in its egotistical philosophizing side, in favour of another, more 'organic' kind of Romanticism disposed to objectivity and the re-integration of human faculties.[26]

Eliot's most important followers continued his hostility to the most flagrant sins of Romanticism (especially in Shelley) without repeating his error of waving the classicist flag. In fact they tended in different and not clearly conscious ways to extend the implicit organicist Romanticism in Eliot's work, inviting Coleridge in through the back door as they kicked Shelley out of the front. The work of F. R. Leavis, especially, shows the strain of divided loyalties to the incompatible positions of Eliot and Lawrence, struggling to define a critical stance that could obey both masters. Selectively systematizing the critical suggestions and skilfully drawing out the romantic implications already present in Eliot's writings, he managed at least to negotiate places for Blake, Wordsworth and Keats in his Eliot-inspired canon of English poetry. In a larger sense, too, Leavis's *Scrutiny* group and the American school of New Criticism both continued, despite their literary hostility to Shelleyism, a Romantic tradition of social and cultural criticism in their common defence of aesthetic values against the degradations of modern industrial capitalism and in their nostalgic attitudes to traditional rural societies or 'organic communities'.

Close Reading and the Rise of New Criticism

By the end of the 1930s, critical writing had a different appearance, in one instantly obvious sense. A typical page in a critical book or essay, especially if concerned with poetry, would, to an extent unprecedented in previous decades, be broken up by frequent passages of quotation from texts, its exposition tending to weave in and out of them. This was a visible manifestation of a new sense of responsibility to the unique particulars of literary works. The logic of this development can be traced, as with so much else, back to Eliot's early essays. In requiring critics to attend to the poem rather than to the poet, Eliot had also given them guidance about what it was they were to seek there. His essays in *Homage to John Dryden* (1924) placed a special value on the ability of the 'Metaphysical' poets of Donne's school to integrate varied experiences into new poetic wholes, their gift for fusing together thought and feeling, in 'a direct sensuous apprehension of thought'.[26] Their omnivorous or unified sensibility is contrasted with the 'dissociated' condition of later English poetry, in which thought and feeling, seriousness and levity, tend to be divided. Similarly the metaphysical 'wit' of Andrew Marvell's poetry is found to embody a flexibility of mind, an urbane awareness of other kinds of experience than the one immediately adopted, which again is lost in later poets. In these essays, as in some of those published in *The Sacred Wood*, Eliot takes care to produce particular exhibits of verse exemplifying these poetic qualities of complex response to experience. If, according to Eliot, poetry gives us more than just a versified 'idea' or feeling, but an intense fusion of associations within the complex concentration of its images, then the reader's and the critic's alertness needs to be of an entirely new kind.

Two important critical projects of the 1920s were dedicated to shaking critics, and readers of poetry at large, out of the habits acquired from Victorian anthologies, and to retraining them according to the new standards required by Eliot. Laura Riding and Robert Graves in their book *A Survey of Modernist Poetry* (1927) mounted a lively defence of modernist verse, arguing by means of detailed explication of poems by Cummings and Eliot that the 'difficulty' of such poetry was attributable to the unwillingness of the Tennyson-loving public to make intelligent efforts, and in particular to its failure to grasp the Eliotic principle of the poem's independence from identifiable personalities. Looking for an easily digested message in poetry, the 'plain reader' was alarmed at the fresh perceptions of the modernist, the entire value of which lay in the fact that they could not be boiled down to a simple prose paraphrase. Taking as an example a poem by Cummings, they analysed it word by word, showing that only those words in that exact order and arrangement could produce the precise effect intended; no simpler statement of an 'idea' could be substituted for it.

At the University of Cambridge, the psychological aesthetic theories of I. A. Richards likewise involved a severe judgement upon the failure of modern readers to keep up with the demands of poetry. Richards did not himself practise much 'close' analysis of poems in the manner pioneered by Riding and Graves, but he insisted like them on the difference between the full meaning of a poem and the crudity of any prose paraphrase of it; and he helpfully classified the numerous ways in which reading of poetry could go wrong. His most celebrated book, *Practical Criticism* (1929), confirmed the hypothesis of Riding and Graves that readers relied heavily on the poet's existing reputation rather than on their own careful attention to the poem itself. The book records the results of an experiment in which Richards gave out to his students and colleagues (the finest young minds in England, one might then assume) copies of poems for critical analysis without disclosing the authors' names. In this exercise in 'blind' critical appreciation, most of the responses (all of them anonymous) showed narrow literal-mindedness and the imposition of wholly inappropriate critical requirements, and many revealed a basic inability to grasp even the plain logical sense of the poems. Richards concluded that a more rigorous training in the reading of poetry was required, and he proposed a number of initial clarifications, beginning with 'The all-important fact for the study of literature . . . that there are several kinds of meaning.'[27] At least four different dimensions of meaning were involved in any utterance: its sense, its feeling, its tone (that is, its implied attitude to the listener or reader), and its intention. The most common error in reading poetry was an over-literal detachment of the plain sense from the full meaning produced in all four dimensions. Richards's conclusion was that 'All respectable poetry invites close reading'[28] rather than dogmatic fault-finding or literal paraphrase.

Richards's larger aim, especially in his earlier books *Principles of Literary Criticism* (1924) and *Science and Poetry* (1926), was to set out a general theory of communication and of value that could justify the place of the arts in the world of modern science. Although it is dressed up in the clinical language of behaviourism and a neurological jargon of 'impulses' and 'stimuli', Richards's theory follows the basic strategy of Matthew Arnold, in which factual knowledge is assigned to the scientists while feelings and values are claimed as the realm of the poets: 'referential' statements that are either true or false belong to the world of fact, but the 'pseudo-statements' of art (which are neither true nor false) belong to the more flexible sphere of 'attitudes' or 'emotive' language. The value of poetry lay not in its factual or doctrinal truth but in its capacity to re-organize our emotional equilibrium, to bring our values into sensitive adjustment. The strictness of Richards's division between poetry and 'beliefs', and his apparent denial that poetry gives us knowledge, were variously disputed by Eliot and the New Critics, but his system is nevertheless in conformity with their view of the poem as a complex organization of attitudes rather than as an abstractable message. He also handed on to the New Critics an important emphasis on the value of irony in poetry, to reinforce Eliot's hints about 'wit'. For Richards as for Eliot, the poet is an agent through whom a multitude of conflicting experiences and impressions are brought into a new order, and the value of poetry lies in its synthesizing power. As Richards presents the matter in *Principles of Literary Criticism*, sentimental poetry provides a simple attitude or mood that would be undermined by being brought into contact with the opposite attitude, whereas the most valuable kind of poetry embodies irony by incorporating opposed attitudes within itself, and is thus immunized from further ironic challenge.[29] It is to this ironic inclusion of opposed attitudes that the *Scrutiny* group and the New Critics generally refer in speaking of a literary work's 'maturity'.

Richards's most precocious student at Cambridge, William Empson, inspired by the detailed analysis performed by Riding and Graves, was encouraged by Richards to develop the logic of 'close reading' in an investigation of multiple meaning in poetry, published as *Seven Types of Ambiguity* (1930). This work of painstaking grammatical analysis attempts to classify various sorts of poetic ambiguity ranging from doubly appropriate similes, through puns, complex metaphors, happy confusions and irresolutions, to full-blown self-contradictions, in a dizzying sequence of analyses (often of single words and phrases) which unravel an unexpected range of semantic possibilities. He finds, in support of Eliot's preferences, that nineteenth-century poetry is only weakly or intermittently ambiguous, whereas the poetry of Shakespeare and of the seventeenth century displays rich ambiguity. No longer just a syntactical or logical problem, ambiguity becomes in Empson an implied criterion of value, closely related to complexity and irony. Empson's approach owes something to Freud's concept of condensation and to Freud's interest in words which carry directly opposed meanings; but his method is also more simply an inversion, as he points out himself, of the usual practices of Shakespeare's editors. The custom in annotating doubtful words, phrases, or syntactical constructions in Shakespeare had been to list all the possible senses including those conjectured by previous editors, but then to dismiss all these interpretations except for the single 'right' reading. Empson, though, instead of regretting or tidying up such ambiguities, celebrates their concentration of multiple associations and admits (in principle) all the possible meanings as contributory to the complex poetic effect. The results are often startling, and to some readers Empson's irreverent tone, especially in the handling of Christian paradoxes, was alarming. The most common objection to the book was that it was merely an exercise in misplaced ingenuity which read more into poems than could possibly be 'there'. Such a response, though, is already built into the open indecisions of Empson's work itself, which admits that his mode of 'verbal analysis' must be complemented by sympathetic appreciation. He lays down no principle or dogma for criticism, but merely reports on the yet unexplored possibilities of 'close reading', passing on to the New Critics an example of intensive attention to paradoxes, ironies, and tensions in poetry.

Empson's interests, partly reflecting those of Richards, were primarily semantic. But the further development of 'close reading' at Cambridge took the different form of a morally-charged critical assessment of the extent to which poets had achieved a unification of 'sensibility' in Eliot's sense. 'Literary criticism', F. R. Leavis declared in 1933, 'provides the test for life and concreteness';[30] and it was as such a test that he deployed close analysis of poetry in his several books and articles of the 1930s, principally in *New Bearings in English Poetry* (1932) and *Revaluation* (1936). Both these works attempt to develop Eliot's suggestions about the 'dissociation of sensibility' in English poetry into a full-scale critical history of English verse, sorting the sound from the unsound according to the essential values identified by Eliot in Shakespeare and the Metaphysical poets: impersonal objectivity, the urbane maturity of 'wit', and the fusion of thought with feeling. Quoting Eliot's critical aphorisms with obsequious frequency, Leavis develops their implied moral valuations – especially in terms of 'maturity' – into an intuitive method of judgement that can inspect the 'words on the page' for health or sickness. In his critical writing, implicit but emphatic criteria, derived from Eliot's essay on Marvell, assert themselves so that poetry affording evidence of a 'concrete' grasp on experience or of the bodily vitality of living speech is highly valued, while poetry that is vague in imagery or remote from spoken English idiom is condemned. Shakespeare, Donne, Marvell, Keats, and Hopkins pass this test, while Milton, Shelley, and most Victorian poets fail it, exemplifying that divorce between thought and feeling which at the same time indicates moral failings of immaturity and self-deception. Leavis is confident that if samples of a poet's work are produced in evidence (and he quotes plentifully), then its value can be empirically and directly felt, primarily in the movement and texture of the verse, and without further reference to such abstractions as form and meaning. He brings in numerous samples as evidence, but what he then does with them is not in most instances analytical. He does provide full critical readings of entire poems by Hopkins and Keats, but usually his quotations are adduced either for purposes of elucidating the sense of 'difficult' poetry or as comparative demonstrations of self-evident virtues and defects. Quotation starts to replace analysis or argument rather than support it, and poets are implicitly 'placed' in relation to one another by the juxtaposition of representative samples rather than by reference to critical principle.

The persuasive force of this kind of 'close' engagement with poetry was considerable, as was witnessed by the large following of disciples attracted to the 'Leavisite' school over the next three decades. The bad habits it cultivated, though, go well beyond the repetitious jargon of approving terms reiterated in Leavis's writing – 'poised maturity', 'consummate control', 'moral seriousness', 'concrete vigour', 'human centrality' and the like. Its confidence in the empirical test of concreteness engendered a kind of dogmatism without precepts, as American critics started to notice in their attempts to elicit from *Scrutiny* some explanation of its critical standards. For while Leavis moved crablike among the poets, never relaxing his grip upon the concrete texture of poetic language where value was located, American criticism, at least in the work of the Nashville 'Fugitives', had begun, without damage to its sense of the concrete, to stand back and re-examine its theoretical foundations.

The core of the major American school that came to be called the New Criticism was formed from the circle of 'Fugitive' poets around John Crowe Ransom and his former Vanderbilt University students Allen Tate and Robert Penn Warren, with another of Tate's students, Cleanth Brooks. To this inner group we can add a few critics from outside the South, including R. P. Blackmur and (with some qualifications) Yvor Winters of Stanford University and the freelance Kenneth Burke. The early phase of this school's remarkable productivity can be defined by the lifetime of Brooks's and Warren's journal *Southern Review* (1935–42), during which period a succession of challenging critical works appeared, from Blackmur's *The Double Agent* (1935) and Tate's *Reactionary Essays* (1936), through Winters's *Primitivism and Decadence* (1937) and Brooks's *Modern Poetry and the Tradition* (1939), to Ransom's *The New Criticism* (1941). The work of this school defined itself negatively against the social concerns of Leftist criticism, insisting on attention to the formal demands of poetry 'as poetry' rather than as doctrine or social documentation, and positively by the adoption and critical revision of concepts derived from Eliot and Richards. Like Richards, the leading New Critics Ransom and Tate were concerned to justify poetry against the claims of science, but they disagreed strongly with his surrender of knowledge and truth to the scientists, which left poetry only with emotive adjustments. For Ransom and Tate, the truths of science are in fact only half-truths, abstractions made for the purposes of instrumental control and thus showing us their objects in only one dimension; poetry gives us knowledge, and of a fuller, three-dimensional kind that preserves the particularity of its objects. Ransom in his *The World's Body* (1938) devised a vivid Southerner's analogy for this contrast, in which the 'efficient self' of practical instrumentality and science is likened to Sherman marching through Georgia destroying everything he could not use, while the 'aesthetic self' is a walker going back over the route, enjoying the countryside.[31] Tate in his *Reactionary Essays* draws upon the anti-rhetorical poetics of Yeats to construct a very similar opposition, in which true poetry is contrasted with the practical and didactic traditions of allegory since Spenser: the poetry of the 'will' simplifies the world into abstractions in order to dominate it, but genuine poetry subordinates the will and its narrow ideas to the full range of experience. As Tate puts it, repeating Wilde's paradox, 'poetry finds its true usefulness in its perfect inutility, a focus of repose for the will-driven intellect,'[32] allowing us to know things as they are, not as we would have them. This kind of anti-utilitarian and anti-rhetorical position was further developed by Ransom in *The New Criticism*, in which the same antinomy is found within each poem, between its 'structure' (by which Ransom means the functional argument or logic) and its 'texture' or perception of heterogeneous detail. Structure is essential, but only to support – as business supports pleasure – the capacity of texture to return us to the full density or 'body' of the world.

Ransom and Tate as critics are principally theorists and defenders of poetry, rather than 'close' analysts, although Tate at least engaged in some detailed reading of specific works, notably an account of his own 'Ode to the Confederate Dead' in *Reason in Madness* (1941). But their theory always points to the importance of complexity and fullness of detail, thus reinforcing the value of close reading against the skimming of poetry for its 'prose' sense. They added to the practice of close reading, too, the important idea of taking the poem as a kind of miniature drama: as Ransom presents it, the poet in donning the 'mask' of metrical form adopts an assumed character, and every poem (not just the obvious examples of Browning's) is to be seen as a dramatic monologue. This dramatic conception, which takes certain characteristic qualities of Donne's lyrics as exemplary, is a significant application of the logic of poetic 'impersonality' that permits the dynamic principle of the poem to be presented as an entirely internal conflict. In the dramatizing terms of New Criticism, partly borrowed from Richards and Empson, the poem encloses an encounter between opposing principles, variously conceived as 'irony', as 'paradox', or as 'tension'. Rather than just reflect an experience outside itself, literature dramatizes experience within the theatre of its form. There arose among the New Critics themselves a theoretical 'tension' around this concept, with Tate and Brooks on the one side speaking in Eliot's terms of poetry's 'fusion' of thought and feeling and of its resolution of opposites, and Ransom (following Empson) on the other side denying that logical oppositions could really be conjured away by poetic magic. The value of such terms as irony and tension lay partly in their hesitating just short of a full Coleridgean affirmation of poetry's reconciling power.

If Ransom and Tate are the theoretical wing of New Criticism, its applied wing is represented most convincingly in the close readings of Cleanth Brooks and R. P. Blackmur. Brooks's *Modern Poetry and the Tradition* follows up the work of Riding and Graves in defending the difficulty of modernist verse by detailed elucidation and justification of the oblique poetic effects achieved by Eliot, Yeats, Auden, Ransom, Tate, and Warren. His lucid defence of the modernist symbol as the counterpart of metaphysical 'wit' draws on the accumulated theoretical resources of the Eliot-Richards-Ransom line to illustrate through a succession of close readings the new poetic values, in particular the incorporation of opposites (intellect and emotion, levity and seriousness) into an inclusive dramatic complexity. The most dedicated of these close readers, though, was Blackmur, whose early books *The Double Agent* (1935) and *The Expense of Greatness* (1941) are remarkable for their intensive focus on technique and diction. His sense of the multiple associations of a word rivals Empson's, although it is harnessed as Empson's is not to purposes of critical valuation. Drawing also on Eliot's impersonal theory to insist on the poet's obligation to objectify feelings in the disciplines of form and 'the superior reality of words',[33] he can write for pages in justification of a single word in a Wallace Stevens poem, or interrogate the vocabulary of E. E. Cummings and Emily Dickinson for its weaknesses. In his undogmatic 'technical' approach, Blackmur is the purest type of the close reader.

In their early phase, the New Critics were mostly freelance essayists like Blackmur and Burke, or poets holding teaching posts remote from the prestigious centres of academic influence (Winters in California, Ransom and Tate in Tennessee, Brooks and Warren in Louisana). At the end of the 1930s, a strategic turn towards implanting New Criticism more firmly in the academic study of literature became evident, partly in professional migrations: in 1937 Ransom moved to Kenyon College, Ohio, where he founded the *Kenyon Review* and established an annual symposium for critics; two years later, Allen Tate took up a writer's fellowship at Princeton, where he arranged for Blackmur (who held no university degree) to establish the first foothold in a teaching career. Warren moved north to the University of Minnesota in 1942. Two young critics with New Critical sympathies, W. K. Wimsatt and René Wellek, found jobs at Yale in 1939 and 1941 respectively; Brooks was to join them there in 1947. This trend was sanctioned and reinforced by two important publications in 1938 that pointed New Criticism in academic directions. One was the textbook anthology *Understanding Poetry* by Brooks and Warren; the other an essay by Ransom, 'Criticism, Inc.', in his *The World's Body*. The Brooks-Warren textbook codified the New Critical approach to poetry in a form that could be taught, guiding teachers and students away from biographical study, message-hunting, or merely effusive 'appreciation' towards the examination of poems as dramatic and organic wholes. This new pedagogic project was a striking success: *Understanding Poetry* went through numerous reprintings and updated editions over the next thirty years, and Brooks soon followed it up with parallel volumes on drama and fiction. Ransom's 'Criticism, Inc.' constituted a call for criticism to become a systematic and professional enterprise based in the universities. Ransom had been encouraged by signs of renewed resistance at the University of Chicago to the predominance of linguistic and historical scholarship, and he proposed (as Leavis did in England) that university departments should subordinate these pursuits to the central activity of critical judgement. The earlier resistance to narrow scholarship by Babbitt and his neo-humanist followers had distracted attention away from literature itself into moral questions, but Ransom's new programme of study would come with a charter of exclusions that would curtail such irrelevances. Thus in 'Criticism, Inc.', Ransom rules out of criticism the discussion of personal impressions of literary works or their effects on audiences; the routines of synopsis and paraphrase; the study of historical or biographical backgrounds and literary analogues; linguistic study and the tracing of allusions; special studies of abstracted 'content' such as geography in Milton; and the moral judgement of literature. What is left is the close study of distinctively literary techniques and their uses. This radical purification of literary study was set by the early 1940s to become a powerful orthodoxy.

Any account of New Criticism needs to reserve a special side-table for Yvor Winters and Kenneth Burke, both of whom are 'impure' exemplars of the school's principles. They are linked to the mainstream Southern group by their common agreement that questions of literary form must take priority over those of biography or of any paraphrasable 'content' in literature; but their interests are contaminated by heretical admixtures and deviations. Winters was regarded by the others as too much of a moralist in the Babbitt tradition. Like Leavis in England, he saw morality as inextricable from literary form, since the writer's technique involved an evaluation of experience; unlike Leavis, he always referred his judgements back to his first principles. His chief contribution to New Critical language was the discovery of a new fallacy, called the 'fallacy of imitative form', in which the writer expresses confusion or disintegration by means of confused or disintegrated forms of expression. In his severe verdict upon the experimentalist poets of modernism in *Primitivism and Decadence* (1937), Winters found this to be a characteristic failing in the work of Pound, Eliot, Cummings, Crane, and others. The artist's duty, he agreed with Babbitt, was to give form to the formless, not to surrender to it; and the resources of traditional metre were the most valuable means to this end. Winters's comparative judgements on particular writers were sometimes eccentric (Robert Bridges and T. Sturge Moore were better poets than Yeats) and rarely argued in close detail, but his principled severity could be very bracing, notably in the devastating assessment of Poe in his *Maule's Curse* (1938). Kenneth Burke is a figure even more remote from the Tate-Ransom-Brooks group, in his radical political sympathies and in his forging of an idiosyncratic critical vocabulary. He is capable of brilliant and intricate 'close readings' in his *The Philosophy of Literary Form* (1941), but these come entangled within the elaboration of an ambitious theoretical programme which invites comparison with the later work of I. A. Richards in his *Philosophy of Rhetoric* (1936). Both theorists were aiming at a general theory of meaning, or a modern version of the medieval syllabus combining rhetoric, grammar, and logic. Burke's attempt, from his early *Counter-statement* (1931) onwards, is to set literary meaning within much larger social, anthropological and psycho- logical contexts than the other New Critics were willing to consider, and his developing view of literature as a form of symbolic or dramatic 'action' or 'strategy' constantly takes him outside the confined textual space of New Critical reading. While other critics contrasted literature with rhetoric, Burke would insist on understanding literature *as* rhetoric, sometimes foreshadowing later models of 'reader-response' theory; and while Ransom and Brooks spoke of dramatic conflict within poems, Burke developed his own theory of the dramatic basis of literature, emphasizing temporal development and process rather than 'spatial' anta- gonism. His work is a curious assemblage of brilliant theoretical sketches which makes the more technical kinds of New Critical reading look introverted by comparison.

Crisis and Criticism

Criticism between the wars was haunted by its strong awareness of cultural collapse and social conflict. Even those critics who seem most eager to isolate the literary work from its social contexts, as in the New Criticism, defend the work's integrity in the name of such social principles as order, tradition, and community. For Eliot, Richards, and their followers in the *Scrutiny* and New Critical circles, the ordered integration embodied in a genuine poem represented a harmony that was to be valued all the more for the contrast it presented to the chaos of contemporary history. Richards and the Leavises placed upon the practice of criticism a decisive responsibility in combating what they saw as the 'levelling-down' of standards in modern 'mass' culture. They feared that the rising tide of popular entertainment in the shape of cinema and pulp fiction would overwhelm the finer traditions of literature unless the discerning minority re-asserted their values. I. A. Richards in *Science and Poetry* (1926) foresaw a catastrophic collapse of older beliefs under the impact of science and the new technologies of cinema and radio, predicting that only the imaginative flexibility of poetry could save us from the consequences. Q. D. Leavis's *Fiction and the Reading Public* (1932) is a prolonged defence of literature's mature awareness against the drug-like or masturbatory fantasies of 'lowbrow' entertainment. Along with F. R. Leavis's *Mass*

Civilisation and Minority Culture (1930), it set the agenda for *Scrutiny*'s vigilant guardianship of 'minority' literary values. The *Scrutiny* critics came to value literature because it preserved, against the now dominant commercially mechanized order of modern life, the maturely integrated mentality of the pre-industrial 'organic community', represented for them in the crafts and rituals of the English village. Their American counterparts, the early New Critics of the Southern group, likewise harked back to 'organic' social traditions of the rural past: Tate and Ransom were both contributors to the Agrarian manifesto *I'll Take My Stand* (1930), which defended the 'traditional' social cohesion, as they represented it, of the South against the rampant industrial development of the North. For both groups, too, the organic integration of the poem represented a kind of sanctuary for traditional values and their enriching concreteness; outside this sanctuary of artistic form, there raged the twin Utopian evils of soulless capitalism and mindless sloganizing communism. Ransom and Tate both defined the unique value of poetry in terms of its distance from utilitarian and practical imperatives, from the abstractions of scientists and social reformers. The political implications of this position were consciously encapsulated in the title of Tate's *Reactionary Essays* (1936).

The taking of political stands in criticism seemed unavoidable. The Cambridge school generated conflicting forms of liberalism (rationalistic in Richards and Empson, organicist in the Leavises), but many other important critics aligned themselves with Left or Right. By and large, the anti-Romantic modernist critics headed Right, while the romantics and realists went Left. Thus Ezra Pound became increasingly involved with Italian Fascism, and T. S. Eliot leaned towards Fascism's more clerical form in Spain. Eliot's *After Strange Gods* (1934) denounced the modern disease of Liberalism, and warned that too many free-thinking Jews would be undesirable in a well-ordered society. After the shock of the Wall Street Crash in 1929, increasing numbers of literary intellectuals declared themselves for the Left: Murry, for instance, converted his *Adelphi* into a Marxist organ, while Read took up anarchism. In the early 1930s, a new generation of critics arrived to proclaim Marxism as the new key to literary problems and to the cultural impasse of a bankrupt civilization. In Britain, these critics were for the most part affiliated directly to the Communist Party, and so were concerned to frame literary discussion within a 'Marxism' increasingly reduced to the propagandist directives of the Stalinized Communist International, in terms of its slogans of 'proletarian literature' and 'socialist realism'. The critical Left in the United States, however, was never securely dominated by Stalinist orthodoxy, being riven by disputes between the Party line and various independent Marxist or semi-Marxist positions more sympathetic to the heresies of Trotsky (whose own *Literature and Revolution* (1924) cast doubt on 'proletarian literature' and on the subordination of artists to the Party). In the simplest terms, the battle-lines of the Red Decade were drawn in literary criticism between the right-wing formalism of Eliot, Tate, and Ransom, and the left-wing propagandism of the *soi-disant* Marxists; at the most abstract level, a religion of Form was opposed to a politics of Content. The most interesting critical responses to the decade of economic and political crisis, however, were looking beyond that crude opposition.

The simpler forms of critical 'proletarianism' were represented in the US by V. F. Calverton in the *Modern Quarterly* and by Granville Hicks in the *New Masses*. Calverton in his *Liberation of American Literature* (1932) and Hicks in *The Great Tradition* (1933) reviewed the ideological tendencies of modern American literature in terms of the degree to which writers had arrived at a progressive political standpoint or had identified themselves with the imminent victory of the proletariat. Henry James and other suspiciously 'negative' or 'pessimistic' writers emerged poorly from such inquests, whose criteria relegated aesthetic value to a position merely supplementary to the current needs of propaganda. At the same time Max Eastman in his *The Literary Mind* (1931) was predicting that criticism would soon be subsumed by psychology and sociology, and was characterizing the modernist writers as a reactionary clique of obscurantists trying to uphold the social prestige of literature against the invincible rise of science. In Britain, the Communist Party critics Christopher Caudwell, Alick West, and Ralph Fox called upon writers to join the socialist ranks, which could save them from decadent pessimism. West, for example, in *Crisis and Criticism* (1937), finds much to admire in *Ulysses*, but finally convicts Joyce for failure to identify with the positive onward movement of society. The British Stalinists, however, had more ambitious aims than their American counterparts: shepherding contemporary writers into the official optimism of the cause was for them only the conclusion of a larger theoretical investigation of literature as an organized form of collective energy. West and Caudwell are at their best when looking for ways beyond the individualist psychology of I. A. Richards to a social conception of poetry: both present the task of poetry as one of rallying the social group's appetite for self-reproduction through productive work. Their activist romantic aesthetic accords rather too well with the tractor-worship evident in Soviet paintings of the time, and tends to make all literature a variant upon the sea-shanty, but the boldness of Caudwell's anthropological and psychological speculations in his *Illusion and Reality* (1937) is often more impressive than this suggests. Caudwell's precocious work includes some interesting critical adaptations of Freud's theory of dreams, and a conception of poetic psychology often more credible than that of Richards, along with some perceptive observations on the social position of writers. It falls into disastrously reductive thinking, though, in its notorious chapters on the history of English 'bourgeois poetry', where the poets are presented largely as mouthpieces for the direct expression of capitalist economic imperatives in successive phases of expansion and decline: Shelley, for instance, here becomes a spokesman for the bourgeoisie in its dynamic phase of industrialization. The crudely economistic scheme is wrapped up in chillingly orthodox political commentary, as when Caudwell compares the unsoundness of Byron with that of the traitor Trotsky.

Association with the Communist Party did not always tie critics to the official literary policy of proletarian triumphalism. An important case of heterodoxy is that of the Harvard professor F. O. Matthiessen, whose communist affiliations were complicated by a Christian-socialist conviction at odds with the optimism of the Party organs. His sympathetic expository work *The Achievement of T. S. Eliot* (1935) openly resists the Leftist tendency to confuse literature with social documentation and propaganda, and it is more interested in New-Critical formal and aesthetic analysis than in any censuring of modernist 'pessimism'. Matthiessen's most influential book, *American Renaissance* (1941) shows a similar unorthodox sympathy for the 'tragic' perspectives of Hawthorne and Melville rather than for the optimism of Emerson, although it values the great nineteenth-century writers in partly political terms for their exploration of the possibilities of democracy. Another significant maverick among the 'fellow-travellers' of American communism was Kenneth Burke, who, as we have seen, shared some formalist principles with the reactionary Agrarians. In his *Counter-statement* (1931), he represented the Agrarians as inadvertent anti-capitalist allies from whom he could borrow elements of his new combination of formalist, Freudian, and Marxist themes. This early work incorporates an astonishing cultural manifesto simply entitled 'Program', which adapts Agrarian anti-industrialism to Burke's more bohemian modernist view in calling for a 'negativist' art that would undermine the values of capitalist efficiency not through proletarian propaganda but by cultivating pleasure against the work-ethic; calling for a drastic reduction of working hours, Burke thus advances an aesthetic for the age of the dole. His imaginative approach to the politics of literature places a new value on 'escapist' writing as a catalyst for dissatisfaction with existing social conditions.

Aside from these idiosyncratic linkings of formalism and Marxism in Burke and Matthiessen, the need for some fruitful synthesis between the two positions was registered more strongly on the American Left in the late 1930s. The left-wing novelist James T. Farrell in his *A Note on Literary Criticism* (1936) rejected the propagandistic prescriptions of Hicks and other would-be commissars of literature, and Bernard Smith in *Forces in American Criticism* (1939) likewise lamented Hicks's crude approach. More significantly, the formerly Party-dominated *Partisan Review* relaunched itself in 1937 on an anti-Stalinist platform, and its leading contributor, Edmund Wilson, published in his *The Triple Thinkers* (1938) a direct rebuttal, by appeal to Marx and Engels themselves, of the Hicksian conception of literature as a class weapon or bearer of virtuous social messages. The *Partisan Review* circle, later to be referred to (like a basketball team) as the 'New York Intellectuals', along with others including Matthiessen, looked to Edmund Wilson as a model of the flexible modern critic, in the first place for the virtues of his *Axel's Castle* (1931), an admirably persuasive account of Symbolism and modernism that includes sensitive studies of Proust, Eliot, Yeats, and Joyce in the historical context of modern literature and thought. Wilson approached literary history from broadly sociological and psychological angles, learning from Marx and Freud but avoiding schematic application of their principles to literary works. Above all he reached out to literary modernism with an imaginative sympathy not found among the censorious dogmatists of Party orthodoxy, elucidating the works of Yeats and Joyce rather than reject them as decadent or pessimistic. Like Murry before him, Wilson disagrees with Eliot's separation of literature from other human interests, and he chides some of the modernists for excessive despair, but he always takes their artistic achievements seriously, just as he always respects the difference between the suggestions of formal art and the direct statements of propaganda. His idea of the future prospects for literature differed sharply from those propagandists who demanded optimistic proletarian novels: for Wilson in *Axel's Castle*, the future belonged to some synthesis of Symbolist and Naturalist principles, of the kind best represented in Joyce's *Ulysses*. Attracting some censure from the New Critics Allen Tate and Cleanth Brooks for his refusal to disconnect literature from its social and psychological contexts, Wilson taught the more independent critics on the American liberal Left – principally the 'New York Intellectuals' – that a duly discriminating formal appreciation of modernist writing could be accommodated with progressive political views. His most talented disciple, Lionel Trilling, a young teacher at Columbia University, developed the literary consequences of the *Partisan Review*'s new anti-Stalinist liberalism in his much-admired critical study *Matthew Arnold* (1939), which presents the dialectical flexibility of Arnold's thought as a model, albeit imperfect, for modern liberals. In the year of the Hitler-Stalin pact, he offered Arnold's sceptical reason as an answer to the dual totalitarian cults of unreflective action.

Marxist criticism called forth a series of scornful responses from the *Scrutiny* group in England, most of them objecting to the communist cult of technological development as a continuation of capitalism's worst features. *Scrutiny* did not, however, reject on principle the idea of literature's economic and social determinations, its own form of criticism being itself 'sociological' although pessimistic. L. C. Knights, the only active socialist in the group, even wrote a study of the economic factor in Renaissance drama, in *Drama and Society in the Age of Johnson* (1937), which warily entertains some Marxist notions; and the Leavises expressed some admiration for the novels of John Dos Passos, whom Granville Hicks had seen as the nearest thing to a great 'proletarian' writer. The predominantly insular and nostalgic bent of the *Scrutiny* circle, though, precluded the kind of positive critical assimilation by which Edmund Wilson and his associates had digested Marx, Freud, Proust and Joyce. The most valuable immediate result of the political polemics of the 1930s in criticism was the synthesizing of a leftward-inclined critical modernism in New York.

Shakespeare in Space

Critical approaches to Shakespeare underwent a remarkable transformation in the 1930s, in which Bradley's conception of character as the key to the plays was overthrown by a new symbolic or 'poetic' understanding of the play as an expanded metaphor or 'spatial' pattern. Before we encounter the work of G. Wilson Knight, the leader of this new school of interpretation, it will be worth briefly reviewing some earlier developments that tended to undermine Bradley's approach.

A strange mood certainly beset the Shakespearean world in the 1920s, a decade that had opened with the publication of *Shakespeare Identified in Edward de Vere, Seventeenth Earl of Oxford* (1920), by one J. Thomas Looney, sparking off the biggest anti-Stratfordian craze since the Bacon boom. A spirit of iconoclasm was abroad in the post-war years, and traditional pieties about Shakespeare were among its victims, as can be seen in the parody of speculative Bardolatry in the 'Scylla and Charybdis' chapter of Joyce's novel *Ulysses* (published by 'Shakespeare & Co.', 1922). T. S. Eliot's definition of the 'objective correlative' was offered to the world in an essay on *Hamlet* in which he insisted that the work was an artistic failure that had attracted all the wrong sorts of attention as a famous enigma. Agreeing with the Shakespearean scholar J. M. Robertson, he found that Shakespeare had failed to transform his obscure feelings into coherent dramatic art. Eliot's respect for Shakespeare's other works, especially *Coriolanus* and *Antony and Cleopatra*, was unaffected, but he expressed impatience with the tendency of critics to project themselves into Shakespearean characters or to detect a philosophical 'meaning' in the plays. His 1927 essay 'Shakespeare and the Stoicism of Seneca' argues that Shakespeare was an impersonal artist, not a philosopher, and that 'none of the plays of Shakespeare has a "meaning" '.[34] In his *Hamlet* essay, Eliot also congratulated the American scholar E. E. Stoll for avoiding character-analysis in favour of examining the play itself. Stoll's *Hamlet* (1919) was one of a succession of studies, culminating in *Art and Artifice in Shakespeare* (1933), in which he dismissed the modern obsession with consistency of character as an anachronistic misunderstanding of Elizabethan theatre. He and other students of Renaissance drama pointed out that the expectations of Elizabethan playgoers differed widely from those of modern audiences, and did not require credible motivation. Thus in the case of *Hamlet*, Stoll argued, the hero's delay is not really a psychological problem but an established convention of revenge drama. Improbabilities of motivation like Othello's sudden jealousy were accepted for the sake of larger dramatic effects of intensity and contrast. Other Shakespeareans tended to agree: J. W. Mackail, for instance, in his *Approach to Shakespeare* (1930), scorned Bradley's obsession with consistent characterization, and followed Stoll in believing that Shakespeare's higher concern for the impact of the dramatic situation as a whole overrode consistency in inessentials.

Another kind of challenge to accepted versions of Shakespeare came from a startling essay by Lytton Strachey on 'Shakespeare's Final Period', first written in 1904, but reprinted at the height of Strachey's fame in his *Books and Characters* (1922). His protest was at the common habit of critics since Dowden of regarding the final period as one of triumphant 'serenity'. Sentimentally besotted by Miranda and the other sweet maids of this period, they were blind to the strong elements of bitterness, violence, and artistic carelessness in the final plays. Strachey's mischievous conjecture was that, far from being 'serene', Shakespeare was by this time bored to death.[35] The hypothesis was taken seriously enough by John Middleton Murry, who devised in his *Discoveries* (1924) an explanation in which Shakespeare had by the time of the last plays accepted defeat in his effort to communicate mystical insights earlier hinted at in the enigmatic poem 'The Phoenix and the Turtle'. Disturbing suggestions began to appear from among the Freudians, notably in a study of *Hamlet* in Ernest Jones's *Essays in Applied Psycho-Analysis* (1923). Jones, following up a suggestion from Freud himself, proposed that Hamlet's delay in dispatching his father's assassin and his mother's bedfellow indicated an unconscious recognition of his own Oedipal desires reflected in Claudius's actions.

The year 1930 was one of further wonders, one of them being the publication of Caroline Spurgeon's lecture *Leading Motives in the Imagery of Shakespeare's Tragedies*. This formed part of a larger project completed in 1935 with her book *Shakespeare's Imagery and What It Tells Us*. Spurgeon's work was devoted to the exhaustive statistical analysis of the playwright's most habitual metaphors and similes; the idea being that they could unconsciously 'give away' secrets of Shakespeare's otherwise inscrutable personality and of his knowledge of the world. *Shakespeare's Imagery* comes complete with charts and tables showing, for instance, that *Troilus and Cressida* yields a record number of 339 images, whereas the *Comedy of Errors* can muster only 60. The recurrence of special categories of image shows that Shakespeare had a good knowledge of gardening, hunting, and housework, and a sympathy for horses, snails, beggars and children (with an 'especial interest in small boys'[36]). Spurgeon even claims that these recurrences can help us build up a portrait of Shakespeare's physical appearance and his character, which displays a 'passion for health, for soundness, cleanliness and wholesomeness in all realms of being . . .'[37] More valuably, Spurgeon goes on to discuss the functioning of imagery in the plays, where it emphasizes dramatic themes or helps create a special atmosphere. As she shows, each play tends to be dominated by a distinctive 'cluster' of recurrent images – of light and darkness in *Romeo and Juliet*, of disease in *Hamlet*, for example. The consequences for interpretation are left open, but it is evident that Spurgeon's new view of imagery as functional rather than merely ornamental suggests a higher importance be granted to the symbolic dimension of the plays, although her own essentially quantitative method could not alone take that further step.

Independently of Spurgeon's research, G. Wilson Knight, then a schoolteacher, had already been pursuing such a symbolic approach under the encouragement of Murry, to whose *Adelphi* he had contributed several articles in the late 1920s. Murry's somewhat mystical approach to Shakespeare, and his tendency to confuse the Bard with Christ, had inspired some of Knight's early insights; but Knight's first major work, *The Wheel of Fire* appeared in 1930 not with Murry's backing (he repudiated it as over-intellectualized) but with that of T. S. Eliot, who wrote for it an introduction in which he congratulated Knight for subordinating character and plot to the whole organic design or 'pattern' of Shakespeare's plays.

Knight's revolutionary revision of Shakespearean interpretation in *The Wheel of Fire* was to some extent inadvertent. He thought of his work rather modestly as continuing Bradley's interest in the special 'atmosphere' of the tragedies, although others recognized it as the boldest overturning of Bradley. This eccentric ultra-romantic Murryite also managed to propose in defence of his methods an unmistakably modernist or Eliotic declaration of the 'spatial' principle in literature:

> A Shakespeare tragedy is set spatially as well as temporally in the mind. By this I mean that there are throughout the play a set of correspondences which relate to each other independently of the time-sequence which is the story: such are the intuition– intelligence opposition active within and across *Troilus and Cressida*, the death-theme in *Hamlet*, the nightmare evil of *Macbeth*. This I have sometimes called the play's 'atmosphere'.[38]

An imaginative interpretation, as distinct from a fault-finding criticism, will need, Knight argues, to put aside limiting conceptions of Shakespeare's intentions, stage conditions, and sources, and above all the irrelevant ethical judgement of characters' motives. We should not look for realistic psychology, but instead 'aim at cutting below the surface to reveal that burning core of mental or spiritual reality from which each play derives its nature and meaning,' and attempt to 'see each play as an

expanded metaphor'.[39] The benefit of this new 'spatial' approach is seen
in several of Knight's individual interpretations of the plays: once we see
the persons of the play as symbols within a larger pattern, supposed faults
or irrelevances in plot- and character-construction melt away, and the
thematic design comes to the fore. Thus in *Macbeth* we have a consistent
atmosphere of nightmarish fear, going beyond the temporal cause-and-
effect logic of the plot; in *King Lear* the larger atmosphere of purgatorial
suffering is more important than any of the persons; in *Othello* a battle
is being fought between cynicism and heroism. Knight's most controversial
symbolic interpretation is of *Hamlet*, in which he sees the Prince as an
agent of poisonous negation set against the more 'human' Claudius in a
thematic conflict of death and life. For Murry and others this was a slander
on the most Shakespearean of heroes. But the advantages of Knight's
method showed most brightly in his reading of two 'problem plays'
hitherto bafflingly resistant to traditional criticism. *Troilus and Cressida*
could now be understood in terms of its central opposition between
romantic intuition and cynical intellect, while *Measure for Measure* could
be conceived as a consistent Christian allegory or parable of justice and
forgiveness, with the Duke cast as God. Knight's work did much to
redeem these plays from moralistic censure and critical neglect, as it
helped also to redeem *Coriolanus* and *Timon of Athens*.

The logic of Knight's new approach is brought out well in the opening
chapter of his sequel, *The Imperial Theme* (1931), where he contrasts the
old ethical criticism with his own 'imaginative' mode of interpretation.
The older school would admire Brutus and Hamlet as 'good' characters,
while condemning Cleopatra as immoral. Knight, however (following
Nietzsche beyond good and evil) sees these persons within the more
important thematic oppositions that they represent, and places Hamlet
and Brutus as agents of the 'evil' theme while Cleopatra is a wholly
positive bearer of the life-force. Not content to dissolve character and
action into 'spatial' oppositions, Knight goes even further by incorporating
entire plays into still larger symbolic patterns tracing the visionary evolution of the 'Shakespeare Progress' from *Julius Caesar* to *The Tempest*. In
The Wheel of Fire, recurrent oppositions like that between love and
cynicism are mapped across several plays, and the tragedies are made to
follow a redemptive Christian scheme in which *Macbeth* is hell, *King Lear*
purgatory, and *Antony and Cleopatra* heaven, while Timon plays the role
of Christ. *The Imperial Theme* constructs still larger patterns with Shakespeare's love-themes and death-themes, and suggests that his constant
symbolic opposition is that between the order of music and the disorder
of tempest. Knight's next book, *The Shakespearian Tempest* (1932), argues
that Shakespeare's entire work forms a unified design to which the
music–tempest opposition is the essential key. Knight's strong disposition
to mysticism thus finally sweeps away the heterogeneous obstacles of
character, plot, and indeed theatre, to trace instead a cosmic 'pattern'. It

was this side of his work that found most favour with T. S. Eliot. From his first encounter with Knight's writings, Eliot began to refer to the 'pattern in Shakespeare's carpet', and to insist that the playwright's works had to be taken as a whole, as in his declaration in the 1932 essay, 'John Ford' that 'The whole of Shakespeare's work is *one* poem'.[40]

Others were keen to develop this new way of reading Shakespeare in rather different directions. A group of young Cambridge critics connected with the launching of *Scrutiny* in 1932 celebrated the overthrow of Bradley by reading Shakespeare's plays 'as poetry', in a less transcendental sense than Knight's. Where Knight was given to telling his readers that 'The spirit of man is each a string vibrating to the sweeping arm of an unseen eternity,' or that in *Antony and Cleopatra* 'we touch the Absolute,'[41] the Cambridge group was more interested in imagery as part of a rich poetic language. Muriel Bradbrook in her *Elizabethan Stage Conditions* (1932) condemned the study of character-development 'apart from the texture of the words in which it is expressed,'[42] since in Shakespeare the dramatist and the poet were inseparable. More aggressively, the co-founder of *Scrutiny*, L. C. Knights, fired off a famous pamphlet mockingly entitled *How Many Children Had Lady Macbeth?* (1933) against the entire line of character-based criticism that had culminated in Bradley, censuring its abstraction of character from the total poetic effect of a Shakespeare play. Against this tradition, he maintained that 'the only profitable approach to Shakespeare is a consideration of his plays as dramatic poems, his use of language to obtain a total complex emotional response.'[43] Previous critics had ignored 'the words on the page,' but we should now return to sensitive appreciation of Shakespeare's handling of words, reading one of his plays 'as we should read any other poem'.[44] Knights appeals directly to new modernist principles, pointing out that if character-creation were the chief critical standard, we would have to throw away *Ulysses*, *To the Lighthouse*, and most of D. H. Lawrence's novels. In fact, 'Macbeth has greater affinity with *The Waste Land* than with *The Doll's House*.'[45] This would seem to be forgetting that it is a play, but then the *Scrutiny* critics made a habit of defying such generic considerations in the name of sheer linguistic energy. Knights goes on to illustrate, even more convincingly than Knight, how a 'poetic' reading of *Macbeth* accounts for supposedly irrelevant or undramatic scenes and speeches, and how the presentation of evil as disorder and deceit in the play permeates its verse.

Unlike G. Wilson Knight, who often ventured definitions of the visionary 'philosophy' of Shakespeare's plays, L. C. Knights maintains a strict Eliotic avoidance of such notions: 'I have called *Macbeth* a statement of evil; but it is a statement not of a philosophy but of ordered emotion.'[46] The other *Scrutiny* critics likewise conduct their appreciations of Shakespeare's verbal texture in terms, derived from Eliot, of the ordering of feeling and of experience. F. R. Leavis himself wrote articles in the 1930s on *Measure for Measure*, *Othello*, and *Antony and Cleopatra*, but the fullest exposition of the *Scrutiny* version of Shakespeare in this period came from D. A. Traversi in his book *Approach to Shakespeare* (1938). This work attempts to construct a narrative of Shakespeare's later work in terms of his reintegration of mind and body, which can be measured in the increased harmonizing of imagery into a rich texture. Thus Shakespeare starts in the sonnets and in *Hamlet* with a loathing of the flesh and a division between expression and experience, but begins to overcome this in *Measure for Measure* and *King Lear*, although he is still struggling for 'ordered significance'. The new sense of maturity and fertility in the imagery attached to Duncan in *Macbeth*, though, points the way to the complete reunion of flesh and value in *Antony and Cleopatra*, where rottenness turns to fertility in this one play 'in which Shakespeare came nearest to unifying his experience into a harmonious and related whole.'[47] Of the late plays, it is *The Winter's Tale* that best embodies this achieved 'maturity' in its reconciliation of spiritual and sensual life, and in its subordination of plot and character to the interplay of poetic imagery. So insistent is the repetitious stress on maturity, fertility, and experience in Traversi's account that it is often hard to tell whether he is discussing Shakespeare's personal and moral qualities or features of the plays; this was a recurrent difficulty with the moral vocabulary of Leavis's followers.

The revolution in Shakespeare criticism did not win unanimous support, and there were significant pockets of Bradleian resistance. H. B. Charlton, who aimed to extend Bradley's methods beyond the tragedies in his *Shakespearian Comedy* (1938), complained of the new cult of imagery:

> Indeed, the present trend of fashionable criticism appears to have little use even for drama. To our most modern coteries, drama is poetry or it is nothing; and by poetry they mean some sort of allegorical arabesque in which the images of Shakespeare's plays are more important than his men and women.[48]

Charlton's traditional view found little use for Shakespeare's late romances, which he dismissed as conventional and lacking in true characterization: even *The Tempest*, he felt, was less profound than *As You Like It* and *Twelfth Night*. Also content to ignore the poetry of the plays in Bradleian fashion was the textual scholar J. Dover Wilson, whose *What Happens in Hamlet* (1935) is like one of Bradley's fussier notes extended for 300 pages in an obsessive sorting out and tidying up of loose threads in the plot of one play. The same kind of 'sleuthing' is conducted at greater length, here into the problem of why Claudius does not react to the players' dumb-show, which in turn leads on to a tour of all the improbabilities and of course to Hamlet's feigned madness. At the same time, the amateur detectives were busy with their usual hobbyist works, including *The Five Authors of 'Shakespeare's Sonnets'* (1923) by H. T. S. Forrest, *Links Between Shakespeare and the Law* (1929) by the Rt Hon Sir Dunbar Plunket

Barton, *Shakespeare, Creator of Freemasonry* (1936) by Alfred Dodd, and *Shakespeare's Vital Secret (Known to to His Queen)* (1937), by R. M. Lucas.

Shakespeare criticism in this phase can be seen as a series of attempts to 'open up' areas of Shakespeare's work not already covered by Bradley's exclusive interest in the tragedies: while Charlton and others worked on the comedies, Wilson Knight revealed the undiscovered problem plays and the Roman plays. The histories eventually fell to the Cambridge scholar E. M. W. Tillyard, who employed the model of hierarchical cosmology developed in A. O. Lovejoy's *The Great Chain of Being* (1936) to argue that Elizabethan culture had, despite appearances, a great reverence for monarchical order. His short book *The Elizabethan World Picture* (1943) and its sequel, *Shakespeare's History Plays* (1944), emerged from a context in which patriotic Englishness had a high wartime value. These were the years of Olivier's film version of *Henry V* (1944), and of Wilson Knight's curious propagandistic writings on the religious significance of kingship in Shakespeare (*The Olive and the Sword*, 1944) and on Britain's messianic destiny as prophesied by Milton (*Chariot of Wrath*, 1942). Unlike Knight's intuitionism, Tillyard's approach to the history plays demanded scholarly reconstruction of their audience's attitudes to history and to royal power. Drawing rather selectively on Elizabethan sermons and chronicles, he represented Shakespeare as an orthodox spokesman for the Tudor version of English history, and thus, against a long sentimental tradition, he argued that Prince Hal's repudiation of Falstaff was the act of Shakespeare's ideal ruler, satisfying the Elizabethan audience's deep attachment to order. In his frequent assumption that Tudor ideology was religiously endorsed in every cottage in the land, Tillyard echoed a commonly held nostalgic view of the 'organically' indivisible vitality of Elizabethan England, which is prominent in the *Scrutiny* critics too. Despite some objections to his princely severity towards Falstaff, Tillyard's was the most generally accepted interpretation of the history plays for the next thirty years.

Theories of the Novel

The interval between the wars was a remarkable period not only of experiment in fictional forms, by Joyce, Woolf, Lawrence, Faulkner and others, but also of advances in the theory of the novel. The antagonistic terms of debate about fiction, already set before the war, were initially cast as an opposition between the aesthetic perfectionism of Flaubert or James and the allegedly mechanical realism of H. G. Wells, Arnold Bennett, and Theodore Dreiser. In the 1920s, however, this conflict rose in some instances above the idealizing or demonizing of personalities into the more impersonal consideration of the basic principles of construction in 'the novel' abstractly conceived and increasingly recognized as the major literary form of the modern world. These discussions took place almost entirely in England, where an established empiricist distrust of theorizing tended to resist or compromise the boldest thinking; in America, criticism of the novel was more closely focused on individual achievements such as that of Melville, or posed in terms of the novelist's relationship to society.

The principal declarations of modernist principle came from Virginia Woolf in her pamphlet *Mr Bennett and Mrs Brown* (1924), and in the essay 'Modern Fiction' in her collection *The Common Reader* (1925). In both works she complains of the limited conceptions of life, character, and 'reality' offered by the novels of Wells, Bennett, and Galsworthy: these materialistic novelists are more interested in social ideals than in human actuality, preferring to describe buildings, furniture and external accessories of life rather than the fluidity and complexity of the soul as explored by the great Russian writers. Woolf saw that 'reality' had become falsely identified with a restricted Edwardian convention of plot-construction, and that it needed to be imagined anew. If the writer were not enslaved to prevailing expectations, 'if he could base his work upon his own feeling and not upon convention, there would be no plot, no comedy, no tragedy, no love interest in the accepted style, and perhaps not a single button sewn on as the Bond Street tailors would have it.'[49] In other essays on Conrad and Russian fiction in *The Common Reader*, and on Hardy in the second *Common Reader* (1932), Woolf continues to contrast the mere transcription of life's surface with true artistic vision and the possibilities of raising the English novel to the status of a respected art.

Similar high hopes for the future of the art animated Percy Lubbock in his major contribution to novelistic theory, *The Craft of Fiction* (1921). The purpose of this work was to rescue the theory of the novel from its confused condition and at last to give it a clear terminology and conceptual system. In a decisive move to impersonality, Lubbock argues that it is time to stop discussing the personalities of novelists and to look instead at novels themselves, to see how they are made. His approach to this task is unmistakably that of a Jamesian disciple, but it is never dogmatic in its exposition of the Master's system. Lubbock's business in this book is to adapt the terms which James had applied to his own novels, and make them into concepts generally applicable to the essential problems of construction encountered in all novels. Inheriting James's predominantly visual metaphors – of pictures and dramatic scenes – Lubbock is to some extent condemned in advance to present fiction as a matter of 'showing' more than of 'telling', and his theoretical distinctions suffer confusion as a result. He starts by admitting that all fiction is necessarily a process of telling and is experienced temporally, but is unable to find a vocabulary for these facts, and so he falls into discussing the novel almost entirely in terms of spatial configuration and vision; unlike some modernists, Lubbock is a 'spatialist' by default rather than on principle. Within these limits, though, he establishes important clarifications of the Jamesian problem of narrative 'point of view'. On this question, Lubbock proceeds from the assumption that the traditional minstrel's method of direct omniscient relation is too primitive, and that its process of telling needs to be disguised so that as far as possible the story should seem to 'tell itself'. Accordingly, a subtler method is to allocate responsibility for the telling of the story to a fictional narrator internal to the imagined world; this has the advantage of accounting for the narrative voice, rather than leaving it hanging above the story. However, the usual first-person kind of internal narrator is unable to analyse his or her own thought-processes, so a more sophisticated method is required to combine the best of both worlds: a third-person account presented mainly as if seen through the eyes of an internal observer but at times allowing this observer to be observed in turn. This last is the method of Flaubert's *Madame Bovary* and of James's *The Ambassadors*, which are presented here as the highest achievements of prestidigitation, achieving the hitherto impossible feat of dramatizing consciousness itself.

Lubbock does not believe, however, that every novel should strain to resemble the late works of James. In the end, method follows the demands of the subject, and there are large-scale subjects that preclude the possibility of having the story tell itself as if it were a piece of theatre. In his contrasting of the panoramic 'picture' (description of settings and summaries of events) with the dramatic 'scene' (presentation of a specific event through dialogue and internal observation), he does recommend that the novelist exploit the dramatic method wherever appropriate, and he deplores Thackeray's failure to take advantage of it in his preference for 'intrusive' commentary; but he can also commend Balzac's predominantly pictorial methods, and censure Tolstoy for the opposite fault of neglecting the benefits of pictorial summary in *Anna Karenina*, where the heroine is inadequately prepared for her scenes. The dramatic method is not to be elevated to a principle in the name of impersonality or any other abstract code, but made use of in the interests only of vividness. Exclusively dramatized novels like James's *The Awkward Age* are not to be imitated as an ideal; rather, a mixture of methods is required, as in the exemplary *Madame Bovary*.

The novelist E. M. Forster responded suspiciously to Lubbock's work as an excessively theoretical project, and he assumed unjustly that Lubbock was forbidding the convincing combination of different methods. In his *Aspects of the Novel* (1927), Forster deliberately adopts a colloquial and unpretentious manner in contrast to Lubbock's theorizing; and although he actually agrees with Lubbock and James about the over-intrusive narrative voices of Thackeray and Fielding, he still maintains, against

James, that the more intense a novelist's interest in method, the less interesting will be his view of life. Technical difficulties can always be overridden, Forster claims, by the novelist's ability to 'bounce' the reader into accepting his world, and the main problem confronting the novelist is not that of point of view but of establishing the right mixture of characters. Rather than waste much time on point of view or even on the concept of form, Forster devotes his attention to the accepted categories of plot and character, with some vaguer observations on 'pattern' and 'rhythm'. His most notable contribution to critical thinking here is a rough distinction between 'flat' characters (usually predictable caricatures) and 'round' ones (those capable of surprising development). A striking feature of his treatment of these issues is his wary distrust of the chronological principle, either in literary history or within the novel itself. 'History develops, Art stands still,' Forster asserts with minor qualifications, and so we are invited to imagine all the novelists of the ages seated around a circular table at the same time, all addressing the same tasks.[50] This synchronism extends to the treatment of time and the chronological succession of the story in novels, which are seen as regrettable and primitive necessities: 'Yes – oh dear yes – the novel tells a story.'[51] The simple sequence of one thing after another that makes a story cannot be done away with as Gertrude Stein has attempted, but its appeal can at least be raised from brute curiosity to sympathetic intelligence by the addition of causality in the form of plot and of 'value' in the evocation of character. Even an expert like Scott has little to give us, being just a storyteller, whereas in *War and Peace* we are rewarded with much more than the mere time-dimension and given a superior sense of space. All this does not make Forster a 'spatialist' in the modernist sense. In his chapter on 'Pattern and Rhythm', for example, where we might expect a discussion of spatially conceived interconnections of motifs, we get only a few remarks on certain plots that involve neat reversals. Forster's synchronism is a defensive stance adopted to guard against the notion that modernist fiction could be 'developing' beyond the boundaries of his Victorian liberalism. This shows up in the only passages of *Aspects* that rise above the normal tone of lethargy into energetic denial. Joyce's *Ulysses* is the occasion for one such moment: this novel is 'a dogged attempt to cover the universe with mud, . . . a simplification of the human character in the interests of Hell.' In the Nighttown episode especially, 'smaller mythologies swarm and pullulate, like vermin between the scales of a poisonous snake.'[52] Joyce has sinned by simplifying the true muddle of human life, Forster concludes. A similar offence is that of Henry James, whose novels sacrifice the confusion of life for the orderly designs of art, so that James's characters are like castrated figures with huge heads and tiny legs. Referring back to an ill-tempered correspondence in which H. G. Wells had challenged James in these terms, Forster sides against James and with Wells; against Art, for Life and its muddle.

Forster's casually untheoretical position, and especially his endorsement of Wellsian 'life' against the artistic cultivation of form, provoked an exasperated response from Virginia Woolf:

> What is this 'Life' that keeps on cropping up so mysteriously and so complacently in books about fiction? Why is it absent in a pattern and present in a tea party? Why is the pleasure that we get from the pattern in *The Golden Bowl* less valuable than the emotion which Trollope gives us when he describes a lady drinking tea in a parsonage?[53]

Forster had ignored the aesthetic functions of the novel and its use of words, Woolf charged, and had treated fiction as an inferior parasite upon the almighty teapot of English social comedy. Similarly disappointed by Forster's invocation of 'life' was the Scottish poet Edwin Muir, whose book *The Structure of the Novel* (1928) attempts a more theoretical classification of novelistic forms. As Muir points out, no novel can be as formless as life itself: 'even *Ulysses* is less confusing than Dublin'.[54] Lubbock's serious attention to form is commended, but his narrowly Jamesian interests and terminology are set aside in favour of a more comprehensive scheme in which Muir maps character and plot onto the co-ordinates of space and time. After disposing of the most basic kinds of adventure-romances under the heading of the Novel of Action, he goes on to develop a contrast between the Character Novel and the Dramatic Novel: the first type deploys relatively 'fixed' characters to illuminate an extensive social panorama (as in Fielding, Thackeray, and Dickens), while the second type shows actively developing characters within a confined sphere that focuses their unfolding destinies (as in the comedies of Austen or the tragedies of Hardy, the Brontës, and Melville). The Character Novel will have the crowded spatial reality of a tableau and a realistic sense of geography, but little sense of time, whereas the Dramatic Novel will have an urgent time-sense but a tightly limited and unvarying location: 'The dramatic novel is limited in Space and free in Time, the character novel limited in Time and free in Space', as Muir summarizes it.[55] Apart from helping to inspire Joseph Frank's reflections on 'spatial form', Muir's work appears not to have won the influential status it deserved. By contrast with Forster's *Aspects*, it goes back rewardingly to first principles of aesthetics (evidently those of Lessing's *Laokoon*), and is able to illuminate the inner logic of recent modernist work, including the novels of Proust, Joyce, and Woolf. It refines Forster's distinction between flat and round characters in such a way as to reveal the satirical possibilities of the flat kind; and it clarifies Woolf's objections to the Wells–Bennett school of social documentation, in an interesting distinction between the 'chronicles' of Tolstoy or Lawrence and the degraded 'period' novel of Edwardian realism. Muir's and Woolf's hopes for a theory of the novel as art were to be compromised, however, by the emergence of an anti-theoretical vitalism from within the English modernist camp itself.

In its most extreme form, the vitalist position is represented by the scattered essays of D. H. Lawrence, whose chief requirement of criticism was that the critic be emotionally alive and instinctively able to tell whether a novel was itself living or tremblingly 'quick', all other critical categories being an irrelevance. As Murry required 'soul' from the novel, Lawrence demanded evidence of a profound 'tremulation' beneath the conscious surface of the work. It is not the characters that matter, he announces in his 1925 essay 'The Novel', since in every great novel the true hero is not any of the persons but the 'nameless flame behind them all'.[56] In an earlier essay, 'Surgery For the Novel – Or a Bomb' (1923), he had complained that the serious modern novel of Joyce, Proust, and Richardson was dying from excessive self-consciousness, and a new current of feeling needed to be tapped if it was to be reborn. When Lawrence speaks of 'the novel' he refers to something like an independent life-form whose glowing vitality is to be distinguished sharply from the novelist's conscious intentions in writing it. In 'The Novel' he takes the case of Tolstoy, whose didactic purpose in *Anna Karenina* is, fortunately, undermined by the contrary sexual energy of 'the novel': 'There you have the greatness of the novel itself. It won't *let* you tell didactic lies, and put them over. Nobody in the world is anything but delighted when Vronsky gets Anna Karenina.'[57] For Lawrence, the value of the novel lies in its inherently fluid relativism, its subversion of 'absolutes' and didactic abstractions. Thus in *Studies in Classic American Literature* he argues that Hawthorne gave his conscious allegiance to official morality, but allowed his 'passional self' to repudiate it when he wrote *The Scarlet Letter*. Lawrence even turns this into a universal rule:

> The artist usually sets out – or used to – to point a moral and adorn a tale. The tale, however, points the other way, as a rule. Two blankly opposing morals, the artist's and the tale's. Never trust the artist. Trust the tale. The proper function of a critic is to save the tale from the artist who created it.[58]

As a general critical principle, this has momentous potential consequences in directing the critic to read – 'imaginatively', as G. Wilson Knight would say – against the grain of the author's supposed intentions. Beyond Knight's Shakespeare studies and a few explorations in psychoanalytic interpretation, though, the invitation was not widely taken up in this period. More seriously attended were Lawrence's several defences of the novel as 'the highest form of human expression so far attained,' and as the 'perfect medium for revealing to us the changing rainbow of our living relationships'.[59] In the posthumously published essay 'Why the Novel Matters', Lawrence claims that as a novelist he considers himself superior to the saint, the poet, and the philosopher, who develop only partial aspects of human life, whereas the novelist affects the 'whole man'. The novel is 'the one bright book of life', of which Homer, Shakespeare, and the Bible were early types.[60] In its flexible refusal to confirm to didactic schemes, the novel can teach us, Lawrence affirms, to develop our instinct for life against conformity to codes of good and evil.

From the debate about the theory of fiction in the 1920s emerged a somewhat different critical impatience with formal categories. The modernist journal *The Calendar of Modern Letters*, to which Muir and Lawrence also contributed, carried in 1926 two short articles by C. H. Rickword (cousin of the editor, Edgell Rickword), which cast doubt upon the value even of such basic terms as character, plot, form, and narrative in the criticism of novels. These notions were, Rickword contended, merely abstractions derived by the reader from the flow of the novel's verbal arrangements. Rickword's point was not clearly elaborated, but as a hint it was eagerly seized upon by the founders of *Scrutiny* a few years later. F. R. Leavis included Rickword's articles in his selection of *Calendar* criticism, *Towards Standards of Criticism* (1933), claiming that they provided the foundation for a new approach to the novel that would be directed to the observable qualities of the novelist's language:

> A novel, like a poem, is made of words; there is nothing else one can point to. We talk of a novelist 'creating characters', but the process of 'creation' is one of putting words together. We discuss the quality of his 'vision', but the only critical judgments we can attach directly to observable parts of his work concern particular arrangements of words – the quality of the response they evoke. Criticism, that is, must be in the first place (and never cease being) a matter of sensibility, of responding sensitively and with precise discrimination to the words on the page.[61]

Leavis believed that this new restriction of the critical discussion to features that could be pointed to was a final repudiation of Lubbock's abstract concern with form, method, structure, and technique. Novels could be treated as poems, in terms of their observable verbal rhythms; indeed, Leavis continued, there was much in common between a poem, a Shakespeare play, and a novel – especially a modernist 'poetic' novel. It is worth nothing here how the new conceptions of Shakespeare and of the novel were mutually reinforcing within the *Scrutiny* circle: while L. C. Knights was justifying a new 'poetic' reading of Shakespeare by reference to the redundancy of 'character' in the modernist novel, Leavis was looking forward to reading novels as if they were poetic dramas.

F. R. Leavis's own development of a new novel criticism was postponed until the late 1940s, while he proceeded to revise the poetic canon. But *Scrutiny* had behind it in the 1930s one considerable assessment of the novel in Q. D. Leavis's *Fiction and the Reading Public* (1932), an ambitious work of 'sociological' literary history which traces the breakdown of a unified reading public into 'lowbrow' and 'highbrow' levels. Q. D. Leavis suggests that since a novel, like a poem, is made of words, the kind of analysis applied by I. A. Richards to poetry could be adapted to fiction, although she acknowledges more clearly than her husband the problems of such an attempt. She regards the best modern novels as 'poetic' in construction, and scorns the Bradleian cult of character in fiction, along with Lubbock's interest in novelistic method. It is not method that makes a novel good or bad, she maintains, but ultimately (as Henry James had implied) the quality of the novelist's mind; and this can be felt by the sensitive critic in the idiom and rhythms of the prose. While her husband tested English verse for its energies and its underlying moral integrity, Q. D. Leavis did the same with English prose, comparing long passages of sentimental modern bestsellers with extracts from *A Passage to India*, revealing what Richards had called 'stock responses' in the former. In her reconstruction of the decline of fiction, the demands made upon readers by novelists started to slacken in the early nineteenth century with Scott, Bulwer-Lytton, Dickens, and Charlotte Brontë, who indulged a new popular demand for daydream fantasies. The resulting clichéd sentimental prose betrayed a moral lapse too, which can be measured in the difference between the 'mature' realism of Jane Austen and the adolescent wish-fulfilments of Charlotte Brontë. In this founding work, the *Scrutiny* group was provided with a mode of direct moral evaluation unencumbered by abstract notions of method. The critical testing of 'life' had superseded the brief flourishing of theory in the 1920s.

In the 1930s, criticism of the novel suffered both from the almost exclusive interest in poetry among Eliot's followers and from the schematic prescriptions offered by Stalinist partisans of 'proletarian fiction' and 'socialist realism' such as Granville Hicks in *The Great Tradition* (1933) and Ralph Fox in *The Novel and the People* (1937). One redeeming feature of the decade is the work of Edmund Wilson, which uses the insights of Marxism more sensitively to examine the implied social criticisms embodied in the works of novelists. His adoption of *Ulysses* as the great modern novel in his early *Axel's Castle* (1931) sets the tone for a series of later essays in which he rescues some modernist heroes from the crude accusation of ignoring social and historical reality: Flaubert and Henry James are redeemed in this way in his *The Triple Thinkers* (1938). More impressive than these is his long essay 'Dickens: The Two Scrooges' in *The Wound and the Bow* (1941), which combines biographical, psychological, sociological, and formal approaches in a major rehabilitation of Dickens as both a great novelist and a great social critic. Drawing attention to Dickens's use of central symbols – the fog in *Bleak House*, the dustheap in *Our Mutual Friend* – Wilson makes Dickens respectable again in Symbolist and modernist terms, comparing him with Kafka and Dostoevsky.

It is worth noting that this reading of Dickens accords with a larger trend in this period, in which certain nineteenth-century novels are rediscovered in terms of their 'poetic' or symbolic virtues. Wilson's recuperation of Dickens's late novels finds its counterpart in the rediscovery of Melville's *Moby Dick* as the great American novel by numerous critics in the 1930s, and in the new value accorded to *Wuthering Heights*, which was allocated a singular position among Victorian novels. David Cecil's *Early Victorian Novelists* (1934), for instance, is a rather half-hearted attempt to rescue Victorian novelists from the disfavour into which they had fallen in the 1920s, but it comes to life in the chapter devoted to *Wuthering Heights*, identifying this novel as the one perfect work of its age, and interpreting it in terms of poetic themes and organic form. Even Q. D. Leavis, who is severe in her judgements on the Victorians, singles out Emily Brontë's novel as one demanding a complex poetic response. Melville, Emily Brontë, and even Dickens, then, were becoming adopted as honorary modernists.

Canons of Modernist Revaluation

In the making and re-making of canons, two major developments stand out in this period. The first and more controversial is the drastic revision of the map of English poetry; the second, eventually more momentous, is the construction of a national literary canon for the United States.

The call to revolution against the received pantheon of English verse had already been raised before the War by Ezra Pound in his attacks on Milton and Victorian poetry, but in the early essays of T. S. Eliot it found a more persuasive echo. Eliot's revised view of 'tradition' proposed that the configuration of past writers is altered by the arrival of the new; which also implied that the literary past would have to be re-assessed in the light of the present generation's needs. Eliot's impact on the canon is sometimes regarded simply in terms of his promotion of John Donne, but in fact it is far more extensive than this. A Donne revival was already on its way, but Eliot both underpinned it with a historical scheme and a criterion of value, and generalized its critical implications, in his observations on the 'dissociation of sensibility'. The qualities of Elizabethan and Jacobean verse in general (but quoted in detail) could now be used to show up deficiencies in the post-Miltonic tradition in accordance with an attractively simple narrative of a Fall from integration. In this story, Milton could be identified as the poet who had eaten, in *Paradise Lost*, the apple of artificial rhetoric, while Shelley could be cast as his anaemic offspring. Eliot's readers were quick to pick up their cue. I. A. Richards, for example, suggested in *Practical Criticism* (1929), that admiration for Shelley or Milton was really a conventional respect for icons of poetic fame, and was not based on qualities of their verse. Professors began to notice in their students an abrupt turn against Shelley; and Edmund Wilson in *Axel's Castle* (1931) warned that a new orthodoxy was already established in the younger generation:

> With the ascendancy of T. S. Eliot, the Elizabethan dramatists have come back into fashion, and the nineteenth-century poets gone out. Milton's poetic reputation has sunk, and Dryden's and Pope's have risen. It is as much as one's life is worth nowadays, among young people, to say an approving word for Shelley or a dubious one about Donne.[62]

Shelley was indeed the usual butt of the *Scrutiny* and New Critical schools, while Donne became a standard of poetic value against whom other poets were to be measured; indeed J. C. Ransom went as far as to claim that he was a better poet than Shakespeare himself.

In the 1930s, Eliot's suggestions were codified into powerful new versions of English poetic history by his followers on each side of the Atlantic. In England, F. R. Leavis set out in *New Bearings in English Poetry* (1932) and *Revaluation* (1936) to realign the English tradition according to Eliot's standards; and in America Cleanth Brooks in *Modern Poetry and the Tradition* (1939) similarly traced a new line of descent from Donne to the modernist poets through the failures of the eighteenth and nineteenth centuries. Leavis's version is by far the more aggressive: *New Bearings* sweeps away all the major Victorian reputations and puts the recently discovered Gerard Manley Hopkins in their place, while *Revaluation* passes severe judgement on Milton and Shelley. The healthy 'line of wit' that Leavis traces in the latter book runs from Jonson and Donne through Carew and Marvell to Pope, while the inferior tradition of melodious preaching is seen to pass from Spenser through Milton to Shelley, Tennyson, and Swinburne. Shelley in particular 'represents pre-eminently the divorce between thought and feeling, intelligence and sensibility, that is characteristic of the nineteenth century.'[63] Leavis is usually elaborately deferent to Eliot in this book, but ventures to prefer Pope over Dryden, and, more interestingly, to smuggle a few Romantics – Blake, Wordsworth, and Keats – back into the canon under cover of their 'concrete' virtues. Brooks in his *Modern Poetry and the Tradition* makes an open appeal for the histories of poetry to be radically rewritten, and sketches out in his final chapter the shape of the new canon. Although based on the same Eliotic criteria of 'wit' and the unification of sensibility, his version is notably less restrictive than that of Leavis, finding room not only for Donne, Marvell, Hopkins, Yeats, and Eliot, but also for Wyatt,

Herrick, Pope, Blake, Coleridge, Keats, Dickinson, Hardy, Frost, Auden, and the American Fugitives.

Brooks's account rather strangely avoids the question of Milton; but in England the status of *Paradise Lost* in the national poetic canon was the subject of impassioned polemic. Eliot's implication that Milton was responsible in some way for the 'dissociation of sensibility' met no resistance from the romantic camp of Murry and Read, which in fact had its own suspicions about Milton's artificial Latinate style. The first significant rejoinder came in E. M. W. Tillyard's *Milton* (1930), and even this accepted Eliot's basic thesis, attempting merely to absolve Milton from personal blame for the defects of eighteenth-century verse. The movement of Miltonoclasm renewed itself in 1936 with a further essay by Eliot regretting Milton's artificial rhetoric,[64] and with a ferocious chapter in Leavis's *Revaluation*, which rails against the monotonous insensitivity of Milton's style in *Paradise Lost* and against its mechanical construction. Leavis's central complaint is that Milton's disembodied style calls too much attention to itself at the expense of sensuous particularity, betraying 'a feeling for words rather than a capacity for feeling through words' to concrete experience.[65] Against this strong trend, C. S. Lewis mounted in *A Preface to Paradise Lost* (1942) a rearguard attempt to justify the ways of Milton to men, but his historical apology for the epic diction of *Paradise Lost* did not answer the critical arguments of Eliot and Leavis so much as declare an incompatibly contrary taste.

Before leaving the English canon, we should notice that although most Victorian and Edwardian literature suffers from canonical relegation under the new modernist scrutiny, a few reputations are singled out for redemption from the sins of the nineteenth century. While some authors are severely reduced in status – Shelley and Tennyson in poetry, Scott and Meredith in prose – others are newly discovered (like Hopkins, first published in 1918) or reappraised in Symbolist terms (like Keats, Emily Brontë, and even, in Edmund Wilson's version, Dickens). Jane Austen, meanwhile, is almost unanimously exempted from the charges of didacticism and sentimentality, levelled at her contemporaries and immediate successors: in the new terminology of sensibility and irony, her status could only benefit from the comparison. The modernist revolution was not, then, an indiscriminate rejection of the nineteenth-century legacy, but an active critical sifting and reshaping of its components. This is particularly clear in the case of the American canon.

Despite the nationalist literary manifestos of Emerson and Whitman in the nineteenth century, the literature of the United States was still largely regarded, until the time of the Great War, as a minor branch of the British tradition. The English departments of American universities scarcely ever bothered to teach it, and the few historical and critical accounts of the subject, like Brander Matthews' *Introduction to the Study of American Literature* (1896) and Barrett Wendell's *Literary History of America* (1900), tended to assess writers by 'genteel' Anglocentric standards receptive to the work of such authors as Washington Irving, William Cullen Bryant, James Russell Lowell, John Greenleaf Whittier, Oliver Wendell Holmes, and Henry Wadsworth Longfellow – the favourites of refined Boston taste. In a major process of canonical revision, this group of writers was to be dislodged, and a new constellation – that of the 'American Renaissance' – installed in its place. To take the most spectacular example of the transformation, in Carl Van Doren's four-volume *Cambridge History of American Literature* (1917–23), Herman Melville is allotted less than four pages of comment; but by the end of the 1930s he was regarded by several critics as America's answer to Shakespeare, and he occupies the highest position in F. O. Matthessien's canon-making work *American Renaissance* (1941). An important impetus to this change was America's entry into the Great War in 1917, and the accompanying sense of larger national destiny after the self-destruction of Europe. The commanding world role of the United States was not supported, critics observed, by an adequate idea of national cultural tradition; and if such a tradition did not exist, it would have to be invented. Van Wyck Brooks submitted an article to the *Dial* in 1918, embodying this need for a canon suitable to modern needs in his title: 'On Creating a Usable Past'. In the post-war years, several American critics devoted themselves energetically to this task. Impatient with the severe Eurocentric classicism of Babbitt and with the narrowness of the 'genteel' Boston canon, they rewrote their country's literary history in the image of democratic nationalism, elevating to central positions the nonconformist energies of Thoreau, Emerson, Whitman, Melville, and Twain, while emphasizing the distinctive Americanness of Hawthorne and Dickinson. In this they had the support and inspiration from England of D. H. Lawrence, whose *Studies in Classic American Literature* (1923) rediscovered a dynamic and uniquely American energy in the works of Hawthorne, Poe, Melville, and Whitman.

The War indeed blew the old humanism of Babbitt and More off course, sweeping their chief disciple, Stuart P. Sherman of the University of Illinois, into the patriotic-democratic cause and into the critical heresy of eulogizing Whitman, as he did in his book *Americans* (1922). Sherman's defection from the humanist camp indicated an important redirection of American criticism, especially in the universities. Scholars gathered in the late 1920s to establish American literature as a serious academic subject, at first in Norman Foerster's collection *The Reinterpretation of American Literature* (1928), then in the journal *American Literature*, launched in 1929. V. L. Parrington in his *Main Currents in American Thought* (1927–30) provided a new democratic and populist interpretation of literary and intellectual history, upon which the Leftist critics of the 1930s built further, notably in V. F. Calverton's *The Liberation of American Literature* (1932). The *Partisan Review* group of the late 1930s had its own Americanist in Alfred Kazin, author of the important survey of American prose, *On Native Grounds* (1942). The crowning work of this movement, combining the social concerns of the 1930s with the New Critics' attention to formal integration, was Matthiessen's *American Renaissance*, which defined the 'central' American canon for the next three decades around the work of Emerson, Thoreau, Hawthorne, Melville, and Whitman. Other critical studies of this period helped to add the names of Dickinson, Twain, and James to the list of major national writers. The United States could now reclaim its literary 'masterpieces', but this critical process had at the same time narrowed the canon to a tiny handful of works selected (especially in Matthiessen's case) according to Symbolist and New Critical principles that involved the exclusion of didactic and social-realist writing such as the novels of Stowe or Howells. Matthiessen's concern for unified sensibility and concrete symbolism had, as in the English case of F. R. Leavis, the canonical effect of exalting but sharply restricting the select exemplars of 'tradition'.

While the academic canon underwent rapid contraction to a core syllabus of truly 'creative' works, the public canon of popular education survived in the reprinting of 'classics' in cheap editions. Indeed, in one form it entered the American academy in so-called 'Great Books' courses pioneered at Columbia and at the University of Chicago. As distinct from the syllabus of English departments, the Great Books course resembled the Everyman Library in scope, ranging from Homer and Plato to Darwin and Freud in an attempt to bring together the landmarks of Western thought, whether 'imaginative' or philosophical, albeit in a disconnected series. The possibilities of the popular reprint itself were extended in the 1930s by the paperback revolution, inaugurated in Britain by Penguin Books. Penguin did not construct any canonical project in their early years, but they did publish in 1938 a revised and updated version of Arnold Bennett's *Literary Taste*, with new twentieth-century lists compiled by Frank Swinnerton. This new guide to literary self-education reveals an interesting compromise between Edwardian and modernist canons, including among major modern writers the old grouping of Wells, Bennett, Galsworthy, Kipling, Shaw, and Bridges, but also alongside them the names of Lawrence, Joyce, Yeats, and Eliot; Woolf, Forster, Auden, and Wyndham Lewis are recommended among 'minor' authors, but then so is P. G. Wodehouse. Swinnerton significantly continues Bennett's policy of including substantial numbers of non-fiction items, including works of science, travel, and philosophy. This was almost the last gasp of the extensive popular canon, soon to be eclipsed by the restrictive model of the academic-modernist syllabus.

The Destructive Element

The major developments in literary theory and critical practice between the wars can be summarized as the effects of a revolutionary purification of criticism, one which repudiated the irrelevances of history and biography all the better to concentrate on the arts of interpretation and analysis, or 'close reading'. The amateur impressionism prevalent before the war came to be challenged and sometimes dislodged by a semi-professional approach to the rigours of reading. The New Criticism, in the widest sense that includes Eliot, Richards, Empson, and the Leavis group, was 'new' chiefly in its sense of responsibility to the objective status of the text, to the overriding authority of 'the words on the page'. In some respects this new obligation seemed to arise from the professional requirements of academic study, as in the case of Richards's model of practical criticism. But the rise of the New Criticism was by no means a simple case of professionalization, and certainly not a direct subordination of literary criticism's free spirit to academic regimentation. By the end of the 1930s, this movement stood ready to dominate the academic conventions of literary study, but its emergence and growth owed much to its insurgent opposition to the habits of the professors; in the simplest terms, its championing of 'criticism' against the routines of philological and historical 'scholarship'. New Criticism, then, was not in the first instance a movement of academics, but a campaign to redirect the attention of academics and their students towards the critical issues defined by small groups of poets writing for 'little magazines' outside or marginal to the universities. The academy asserted its growing weight in this period less as a base for the leading critics than as the decisive audience for a new critical writing. Many of the important critics of the period – Eliot, Woolf, Lubbock, Wilson, Murry, Lawrence – were working from well outside the academic sphere, and some less substantial figures like H. L. Mencken were indeed sarcastically anti-academic; while most of those who held some teaching position, like Richards, Empson, Leavis, Tate, Wilson Knight, Blackmur, Winters, and Brooks, were in temporary or insecure positions, usually remote from the centres of academic power, and typically publishing in non-academic little magazines. *Scrutiny*, for instance, was produced from a private home in Cambridge, and was not an authorized academic journal. In fact, until John Crowe Ransom launched the *Kenyon Review* in 1939, there was, strictly speaking, scarcely such a thing as an academic journal of literary criticism.

That this breakthrough into academic influence should have taken place in the United States rather than in Britain was one more sign of the robustness of the American critical scene. American criticism did in fact go through a comparatively thin period in the 1920s, but this was more than made up for by the energy and quality of critical discussion in the following decade, which threw up two remarkably productive schools around Ransom and Edmund Wilson. The strongest phase of English-based criticism came in the fifteen years following the Armistice: this period is rightly regarded as that of a renaissance in English criticism, including as it does the best of Eliot, Richards, Lawrence, Woolf, Murry, Empson, Wilson Knight, and Lubbock, and the launching of such journals as the *Criterion*, the *Adelphi*, the *Calendar of Modern Letters*, and *Scrutiny*; it witnessed too some sudden advances in the theory of the novel, and some spectacular innovations in Shakespeare criticism. The English did not, however, look after their critics, and much of this promise was dissipated by death, exile, and eccentric decline: a cruelly wasteful case was that of William Empson, the brightest young critic of his generation, who was expelled from his Cambridge college for possessing condoms, and thus spent most of the 1930s in China and Japan. Before the Great War, American critics like James and Pound emigrated to England; after it, English critics emigrated, albeit temporarily, to North America: Lawrence to New Mexico, Knight to Toronto, Richards to Cambridge, Massachusetts. The cultural centre of gravity was already shifting from London.

A further momentous shift in critical culture was beginning to show itself in this period: the arrival of women as critics and literary scholars in significant numbers, particularly in British academic life in the 1930s. The most prominent figure in this development, Virginia Woolf, was in some respects unrepresentative of its typical features, both in her exclusively private education and in her standing as a leading novelist and publisher. For the most part, women in criticism were products of the recent opening of university courses to female students. Maud Bodkin, for instance, had studied at the University College of Wales in the 1890s, while Queenie Leavis and Muriel Bradbook emerged later from Girton College, Cambridge. Women were particularly prominent in Renaissance literary studies: here the work of Bradbrook and Spurgeon, as of Una Ellis-Fermor and (in the USA) Lily B. Campbell, was of recognized importance. Meanwhile women made their mark in other fields of specialist research: Edith Birkhead's *The Tale of Terror* (1928), for instance, is still cited as an authority, while Mary Lascelles's *Jane Austen and Her Art* (1939) was a landmark in its field. The American poet Laura Riding could claim not only to have established an early link between the Tennessee 'Fugitives' and British criticism, but also to have been a co-founder of the entire modern tradition of 'close reading', through her collaboration with Robert Graves in *A Survey of Modernist Poetry* (1927). Virginia Woolf should not be regarded, then, as a lone figure in this world, but rather as a particularly versatile and subtle essayist, standing somewhat apart from her generation of specialist women scholars as an all-round woman of letters. Her special eminence in the history of criticism is as the founder of modern feminist criticism. It is possible, with a little special pleading, to deny her this title in favour of Rebecca West,[66] but not to ignore the importance of her essay *A Room of One's Own* (1929) as a landmark in modern literary culture and as a classic of feminist argument. By the now famous device of imagining an equally talented sister for Shakespeare, Woolf reviews the question of women's literary achievements in the context of the obstacles – economic, social, ideological – that stand in their way, and in so doing she exposes major injustices distorting the worlds of learning and literature themselves.

The appearance of a feminist criticism was one aspect of a wider mood of restless disobedience and irreverence that was abroad in the 1920s and beyond. This manifested itself in various ways in the critical writing of the period, especially in aberrations of tone: violently destructive in Hulme and Pound, pontifical in Eliot, hysterical in Lawrence, apocalyptic in Murry and Knight, bitterly suspicious in Tate and Leavis, 'clinical' in Richards. While the civilities of public discussion were kept up, and the principal interlocutors were referred to as Mr Eliot or Mrs Woolf, it was in general a time of lively ill-will, destructiveness, and contempt in literary criticism, by comparison with the clubbish tolerance prevailing in the pre-war years; and the chief victims of this mood were the leading writers of the pre-war period. *The Calendar of Modern Letters* specialized in publishing demolitions of the great Edwardians, and its editor, Edgell Rickword, collected a number of them in book form as *Scrutinies* (1928), including a brilliant assault on Kipling by Robert Graves, a drubbing for Galsworthy by D. H. Lawrence, and a cruelly funny caricature of the dog-loving Georgian poets by Roy Campbell; as was to be expected, the reputations of Bennett, Shaw, and Wells were kicked about elsewhere in the same book. F. R. and Q. D. Leavis were greatly impressed by this work, and attempted to keep up the arts of hostile criticism in *Scrutiny*.

The obverse of this iconoclastic spirit was the cultic fervour which sometimes surrounded the new 'mission' of criticism. Richards spoke of critical reading as a kind of salvation, and treated metaphor as a redemptive sacrament, and, in general, the New Critics followed him in this, likening the paradoxes of the poem's organic form to those of their own Christian faith. Richards himself, like his student Empson, was a rationalist who saw more sense in Confucianism than in Christianity, but his resort to the Coleridgean model of integration and psychic healing through poetry only reinforced the Christian emphasis so evident in this period. Christian critics did not have a monopoly over critical discussion (although it helped to count Eliot among one's fellows), but they did benefit from a conventional deference which prevented outsiders from disputing their sacred ground. The religious quarrels in criticism were *between* Christian critics of differing bents, notably the battle between the 'orthodox' Eliot and the ultra-Protestant Lawrence and Murry. Anti-semitism in the English departments of the universities had so far inhibited the emergence of a distinctively Jewish voice, although Lionel Trilling and others of the New York intellectual circle were already showing more interest in Freud and Marx than in Newman and Hopkins. The gentile atheists were in some disarray, but the outcast Empson awaited his vengeance.

No survey of the critical culture of the time would be complete without some notice of the disastrous fashion it inflicted upon critical book titles. The seminal book of the period – Eliot's *The Sacred Wood* – had borrowed its title from James Frazer's great anthropological survey, *The Golden Bough*, and in turn it passed on a habit of naming critical works with this maddeningly cryptic article–adjective–noun formula, as if they were Henry James novels; a convention that persisted into the 1960s. Any reader who has browsed through shelves of twentieth-century criticism will have suffered the exasperations of this misplaced symbolism, which has given us such works as *The Stricken Deer* (D. Cecil, 1929), *The Burning Oracle* (G. W. Knight, 1939), *The Starlit Dome* (Knight again, 1941), *The Well Wrought Urn* (C. Brooks, 1947), *The Hovering Fly* (A. Tate, 1948), *The Complex Fate* (M. Bewley, 1952), *The Inmost Leaf* (A. Kazin, 1955), *The Charted Mirror* (J. Holloway, 1960), *The Tangled Bank* (S. E. Hyman, 1962), *The Widening Gyre* (J. Frank, 1963), and, most ludicrous of all, *The Broken Cistern* (B. Dobrée, 1954), which is in fact not about faulty plumbing but a study of public poetry. In their devotion to the magic of the Symbol, many critics seem to have rejected the denotative function of the book title as some kind of utilitarian vulgarity.

The legacy of this period in criticism is normally defined in terms of the triumph of New Criticism, the emergence of the *Scrutiny* group, and sometimes that of the New York Intellectuals. These were indeed major developments, all of which dominated the post-war scene; but they are not the whole story. There is a remarkable range of new thinking and of exciting redirection in this period's work: the invention of American Literature, the theorizing of the novel, the revolution in Shakespearean interpretation, the discovery of Marxism and psychoanalysis, and the battle between classical and romantic principles all animate this heroic phase of modern criticism. In our own recent times, some scholars have gone back to particular figures in the inter-war period with a new sympathy: the critical writings of Virginia Woolf, in particular, have attracted a great deal more attention as founding documents of modern literary feminism; Kenneth Burke has been adopted by some others as the missing link between radical and formalist traditions; and William Empson is being re-read as something like the first post-structuralist critic. As our preoccupations evolve, we shall continue to rediscover unexpected echoes and challenges in the work of these decades, when criticism was quickened by its belief in itself as a 'central' and decisive cultural force.

Notes

1. T. S. Eliot, *The Sacred Wood: Essays on Poetry and Criticism* (1920; 7th edn, 1950), pp. 56, 53.
2. T. S. Eliot *Selected Essays* (1932; 3rd edn, 1951), p. 288 (from the 1921 essay 'The Metaphysical Poets').
3. Joseph Frank, 'Spatial Form in Modern Literature', *Sewanee Review* 53 (1945); reprinted in Frank, *The Idea of Spatial Form* (New Brunswick, NJ, 1991), pp. 5–66.
4. Eliot, *Sacred Wood*, p. 32.
5. J. M. Murry 'The Sacred Wood', *New Republic* April 13, 1921, pp. 194–5; reprinted in Malcolm Woodfield (ed.), *Defending Romanticism: Selected Criticism of John Middleton Murry* (Bristol, 1989), pp. 94–8.
6. Irving Babbitt, *Rousseau and Romanticism* (Boston, MA, 1919), p. 260.
7. Babbitt, *Rousseau*, p. 367.
8. T. E. Hulme, *Speculations* ed. Herbert Read (1924), p. 118.
9. Hulme, *Speculations*, p. 126.
10. Hulme, *Speculations*, pp. 113, 133.
11. Eliot, *Sacred Wood*, p. 58.
12. Eliot, *Sacred Wood*, p. 100.
13. Eliot, *Sacred Wood*, p. 54.
14. J. M. Murry, 'On Fear; and on Romanticism', *Adelphi* l:iv (September, 1923), p. 275; reprinted (as 'On Editing; and on Romanticism') in J. M. Murry, *To the Unknown God* (1924), p. 82.
15. Eliot, *Selected Essays*, p. 26.
16. Eliot, *Selected Essays*, p. 25.
17. Frank Kermode (ed.), *Selected Prose of T. S. Eliot* (1975), p. 177 (from 'Ulysses, Order, and Myth').
18. Herbert Grierson, *The Background of English Literature and Other Essays* (1925; Harmondsworth, 1962), pp. 221–49.
19. Woodfield (ed.), *Defending Romanticism*, pp. 181, 180.
20. Woodfield (ed.), *Defending Romanticism*, p. 145.
21. Woodfield (ed.), *Defending Romanticism*, p. 133.
22. J. M. Murry, *Discoveries* (1924, revised 1930), p. 17.
23. D. H. Lawrence, *Selected Literary Criticism* ed. Anthony Beal (1956), p. 213.
24. Wyndham Lewis, *Men Without Art* (1934), p. 194.
25. This distinction between solipsistic and objective-organic Romanticisms was formulated by Murry himself in his 1923 essay 'More About Romanticism': see J. M. Murry, *To the Unknown God* (1924), pp. 134–51.
26. Eliot, *Selected Essays*, p. 286 (from 'The Metaphysical Poets').
27. I. A. Richards, *Practical Criticism* (1929), p. 180.
28. Richards, *Practical Criticism*, p. 203.
29. I. A. Richards, *Principles of Literary Criticism* (1924; reset 1967), pp. 196–8.
30. F. R. Leavis (ed.), *Towards Standards of Criticism: Selections from The Calendar of Modern Letters, 1925–7* (1933), p. 9.
31. John Crowe Ransom, *The World's Body* (New York, 1938), p. 250.
32. Allen Tate, *Collected Essays* (Denver, CO, 1959), p. 113 (from the 1934 essay 'Three Types of Poetry').
33. R. P. Blackmur, *The Double Agent: Essays in Craft and Elucidation* (New York, 1935), p. 94 (from the 1931 essay 'Examples of Wallace Stevens').
34. Eliot, *Selected Essays*, p. 135.
35. Lytton Strachey, *Books and Characters, French and English* (1922), pp. 47–64. The essay can also be found in Strachey's posthumous collection *Literary Essays* (1948).

36. Caroline F. E. Spurgeon, *Shakespeare's Imagery and What It Tells Us* (Cambridge, 1935), p. 139.
37. Spurgeon, *Shakespeare's Imagery*, p. 206.
38. G. Wilson Knight, *The Wheel of Fire: Essays in Interpretation of Shakespeare's Sombre Tragedies* (1930; 4th edn, as *The Wheel of Fire: Interpretations of Shakespearian Tragedy*, 1949), p. 3.
39. Knight, *Wheel of Fire*, pp. 14, 15.
40. Eliot, *Selected Essays*, pp. 245 (from 'Dante', 1929), 203.
41. G. Wilson Knight, *The Imperial Theme: Further Interpretations of Shakespeare's Tragedies, Including the Roman Plays* (1931; 3rd edn, 1951), pp. 322, 326.
42. M. C. Bradbrook, *Elizabethan Stage Conditions: A Study of Their Place in the Interpretation of Shakespeare's Plays* (Cambridge, 1932), p. 127.
43. L. C. Knights, *How Many Children Had Lady Macbeth? An Essay in the Theory and Practice of Shakespeare Criticism* (Cambridge, 1933), pp. 10–11.
44. Knights, *How Many Children*, p. 31.
45. Knights, *How Many Children*, p. 34.
46. Knights, *How Many Children*, p. 53.
47. D. A. Traversi, *Approach to Shakespeare* (1938), p. 127.
48. H. B. Charlton, *Shakespearian Comedy* (1938), p. 11.
49. Virginia Woolf, *The Common Reader* (1925; 1962), p. 189 (from 'Modern Fiction').
50. E. M. Forster, *Aspects of the Novel* (1927; Harmondsworth, 1962), p. 16. For a fuller account of *Aspects* and its contexts, see S. P. Rosenbaum, '*Aspects of the Novel* and Literary History', in J. S. Herz and R. K. Martin (eds), *E. M. Forster: Centenary Revaluations* (Toronto, 1982), pp. 55–83.
51. Forster, *Aspects*, p. 34.
52. Forster, *Aspects*, pp. 125–6, 127.
53. Virginia Woolf *A Woman's Essays* ed. Rachel Bowlby (Harmondsworth, 1992), p. 123 (from 'The Art of Fiction', a review of Forster's *Aspects of the Novel* published in the *Nation and Athenaeum* of 12 November, 1927).
54. Edwin Muir, *The Structure of the Novel* (1928), p. 11.
55. Muir, *The Structure of the Novel*, p. 88.
56. D. H. Lawrence, *A Selection from Phoenix* ed. A. A. H. Inglis (Harmondsworth, 1971), p. 165.
57. Lawrence, *Selection from Phoenix*, p. 162.
58. D. H. Lawrence, *Studies in Classic American Literature* (1923; Harmondsworth, 1971), p. 8.
59. Lawrence, *Selection from Phoenix*, p. 161 (from 'The Novel'); *Selected Literary Criticism*, p. 113 (from the 1925 essay 'Morality and the Novel').
60. Lawrence, *Selected Literary Criticism*, p. 105.
61. Leavis (ed.), *Towards Standards of Criticism*, p. 16.
62. Edmund Wilson, *Axel's Castle: A Study in the Imaginative Literature of 1870–1930* (New York, 1931), pp. 116–17.
63. F. R. Leavis, *Revaluation: Tradition and Development in English Poetry* (1936; Harmondsworth, 1972), p. 15.
64. 'A Note on the Verse of John Milton', in *Essays and Studies* (English Association, 1936); reprinted as 'Milton I' in Kermode (ed.), *Selected Prose*, pp. 258–64.
65. Leavis, *Revaluation*, p. 53.
66. See Maggie Humm, *Feminist Criticism: Women as Contemporary Critics* (Brighton, 1986), pp. 155–76.

Chapter 4
Beyond the New Criticism: 1945–1968

The Critical Agenda

In the decades following the Second World War, literary criticism found itself enjoying mixed fortunes. Worldly success, in the form of established positions in an expanding university system and the flourishing of academic literary journals, came along with a gnawing self-doubt and loss of conviction about the purpose of the critical enterprise. The horrors of Auschwitz and Hiroshima were themselves deeply corrosive, undermining certain central assumptions about the humanizing aims of literary study. As George Steiner suggested in his *Language and Silence* (1967), the concentration camp commandants who were moved by Goethe's poetry but unmoved by their victims seemed to cast doubt on the Arnoldian belief in literature's morally enriching value: might literary self-cultivation actually be, in moral terms, merely useless or even distracting?[1] In a more mundane sense, too, the incorporation of criticism into a large educational bureaucracy threatened to replace the formerly independent critical vitality of the pre-war little magazine tradition with the routine functions of a corporate machine. John Crowe Ransom's half-humorous prophecy of 'Criticism, Inc.' seemed to many observers to be coming grimly true, with the authentic critical element vanishing beneath reams of automatized interpretations. Looking back on post-war developments in criticism in 1970, Malcolm Bradbury complained of the proliferation of 'minor articles in minor journals about minor symbols and their minor function in a minor work by a minor writer'.[2] Post-war criticism was frequently unsettled by this suspicion that it had somehow lost – or sold – its soul.

The important developments in the theory and practice of criticism between 1945 and 1968 are best understood in terms of emergent challenges to the dominance of New Criticism and its English counterpart, the Leavisite current. After the war, the New-Critical model of reading began to appear no longer as an exciting revolutionary cause but as an orthodoxy of the classrooms; and one that invited challenge from the more adventurous polemicists in the field of literary argument. The scene presented in the 1950s, then, is one of contradiction and transition: the New-Critical and Leavisite positions attain their most powerful influence, but this very success provokes a countervailing impatience and readiness to contest their principles. As the New Critics became more confident in outlawing supposed critical heresies – as in W. K. Wimsatt's *The Verbal Icon* (1954) – or in announcing tightly restricted canons – as in F. R. Leavis's *The Great Tradition* (1948) – so it became easier, and more tempting, to represent their positions as narrow prejudices and constraints upon genuine imaginative response. New Criticism attracted a variety of antagonists, whose different grounds of objection will be reviewed in more detail in the third section of this chapter. For the moment, it is worth noting briefly just the range of contrary opinion. Some critics objected first to the limits of the New Critical canon, in particular to the relegation of the Romantic and Victorian traditions carried out under Eliot's influence. The camp of Romantic revivalists included several of the more important new arrivals on the post-war critical scene: Northrop Frye, M. H. Abrams, Geoffrey Hartman, and Harold Bloom among them. Others, such as J. Hillis Miller and Robert Langbaum, set out to show that the Victorian poets were seriously 'modern' writers. From the distinct starting-point of critical method, a more substantive body of objectors found fault with the New Critics' intensive focus on verbal texture at the expense of larger structures and meanings in (or among) literary works. Here the 'Chicago Critics', in the first place R. S. Crane and Elder Olsen, found common cause with the Toronto-based theorist Northrop Frye and other 'myth' critics. Those critics who maintained an interest in the connections between literature and its social and cultural environments of course resisted the New Critical separation of text from context. This camp included Lionel Trilling and Philip Rahv, with their associates in the New York circle, along with socialist critics in Britain, such as Raymond Williams. Finally, we can identify a British strain of counter-modernism which, in the work of such critics as Donald Davie, Graham Hough, and Frank Kermode, begins to question the founding principles, chiefly of Eliot, Pound, and Hulme, upon which New Critical practice was based. For these critics, some of them echoing the themes of the 'Movement' poets around Larkin and Amis, the uppermost question was the degree to which the modernist cult of the symbol had destroyed the rational basis of communication between writers and readers.

The problem of modernism loomed large for post-war critics, and necessarily presented itself now largely as an historical question, no longer as an issue of immediate partisanship as it had been for, say, Leavis and Tate in the early 1930s. Defenders of modernist writing had not only to explicate difficult works, but to justify modernist methods in a changed cultural context, and against a background of some political suspicion. Ezra Pound, for instance, looked rather less impressive as a cultural hero after his wartime broadcasts from Rome on behalf of Mussolini's Fascism; and the authoritarian streak in Eliot, Yeats, and Lawrence stood out more disturbingly to those readers who had narrowly escaped the Holocaust, or merely survived a war against Fascist powers. The leading modernist writers nevertheless found in this period their enthusiastic apostles – Hugh Kenner in *The Poetry of Ezra Pound* (1951) and *The Invisible Poet: T. S. Eliot* (1959), F. R. Leavis in *D. H. Lawrence, Novelist* (1955) – and their more sober memorialists, notably Richard Ellmann in his monumental biography *James Joyce* (1959). The Edinburgh publishers Oliver & Boyd launched a successful series of short studies of modern writers, under the title 'Writers and Critics': it included Frank Kermode's *Wallace Stevens* (1960) and Northrop Frye's *T. S. Eliot* (1963). Modernism was the material for several important critical surveys: G. S. Fraser's *The Modern Writer and His World* (1953; revised 1964), A. Alvarez's *The Shaping Spirit* (1958) and Stephen Spender's *The Struggle of the Modern* (1963), for instance. It was anthologized in a substantial sourcebook of manifestos and key documents by Richard Ellmann and Charles Feidelson in their *The Modern Tradition* (1965), and was boiled down to a reading list by Cyril Connolly in *The Modern Movement: 100 Key Books* (1965). And despite the new sense of distance from the high modernism of the 1920s, reinforced by the deaths of Yeats, Woolf, and Joyce, there was as yet no agreement that the 'modern movement' was finished. The work of the still active W. H. Auden, for example, became the subject of several critical works in this period, among them Richard Hoggart's *Auden* (1951) and M. K. Spears's *The Poetry of W. H. Auden* (1963). Furthermore, new kinds of radical experiment in literature had arisen, the most important of these being the work of Samuel Beckett and of related 'absurdist' playwrights. Hugh Kenner's *Samuel Beckett: A Critical Study* (1962) was only one of several attempts to elucidate this latest modernist enigma. Martin Esslin's more comprehensive *The Theatre of the Absurd* (1961) rapidly became an indispensable guide to the new wave in European drama. Taking a wider view of the European cultural scene, Susan Sontag kept the readers of New York magazines up to date with Lukács, Camus, Barthes, Lévi-Strauss, Sartre, Sarraute, Pavese, Weiss, Ionesco, Bresson, Godard, and Resnais, collecting her articles in *Against Interpretation* (1966).

   While most of these accounts of modernist writing were either celebratory or apologetic, some others were anxiously sceptical about the value of modernist experiment, and about the legacy it had left for the current generation of readers and writers. From this quarter came some violent diatribes like Karl Shapiro's anti-intellectual essay *In Defense of Ignorance* (1960), but also a few soberly considered re-assessments, of which Graham Hough's *Image and Experience* (1960) gives us the clearest sense of criticism's predicaments at this time. Its long opening essay, 'Reflections on a Literary Revolution', voices several doubts about modernist poetry and its cultivation of the image at the expense of logically connected discourse; and it accuses Eliot and Pound of cutting poetry off from Dr Johnson's 'common reader'. The large reading public once enjoyed by Tennyson has, Hough claims, been frightened away, and contemporary poetry is read – and indeed written – only by students and professors in the universities. Meanwhile modern criticism, yoked to the modernist revolution, has largely abandoned its tasks of judging and valuing contemporary works, preferring instead the lesser functions of 'panegyric, extenuation, exegesis – everything in fact from log-rolling to what is called explication'.[3] Hough's view helps to bring into focus a significant shift in the balance of critical effort away from the defence of modern poetry, and towards the consideration either of more public genres (the novel, the drama) or of the writer's incorporation into a wider culture. Thus the modernist conception of the *avant-garde* poet battling against society and the common language to preserve his or her individual vision tends now to give way to an image of the storyteller using the common language to record or transcribe fictions *on behalf of* society. Whether in Northrop Frye's myth criticism or in the quasi-Marxist literary history of Raymond Williams, the writer appears in this humbler role, as a scribe to social ideology or to the collective mythic dream.[4]

The cultural configuration of the post-war years was in many ways favourable to such a recuperation of the writer into the collective structures of language and culture. The notion of the 'committed' writer, emerging from French existentialism; the impact of neo-realist cinema from Italy; and the sudden celebrity of George Orwell – all seemed to encourage a shift of attention from the anti-social poet to the socially responsible novelist. In any case, a pronounced lurch towards prose fiction is evident in post-war criticism. The career of F. R. Leavis, who published books on poetry before the war, and books on the novel after the war, is not exactly typical, but it it still symptomatic. Other leading critics in the post-war years show the same kind of bias: Lionel Trilling, who had written on Arnold before the war, published in 1950 his most influential collection of essays, *Liberal Imagination*, which contained several important studies in the novel, but only one essay on poetry. As we shall see, this period produced a remarkable body of writings on the novel, including not just Leavis's *The Great Tradition*, but also Wayne C. Booth's *The Rhetoric of Fiction* (1961), Ian Watt's *The Rise of the Novel* (1957), Dorothy Van Ghent's *The English Novel: Form and Function* (1953), and David Lodge's *Language of Fiction* (1966). These were general studies, but there was a further wealth of critical work on individual novelists, notably J. Hillis Miller's *Charles Dickens* (1958), and W. J. Harvey's *The Art of George Eliot* (1961). The Victorian novelists, in fact, benefited particularly from this flourishing of novel-criticism, and made up in the 1960s what their reputations had lost in the 1920s. A remarkable instance is the critical fate of George Eliot, who had suffered decades of neglect and lukewarm condescension – from David Cecil and others – until the immediate post-war years, when Leavis's *The Great Tradition* and Joan Bennett's *George Eliot* (1948) both made serious claims for her work. Within a few years, a new critical industry had revived around her fiction, and *Middlemarch* was being spoken of as the summit of achievement in English fiction, as though this had always been agreed upon.

The new attention to the novel, important enough in itself, was also a symptom of a general shift from the intensive to the extensive, or from the smaller to the larger scale in literary studies: typically from the scrutiny of local ambiguities in short lyrics to the comparison of thematic structures among groups of novels or plays. As central critical terms, irony, ambiguity, and paradox gave way to plot, structure, myth, and fiction, as the new terminologies of Frye, Crane, Kermode, and Williams took hold. At a more abstract level still, the turn to fiction implied, and indeed culminated in, a discarding of 'spatial' models of literature and a return to temporality: Frank Kermode's *The Sense of an Ending* (1967) exemplifies and extends the tendencies in this period to reinstate *narrative* as the master term of cultural analysis. Northrop Frye's spatialized scheme of narrative categories in *Anatomy of Criticism* was one step towards a renewed appreciation of narrative; but in its emphasis on the universality of 'myth' and metaphor, it was not good enough for Kermode, who eschewed the circular patterns of 'myth' for the linear, time-bound explorations of 'fiction'. Kermode and Frye agreed, however, on two significant points: that historical and scientific narratives were myths or 'fictions', and that the Bible was the model and source-book for all later Western narratives.

The question of literature and religion was for various reasons a prominent and controversial one in this period, as we shall see later. It was to some extent artificially emphasized by the ideological conditions of the Cold War, in which a number of intellectuals who had formerly been optimistic Communists lurched contritely into pessimistic Christianity of a kind that concentrated all its attention on Original Sin rather than on redemption. In the climate which generated William Golding's novel *Lord of the Flies* (1954), 'Evil' was regarded as the great problem of the day, and much literary discussion was accordingly devoted to the wisdom of Dostoevsky and to the inescapably 'tragic condition' of Man. As a literary-critical phenomenon, though, this trend is less interesting than the resistance to it, which is vehement in the essays of Philip Rahv and in Raymond Williams's *Modern Tragedy* (1966), and above all in William Empson's *Milton's God* (1961). Similarly, the larger tides of McCarthyism and of Cold-War paranoia left criticism relatively untouched. It is possible to attribute the strength of New Criticism in the early 1950s, and the ahistorical abstractions of Frye's scheme, to a Cold-War taboo on the discussion of literature's social and historical dimensions, but any such taboo seems to have been honoured more in the breach than in the observance: among leftist critics like Philip Rahv and Raymond Williams, but also among mainstream liberal critics, the turn to prose fiction was precisely a way of keeping that discussion alive.

High-Tide of New Criticism

For the New Critics in the United States, and for the Leavis group in England, the immediate post-war period was one of triumphant consolidation. A day of reckoning was to come, which can be dated somewhere in or around the year 1957; but even after the arrival of substantial opponents, the critical positions of these two groups enjoyed a significant afterlife in the expanding education system of the 1960s. After the War, American New Criticism entered a final flourishing phase in which the founding fathers – Ransom and Tate, Winters and Blackmur – gave way to the newer talents of Cleanth Brooks and W. K. Wimsatt, who were colleagues at Yale from 1947. The most illustrious works of this phase were Brooks's *The Well Wrought Urn* (1947), Wimsatt's *The Verbal Icon* (1954), and their joint production, *Literary Criticism: A Short History* (1957). Along with these should be placed another Yale production, René Wellek's and Austin Warren's *Theory of Literature* (1949). The English group around F. R. and Q. D. Leavis mourned the financial collapse of its journal *Scrutiny* in 1953, but soon found that back numbers were in such demand that Cambridge University Press reprinted the entire set of twenty volumes in 1962. The principal works of the group in this phase were those of F. R. Leavis – *The Great Tradition* (1948) and *D. H. Lawrence, Novelist* (1955), with the essay-collection *The Common Pursuit* – and of L. C. Knights – *Some Shakespearean Themes* (1959) and the essays collected in *Explorations* (1946) and *Further Explorations* (1965). Just as the American New Critics had a profound effect on university teaching through the textbooks of Brooks and his collaborators, so in England the 'Leavisites' spread their influence through a seven-volume work of literary history and reference, the *Pelican Guide to English Literature* (ed. Boris Ford, 1954–61), which was for twenty years constantly consulted by students and teachers in Britain.

As in its early phase, New Criticism in America established its authority through a combination of argument in literary theory with exemplary explications in the arena of practical criticism. The most important theoretical arguments in the post-war years were advanced from Yale by W. K. Wimsatt and René Wellek, while the models of close reading were offered, as in the past, by Cleanth Brooks. Wellek's collaboration with his former colleague Austin Warren of the University of Iowa in their

Theory of Literature is especially notable as an attempt to found modern literary criticism and literary history upon the basis of a scientific literary theory. 'Literary theory', they write, echoing a familiar New-Critical insistence '. . . is the great need of literary scholarship today.'[5] Their own theory draws variously upon Kant's aesthetics, Roman Ingarden's model of the 'intersubjective' status of the art-work, and the scientific formalism of the Prague Linguistic Circle, of which Wellek had been a member before the War. In this least provincial of New-Critical works, European thought is to the fore, and the authors have their eyes on the development of Comparative Literature (Wellek's institutional domain) rather than on the Anglophone cultural traditions. Wellek, who wrote most of the book, was, long before the later controversies over structuralism, an early champion of theory against the romantic Leavisite cult of concrete particulars, the first theorist writing in English to describe the work of art as 'a whole system of signs, or structure of signs',[6] and among the first to discuss the Russian Formalists' distinction between plot and story in narrative. Following a broadly formalist line of argument, these two authors divide the various kinds of literary study into 'intrinsic' and 'extrinsic' approaches, and go on to claim that the 'extrinsic' traditions of biographical, psychological, philosophical, or sociological interpretation involve fatal confusions of cause with effect, and thus must be subordinated to 'intrinsic' analyses which respect the special status of the art-work. *Theory of Literature* is a careful and systematic survey of some of the major problems in literary study, executed in a rather ponderous manner. It is unmistakably a textbook, and one that was widely adopted as the basis for comparative literary studies in various parts of the world. In the third edition (1962), Wellek noted with satisfaction that the book had been translated into Spanish, Italian, Japanese, Korean, German, Portuguese, Hebrew, and Gujarati.

More elegant and in other ways more impressive as a defence of New-Critical principle is Wimsatt's volume of essays, *The Verbal Icon*, which contains several subtle considerations of the nature of metaphor, along with two celebrated essays written in collaboration with Monroe C. Beardsley defining the twin 'fallacies' of affectivism and intentionalism, against which it is necessary to defend 'objective criticism'. Wimsatt was, like Wellek, a serious historian of literary theory, aware both of recurrent problems in aesthetic and critical debate and of recent difficulties in New-Critical thinking itself, especially in the work of I. A. Richards. Wimsatt's aim is, in part, to overcome the split between technique and value which he detects in Richards's theory of 'emotive language', and to correct what he sees as Richards's bias towards psychology. His effort to integrate valuation with technical analysis leads him, in the essay on 'The Concrete Universal', to formulate as a law that identification of poetic unity with maturity which Leavis had already asserted as an intuition:

. . . the rhetorical structure of the concrete universal, the
complexity and unity of the poem, is also its maturity or
sophistication or richness or depth, and hence its value.
Complexity of form is sophistication of content. The unity and
maturity of good poems are two sides of the same thing.[7]

If this is the case, then, as Wimsatt goes on to argue in another essay,
the explication of a poem's implicit order and coherence *is* the full
criticism of the poem, and does not require a separate value-judgement
appended to the technical description. Much of Wimsatt's thinking
revolves around such problems of integration and fusion: thus metaphor
is, as Coleridge suggested, a fusion of the abstract and the concrete, and
poetry is a fusion of material and idea, sound and sense. However,
Wimsatt also insists that unity must imply heterogeneity and conflict, and
that metaphor relies upon difference as well as likeness. With the other
New Critics, Wimsatt is pulled in two directions: towards the monistic
union of word and thing, as in the 'icon' of his title (the sign that shares
in the properties of its referents, as in onomatopoeia), and towards the
dualistic 'tension' between contending intellectual and sensory dimensions
in poetry. In principle, he holds to the latter position, insisting on the
conceptual element in metaphor, and reminding us that verbal art is an
intellectual art; but we can often see him tempted away from conceptual
meaning towards pure 'being' in poetry. His hesitations and compromises
on this crucial point are the most intelligently formulated that one can
find among the New Critics.

The pair of essays composed with Beardsley on the 'fallacies' of critical
method have acquired a reputation for arrant dogmatism and for fetishizing the literary text as an 'object'. There is some basis for such charges,
but it is often forgotten by those who repeat them that Wimsatt was
perfectly well aware that the text as 'object' is simply a necessary abstraction invoked for the purposes of analysis. Likewise overlooked is his
concession that not all uses of biographical evidence in criticism are
distracting or irrelevant; usually he and Beardsley are hastily accused of
'outlawing' any reference to the author. The essays themselves – 'The
Intentional Fallacy' (1946) and 'The Affective Fallacy' (1949) – are admirably lucid in their most important propositions, distilling an entire tradition of critical argument since Eliot (or since Wilde) into a few essential
formulae. They are also, in substance, the founding documents of post-
war American literary theory: besides declaring an end to the older
traditions of biographical and impressionistic criticism, their clarification
of the distinction between private motive and public language anticipates
some of the principles of structuralism and post-structuralism – notably
the idea that language is not in the possession or control of any of its
users. For Wimsatt and Beardsley in 'The Intentional Fallacy', the poem
(or other text) 'belongs' not to the author but to the public, and by

entering the realm of language has released itself from the author's power to control its meanings. The author's prior intention is either unavailable to us – except as transformed into the work itself – or, if separately available, superseded by the work. Even in a lyric poem, we should impute the thoughts and attitudes of the work in the first place to the dramatic 'speaker' rather than to the author, because a poem is (as the other New Critics had insisted earlier) a dramatic verbal performance, not a pragmatic communication of information. As they extended their case in 'The Affective Fallacy', Wimsatt and Beardsley argue that the intentional fallacy, which confuses a poem with its causes, resulting in biographical irrelevance, has its counterpart in the fallacious confusion between the poem and its psychological effects ('affects') upon readers, resulting in impressionism; in either case, the poem itself is occluded and critical standards are surrendered to relativism. The Affective Fallacy had claimed as one of its many victims the pioneer of New Criticism itself, I. A. Richards, who was diverted from poems to the putative adjustments of impulse and attitudes in the minds of readers. By marking off so sharply the symmetrical paths of diversion from criticism's proper aim, Wimsatt and Beardsley hoped to stabilize the true 'object' of critical attention. The terms in which they attempt this betray a strong professional partiality: the critic, they argue, should not be merely a reporter of his own responses to works, but an explicator of meanings, a teacher.

The most persuasive of practical explicators in this school remained Cleanth Brooks, whose book *The Well Wrought Urn* contains the best-known examples of 'close reading' for irony and paradox. Brooks, too, has his theoretical side, and warns against certain errors in critical method. In his case, in the chapter-title 'The Heresy of Paraphrase', the warning is against confusing the poem with a summary of its 'statement'. Again, it is worth noting here that Brooks does not forbid paraphrases of poems, but simply warns against mistaking them for the fuller meanings of the poems themselves. For Brooks, a poem is a structure of dramatized attitudes, not a sequence of logical propositions; it is more like a ballet or a play than a statement. Like Wimsatt, he quotes from Archibald Macleish the slogan 'A poem should not mean but be'. The poem then communicates not a separable 'content' but the entirety of its ordered values and meanings, so that if we insist on speaking of a poem as a communication we can only conclude tautologically that 'the poem says what the poem says';[8] but it is better to regard the poet less as a communicator than as a 'maker', who fashions an ordered model of experience. Thus, when we find what looks like a philosophical assertion in a poem – as with the announcement in Keats's 'Ode on a Grecian Urn' that 'Beauty is truth, truth beauty', we must read it within its dramatic context rather than isolate it as the poem's supposed meaning. The value of Brooks's close readings of chosen poetic texts from Donne and Shakespeare to Tennyson and Yeats in *The Well Wrought Urn* lies chiefly in their exhibition of complexity in poems or poets usually considered 'simple'. It is one thing to bring out the paradoxes in a Donne poem, as he does in the first chapter on 'The Canonization', but quite another to demonstrate that Gray's Elegy, or Wordsworth's Immortality Ode, or Tennyson's 'Tears, Idle Tears' are all just as 'difficult', just as ironic or paradoxical, as Donne or Eliot. The 'maturity' that Brooks attributed to Donne on the basis of his ability to accommodate opposing attitudes is, in this extended account, the property of all genuine poets, not just those favoured in Eliot's or Leavis's canon. From one side, this seems to testify to Brooks's more catholic generosity; but from the other it can appear to involve the uniform attribution of exactly the same predictable qualities (irony, ambiguity, paradox – Brooks himself apologizes for the iteration of these now well-worn terms) to every significant poet, regardless of historical differences.

Out on the fringes of the New-Critical movement, the mavericks William Empson and Kenneth Burke looked even more isolated as they insisted, against Wimsatt's injunctions, on referring to authors' intentions and moods, fallacy or no fallacy. Always more ambitious in scope than the formalists of Yale, Burke continued to elaborate his theories of language, social ritual and 'dramatism' in *A Grammar of Motives* (1945), *A Rhetoric of Motives* (1950), and *Language as Symbolic Action* (1966), extending his interpretations of catharsis in literary works into general propositions about signification, rhetoric, and ideology. William Empson's *The Structure of Complex Words* (1951) is a further study in 'verbal analysis', but this time removed from literary criticism into the theory of lexicography: an elaborated response to the *Oxford English Dictionary*, this book attempts a more precise method of classification for the multiple senses of a word, distinguishing various kinds of implication, connotation, and contextually-influenced meaning. Its studies of individual words – *all, fool, dog, honest*, and *sense* – are sometimes fascinating, although many readers have found Empson's attempt to summarize his argument in algebraic equations too much for them. Another critic now finding himself increasingly remote from the centres of New-Critical orthodoxy was R. P. Blackmur. The strongest parts of his collections *Language as Gesture* (1952) and *The Lion and the Honeycomb* (1955) are the essays reprinted from his pre-war books; many of the post-war essays are exasperatingly obscure in their resort to a private vocabulary, as when Blackmur writes that 'The critic's job is to put us into maximum relation to the burden of our momentum, which means he has to run the risk of a greater degree of consciousness than his mind is fit for.'[9] Where Blackmur does make sense, he is often expressing disaffection with the development of New Criticism into a narrow orthodoxy: in the title essay of *The Lion and the Honeycomb* he fears that this modern school will soon become sterile unless it renews its Coleridgean psychology with fresh perspectives from Aristotelian poetics. In another essay, 'A Burden for Critics', he complains that New Criticism has failed to pass from technical analysis to fully critical comparison and judgement, and that its confidence with the shorter poems of Eliot and Yeats is balanced by an incapacity to deal with the major works of Dante, Chaucer, Racine, or Goethe. While Blackmur implied that the game was up for New Criticism, one of the fathers of the school, Allen Tate, underlined this sense of exhaustion by publishing a lecture entitled 'Is Literary Criticism Possible?' (1951) – with an emphatically negative answer to his own question. Like Blackmur, Tate declared that stylistic analysis on its own was insufficient, while the larger evaluative sense was both indefinable and (more damagingly for the efforts of Brooks and Wimsatt) unteachable: to imagine that the insights of critical evaluation could be taught to college students was, for the increasingly weary Tate, merely another of the illusions of modern democracy.

The post-war phase of the *Scrutiny* group in Britain is marked, not by any narrowness of technical analysis, but by a change of emphasis in F. R. Leavis's work that can be described simply enough as a lurch towards Romanticism, especially the Romanticism of Murry and Lawrence. Even in the 1930s, Leavis had mixed his deference to T. S. Eliot and his idea of 'tradition' with some dismay at Eliot's dismissal of D. H. Lawrence as a spiritually sick heretic. Torn between two masters, Leavis found himself drawn increasingly to Lawrence's militant English Protestantism, and repelled from Eliot's cosmopolitan Anglo-Catholic stance. In *The Common Pursuit* (1952) he reprints his early defences of Lawrence against Eliot, including an essay that refers to Lawrence not only, implausibly enough, as 'the finest literary critic of our time', but as 'the representative of health and sanity'.[10] Eliot, meanwhile, is referred to as a spent critical force, and the Protestant-Romantic tradition which he had scorned in *The Sacred Wood* finds its way back to favour in Leavis's praise for Bunyan and Blake. In an essay on Swift, for instance, Leavis concedes that the author of *Gulliver's Travels* is a great writer, but notes that he is also coldly negative and egotistical, not really intelligent or self-aware; in a classic instance of his method of comparative 'placing', Leavis delivers his verdict: 'We shall not find Swift remarkable for intelligence if we think of Blake.'[11] He had already shown in *The Great Tradition* his preference for the moral intensity of George Eliot over the ironies of Fielding, Sterne, or Joyce; in his *D. H. Lawrence, Novelist* (1955), he goes on to contrast the reverently life-affirming genius of Lawrence with the life-denying cynicism of Joyce and Flaubert. This book does have, incidentally, some quite valuable commentary on incidents in *The Rainbow* and *Women in Love*, but it is notable chiefly as evidence of the collapse of Leavis's critical sense, sacrificed in abject surrender to Lawrence, whose work is 'an immense body of living creation in which a supreme vital intelligence is the creative spirit – a spirit informed by an almost infallible sense for health and sanity.' By the end of this work, indeed, an 'almost' infallible sense in

Lawrence has become absolutely infallible: 'an infallible centrality of judgement' and 'an unfailingly sure sense of the difference between that which makes for life and that which makes against it'.[12] Blinded by animosity towards the Bloomsbury group, the BBC, and the sinister London literary 'establishment', Leavis could not see that he was turning Lawrence into a Protestant Pope, and himself into a repetitively dogmatic apologist. Also lost in this process was Leavis's former sense of verbal complexity: now all that mattered was whether you were 'for' life or 'against' it. By the time Leavis came to review Eliot's *On Poetry and Poets* (1957), it was clear that Eliot himself was anti-life. Had he not disastrously and blasphemously preferred James Joyce to Lawrence? As in the Bolshevik party under Stalin, the leaders of the revolution were the most vulnerable to excommunication. Thus the most aggressive of Eliot's English disciples came to arraign his old master on charges of Flaubertianism, even repudiating with contempt the most important of his scriptures, the essay on 'Tradition and the Individual Talent': 'the falsity and gratuitousness of its doctrine of impersonality are surely plain enough', Leavis writes, with all the confidence of infallibility.[13]

Like other evangelical movements, 'Leavisism' enjoyed an influx of converts, not only in England but in India and as far afield as Australia, where earnest young university teachers would explain why Lawrence's story *The Captain's Doll* represented the most consummate judgement on the relations between men and women, and which of the English poets had achieved poised maturity. As the universities expanded, growing numbers of students of 'English' could refer either to the new paperback editions of Leavis's works or to the collaborative literary history of his associates and students, the *Pelican Guide to English Literature*, the strength of which lay in the consistency of its position on the course of the cultural 'tradition'. Its weakness, spectacularly illustrated at the start of the first volume by John Speirs's survey of medieval verse, was its nostalgic version of social history. Thus Speirs assures us that the community behind Chaucer's poetry is a harmonious whole (this despite the Peasants' Revolt, forgotten in this account), and that most medieval literature springs from communal dancing around maypoles and other survivals of archaic tree-worship, or in some cases goat-worship. In the cultural disorder of the 1960s, someone, at least, was standing up for Merrie England, even if it meant invoking what Eliot might have called strange gods.

Alternatives to New Criticism

Objections to the perceived narrowness of New Criticism were voiced from several quarters in the post-war years, accumulating by the end of the 1950s to constitute a collective determination to pass beyond its limits. Some of the complaints against the now dominant academic tendency were accompanied by alternative programmes of critical work, ranging from corrections of emphasis to entire new systems of literary theory. For the sake of convenience, it will be worth reviewing these positions in turn, starting with the New York critics around Lionel Trilling, moving on to the Chicago critics led by R. S. Crane and to the work of Northrop Frye in Toronto (with other Romanticists and 'myth' critics), before examining a more mixed array of critics in Britain.

For Trilling, as for Philip Rahv and other New York critics in the *Partisan Review* circle, the most important principle was that literature was, in Matthew Arnold's phrase, a criticism of life, and thus could not without severe distortion be isolated from its philosophical, social, historical, and psychological contexts. Literature carried a moral value, and could not be disentangled from ideas and ideologies, however hard Eliot and his followers might try to insulate it. From this position, the close textual analyses of the New Critics appeared to involve an offensive trivializing and a misguided purification of literature. Against some of the cruder varieties of Leftist criticism in the 1930s, these critics had protested that literary works should not be treated as simple sociological or biographical documents; now they had to protest against the opposite 'formalist' error of treating novels and poems as if they had no content at all. Trilling's most important book, *The Liberal Imagination* (1950), ends with an essay, 'The Meaning of a Literary Idea', which confronts directly the principle announced by Wellek and Warren, that literature can make use of ideas only when they cease to be ideas, becoming instead symbols or myths. While agreeing that art should not be confused with philosophy, Trilling accuses Wellek, Warren, and Eliot of 'dealing with art as if it were a unitary thing, . . . making reference only to its "purely" aesthetic element, requiring that every work of art serve our contemplation by being wholly self-contained and without relation to action.' In the same essay, Trilling counters the New-Critical emphasis on the supra-rational properties of symbolism and metaphor by claiming that 'Poetry is closer to rhetoric than we today are willing to admit; syntax plays a greater part in it than our current theory grants, and syntax connects poetry with rational thought . . .'[14] Confronting the New Critics again in the essay 'The Sense of the Past', Trilling complains that 'they make the elucidation of poetic ambiguity or irony a kind of intellectual calisthenic ritual', and that 'they forget that the literary work is ineluctably a historical fact, and, what is more important, that its historicity is a fact in our aesthetic experience.'[15] Attempting to abolish historical distance and thus to make the poem more immediate, the New Critics had torn away that inescapable 'pastness' that is a part of the poem's fuller present meaning.

Trilling's own critical interests lay largely, as he put it, 'at the dark and bloody crossroads where literature and politics meet.'[16] This meant that he addressed writers first as critics of their own societies, but also that he was concerned to correct the imaginative deficiencies of the 'progressive' or liberal sub-culture to which he belonged, unsettling its sentimental conception of 'reality' and its righteous self-congratulations. Discussing Henry James's novels *The Princess Casamassima* and *The Bostonians*, for instance, he claims that they show the selfless instincts of humanitarianism to be potentially just as dangerous as more selfish motives. For Trilling, the encounter with literature was to be an exercise in extending our 'moral imagination', stretching it beyond our currently too simple ideas of reality. Reacting against the 'optimism' of liberal opinion in the 1930s, Trilling went some way with the tide of post-war ideology in valuing the 'tragic vision', adopting as his favoured tragic thinker Sigmund Freud. His encounters with Freud are notable for establishing responsible uses of psychoanalysis in modern Anglophone criticism, raising the discussion well above the levels of crude pathology that had prevailed in this field before. In his essay 'Art and Neurosis', and in the more substantial 'Freud and Literature', Trilling rejects the view of the artist as a 'wounded' neurotic, as employed by Edmund Wilson. Although Freud himself had indulged this notion, it is insufficiently Freudian, Trilling argues, both because we are *all* neurotics (and so the artist is not special in this respect), and because neurosis is an active process rather than a passively-received scar. Despite Freud's weakness on this point, Trilling salutes him as the most important contributor to our ideas of art since Aristotle, especially for demonstrating that poetry is not an aberration but basic to the constitution of the mind. Looking at this the other way round, psychoanalysis can be seen as a kind of poetics: 'a science of tropes, of metaphor and its variants, synecdoche and metonymy.'[17] In Trilling's sophisticated understanding of the implications of Freud for literary interpretation, the point is no longer to reduce the work to a simple pathological symptom (there can be no 'single meaning' to a work of art, he insists), but to bring out its multiple, ambiguous, and contradictory significances.

Philip Rahv, who also wrote a valuable essay on Freud and literature, is more impressive as a sceptical monitor of critical fashion ('*Zeitgeist* palaver', as he called it) than as a critic in his own right. His major collection *Literature and the Sixth Sense* (1969) includes devastating essays on 'proletarian' literature in the 1930s, and on Leavis's over-valuation of Lawrence, but the chief target of his polemics is the critical tradition of Eliot and his followers. His essay 'Fiction and the Criticism of Fiction' objects to the New Critics' indiscriminate importation into the study of prose fiction of procedures designed for the close analysis of poetry, and to their fetishizing of 'technique' and symbolic patterns. In general, the New Critics were attempting, in the interests of a reactionary idealism, to purge art of its worldly particulars, converting it into a spiritual scheme. In another essay, 'The Myth and the Powerhouse' (1953), Rahv derides the contemporary critical cult of 'myth' as a regressive romantic attempt to escape from history and time into a supposedly timeless order; and this was before the new wave of 'myth criticism' had fully asserted itself. By 1958, Rahv was able to announce at last that New Criticism had exhausted itself into terminal dullness. Rahv's great merit was to recognize that criticism is 'a mixed discourse'[18] requiring good judgement in the mixing of interests for its various occasions; any code of proscription that would debar alleged 'extra-literary' interests could only reduce it to a depleted routine.

A more theoretically-based set of objections to New Criticism emerged from literary scholars at the University of Chicago, in their journal *Modern Philology*, in a collaborative work, *Critics and Criticism, Ancient and Modern* (edited by R. S. Crane, 1952), and in R. S. Crane's book *The Languages of Criticism and the Structure of Poetry* (1953). The Chicago critics – Crane, Elder Olson, W. R. Keast, Richard McKeon and others – conducted collaborative research into the history of criticism, which led them to emphasize the virtues of Aristotle's inductive method and his discrimination of poetic genres. The importance of generic distinctions between *kinds* of literary work lay at the root of their quarrel with Ransom, Brooks, and other New Critics. Citing L. C. Knights's assertion that *Macbeth* is a poem like *The Waste Land*, Crane accused the New Critics in general of obliterating the proper distinctions between different literary forms and functions in their zeal to distinguish poetic language (as if that were a single entity) from practical or scientific languages. Thus the New Critics 'continue to read all poems as if their authors had constructed them on identical principles, confusing, for instance, mimetic forms with didactic, and treating lyrics and novels, tragedies and essays, by means of the same distinctions . . .'[19] As Crane argues against Cleanth Brooks, poets do not write 'poetry' but specific kinds of poems, which present them with identifiable formal problems; and if you define poetry by its medium alone – that is, by its non-referential language – you will reduce it to irony or paradox (which are not, in any case, unique to poetry), while neglecting the specific functions of poems. This was in itself a formidable illumination of the dangers implicit in New-Critical theory, and it implied too an alternative method, starting not from linguistic qualities like paradox but from the formal principles and intended effects of the work in question. The Chicago critics spent far more time on literary theory than they did on the direct analyses of literary works, but one essay in *Critics and Criticism* – R. S. Crane's 'The Concept of Plot and the Plot of *Tom Jones*' – may stand as a model of the method they were recommending. Crane takes as his central concept here the Aristotelian idea of 'plot', in the higher sense, as a synthesis of parts working towards a single effect, and insists that plots need to be differentiated: there are plots of action, of character, and of thought, and *Tom Jones* is a plot of action – but again, of a specific kind, namely a comic plot. Crane outlines not just the underlying structural unity of the novel, but the particular problems which its author faced in maintaining the integrity of its comic plot against the intrusion of unsuitable responses from readers, especially in the handling of our sympathies with the various characters. Here, the success of the novel is to be judged by reference to the task Fielding set himself. But, as Crane argued elsewhere, this method does not lead us into the 'intentional fallacy' of relying on inaccessible private motives, since the author's intention can be assumed to be the overcoming of publicly observable formal problems in the chosen literary genre.

Crane admitted that his method in the essay on *Tom Jones* could not be the last word on that novel; it was a formal criticism only, and fell short of the kind of 'qualitative' criticism practised by Leavis. Thus it could show how well Fielding had handled the difficulties of holding together a complex comic plot, but it could not place Fielding's achievement in terms of 'seriousness', 'greatness', or any of Leavis's other imposing watchwords. Crane and the other Chicago critics held to the doctrine of pluralism in literary-critical debate: no critical school could rightly claim a monopoly of the truth about literature, because there were several valuable approaches, each one making sense in its own terms. This did not mean, however, that some methods were not preferable to others: the Chicago critics clearly preferred the ancient school of Aristotle to the modern school of Coleridge, and for clearly explicable reasons. Aristotle's inductive method, which derives its categories from observing actual literary works, is to be preferred, they say, to the modern habit of deciding in advance what are the essential properties of all poetry and then (inevitably) finding them illustrated in the works examined. To the New Critics, though, it appeared that Crane and his associates were hiding, behind their protestations of pluralism, a dogmatic neoclassical system of generic categories; W. K. Wimsatt replied to the Chicago group in these terms in his review of *Critics and Criticism*, later reprinted in *The Verbal Icon*. After the early 1950s, when Crane and some of his collaborators went into retirement, the Chicago critics did not press home their case against the errors of modern criticism. Their direct legacy includes the work of their younger associate, Wayne C. Booth, while their indirect influence was felt more widely in a renewed sense of the importance of genre.

As the authority of Eliot and his disciples began to come under assault, the repressed tradition of Romanticism inevitably reasserted itself, and most strongly in North America. At Cornell University, M. H. Abrams conducted a reasoned historical account, and defence, of Romantic literary theory in *The Mirror and the Lamp* (1953). Two younger critics at Yale, Geoffrey Hartman and Harold Bloom, came forward in the 1950s with new accounts of Wordsworth and Shelley, pitched directly against the orthodox devaluation of Romantic poetry. For Bloom in *Shelley's Mythmaking* (1959) and *The Visionary Company* (1961), as for Hartman in *The Unmediated Vision* (1954) and in *Wordsworth's Poetry* (1964), the Romantics were not sentimental nature-worshippers as Babbitt had believed, but heroes of visionary consciousness, attempting to humanize the world of Nature or to bring it into a reciprocal relation with the mythic imagination. These young critical heretics had been pre-empted as defenders of Romantic poetry, however, by a Canadian critic writing on William Blake. This was Northrop Frye of the University of Toronto, whose book *Fearful Symmetry: A Study of William Blake* (1947) launched the post-war 'Romantic revival' in criticism, and along with it Frye's own extraordinary career of critical system-building.

Frye's surprising argument in *Fearful Symmetry* is that Blake is not an eccentric but a normal kind of poet; it is we, as modern readers, who are the eccentrics in that we have lost the art of reading allegorically as Spenser's or Dante's readers were skilled in doing and as Blake himself did. Although he does not mention him by name, Frye is constructing here a case against Eliot, at least the Eliot who regretted Blake's Protestant thinness of cultural inheritance, his cranky production of home-made mythologies. In Frye's view, Blake was not indulging merely private visions and symbolic significances but drawing upon a universally shared iconography of the human imagination, which can be reconstructed in terms of explicable meanings. Frye accordingly offers extended readings of Blake's prophetic books, although his real focus is upon the larger 'system' which is made up from the entire work of the poet. Philosophical, mythological, and cosmological systems are, for Frye, kinds of artwork, which can be appreciated in terms of their inner coherence, and likewise the larger whole which is an artist's entire *oeuvre* is itself to be regarded as a single work of art made from contributory parts like the Bible or a cathedral. This implies, more generally, that we should not confine our responses to single works, in New-Critical fashion, but instead look at the writer's entire 'world' or mythopoetic power as embodied in the *oeuvre*. In this first instalment of his own system, Frye already promises that 'the interpretation of Blake is only the beginning of a complete revolution in one's reading of all poetry.'[20]

The second instalment of Frye's critical revolution was the spectacularly bold scheme of literary categories outlined in *Anatomy of Criticism* (1957). This book is the single most momentous work of literary theory in its generation, combining as it does a polemical defence of criticism as a value-free 'science' with a persuasive new classification of literary genres. As if inspired by Blake, Frye builds here a free-standing, all-inclusive, and fearfully symmetrical system of types, modes, forms and genres, all adding up to the constitution of a 'self-contained literary universe' or 'total body of vision'.[21] Part of the excitement of Frye's new model of literary study at that time lay in the abrupt shift of focus from the New-Critical close scrutiny of a short poem to the consideration of the entire literary 'system' as a beautifully self-regulating world of meanings. One of his starting-points was T. S. Eliot's idea of tradition as an 'ideal order' of works existing in relation to one another and independent of time or circumstance. Another appears to have been the example of the Chicago critics, with their 'inductive' principles and their emphasis on the determining importance of literary genres. In any case, the result was a drastic 'standing back' from the local particulars of a given work (Frye regarded New-Critical methods as a kind of provincialism) the better to see the higher categories, conventions and types of which that work was but an instance; a turn, in other words, from critical appreciation to literary science, or from aesthetics to anthropology.

Frye's purpose in *Anatomy of Criticism* is nothing less than the reformation of literary study from the ground up, through the exposition of a central theory comparable to that of evolution in biological science. By those standards it would have been remarkable if he had succeeded, where even Aristotle had fallen short. But to witness his attempt is still bracing, instructive, and even at times intoxicating. His first move is to go back to a problem built into the foundations of academic literary study: the conflict between Taste and Knowledge. Frye's answer here, like R. G. Moulton's in an earlier generation, is the simple and drastic one of setting aside Taste, judgement, and appreciation as matters of upper-class gossip and subjective valuation, upon which no systematic Knowledge could be founded. Tributes to the 'greatness' of an author, or comparisons between the relative maturities of Milton and Shelley, were for Frye largely exercises in empty rhetoric. Knowledge, on the other hand, must start from an acceptance of literature in its totality, without the discrimination of a privileged 'tradition'. This did not mean that all works were just as good as one another; only that the preferences of trained taste could not be established by argument or tied consistently to objective qualities of literary works. These principles are of course, as Frye well knew, the diametrical opposites of those upheld in the Arnoldian tradition culminating in Leavis, for whom discrimination was the beginning and end of criticism. By pursuing so resolutely the road of value-free Knowledge, Frye laid the foundations in his *Anatomy* for the enormous subsequent development of academic literary theory.

Beyond its initial polemical premises, the *Anatomy* is devoted, as its title implies, to the elaboration of a complicated taxonomy or classification of the fundamental types of literature and of criticism. Frye begins by outlining, with the help of Aristotle, a model of five fictional modes which are distinguished according to the hero's degree of superiority to other persons and to his environment: at the top, we have the divine hero of myth, and below him the heroes of romance, of the 'high mimetic mode' (i.e. epic and tragedy), of the 'low mimetic mode' (i.e. comedy and realistic fiction), and finally the inferior hero of the ironic mode. The history of Western fiction, Frye argues, is that of a descent down this modal ladder, from the sublimely mythic to the ridiculously realistic and ironic. Moving on to the theory of literary symbolism, Frye then revives the medieval scheme of multiple significance with its four 'levels' of literal, allegorical, moral, and anagogic meanings, adapting it freely to produce a stratified scheme both of meanings and of matching critical approaches: thus critical commentary is a form of allegory, while the highest kind of meaning is the anagogical or universal kind that presents a 'total dream' or organized model of human desire, as in holy scriptures or mythopoeic works like Blake's prophetic books. Among critical approaches, the corresponding higher varieties are the archetypal and the (as yet unrealized) anagogic kinds, which are distinguished by assuming the larger context of literature as a whole. 'Poetry', Frye tells us 'can only be made out of other poems; novels out of other novels. Literature shapes itself, and is not shaped externally'.[22] The ultimate goal of the critic must then be the anagogic or totalizing project of discerning behind all literary phenomena the archetypal Poem or Novel of which all the rest are imitations; or recognizing the originating Word from which the Creation follows. In the third of the four essays making up the *Anatomy*, Frye proceeds to categorize literary archetypes in a fourfold scheme of basic narrative patterns corresponding to the seasons: comedy (Spring), romance (Summer), tragedy (Autumn), and irony or satire (Winter), all four being but 'episodes in a total quest-myth'.[23] By this stage Frye's all-devouring theoretical system has brought us back to the perfect reconciliation of 'science' and 'religion' that is speculative anthropology in the tradition of Sir James Frazer and Jessie Weston. In other words, although Frye is not a card-carrying Jungian like Maud Bodkin, he has subordinated all other critical approaches to the master-code of myth criticism.

From its origins among psychoanalysts and anthropologists, myth criticism, or the interpretation of literature in terms of perennial motifs and themes, had made little significant headway before the Second World War. The post-war years, however, provided it with a new lease of life, hoisting the idea of 'myth' to the centre of intellectual discussion. The leading philosopher of myth, Ernst Cassirer, published his *Essay on Man* in 1944, two years after his disciple, Susanne K. Langer, had brought out her *Philosophy in a New Key*. In Europe, Robert Graves's *The White Goddess* appeared in 1948, and Mircea Eliade's *Le Mythe de l'éternel retour* in the following year. From the high Jungian school of mythography came Joseph Campbell's *The Hero With a Thousand Faces* (1949), and in the same year a number of myth-critical books by American literary scholars, including Francis Fergusson's *The Idea of a Theater* and Richard Chase's *Quest for Myth*. Soon, even W. H. Auden was joining in, with a study of the sea in literature, *The Enchafèd Flood* (1951). It was, as Philip Rahv observed in 1953, an age of 'mythomania'. The typical procedure among literary myth critics was to treat numerous individual literary works (or rather, their abstracted stories) as instances of a single and universal story, which is, where possible, further treated as a version of a religious ritual enacting the mystery of death and rebirth: thus all heroes are Osiris or Lancelot or Orpheus or Jesus, all quests are for the Grail or the Golden Fleece, all happy endings are rebirths. So for Richard Chase in his *Herman Melville* (1949), Captain Ahab is, not surprisingly, a version of Prometheus; but then so is everyone else in Melville's fiction, except for Billy Budd, who is the scapegoat-god (Jesus, Osiris, and the rest) of whom the Cambridge anthropologists had written. In his *Quest for Myth*, Chase attempts, with some embarrassment and discomfort, to sketch the outlines of a founding story of the hero withdrawing from and returning to his community, as a basis for interpreting poems by Donne, Wordsworth, and Auden; but by the time he published *The American Novel and Its Tradition* (1957), Chase had given up on myth criticism entirely, having found that it set a restricted agenda of 'reconciliation' that could not recognize contradiction or historical conflict in literature. Frances Fergusson was on safer ground in his *The Idea of a Theater*, principally because drama actually *is* a kind of ritual, not just the supposed echo of one. Predictably enough, he draws upon the work of the anthropologists in seeing the tragic hero as a scapegoated and dismembered god, whose sufferings bring regeneration to his society. Less predictably, he steps outside the theatre to consider Dante as the highest kind of artist, one who embraces the entire cycle of death and resurrection, not just its tragic moment. For Fergusson, as for Frye or for Wilson Knight, the cycle's the thing.

The most irreverently controversial of the American 'myth' critics was Leslie Fiedler, a professor at the University of Montana. Taking his bearings from Freud and Trilling in his essays collected in *No! in Thunder* (1960), Fiedler argued against the New Critics that the most valuable study of literature was to be focused on its mythic dimension rather than on its verbal complexity. Although he was close to the position of the New York group in his Freudianism and his view that art must challenge liberal pieties, he still managed to scandalize readers of *Partisan Review* in 1948 with an astonishing article, 'Come Back to the Raft Ag'in, Huck Honey!', in which he proposed that the secret of American fiction is a recurrent homoerotic fantasy of interracial male bonding (as with Natty Bumppo and Chingachgook, Ishmael and Queequeg, Huck and Jim). He developed this thesis into a full-length psycho-history of the American imagination in his *Love and Death in the American Novel* (1960), arguing that the major tradition in America has been one of Gothic terror, in contrast with the European tradition of adultery and courtship in fiction; ill at ease with adult sexuality, the (white male) American writer dreams of escaping the feminine domestic world into a natural idyll in which he can assuage the national guilt for genocide and slavery by embracing a dark-skinned brother. The distinctive feature of Fiedler's myth criticism is that, unlike the universalism of the Jungians or of Frye, it allows for culturally-specific myths, and focuses especially on stereotypes generated by particular racial, sexual and religious antagonisms. From his early work in *The Jew in the American Novel* (1959) to the later study of racial and sexual outcasts in *The Stranger in Shakespeare* (1972), he laid the basis for future work on the representation by dominant cultures of their feared 'Others'.

While the break-up of the New-Critical hegemony in North America was leading criticism into a more adventurous phase of Romantic flamboyance, the equivalent moment in Britain encouraged calls for caution, safe consensus, and civilized decorum. The critical revolution of the 1920s and 1930s came in for retrospective censure for its unbalanced excesses of emphasis, which now needed the correction of moderate good sense. In response to the sclerotic dogmatism of *Scrutiny*, the Oxford scholar F. W. Bateson launched the rival journal *Essays in Criticism* in 1951, attracting contributions from several younger academic critics and from writers who came to be identified with the counter-modernist 'Movement' of the 1950s (Kingsley Amis, John Wain, D. J. Enright, and others). Bateson's editorial manifesto of 1953, 'The Function of Criticism at the Present Time', regrets what he calls the irresponsibility of the New Critics (including Leavis and Wilson Knight). The older generation of critics was culpable, Bateson announced, both for evading its social responsibilities and for wilfully ignoring the contexts of the works it analysed: Cleanth Brooks, for example, was practising a form of escapism by cutting poems off entirely from their social occasions. On the other hand, the merely 'sociological' critics (Bateson unfairly named Edmund Wilson and Lionel Trilling here) could not be relied upon to respect the complexity of literary texts. Accordingly, there needed to be a new compromise reconciling the best traditions of scholarship and criticism, of contextual and textual studies. This rejection of the modernist pioneers in the name of a new sense of responsibility is a general trend that can be traced across the work of four new British critics, all of whom contributed to early issues of *Essays in Criticism*: Donald Davie, Graham Hough, Raymond Williams, and Frank Kermode.

Donald Davie's first two books, *Purity of Diction in English Verse* (1952) and *Articulate Energy* (1955), open up a campaign to revive in poetry those virtues of traditional syntax dismissed by Imagist orthodoxy. Davie identifies Pound and Eliot as – despite appearances – heirs of the Romantics, finally tearing up the old eighteenth-century contract between author and reader. Agreeing with the Chicago critics, he calls for a revival of older generic classifications; and against Leavis and the New Critics he scorns the cult of concreteness in poetry, defending instead the highly abstract language of Wordsworth's *Prelude*, the pleasures of which lie in appreciation of syntactical continuity and control. Davie indeed draws a direct connection between the obscurantist abandonment of syntax in the Symbolist-Imagist tradition and the destruction of social and political consensus in Eliot's and Pound's ultra-right politics, claiming that 'the development from imagism in poetry to fascism in politics is clear and unbroken', and that 'to dislocate syntax in poetry is to threaten the rule of law in the civilized community.'[24]

Graham Hough, as we have noted already, expressed in his *Image and Experience* (1960) a strong unease about the fate of the modernist revolution in poetics, which he contrasted with the Romantic literary revolution of the early nineteenth century. Whereas the Romantics had led a genuine and inevitable spiritual renaissance, and had thus founded an authentic new tradition, the Imagists and their associates had attempted a merely 'technical' insurrection against the norms of accepted language, producing only a dead-end for modern poetry:

> The wilful Alexandrianism, the allusiveness and multiplicity of reference, above all, the deliberate cultivation of modes of organisation that are utterly at variance with those of ordinary discourse – these are the main reasons for the disappearance of Johnson's common reader.[25]

As in criticism Wilson Knight had replaced character in action with patterns of imagery, so in poetry Pound and Eliot had elevated the juxtaposition of images above the narrative or discursive connections of plot or of 'ordinary discourse'. The result was that readers had given up on poetry altogether and spent their time on sociological commentaries instead. For Hough as for Davie, it was deplorable that basic syntactical connection had been destroyed. A poem, he insists, ought to make the same kind of sense as any other discourse, and of course it still does in the work of those poets overlooked by modernist orthodoxy: Thomas Hardy, Robert Frost, Robert Graves, John Crowe Ransom, Edwin Muir and John Betjeman – who together constitute a 'main road' of twentieth-century verse from which the Imagist line has been a fruitless detour. Without pretending that modernism and its codes of impersonality had never happened, we should, says Hough, revive the principle of Wordsworth, that a poet is a man speaking to men.

While Davie and Hough announced dissenting positions and recorded protests against what they saw as the extreme consequences of literary modernism, Frank Kermode in *Romantic Image* (1957) and Raymond Williams in *Culture and Society, 1780–1950* (1958) attempted the more valuable task of tackling the same problem through historical investigation, reconstructing the cultural developments that had culminated in the new orthodoxies of Eliot and the New Critics. Both of them disentangle the complicated meanings attached to central terms of modern cultural analysis, and both begin with the Romantic poets and their sense of disconnection or alienation from society. But while Kermode studies the evolution of the term 'Image' as a kind of key to modern literary and critical assumptions, Williams investigates a cluster of 'keywords' grouped around the word 'Culture', as a way of understanding modern bourgeois society in Britain and the traditions of imaginative resistance to it. Kermode looks forward to a new phase of poetry that can move beyond the irrationalism of the Symbolists and Imagists, incorporating 'the ordinary syntax of the daily life of action'.[26] Williams more ambitiously looks forward to the socialist goal of a 'common culture' no longer stratified by the élitist principles of Eliot and Leavis. Williams's work, although at this stage still tied to some of the habits and conventions of the Leavis group, points beyond literary criticism to a larger project of cultural history: *Culture and Society* looks well beyond the high literary tradition to trace a line of social criticism and reform including Cobbett, Owen, Bentham, Carlyle, Gaskell, Ruskin, Morris, Gissing, Tawney, and Orwell. In so far as it attempts critical discrimination (and Williams does sometimes set out to evaluate an author's sensibility), it is usually in order to take bearings for social renewal in the present. Williams's next book, *The Long Revolution* (1961) included a sequence of studies in the sociology of literature and drama – on the histories of journalism, publishing, theatres, and schools – which, along with some of the contemporary work of Richard Hoggart, went some way towards founding a new discourse that would soon rival the authority of literary criticism: that of Cultural Studies.

Kermode's account of the development of modern poetics in *Romantic Image* was notable as the most persuasive illustration of the oft-repeated charge that Eliot and the other modernists were in fact heirs of Romanticism despite their own protestations. Kermode shows how Eliot's own doctrine of the 'dissociation of sensibility' (which Kermode here demolishes), along with Hulme's and Pound's idea of the 'image', is derived from the Romantic tradition of Keats, Coleridge, Baudelaire, and the Pre-Raphaelites, filtered through the decadent or Symbolist line of Pater, Symons, and Yeats. He traces a fascinating line of privileged images – the female dancer, the female dreamer – showing meanwhile how such images form part of a long Romantic campaign against public rationality, ordinary discourse, and intellect itself, which is magically dissolved into the concreteness of the dancing body. Kermode closes this book with a prediction that order and reason would return to poetry. In his next work, *Wallace Stevens* (1960), he could announce that it had: here was a modern American poet, largely overlooked by British critics, who had convincingly balanced the claims of the image with those of discursive philosophical reasoning in verse. His immersion in Stevens's poetics had further results in the arguments of Kermode's major work of the 1960s, *The Sense of an Ending* (1967), which is in many ways the culminating theoretical work of this period. This curiously eclectic book, the argument of which ranges from Homer to Robbe-Grillet, from Augustine to modern physics, is in one sense a series of sermons on Wallace Stevens's conception of poetry as the 'supreme fiction'. Kermode compares literary fictions with other kinds of narrative in theology and history, in order to ask how fictions 'make sense of the world' for us. The answer he proposes is that literary fictions, like the fictions of history and theology, give a redemptive structure to time, converting it from *chronos* (meaningless succession of passing time) into *kairos* (time made significant or 'critical'), giving us a world formed into beginnings, middles, ends, progresses, declines, and catastrophes. Here, interestingly, Kermode stubbornly resists the common temptation to speak of literature 'overcoming' or transcending time through spatial patterning: temporality for him as for Aristotle is inescapable, and so-called 'spatial form' in literature is simply a misapplied metaphor. Kermode comes into collision here not only with Joseph Frank but also with Northrop Frye, whose predominantly spatial model of archetypes he resists, setting up a central opposition between myth, which is circular, self-confirming, and absolute in its demand for assent, and fiction, which is linear, self-conscious and exploratory: posing the contrast with brutal harshness, Kermode gives *King Lear* as an example of fiction, the Nazi ideology of anti-semitism as a myth. A myth is a fiction that has forgotten that it is a fiction; and this potential for regressive amnesia is present, Kermode suggests, in all fictions, requiring a countervailing scepticism to hold it in check. His own vigilant scepticism in this and previous works established Kermode as the critic best equipped to undertake the modern critical task of 'making sense of the ways we make sense of the world.'[27]

More Shakespearean Themes

As in other spheres, the modernist revolution rolled on in Shakespeare studies, still led by the innovators of the 1930s; but it encountered in this period new strains of scepticism and theoretical resistance. The school of symbolic or poetic interpretation founded in Britain appeared to make new conquests in America, but as it expanded so it stirred into action opposing styles of reading.

The leader of the Shakespearean revolution, G. Wilson Knight, showed no sign of relaxing his efforts, even twenty years after his entrance upon the critical stage. In the post-war years he brought out yet another two Shakespearean books, *The Crown of Life* (1947) on the last plays, and *The Mutual Flame* (1955) on the sonnets. Both works show a certain loss of focus, as Knight spends more time drawing links between Shakespeare, Nietzsche, and the English Romantic poets than in illuminating the works of Shakespeare himself. Beyond the detection of echoes from previous plays in Shakespeare's last phase, Knight has little to offer in *The Crown of Life* except some odd rumination on eternal harmonies and spiritual radiations, and the unexpected argument that Shakespeare's crowning achievement is not, after all, *The Tempest* but *Henry VIII*. This curious judgement follows from Knight's intensely patriotic phase during the War, when he came to regard the major English poets as prophets of national destiny and thus, in his mind, as reverent royalists. Even *The Tempest* itself, in this account, becomes a vision of the English soul and its imperial destinies. *The Mutual Flame* has at least a more coherent argument on the sonnets, although its section on 'The Phoenix and the Turtle' is somewhat tangled. Knight reads the sonnet-sequence as an 'integration-quest', in which Shakespeare seeks to balance his masculine and feminine aspects into a higher union of androgyny, which Knight calls bisexual.

> The perfectly integrated state, which we may call the Christ-state, is necessarily unmarried, since no partner can, for the bisexual integration, be needed, both sexes being complete, and at one, within. The Sonnets show the way towards this state of being.[28]

Knight had in 1950 become a confirmed Spiritualist, and in his later manner of interpretation it shows, chiefly in disconnected ramblings about higher awareness and eternal insights.

His near-namesake, L. C. Knights of *Scrutiny* and of Sheffield and Bristol Universities, offered the more acceptable face of the new Shake-spearean interpretation in his *An Approach to Hamlet* (1959) and *Some Shakespearean Themes* (1960). A good deal less iconoclastic than in his earlier days, Knights sets out in his *Hamlet* essay to rescue Shakespeare from T. S. Eliot's diagnosis of an unspecified psychological 'problem' in the playwright that had been unsuccessfully expressed in the play. Drawing on an analysis of Othello as a self-deceiving narcissist, published some years before by F. R. Leavis, Knights insists that the problem – defined as self-regarding immaturity – is Prince Hamlet's, not his creator's. The aim of *Some Shakespearean Themes* is the familiar one of tracing the Shakespeare Progress from the early work to the last plays, more or less as D. A. Traversi had done, and again in terms of richly mature ordering of experience. Knights does take the further risk of speaking of Shakespeare's 'philosophical' achievement, and of his thought rather than just his con-crete apprehension of experience. The turning point of Shakespeare's development, for Knights, is *King Lear*, in which the momentous questions posed in earlier plays – like 'What is essential human nature?' – receive at last their affirmative answers, although as valued experiences rather than as maxims. The edge has come off Knights's critical work in these books, and the only surprise in them is the degree to which they shuffle back to Bradleian character- and author-study.

A more significant and more confident extension of the revolution declared by Knights in 1933 was to be found in the adoption of 'symbolic' interpretations by American 'New Critics' such as Cleanth Brooks. In his *The Well Wrought Urn* (1947), Brooks included only one chapter on a dramatic work: an essay on symbolism in *Macbeth* that had been published previously under the title 'Shakespeare as a Symbolist Poet'. Placed immediately after a chapter on Donne's paradoxes, the *Macbeth* essay invites us to treat the play as we would a metaphysical poem, examining selected 'difficult' passages in close detail in order to show hitherto unrevealed layers of sense. Here Brooks acknowledges Caroline Spurgeon's work on the play's imagery of garments and coverings, but sees it as defective in that Spurgeon had failed to notice the symbolic significance of babies. Raiding different parts of the play for images of babies and of cloaks, Brooks then brings these elements together to suggest a dominant meaning in terms that resemble later structuralist emphases: the underlying opposition in the play is revealed to be that between the Naked and the Clothed. Brooks had by this time collaborated on a textbook, *Understanding Drama* (1945) with one of his colleagues at Louisiana State University, Robert B. Heilman, who was also publishing on Shakespeare in these years. Heilman's books *This Great Stage: Image and Structure in 'King Lear*' (1948) and *Magic in the Web: Action and Language in 'Othello'* (1956) announce at some length, and long after Wilson Knight's first works, that Shakespeare's plays are extended metaphors made up of patterns of imagery which, when unravelled, point us in the direction of the great questions of life, death, appearance, and reality. Heilman was an enthusiastic, if not very careful New Critic, excited by the possibility of reading any literary work as a 'poem' (indeed, he published an article in 1948 on '*The Turn of the Screw* as Poem'). His misfortune was that he came to the attention of the Chicago critics.

In the pages of *Modern Philology*, Cleanth Brooks came to be identified as the New Critic who most consistently disregarded fundamental distinctions between kinds of poem, reducing them all to samples of the same kind of paradoxical language. Earlier examples of the same logic, notably L. C. Knights's claim that *Macbeth* is a poem like 'The Waste Land', were also quoted with horror in Chicago. The last straw was Heilman's *The Great Stage*, which was reviewed by W. R. Keast in 1949. Keast objected vehemently to what he saw as Heilman's imposition of an arbitrary theory of symbolism onto *King Lear*, that is, to Heilman's assumption that imagery is the primary element in drama, to which plot and character are secondary. This leads to the attribution of 'symbolic' meanings to elements

of the play and its language that could be accounted for more simply by
their functions in the plot or action. And Keast pressed the complaint
further: to dwell on the 'verbal patterns' of a Shakespeare play as if they
were the primary basis of its meaning was bound to be fruitless, since
the significance of such patterns always depended upon their contexts,
and thus in turn on plot, character, and genre. The New-Critical
approach had the effect of dissolving the specific moral and emotional
effect of a Shakespeare tragedy into merely intellectual platitudes in which
the tragic element is forgotten altogether. As Keast pointed out, it was the
habit of this school of interpretation to take the tragic suffering out of
tragedy, seeing only triumphant insight and affirmation in its place.

As the shortcomings of the school of 'symbolic' interpretation became
more apparent in these debates, so the ground was cleared for a less
genre-blind approach to Shakespeare. The most successful model of such
a new departure was presented by Northrop Frye in his two Shakespearean
works, *A Natural Perspective: The Development of Shakespearean Comedy and
Romance* (1965) and *Fools of Time: Studies in Shakespearean Tragedy* (1967).
Frye inherited certain principles from G. Wilson Knight – the priority
of value-free interpretation over criticism, a Nietzschean disdain for moral
'messages' in literature – but he was in the end a very different kind of
Romantic. Where Knight had scoured a play's recurrent imagery for clues
to the nature of Shakespeare's originating visionary insight, Frye turns his
attention to the recurrence of certain plot-structures and stock character-
types across the whole Shakespearean *oeuvre* and beyond it in world
drama. This shift of focus, in which Frye 'stands back from' the individual
work, exposes the difference between the Romantic Bardolater, whose
quest is for the fountain of individual genius, and the Romantic folklorist,
who goes in search of the collective imagination and its inner logic. Like
E. E. Stoll before him, Frye insists that convention is the key to Shakespeare's work: the plays are not allegories concealing personal moral
attitudes, but objective models of human desire, based firmly upon older
dramatic conventions. For Frye, the inherited convention or dramatic
structure is always prior to the 'attitude' of the play: thus, for instance,
the forgiving of the villainous character at the end of a Shakespearean
comedy is 'primarily structural, not moral: Shakespeare's emphasis on
reconciliation is a technical emphasis rather than an oozing through of
personal benevolence.'[29] Similarly,

> *Macbeth* is not a play about the moral crime of murder; it is a
> play about the dramatically conventional crime of killing the
> lawful and anointed king. The convention gives a ritual quality
> to the action, and the element of reversed magic to the imagery
> that enables the poet to identify the actors with the powers of
> nature . . . Accept the convention, and the play is all right; reject
> it, and the play is all wrong.[30]

In an important sense, the true begetter of the play is not Shakespeare but the inherited convention of tragedy or comedy, which in turn is descended from ancient myth.

Frye has his own preferences among conventions: as he admits at the start of *A Natural Perspective*, he inclines towards comedy and romance rather than tragedy or ironic realism; towards the Pleasure Principle rather than the Reality Principle. This temperamental bias, supported by the 'comic' teleology of his Christian faith, makes Frye a more exciting guide to comic conventions than to Shakespearean tragedy. In *A Natural Perspective* Frye illuminates the logic of Shakespearean romantic comedy by referring us back to the typical structure of New Comedy in Plautus and Terence, with its contest between the younger generation and the older, and its progression from ritual abstinence through licence to festive social renewal, Simplifying the pattern in Freudian terms, Frye presents this form of comedy as a victory of the Pleasure Principle over the social obstacles placed against it. Reflecting more generally on the nature of comedy, Frye tells us that it is more primitive and folkloric than tragedy, and that it moves in the direction of identity (at the social level, marriage and festivity; at the individual level, release from the bondage of the obsessive 'humour'). Ultimately, it re-enacts the positive half of the natural cycle, leading us from winter to spring, in a ritual of rebirth.

The problem with tragedy, as Frye himself explains, is that it individualizes its audience, while comedy binds them in collective celebration; and so tragedy goes against the anthropologizing grain of Frye's project. His examination of tragic conventions in *Fools of Time* does yield some valuable distinctions – between tragedy and melodrama, for instance – and it makes a suggestive connection between Freud's mythography of the 'primal father' devoured by his guilty sons and the Shakespearean figure of the Fallen Prince (Duncan, old Hamlet, Richard II, Julius Caesar); but it is primarily an exercise, albeit a brilliant one, in Frye's favourite pastime, taxonomy. In this account, there are three kinds of tragedy: tragedies of order, following from the fall of a prince such as Agamemnon (in Shakespeare, *Julius Caesar, Hamlet, Macbeth*); tragedies of passion, in which a protagonist such as Antigone is torn between social and personal duties in a divided world (*Romeo and Juliet, Troilus and Cressida, Antony and Cleopatra, Coriolanus*); and tragedies of isolation, in which a hero such as Oedipus conducts his search for individual identity (*King Lear, Othello, Timon of Athens*). Frye is at his best here in following through the patterns of character-type thrown up by each of these categories. Thus each tragedy of order has an order-figure, a rebel-figure and a nemesis-figure, while in the tragedies of passion an Adonis-figure is repeatedly bewitched by an archetypal Temptress and counselled by a mythic Jester (Mercutio, Pandarus, Enobarbus). At this level of analysis Frye could claim that, although following where G. Wilson Knight had led – especially in the account of storms and tempests in *A Natural*

Perspective – he had more convincingly answered T. S. Eliot's demand for elucidation of the 'pattern in the carpet' of Shakespeare's work taken as a whole.

The Rise of the Novel

As we have noted above, the post-war decades were remarkable for a flourishing of critical interest in the novel, both in theoretical studies and in works focused on individual authors. The secondary literature of 'the novel' expands in all directions in this period, taking in popularly accessible essays and guides like those of V. S. Pritchett in *The Living Novel* (1946) and of Walter Allen in *The English Novel* (1954) and *Tradition and Dream* (1964), along with technical academic analyses like those of Wayne C. Booth and David Lodge. In so far as it generalizes from the specific cases before it, and it does this often enough, criticism in the 1950s and 60s refers back repeatedly to a fundamental dilemma formulated earlier by Henry James: resolving the rival claims of artistic form or 'pattern' in the novel with those of 'lived experience'. Before the war, James himself had become associated – both by friends like Lubbock and by enemies like Wells and Forster – with the formalist or aestheticist solution to this problem, with Art rather than with Life, but Q. D. Leavis and others in the *Scrutiny* group had tried to realign him with a version of realism, stressing his engagement with irreducible moral complexities. In one way or another, the various critical positions of this period arrive at a compromise settlement, formulating the novel's dual responsibilities to aesthetic form and to moral value, to Art and to Life. Truisms abound in this field, and it is hard to distinguish one critic from another at this abstractly formulaic level. Differences, however, emerge when they descend to particular cases in order to exemplify the ideal balance; and a larger tension can be observed between American critics, who often incline towards symbolism and romance in fiction, and British critics who cling to the realist tradition.

If it is possible to speak of a general direction in which the novel-criticism of this period tends, then it is towards a complication or qualification of the modernist or Symbolist position, one in which the emphasis on aesthetic pattern or scheme is balanced by recognition of the claims of 'character' and worldly contingency. The high modernist phase of the 1940s was one in which the novel was to be described as a kind of 'poem', organized by thematic and symbolic contrasts rather than by plot and character. Thus *Scrutiny* ran a series of articles by F. R. Leavis and others under the general title 'The Novel as Dramatic Poem', and in the

United States Robert B. Heilman wrote of Henry James's *The Turn of the Screw* as a poem. This line of argument culminates in Leavis's *D. H. Lawrence, Novelist* (1955), with its repeated emphasis on the 'poetic' qualities of *The Rainbow* and its continuation of 'the tradition' descending from *Sir Gawain and the Green Knight*. In America, the most influential statement of the equivalent New-Critical position was Mark Schorer's much-reprinted essay 'Technique as Discovery' (1948), which follows T. S. Eliot in stressing the crucial difference between 'raw' experience and its transformation or objectification into art. Schorer is extremely vague about what he means by 'technique' here (it seems to include style, convention, and several other things, and to carry the implication that most writers have no technique), but he is clear in his formalist insistence that it does not follow after an already-given subject-matter; rather, it 'discovers' or defines a new subject-matter that could not have existed before. This is, for Schorer, a way of describing the difference between bad novels like Defoe's *Moll Flanders*, Wells's *Tono-Bungay* or Lawrence's *Sons and Lovers*, which merely reproduce an undigested slice of social history or of personal experience, and good novels like *Ulysses, A Portrait of the Artist as a Young Man*, and *Wuthering Heights*, which give order and value to experience through style and technical control. Schorer's position is clearly a much simplified version of Henry James's hostility to the untreated 'lump' or slice of life, and it is partly an intervention into contemporary American taste, elevating Faulkner and Hemingway above the social realism of James T. Farrell and others.

The English critical school around F. R. Leavis, although it was still in principle committed to the virtues of the modernist 'poetic' novel, was unwilling to celebrate it in such simple terms as 'technique', for fear of falling into the error of aestheticism – a life-denying heresy associated with Flaubert and Joyce. Still shuddering with revulsion at the effete Decadence of the 1890s, the Leavis group insisted that artistic control or 'form' in the novel was not an alternative to moral and social responsibility, but the very signature of moral gravity. Thus, in one of his repeated attempts to distinguish the healthy English tradition from the sterility of Flaubert, F. R. Leavis asks in his *The Great Tradition*:

> Is there any great novelist whose preoccupation with 'form' is not a matter of his responsibility towards a rich human interest, or complexity of interests, profoundly realized? – a responsibility involving, of its very nature, imaginative sympathy, moral discrimination, and judgement of relative human value?'[31]

By this standard Joseph Conrad is judged a greater novelist than Flaubert because of his greater interest in humanity, and his stronger moral pre-occupations. In a series of breathtakingly abrupt verdicts, Defoe, Fielding, Sterne, Thackeray, Dickens, the Brontës, and Hardy are all dismissed by

Leavis as insufficiently serious. Henry James, meanwhile, is carefully detached from Flaubert's school and instead soldered onto the English provincial tradition of Austen and George Eliot. Thus the organizing principle of fiction, that distinguishes it from mere social reporting, is now no longer 'form', in the abstractly aesthetic sense, but an 'informing' moral intensity or reverence for life.

A similar attempt to evade the aestheticist connotations of 'form' by substituting for it a more wholesome term is to be found in Leavis's disciple Arnold Kettle, author of *An Introduction to the English Novel* (2 vols., 1951–53). Kettle thought of himself as a Marxist critic, and borrowed some of his terms from the Hungarian Marxist Georg Lukács, but in practice he formed a kind of Popular Front with the Leavisites which often left him indistinguishable from them. Drawing on Lukács, Kettle insisted that the 'raw' reflection of life in fiction was insufficient, and required the imposition of 'pattern' or overall significance; on the other hand, if this pattern was derived from a one-sidedly pessimistic world-view, as with *Middlemarch* or the novels of Hardy, the author could be chided for undialectical determinism, decadence, and even (in the case of Joyce's *Ulysses*) with 'sterility'. Kettle is on firmer ground when he draws detailed connections between novels and the social tensions of their time.

A more impressive synthesis of formal and moral approaches to the novel is offered in Dorothy Van Ghent's *The English Novel: Form and Function* (1953). More consistently than Leavis, Van Ghent believes that 'we cannot dissociate an author's conception of life, and its "value" and "significance", from the aesthetic structure of the literary work.'[32] Novels embody moral ideas and attitudes, but these are implicit, embodied in the fictional 'world' and its events; and only if the novel achieves convincing unity will its world-view count for us. Van Ghent's procedures are those of the classroom, her book having grown from her courses at Kansas University, and she is appropriately clear about her methods: of every novel we must ask 'what are its elements? how are they made to cohere in a unity? how are its special technical devices . . . appropriate to the making of this particular world?'[33] She asks these questions of eighteen novels, from *Don Quixote* to *A Portrait of the Artist as a Young Man*, and, as we might expect from a critic so clearly influenced by New-Critical and Leavisite positions, she favours Lawrence, Joyce, and Emily Brontë over Walter Scott and George Meredith, and she agrees with Lubbock in complaining of the disorganized state of *Vanity Fair*. But she is no mere follower of fashion: her readings are fresh and intellectually lively, never more so than in her chapter on *Wuthering Heights*, which includes not only an 'archetypal' study of Heathcliff but also a sophisticated proto-structuralist exposition of the fundamental binary oppositions (culture/nature, limitation/excess) governing the novel. Van Ghent's ability to define the special characteristics of a novelist's 'world' is further illustrated in her article, 'The Dickens World: A View From Todgers's' (1950), a brilliant examination of the ways in which things become like people and people like things in Dickens's novels. This kind of attempt to evoke the underlying logic of an author's imaginative 'world' was more commonly attempted in this period, as the New-Critical concentration on the short work gave way to new approaches to authors and *oeuvres*, as in Frye's work on Blake and Shakespeare. An important example is J. Hillis Miller's *Charles Dickens: The World of His Novels* (1958), which sets out to define the characteristics of Dickens's imagination, and in particular the ways in which it attempted to assimilate the complexity of the modern urban world.

The positions of Leavis and Van Ghent can be seen as qualified versions of New-Critical formalism, combining 'moral vision' with formal integrity. But there were also in this period several critical positions on the novel that more clearly distanced themselves from New Criticism. The most frontally polemical was Philip Rahv's, summed up in his essay 'Fiction and the Criticism of Fiction' (1956), which attacked Mark Schorer's obsession with 'technique'. Closely related to this, although less polemical, was the position developed by Lionel Trilling in the essays collected in *The Liberal Imagination* (1950). Like Rahv, Trilling objected to the artificial imposition of 'poetic' patterns of symbolism onto novels, and he insisted that novels could deal openly with ideas, not just symbols. Both critics also shared a suspicion of what they saw as a sentimental cult of 'Reality' in American culture, opposing itself to intellectual clarity. Middlebrow 'realism' in the tradition of Dreiser and Steinbeck, and academic Symbolism as practised by the New Critics were twin evils of simplification, both tending to obliterate that particular kind of attention to human behaviour that is most valuable in novels. In his essay 'Manners, Morals, and the Novel', Trilling declares memorably that 'the most effective agent of the moral imagination has been the novel of the last two hundred years.'[34] But, as Trilling explains, this means that the novel must complicate, not confirm, our previous notions of reality, and it does so best when it pays close attention to 'manners' and thus to character. We may have broadened our social sympathies, Trilling feels, but 'we have lost something of our power of love, for our novels can never create characters who truly exist.'[35]

In Britain, where an anti-symbolist preference for 'Life' over aesthetic pattern held a firmer grip on criticism, a similar conception of the novelist's 'love' as embodied in characters was developed at length by John Bayley in *The Characters of Love* (1960). For Bayley, 'love' implies the novelist's delight in a character's freedom or independent existence, as opposed to the solipsistic projection of one's own personality. He complains that modern artists such as Lawrence or Proust feel that they need to reveal some insight about the Human Condition, to impose on their readers some view of the world, whereas the great artists of the past

– Chaucer, Shakespeare, Dickens, Tolstoy – could take human reality (or 'Nature') for granted, delighting in the personalities of others for their own sakes. In asserting 'the supremacy of personality in the greatest literature',[36] Bayley might seem to be challenging Eliot's principles, but in fact his position is descended from Eliot, particularly in its nostalgia for pre-ideological spontaneity and in its rejection of Romantic solipsism. The 'personality' celebrated here is not that of the artist – who remains impersonal – but of the character. This places Bayley on the side of Eliot, against the school of Lawrence, Murry, and Leavis; but at the same time distances him from the modern symbolist tradition. Bayley is aware of, and sometimes embarrassed by, the evident conservatism of his position, which sometimes makes E. M. Forster look like a Parisian Surrealist; and he is prepared to turn some genial mockery upon his own claims: 'I may seem to be suggesting that English writers traditionally love their characters, as the English are said to love their dogs, more than the writers of other nations. And I believe that in practice this may well be so.'[37] In fact his defence of 'character' has the effect of rewarding at least a few non-English authors – Scott, and especially Tolstoy – with a higher standing than modernist orthodoxy would allow them.

A growing counter-modernist trend in novel criticism revealed itself in the publication of Barbara Hardy's *The Appropriate Form* (1964) and W. J. Harvey's *Character and the Novel* (1965). Both these critics align themselves (despite expressed awareness of his shortcomings) with E. M. Forster's suspicion of aesthetic schematism. Although never 'naïvely' devoted to the direct imitation of Life's sacred muddle, they pay their highest compliments to those novelists who place truthfulness and fullness of representation above formal design. Hardy makes a familiar kind of contrast between 'dogmatic form' – in which the plot is arranged according to the providential design of an ideology, as in *Jane Eyre* – and 'expansive form', which is more various and free-flowing in its commitment to truth-telling, as in *Anna Karenina* and (despite its de-sexualized climax) *Middlemarch*. She regrets the recent importation from Shakespearean studies of a critical over-emphasis on theme and symbolism, and insists that the novel, unlike the dramatic poem, relies on realistic rendition of local detail. Against James and his followers, she justifies the large, loose baggy monsters as the highest types of novelistic art. W. J. Harvey's book likewise conducts a defence of Tolstoy (here, *War and Peace* rather than *Anna Karenina*) against the James-Lubbock camp; and, like Barbara Hardy, he suggests that there is a higher kind of 'form' that encompasses the full variety of experience rather than just schematic symmetry. Reviving the importance of character is not, for him, a question of abandoning our sense of form; rather, it involves an appreciation of those greatest novels in which the rendering of character overflows the necessities of form. As in Bayley's more overt case, there is an implication in Harvey and Hardy – not unconnected with liberalism of

the Cold-War period – that 'form' is the realm of necessity while 'character' is the realm of freedom. 'Form' is referred to as simple and diagram-
matic, while 'character' is richly varied. Something like this opposition
surfaces in the far more sophisticated meditations of Kermode's *The Sense
of an Ending* (1967). For Kermode, literary fiction is to be distinguished
from the atavistic certitudes of myth, partly on the basis of its inescapably
temporal dimension, which undermines talk of 'spatial form' or eternal
cycles of recurrence. But this temporal organization itself betrays a recurring tension between two kinds of time: *kairos*, or significant time
(typically, time as crisis), and *chronos*, or mere passing time. Fiction must
organize itself in terms of significant time – beginnings, climaxes, ends –
but if it gives us nothing but this 'redeemed' time, in which ends are
contained in their beginnings, then it will be too easily consoling, too
childish or escapist an expression of regressive fantasy. There must rather
be a counterweight of contingency or openness to reality, a certain degree
of disappointment and surprise, and of that anti-poetic scepticism which
has sustained the novel since Cervantes. In other words, despite some of
the implications of post-Symbolist critics, the novel cannot become fully
'poetic'.

The most substantial contribution to the theory of the novel in this
period, Wayne C. Booth's *The Rhetoric of Fiction* (1961), also belongs in
part to the counter-modernist movement of the times. Formed in the
Chicago school, Booth subjected some of the more important axioms of
modernist criticism to extended sceptical scrutiny, dissolving the crucial
received distinction between 'telling' and 'showing'. As his title indicates,
Booth is interested in the rhetorical dimension of fiction, one that had
been neglected in most modernist accounts (Kenneth Burke aside); and
so, for him, a novel is necessarily a persuasive 'telling', a manipulation of
a reader by an author, however indirect the means. The common injunctions, derived from James and Lubbock, to 'dramatize' one's story, to
'show' its events while concealing one's own narrative construction of
them, are shown to be founded on misleading metaphors. Strictly speaking, as Booth argues, the author cannot really 'disappear' behind his or
her tale, and nor can the events of the story really just present themselves
neutrally. Every apparently impartial 'showing' turns out to be an oblique
form of partial telling. Even in the drama – the modernists' ideal model
of impersonal showing – the selection and disposition of event and
dialogue implies a responsible agent who has made certain judgements
and valuations. And even though the real author usually does, as the
modernists promised, disappear from the work, we readers or auditors
inevitably posit an 'Implied Author' as the agent responsible for putting
in place the fictional world of the play or novel and its *dramatis personae*.
In certain prose fictions with a first-person narrator (Huckleberry Finn,
say), the important effect of irony depends on the reader's perception of
a gulf between the narrator's view and the values attributed to the Implied

Author. 'Telling', or narrative voice, then, is decisive in the analysis of novels. Aside from, although prompted by, his quarrel with the James-Lubbock tradition, Booth embarks upon an extended elucidation of the problems of narrative voice and irony, replacing the rough-and-ready distinction between first- and third-person narrators with a more sensitive set of distinctions between 'dramatized' and 'undramatized', 'reliable' and 'unreliable' narrators, and clarifying the basis of the 'omniscient' narrator's special privileges. As literary criticism, *The Rhetoric of Fiction* has its shortcomings, notably a narrow lack of sympathy with Joyce and other modernist novelists, but as a study in the principles of narrative voice, it is a landmark in modern theory.

Next to Booth's work, the single most influential book on the novel in this period was Ian Watt's literary-historical work *The Rise of the Novel* (1957), which opened up the question of fictional realism as a combination of formal and ideological elements – of descriptive particularity with moral judgement. This work has subsequently become the target of innumerable attacks, notably for its elimination of women writers from the account of the English novel's origins. In its time, its achievement was to have clarified the problem of realism as a peculiar hybrid of conventions arising in a specific period. Influenced in part by Q. D. Leavis's account of the reading public, and borrowing some ideas in diluted form from Marxist cultural analysis, Watt linked the rise of the novel with the rise of the bourgeoisie, arguing that a new sense of individualism was a necessary condition for the emergence of modern fiction. The greater part of the work is devoted to studying the ways in which Defoe, Richardson, and Fielding established a newly individual sense of the world's reality in their novels. The prior history of prose fables and romances goes unremarked, and the difficult case of Swift's *Gulliver's Travels* receives no mention. Watt's book is one in which 'the novel' is equated with whichever fictions can be seen as preparing the way for Austen and the nineteenth-century realists; in short, with the work of three men writing in a new minority tradition. By way of counterbalance to the violently anti-realist pronouncements of the early modernists, it encouraged a new respect for realism as a method and an attitude that had, in its day, been as revolutionary as Imagism itself. Realist novelists could now be recovered as heroes of Western art and intellectual liberation, in such critical accounts as Harry Levin's *The Gates of Horn* (1963), which examines Stendhal, Balzac, Flaubert, Zola, and Proust. Raymond Williams, meanwhile, called for a renewal of realism in contemporary fictional practice, in his *The Long Revolution* (1961).

The new favour in which novelistic realism found itself among British critics contrasted oddly with the enthusiasm for 'romance' in North America, encouraged by Frye and others. In fact we find here a strange inversion of the transatlantic conflicts at the end of the nineteenth century, when 'realism' was discussed in Britain as an alien American creed, while 'romance' was the native gift. In the 1950s, romance was being spoken of as distinctively American, realism as almost peculiarly English. Lionel Trilling observed, with regret, in *The Liberal Imagination* that the American novel typically diverges from the investigation of social reality. Two books published in 1957 – Harry Levin's *The Power of Blackness* and Richard Chase's *The American Novel and Its Tradition* – pressed this argument further, claiming that prose romance was the special glory of American literature, yielding psychological insights unknown to the realist traditions of Europe. While Levin focused on the works of Poe, Hawthorne, and Melville, Chase constructed a longer romance tradition from Charles Brockden Brown to William Faulkner. Further elaborations of this thesis, in which the American soul takes flight from actuality into solipsistic dream or Gothic nightmare, include Leslie Fiedler's *Love and Death in the American Novel* (1960) and Richard Poirier's *A World Elsewhere* (1966). The ideological implications generated by this consensus in the building of 'American Literature' as a discipline included the assumption of an American exceptionalism in the supposed 'freedom' of its authors from social determinations; with the corollary that a social-problem novelist such as Dreiser or Dos Passos must be in some essential way unAmerican.

Canons for Courses

In the post-war period, literary canons came under increasing pressure from the burgeoning educational system: as the universities and colleges expanded, so the canon contracted to fit the constraints of the course syllabus. The older canons of self-education and broad reading gave way to a generically restricted conception of autonomous 'literature' that excluded such forms as travel writing, history, biography, or essays. For the purposes of the literature course, literature meant novels, plays, and poems. The assumed definition relied on the New-Critical distinction between autonomous symbolic forms and those kinds of writing that are entangled with external reference and ulterior motives. Moreover, the limited time allowed for an academic course tended to reduce literature still further to 'great' novels, plays, and poems.

An older, pre-academic model of the canon survived in T. S. Eliot's published lecture *What Is a Classic?* (1945), in which England's leading critic explained that no modern European language had a true classic author of the kind represented by Virgil; they might have 'great' authors like Shakespeare or Goethe, but not such poets as could realize finally all the possibilities of their language. Classic authors, in Eliot's sense, must not only be dead, but they must also be the culminating points of dead languages. This lecture, with its strongly Arnoldian suspicion of 'provincialism', represents Eliot's pan-European standpoint, one in which national literatures are all to be subordinated to an inclusive idea of the European mind. A more generous version of this internationalist impulse is found embodied in the Penguin Classics series, inaugurated in the same year as Eliot's lecture with E. V. Rieu's prose translation of the *Odyssey*. This series became the paperback heir of the Everyman enterprise, although it was confined to literature in translation, from Homer to Zola (chiefly Greek, Latin, French, German, Italian, and Russian, but including the Middle English of Chaucer and Langland). It placed translations of 'great books', many of them refreshingly up-to-date in style, into the pockets of the intellectually hungry post-war generations, as did its counterparts in the United States like the Signet Classics and Rinehart Editions.

These were books for a wide, educated public. The impact of the academic course and its special needs can be detected in the appearance of several new literary 'classics' series in the 1960s, among them the Penguin English Library (from 1966) and the Norton Critical Editions (from 1961). The Penguin English Library complemented the foreign-language classics by providing cheap texts of canonical English works – excluding Shakespeare and the poets, who had their own series – with explanatory endnotes and introductions by academic or other authorities: Q. D. Leavis wrote the introduction to *Jane Eyre*, for example. The first ten titles in the series included two novels apiece by Austen and Dickens, along with *The Pilgrim's Progress, Robinson Crusoe, Tom Jones, Wuthering Heights*, and *Middlemarch*. The Norton series embraced Shakespeare and some translated classics, but in a fashion more ambitiously directed towards the requirements of students and teachers: each volume contained along with the primary text a bibliography, contemporary responses to the work, and a small library of modern critical essays upon it. Each series was designed with the newly expanded student market in mind, Penguin aiming for the fairly traditional British course in 'English Literature', Norton at the 'Great Books' and 'American Literature' courses as well. Since 1961, the appearance of a Norton Critical Edition has been a useful guide to a work's standing in American classrooms. The first in the series were *Gulliver's Travels, The Scarlet Letter, The Adventures of Huckleberry Finn, The Red Badge of Courage, Henry IV, Part One, Wuthering Heights, Hamlet, Heart of Darkness, The Ambassadors, Madame Bovary* (translated by Paul de Man), *Crime and Punishment, Great Expectations*, and *Tess of the D'Urbervilles*, while other titles published in the first decade included *Emma, Candide, Hard Times, Anna Karenina*, a selection of Donne's poetry, and *Moby Dick*. The Twentieth Century Views series of critical essay-collections, meanwhile, placed greater emphasis on modern European writers: its first twenty-one titles included volumes on Camus, Proust,

Brecht, Lorca, Kafka, and Sartre, but only two collections devoted to English-born authors (Fielding and Donne).

The restriction of the canon to those few masterpieces likely to be found on a university syllabus was not merely a matter of the blind operation of market forces through publishers' series. Academic critics intervened actively to shorten the list of true 'classics', none more forcibly than F. R. Leavis in *The Great Tradition*, which notoriously opens with the declaration that the great English novelists are Jane Austen, George Eliot, Henry James, and Joseph Conrad, the others – from Defoe and Fielding onwards – being in some way overrated. Leavis presented his exclusive list as a reaction against the uncritical puffing of such minor Victorian novelists as Marryat, Trollope, Yonge, and Read; but then, as his enumeration of minor novelists goes on to include Scott, Thackeray, Gaskell, Charlotte Brontë, Fielding, Hardy, and even Dickens, one wonders who is confounding major with minor. It would be quite unfair to pretend that Leavis appreciated only four novelists: in *The Great Tradition* itself there are admiring words for Emily Brontë, and a special appendix which spares *Hard Times* from the general depreciation of Dickens (largely because its anti-utilitarian position echoes that of Lawrence and of Leavis himself). Having suffered some censure from Lionel Trilling and others for his failure to include Dickens in his 'tradition', Leavis in his next book, *D. H. Lawrence, Novelist*, offers a more generous – but less often quoted – list of the great novelists in English: Austen, Hawthorne, Dickens, Eliot, James, Melville, Twain, Conrad, and Lawrence; and even this, he says, is not exhaustive. The problem with Leavis's canon lies not so much with the numbers of authors allowed on the list, as with the category of 'greatness' itself, and with its life-is-too-short assumption of finite reading time – a universalizing, this, of the student condition. It is often supposed that Leavis's fiercely exclusive insistence upon reducing the canon of English literature to a small number of works or authors was animated by personal narrowness or puritanical zeal. 'Another book to cross off your list', as Frederick C. Crews mockingly summarized this attitude.[38] But although these factors may have played their part, it is evident from such works as *English Literature in Our Time and The University* (1969) that he was prompted most of all by the brevity of the three-year degree course taken by his Cambridge students: he simply wanted to ensure that in the short time available for their studies, they should read nothing but the greatest. Time's winged chariot – or at least the Board of Examiners – forbade wasting precious hours on minor novelists. Although driven by the best of motives as a teacher, Leavis was guilty of a certain professional blindness in assuming that the reading of literature is an activity that one cannot continue after leaving university.

In its fully extended form, which of course includes drama and poetry as well as novels, the canon of Leavis's more ecumenical followers is displayed in the seven volumes of Boris Ford's *Pelican Guide to English*

Literature. Here, even such questionable Victorian authors as Thackeray, Trollope, and Meredith are awarded their chapter or section in the volume *From Dickens to Hardy* (1958), although there is no chapter for Gaskell, Gissing, Stevenson, Christina Rossetti, Swinburne, or Wilde. In the earlier volumes, there is no substantial consideration of prose romances: Malory is out, as is Sidney, while Bunyan is in. Non-fiction prose writers, though (known to Leavis's Cambridge students as the 'English Moralists' – the title of a compulsory examination paper), are included throughout the series, from Bacon, Browne, and Hobbes to Addison, Johnson, Carlyle, and Ruskin; but Pepys, Boswell, Gibbon, De Quincey, Hazlitt, and Pater are overlooked, several of these being immoralists. The volume *From Dryden to Johnson* (1957) covers the novelists usually considered by previous standard histories, despite Leavis's own dismissal of several of them: Defoe, Swift, Richardson, Fielding, Smollett, even Sterne (a nasty trifler, we are told in *The Great Tradition*). The volume on the Romantic period, *From Blake to Byron* (1957), includes both Austen and Scott (but not Godwin, Radcliffe, Mary Shelley, Edgeworth, and Peacock) to represent prose fiction. Among the poets, it adds only Crabbe to the expected list of seven major names; Clare is passed over, as is Southey. Joyce, Woolf, and Auden are all fairly represented in the final volume, *The Modern Age* (1961), again despite Leavis's own antipathies; even Shaw has his place here, although the editors draw the line at the virtually unmentionable Bennett, Wells, and Huxley. Taken as a whole, this is by no means a fanatically curtailed canon, although it does tend to isolate eight or ten 'major' figures in each period from the larger pool of 'minor' writers. It represents a long-standing Leavisian compromise between Eliot's tradition of 'wit' and the provincial-puritan line of social protest (Langland-Bunyan-Crabbe-Lawrence), further relaxed by younger critics who admired the general principles of Leavis's approach without sharing his exact set of prejudices.

The perceived exclusivity of Leavis's own model of the canon was regretted by many objectors, on several grounds. George Steiner charged Leavis with provincialism, for turning his back on such European writers as Flaubert and Proust. Others noticed his increasingly severe verdicts on almost anything written after Lawrence's death in 1930. In particular, the younger critics who contributed to the early volumes of *Critical Quarterly* (founded 1959), while acknowledging Leavis's importance, were eager to distance themselves from his hostility to contemporary writing. Its editors, C. B. Cox and A. E. Dyson, encouraged a lively interest in the most recent literature, and published new poems by Larkin, Hughes, Plath, Gunn, Tomlinson, and others, alongside critical articles by Raymond Williams, David Holbrook, Bernard Bergonzi, and Malcolm Bradbury. Through its close relationship with schoolteachers, the *Critical Quarterly* did much to bring about the canonizing in Britain of such modern poets as Larkin, R. S. Thomas, and Ted Hughes. This result was further encouraged by A. Alvarez's landmark anthology *The New Poetry* (1962; revised 1966), which established Hughes, Gunn, and Sylvia Plath as fixtures in the classroom, and as successors to Larkin. It was through the classrooms of a new mass education system that some recent prose fictions also found themselves quite suddenly canonized. Two spectacular cases here were Orwell's *Animal Farm* (1945) and Golding's *Lord of the Flies* (1954), both of them conventionally short fables with obvious appeal to adolescents. It cannot be an accident that they both also offered fertile ground for basic indoctrination in the major ideological themes of the Cold War, seeming to prove that radical social change is futile because of the inherently aggressive and possessive characteristics of an unchanging 'human nature'. British schools bought these texts in thousands.

In the United States, where the polemics for and against Leavis tended to mean very little, the processes of canon-formation proceeded more quietly, with the canon of American literature built consensually on the foundations laid by Matthiessen. Thus the accepted major American authors since 1800 were Poe, Emerson, Hawthorne, Thoreau, Melville, Whitman, Dickinson, James, Twain, Crane, and Eliot, with the possible addition of Pound, Faulkner, Stevens, and Fitzgerald. Faulkner's reputation in particular was boosted by the award of the Nobel prize in 1950, after which numerous studies of his work appeared, chiefly from the academic presses.

The bigger disputes involved the English canons, of poetry and of fiction. Here, North American critics such as Frye, Abrams, Hartman, and Bloom were working to dislodge Eliot's canon, attempting to redeem Blake, Shelley, and indeed the longer Protestant-Romantic line of poets since Spenser and Milton. Critics in Britain, meanwhile, concentrated on defending the tradition of realist fiction against its various modernist detractors: there were numerous defences of Dickens and George Eliot, and, from Ian Watt, an account of Defoe and Fielding to set against Leavis's dismissals. Meanwhile, Raymond Williams's *Culture and Society* is devoted almost entirely to 'minor' and indeed non-literary figures, paying close attention to precisely those lesser Victorian novelists that Leavis had invited us to forget: Gaskell, Kingsley, Mallock, and Gissing. Northrop Frye's value-free system had in principle done away with canons of major and minor authors; but Williams's project of cultural history (by no means value-free) was beginning to look beyond the 'great' figures in practice.

The Babel of Interpretations

By comparison with the inter-war years of critical revolution, which enjoyed a certain freedom of improvisation in the development of new critical arguments, the Cold War decades in literary criticism were marked by a more cautious, reflective, and self-conscious spirit. This was a period of metacritical retrospection and of carefully ruminated theory. As Graham Hough noted, with some regret, in his *Image and Experience* (1960), 'About forty years ago it was possible to be deeply engaged with literature, as a writer or a student, yet to be entirely innocent of any concern with literary theory. This is hardly possible now.'[39] Although the loss of such innocence can be traced back – as Hough himself traces it – to the days of Hulme and Pound, its full consequences came to be felt only after the first phase of the New Criticism; that is, in the late 1940s. Between the wars, for instance, there had been no substantial work of critical history, and Saintsbury was the last important authority. In the 1950s, though, we have Wimsatt's and Brooks's *Literary Criticism: A Short History* (1957), the first two volumes of René Wellek's enormous *History of Modern Criticism 1750–1950* (1955), and M. H. Abrams's *The Mirror and the Lamp* (1953). The Chicago critics in these years published their collaborative investigations into literary theory since Aristotle in *Critics and Criticism, Ancient and Modern* (1952), followed by R. S. Crane's metacritical work *The Languages of Criticism and the Structure of Poetry* (1953). Northrop Frye's major work, *Anatomy of Criticism* (1957) is an extended metacritical polemic and theoretical treatise involving, as its title implies, a classification of the possible kinds of critical thought. Leaving aside such substantial theoretical works as Wimsatt's *The Verbal Icon* (1954) or Wellek's and Warren's *Theory of Literature* (1949), one can point also to a number of books dealing with the problems of twentieth-century criticism itself: Stanley Edgar Hyman's *The Armed Vision* (1948), Murray Kreiger's *The New Apologists for Poetry* (1956), Graham Hough's *Image and Experience*, and John Casey's *The Language of Criticism* (1966). It should be noticed that all of these works were written by university teachers, awareness of literary theory and its history having become something of a professional requirement, at least in the United States.

The general incorporation of criticism into the academy brought with it a professional code of pluralism, according to which critics of different schools and persuasions were to be understood as contributing, each in their different way, a particular kind of insight to the total body of literary understanding and appreciation. No single critic or school, it was accepted, could decently claim to have the uniquely true approach to literature, and thus no unseemly warfare (or even discussion) need break out between competing schools, if each agreed not to challenge the claims of the others. The protocols of peaceful co-existence, or of what Gerald Graff has since called this 'guild mentality' of modern academic criticism[40] were spelt out by R. S. Crane in the Chicago manifestos of the early 1950s, and in somewhat different terms by Northrop Frye in *Anatomy of Criticism* and by Wellek and Warren in *Theory of Literature*. To an anti-academic modernist like Ezra Pound, such an arrangement would have seemed preposterous, if not downright corrupt, but in the literature departments of the universities, it settled in as a way of getting by. The first result of professional pluralism was the overproduction of interpretations or 'readings' (a newly favoured term at this time) of literary texts, unchecked by common norms of credibility. The monuments to this phase of educational boom are the critical 'casebooks' which flourished in the 1960s. Whether in the Macmillan Casebook series published in London, or in Prentice-Hall's Twentieth Century Views series from New Jersey, the volume devoted to any given author or text could be relied upon to reprint critical essays from several mutually incompatible positions (a myth critic, a historicist, a biographer, a Freudian, a formalist, a Catholic existentialist, and so forth), displaying the wondrous variety of the critical spectrum. To sceptical eyes, it looked more like a 'Babel of Interpretations', as E. D. Hirsch called it.[41]

Hirsch, in his work of hermeneutic theory, *Validity in Interpretation* (1967), challenged what he saw as a now widespread agnosticism about the determinable meaning of any text, fostered by the prestige of T. S. Eliot's model of impersonality, by misreadings of the Beardsley and Wimsatt article on 'The Intentional Fallacy', and by the distinct modern current of historical relativism. Unpicking the issues with great care, he exposed a number of elementary confusions about the author's relation to his or her text, although not without generating further difficulties in trying to explain how an author's meaning might be recovered. His attempt to reinstate an 'intentionalist' position, in which the 'author's meaning' is the true goal of interpretation, hinges upon a central distinction between the original *meaning* intended by the author, and the *significance(s)* that the text may subsequently acquire: the meaning is constant, but significances may change with each reading. Hirsch does not claim that we can achieve certainty about the author's meaning, but insists that we should aim to reach agreement about the most probable intention, at least in terms of the basic conventions within which the author was working. Otherwise, as he warns, we are afloat upon the seas of indeterminacy.

This was one way of dealing with the proliferation of interpretations: trying to reduce it to a smaller set of plausible versions, tied to a fixed centre of meaning. Another course taken in the 1960s was that of abandoning interpretation altogether. This position, adopted by Susan Sontag in the title essay of her wide-ranging collection *Against Interpretation* (1966), represents both a radical departure from current academic practice

and at the same time a return to the high formalist orthodoxy of
Eliot, and indeed of Oscar Wilde. Representing the contemporary urge
to interpret as the intellect's vengeful assault upon art, Sontag condemns
the misguided search for a 'content' behind the surface appearances of
an artistic work, and calls for a new kind of commentary directed at its
formal and sensory dimensions – an 'erotics of art' rather than a hermen-
eutics, as she puts it, anticipating Roland Barthes's later formulations of
textual pleasure.[42] Expanding upon this position in her essay, 'On Style',
she maintains that a work of art is not a statement so much as an
experience, and one that can enhance our capacity for moral choice
without itself advocating a moral position. In the final essay of *Against
Interpretation*, 'One Culture and the New Sensibility', Sontag suggests that
the cultural formation in which literature was once central is becoming
obsolete, overtaken by the rising importance of 'contentless' arts such as
cinema, music, and architecture. Commentary on the 'content' of literary
works, or development of their ideas – so important to such a critic as
Lionel Trilling, for instance – is now redundant, as 'high' and 'low'
cultures blend together and the long reign of Matthew Arnold draws to
a close. Sontag's fleeting but prescient encounter with literary-critical
issues in the 1960s heralds the arrival of postmodernist themes in later
years.

Sontag was the youngest, and Trilling the oldest, of an important
cohort of post-war critics from Jewish backgrounds. This new presence
of Jewish intellectuals at the centre of literary-critical debates is one of
the distinctive developments of the period in terms of the personnel
of criticism; the other, more obvious trends being the increasing predominance of academic critics over public or journalistic kinds, and the number
of professional interpreters supported by the large American university
system compared with the state of affairs in Britain or its former colonies.
The hegemony of Christian critics, led by T. S. Eliot, began to slacken
in this period, although it was still possible for Wimsatt and Brooks in
their *Literary Criticism* to conclude, in the tones of a medieval bishop,
that the most plausible kind of literary theory would need to be in accord
with the dogma of the Incarnation rather than with the Gnostic or
Manichaean heresies.[43] Wimsatt, a Roman Catholic, also concludes *The
Verbal Icon* with an essay on 'Poetry and Christianity' that identifies the
defence of poetry with the defence of religion.[44] Carefully avoiding any
doctrinal dispute with such churchmen, the freethinking Jews against
whom Eliot had warned the world in the 1930s nonetheless took up
their eminent places in the world of criticism: Trilling was there at
Columbia, M. H. Abrams at Cornell, Harold Bloom at Yale, Geoffrey
Hartman at Yale and Cornell, Leslie Fiedler at Montana, George Steiner
at Princeton and the less hospitable Cambridge, England, Richard
Ellmann at Northwestern, Harry Levin at Harvard; Susan Sontag was a
freelance teacher and writer in New York. In such company, the presump-

tion of universal assent to the doctrines of Christianity, so often made in critical writing during the New Critics' heyday, could no longer be made in the 1960s or after.

A more spectacular affront to the position of Christian criticism came from a gentile atheist, William Empson. Returning to England in 1953 after a long stint in China, Empson claimed to notice a new impudence among Christian ideologues, who were now openly boasting of their creed's sadism. His irritation at what he called the 'neo-Christian' movement in literary criticism – including such figures as C. S. Lewis and Hugh Kenner – led to the writing of *Milton's God* (1961), which is both an interpretation of *Paradise Lost* and an extended diatribe against Christianity, 'the most insinuating of all organized evils'.[45] Noticing the discomfort with which Christian critics approach the action of *Paradise Lost*, Empson takes the side of Shelley in pointing out that 'the reason why the poem is so good is that it makes God so bad'.[46] This is a poorly organized and rambling, but nevertheless a shocking work, whose bluntness exposes the prior consensus by which Leavis, for example, refers to Christianity in Milton's work as if – Empson notices – it were merely a neutral topic. Empson violated an important taboo here, indicating again that in the debates of the 1960s, the floodgates of some kind of anarchy were creaking open.

Notes

1. George Steiner, *Language and Silence* (1967; abridged edn, Harmondsworth, 1969), pp. 22–4, 83–4.
2. Malcolm Bradbury, 'Introduction: The State of Criticism Today', in M. Bradbury and D. Palmer (eds), *Contemporary Criticism* (1970), p. 24.
3. Graham Hough, *Image and Experience* (1960), p. 45.
4. Bradbury (op. cit., pp. 30–5) also comments on this process.
5. René Wellek and Austin Warren, *Theory of Literature* (1949; 3rd edn, Harmondsworth, 1963), p. 19.
6 Wellek and Warren, *Theory of Literature*, p. 141.
7. W. K. Wimsatt, *The Verbal Icon: Studies in the Meaning of Poetry* (Lexington, KY, 1954; London, 1970), p. 82.
8. Cleanth Brooks, *The Well Wrought Urn* (New York, 1947), p. 74.
9. R. P. Blackmur, *The Lion and the Honeycomb* (New York, 1955), p. 198.
10. F. R. Leavis, *The Common Pursuit* (1952; Harmondsworth, 1962), pp. 233, 238.
11. Leavis, *Common Pursuit*, p. 87.
12. F. R. Leavis, *D. H. Lawrence, Novelist* (1955; Harmondsworth, 1964), pp. 81, 377.
13. F. R. Leavis, *'Anna Karenina' and Other Essays* (1967), p. 179.
14. Lionel Trilling, *The Liberal Imagination: Essays on Literature and Society* (New York, 1950; London, 1961), pp. 289, 290. This point about rationality and syntax was

soon to be taken up by the British critics Donald Davie, Frank Kermode, and Graham Hough in their re-assessments of the Symbolist tradition.

15. Trilling, *Liberal Imagination*, pp. 183, 184.
16. Trilling, *Liberal Imagination*, p. 11.
17. Trilling, *Liberal Imagination*, p. 53.
18. Philip Rahv, *Literature and the Sixth Sense* (Boston, 1969; London, 1970), p. 250.
19. R. S. Crane, Introduction to *Critics and Criticism, Ancient and Modern* (Chicago, 1952), p. 15.
20. Northrop Frye, *Fearful Symmetry: A Study of William Blake* (Princeton, NJ, 1947), p. 11.
21. Northrop Frye, *Anatomy of Criticism* (Princeton, NJ, 1957), pp. 118, 55.
22. Frye, *Anatomy of Criticism*, p. 97.
23. Frye, *Anatomy of Criticism*, p. 215.
24. Donald Davie, *Purity of Diction in English Verse; and Articulate Energy* (Harmondsworth, 1992), p. 86.
25. Hough, *Image and Experience*, p. 26.
26. Frank Kermode, *Romantic Image* (1957; 1971), p. 176.
27. Frank Kermode, *The Sense of an Ending: Studies in the Theory of Fiction* (New York, 1967), p. 31.
28. G. Wilson Knight, *The Mutual Flame* (1955), p. 34.
29. Northrop Frye, *A Natural Perspective: The Development of Shakespearean Comedy and Romance* (New York, 1965), p. 111.
30. Frye, *Natural Perspective*, pp. 62–3.
31. F. R. Leavis, *The Great Tradition* (1948; Harmondsworth, 1972), p. 41.
32. Dorothy Van Ghent, *The English Novel: Form and Function* (1953; New York, 1967), p. 139.
33. Van Ghent, *English Novel*, pp. 48–9.
34. Trilling, *Liberal Imagination*, p. 222.
35. Trilling, *Liberal Imagination*, p. 217.
36. John Bayley, *The Characters of Love: A Study in the Literature of Personality* (1960), p. 266.
37. Bayley, *Characters of Love*, p. 273.
38. Frederick C. Crews, *The Pooh Perplex: A Freshman Casebook* (New York, 1963), p. 101. The quoted phrase is a chapter heading from Crews's burlesque of modern critical schools; here, 'Dr Simon Lacerous' manages to reduce the number of great English novelists to just one: D. H. Lawrence.
39. Hough, *Image and Experience*, p. 28.
40. Gerald Graff, *Professing Literature: An Institutional History* (Chicago, 1987), p. 228.
41. E. D. Hirsch, Jr, *Validity in Interpretation* (New Haven, CT, 1967), p. 127.
42. Susan Sontag, *Against Interpretation* (New York, 1964), p. 14.
43. William K. Wimsatt, Jr, and Cleanth Brooks, *Literary Criticism: A Short History* (New York, 1957), p. 746.
44. Wimsatt, *Verbal Icon*, p. 276.
45. William Empson, *Milton's God* (1961), p. 253.
46. Empson, *Milton's God*, p. 13.

Chapter 5
Literary Theory and Textual Politics: Since 1968

'Theory' and the Critical Agenda

After the turmoil of the year 1968, criticism, along with much else in Western intellectual life, became caught up in conflicts over the politics of culture, of cultural institutions, and of language. From the Parisian epicentre of student revolt, new theoretical vocabularies passed suddenly into the hitherto insulated world of Anglophone literary debate. Criticism, in its then usual senses of appreciation and evaluation of poems, plays, or novels, was quickly overwhelmed by the growth of what became known simply as 'Theory'. This entity, regarded in some quarters as a sinister invasion force, was a variegated cargo of literary and linguistic theories of continental European origin, underpinned by larger intellectual systems such as Marxism, psychoanalysis, and post-Nietzschean philosophy, all given a new edge by contemporary radical movements ranging from feminism and gay liberationism to civil libertarianism and anti-imperialism. Clearly the most spectacular changes in literary criticism and associated discourses were those consequent upon the relatively abrupt arrival in the English-speaking world of 'Theory' in this complex form. It should not be assumed, though, that literary theory burst suddenly into existence in the late 1960s. On the contrary, it is at least as old as Aristotle, and enjoyed an important resurgence in North America in the 1940s and 50s, in the work of the New Critics, of Frye, and of the Chicago school. Nor can one pretend that criticism suddenly became 'politicized' in this period: it had always had significant political implications, even if these had been taken for granted in the largely conservative consensus of early twentieth-century criticism. The new – and, for many, disorienting – factor was the conjunction of numerous unfamiliar literary and cultural theories with a widespread insurgence against the traditional forms of cultural authority, including those of the academy in which criticism had become institutionalized. Arcane linguistic theories of signification mixed with gut politics of anti-authoritarian suspicion to condemn existing methods of literary study as 'naïve' in their blindness to ideological implications. The arrival of 'Theory', then, presented itself as a loss of innocence in which the empiricist habits of thought prevalent in Anglo-Saxon culture were torn aside in order to expose the complicity of traditional humanistic study with oppressive ideologies and dominant systems of power. In the period of protest against the Vietnam War and of numerous bloody clashes between students and police in various parts of the world, and in the disillusionment of the Watergate scandal, the liberal-democratic state forfeited its benign appearance and came to be regarded by younger intellectuals especially as a thinly-veiled dictator-ship, of which the educational system was merely one more arm, despite its vaunted idealism and independence.

Such, at least, was the common view of the 'children of '68', whose political perspectives tended strongly towards 'ultra-leftism', that is to say, the simple equation of liberal democracy with Fascism, of education with propaganda. Literary critics were, however, by no means suddenly converted wholesale to such notions, which filtered up through the lower ranks of the academy in the 1970s. The initial encounters between Anglophone critics and continental theory were a good deal more tenta-tive, deriving from a sense of the exhaustion of such established traditions as New Criticism, and a curiosity about the large intellectual claims of – in the first place – French structuralism. As interest in these continental systems grew apace, it appeared that literary criticism, whose autonomy had been so fiercely defended by the New Critics and Leavisites, was now being swallowed up by the larger intellectual domain of the 'human sciences': anthropology, sociology, psychology, linguistics, political theory, history, and philosophy. To the horror of those for whom literary criticism was a unique and distinctively 'central' activity, literature seemed now to have been stripped of its privileges, colonized by essentially unsympathetic powers, and subjected to interrogation in strange tongues.

'Theory' was never an internally harmonious movement, incorporating as it did a number of mutually antagonistic positions. Nevertheless, the various tributaries of what in the 1970s appeared to be a common cause shared an agenda and a set of central preoccupations. Three of its leading items should be introduced here: the primacy of Language, the dethrone-ment of the 'subject', and the dissolution of 'unity'.

One of the more significant conclusions drawn by French intellectuals from the defeat of the 1968 general strike and accompanying student revolt was that the greatest power lay not in some external institution like the riot police or the legislature but in language itself – hence its honorific capitalization as Language. For the psychoanalyst Jacques Lacan, it was our entry as infants into the 'Symbolic Order' of Language that formed our entire psyche, while for the historian Michel Foucault, Power was Language and Language was Power, locked together in those authoritative 'discourses' that permitted us to speak and think only in certain recognized ways. We were all trapped in the cramped cells of the pronoun system, condemned by Language to act the part of an 'I' or a 'You', all unwittingly controlled and policed by our own tongues. It was not we who used and spoke the language, but Language which used and spoke us. And Language was not an innocent or neutral medium, but saturated with oppressive authority, classifying, labelling and defining the human beings who imagined they were its masters. Perhaps more importantly in the context of literary criticism, the meaning of a text was not something found through and beyond Language, but something produced entirely *by* Language. In the structuralist tradition inaugurated by the Swiss linguist Ferdinand de Saussure in his *Cours de linguistique générale* (1916), Language is disconnected from the things outside of itself that it talks about (its 'referents'), and considered purely as a system of distinctions between and among its own elements ('signs'). Accordingly, Language can no longer be regarded as a window through which an external reality can be perceived; rather, it is the very means by which that 'reality' itself is *constructed*. Hence its vital political importance: if reality is to be changed, it can only be by some unimaginable remaking of Language, some reversing of the signs. If Language is the realm of differentiation, nothing can come into being except by its blessing. And it is important to note that the 'Language' invoked in this intellectual tradition is not anything so messy as an actual tongue like Swahili or Welsh, but rather a pure principle of differentiation as such, a generalization of Saussure's claim that Language is a system of differences. This is why the literary-critical consequences took the form, not of directly linguistic analysis of texts, as in stylistics for example, but of continuing assaults upon the principle of mimesis or the imitation of life in literature. The principal issue was whether literature 'reflected' a pre-existing reality outside it, or whether it 'constructed' a new reality. The advocates of 'Theory' insisted upon the linguistic construction of reality, and implied that the aesthetic theory and practice of realism in literature was inherently reactionary. In this new discourse, 'reality' appeared to have been swallowed up entirely by Language, and literature by 'textuality': if literary works were to be seen as referring to anything at all, it must be to Language and the work's own linguistic status. Texts fed upon themselves or upon other texts, and thus all writing was a kind of rewriting, whether as parody, as pastiche, as revision, as antiphony, or as allusion.

If everything is constructed in Language, then the chief victim of this revelation is the individual, as author of his or her own destiny and creator of meanings. For most of the advocates of the new 'Theory', the received idea of the autonomous human individual was a fantasy projected by liberal bourgeois ideology, rather casually labelled 'humanism' by its radical challengers. Marx and Freud had already undermined this mythic hero by showing how his 'free' actions were in fact determined by forces beyond his control or even knowledge. Now the rediscovery of Saussure's linguistic principles added the determining power of Language to those of material production and the Unconscious: we are free to speak, but only what Language permits. 'Man' in the optimistic humanist sense, was dead, replaced by the rather wretched creature referred to as 'the subject'. The point of this punning title was to emphasize the illusion of individual self-determination as a linguistic/political mirage: the 'subject' is merely an empty grammatical category (the subject of a sentence, such as an 'I') which we may occupy without recognizing that it *subjects* us to the higher laws of Language and culture. Thus our subjectivity is an effect of Language, combining apparent sovereignty with real servitude, and allowing us to take up only those roles or 'subject-positions' that are already ordained for us by the linguistic and cultural system into which we are 'inscribed'. The theoretical principle that sanctioned the demotion of the humanist individual to the sorry condition of subjecthood was Saussure's assertion of the primacy of linguistic system (*langue*) over linguistic event (*parole*): any individual utterance or *parole* relies on a prior system of distinctions and rules if it is to have any meaning at all, and thus stands as an instance of the system, not as a freely invented expression. According to the same logic, the supposedly sovereign individual is in fact little more than the ventriloquist's dummy of a Language that is always in place before he is. In literary-critical terms, such arguments were directed against the myth of the Author as the validating source of the text's meanings, most famously in Roland Barthes' essay in 1968, 'The Death of the Author'. As Barthes declared there, if the author is dethroned from his godlike position as guarantor of stable meanings, then the consequence should be the liberation of the reader.

In the older modernist scheme, the key to literary art was the rendering of 'consciousness', and the health or integrity of the author's own consciousness would find its counterpart in the underlying unity of the work of art. The modernist principle of impersonality may have discouraged the exhibition of idiosyncratic opinion and certain kinds of overt self-regard, as it simultaneously debarred biographical inquisitiveness on the part of the critic; but it did so all the better to test the author's primary qualities of perception, sensitivity, and equilibrium. If the author's sensibility were strong enough to overcome (in I. A. Richards's terms) the chaos of conflicting impulses and impressions, then human consciousness would assert its ability to impose order upon the world, here in the shape of an organically unified work of art. As both Henry James and F. R. Leavis believed, the author's quality of mind is reflected in the quality of the literary work: to speak of the maturity or integrity of one is to commend the other. But once we deny the sovereignty of consciousness, surrendering its powers to Language, then, just as surely as the individual gives way to the 'subject', so Literature gives way to 'writing' (*écriture*), and the artistic 'work', considered as the product of an integral mind, must give way to the *text*, that is, to a web of signs with no organizing centre. At the end of this chain of iconoclasms lies the destruction of one of the most sacred principles of modern criticism and aesthetics: the organic unity of the art-work. The most striking feature of literary-critical discourse under the new reign of Theory since the 1960s, indeed, has been the complete reversal of critical arguments and values on the question of unity. In previous decades, it had been the purpose of count-less critical essays to vindicate the unity of an apparently self-divided or disorganized work – to show that all its loose ends or digressions actually served to reinforce its central theme, for example. Now that aesthetic unity was to be interpreted suspiciously as an ideological projection of the repressive conformity required by the modern corporate state, it became, for many critics, a political duty to demonstrate the exact opposite: that the apparently unified text was really riven with irreconcil-able self-contradictions and fundamental instabilities. The pious jargon of formal harmony employed by the old schools (integration, poise, organic wholeness) was abruptly abandoned in favour of a grimly violent new set of metaphors suited more to the military hospital than to the library. Literary form was now to be spoken of in terms of deformity and internal breakage, and poems were to be 'interrogated' so as to reveal their wounds, mutilations, amputations, scars, lesions, sutures, punctures, fis-sures, fractures, and ruptures. And as the figurative 'body' of the text was cut up, so was its 'voice', which now became a pandemonium of contend-ing cries: as the new vocabularies had it, the text was to be seen as polyvalent, multivocal, polyphonic, dialogic, multi-accentual, and prefer-ably convulsed in schizophrenic babble.

The drastic reversal of perspective in which unity was eclipsed by its opposites was both a genuine correction of previous blindnesses and at the same time a knee-jerk reflex inversion of values, justified on indiscriminate 'political' grounds that owed more to sentimentality than to political clarity. The partisans of 'Theory', whether neo-Marxist, psychoanalytic-feminist, or post-structuralist, exposed previously occluded or ignored dimensions of internal conflict and impasse in literary texts, often in a lively and refreshing manner. They also tended to encourage an easy equation between cultural and political radicalisms, contrasting the 'closed' literary text of the nineteenth century, say, with the 'open' work of twentieth-century modernism, as if the difference between them was the same as that between despotism and democracy. Theorists of the New Left and of the emerging social movements such as feminism in the 1970s, less interested in social and economic transformation than in 'demystifying' the dominant ideological representations, looked back to the European modernist avant-garde for a model of cultural subversion. Drawing upon a theoretical tradition that included the writings of the Russian Formalist group around Victor Shklovsky, those of Bertolt Brecht, the tradition of the Frankfurt School of Marxism, and the more recent work of Roland Barthes in his book *S/Z* (1970), they learned to look upon everyday experience and language as a treadmill of 'automatized' habit and ideological complacency from which we needed to be jolted by the artist's shock-tactics. Literary works that seemed to offer a coherent imitation of life and a cast of credible characters with whom the reader might sympathize were to be deemed regressive, regardless of their ostensible political tendency, while works that resisted habitual modes of understanding by deforming language and narrative structure drastically were to be honoured as revolutionary texts. According to this kind of politicized formalism, Zola's *Germinal* or Stowe's *Uncle Tom's Cabin* might be condemned as (in Barthes' terms) 'readerly' texts with pre-established 'closed' meanings which the reader gulped down in docile passivity, while Pound's *Cantos* or Joyce's *Finnegans Wake* could be commended as 'writerly' works that challenged the reader to participate in creating their 'open' range of meanings. According to the simplest versions of this antinomy, realism, or even the notion of reference to a reality outside language, is all constraint and fixity, modernism and its successor, 'postmodernism', are all liberation and fluidity. As early as 1979, Gerald Graff was noticing how this 'premature politicization of terms' resembled a moralistic melodrama in which Good (fictive openness) battled against Evil (mimetic closure).[1]

Not all of the critical positions inspired by the political insurgence of 1968 and after were tied in this way to a modernist tradition of formalist linguistic radicalism. There remained a body of Marxist criticism, informed by Georg Lukács and Raymond Williams, for which literary realism still had positive value and modernism had a dubious political record. A similar respect for realist traditions can be found in much American and British feminist criticism, in which *Uncle Tom's Cabin* is – with whatever reservations – generally regarded as a more liberating work than Pound's *Cantos*, and literary texts are commonly seen as referring to realities of social injustice rather than to their own fictiveness. Even so, it is noticeable that these positions usually retain the assumption that literary works are valuable to the extent that they 'subvert' the dominant ideology or 'transgress' some restrictive boundary imposed by it. The melodrama (if it is that) of toppled ogres and of barriers endlessly broken seems stubbornly persistent. Critical and theoretical debate since 1968 has involved several ferocious contests, between formalist and historicist camps, and on many other fronts; but the old humanist doctrine that the best literature is – and should be – liberating has commanded remarkably broad assent.

Textualities: Structuralism and Beyond

Although there were signs of some attention in the 1960s to linguistic and anthropological theories of the kind known as 'structuralist' – notably the holding of a conference on structuralism at Johns Hopkins University in 1966 – it was in the 1970s that the appeal of 'structural analysis' asserted itself so far as to impinge upon literary-critical debate in the English-speaking world. This despite the fact that in France, the structuralist 'moment' had already passed by the late 1960s. The most obvious indication that a powerful but unfamiliar school of thought had arrived was the appearance of numerous guides, synopses, and introductory works on structuralism, many of them directed towards those engaged in literary study: Robert Scholes's *Structuralism in Literature: An Introduction* (1974), Jonathan Culler's *Saussure* (1976), and Terence Hawkes's *Structuralism and Semiotics* (1977) were widely-consulted beginners' guides, while the more substantial critical engagements with – and adaptations of – the new movement included Fredric Jameson's *The Prison-House of Language* (1972), David Lodge's *The Modes of Modern Writing* (1977) and Jonathan Culler's *Structuralist Poetics* (1975). These accompanied a wave of translations and reprints which put into circulation the writings of Saussure, Lévi-Strauss, Jakobson, Barthes, Todorov, and Genette, along with those of their long-forgotten precursors, the Russian Formalist group of Shklovsky, Eikhenbaum, and Tynianov.

The radical shift of focus encouraged by such works was a redirection of attention from the properties of individual works or authors to the underlying 'codes' governing literary (and other) works in general: what mattered now was not so much what a novel or poem might mean, but *how* it produced its meanings, or how readers produced meanings from it. As Jonathan Culler insisted in *Structuralist Poetics* and later works, the Anglo-American assumption that the goal of criticism was the production of improved interpretations of individual works should now be abandoned in favour of a new programme of investigation whose purpose would instead be to make explicit the implicit workings of the linguistic and literary conventions upon which the effects that we call 'literature' depend. Culler draws upon Noam Chomsky's concept of linguistic 'competence' or implicit awareness of rules, extending it into the idea of 'literary competence', or the ability of readers to recognize literary works and to assimilate them appropriately. As structuralism's founder, Ferdinand de Saussure had redirected linguistic study away from the individual utterance (*parole*) to the rules of the language as a whole (*langue*), so Culler hopes to move literary discussion away from criticism towards poetics, by which he means the study of the conventions and expectations operating in the way that we read texts – how we expect (and usually therefore produce) significance, coherence, and binary thematic oppositions in a literary work. A somewhat similar kind of reorientation, away from critical interpretation and towards the 'scientific' study of conventions, had been proposed before by Northrop Frye, whom Culler acknowledges; but there is still a substantial difference between Frye's construction of a universal taxonomy of genres and Culler's structuralist investigation into the operations of what he calls 'naturalization' performed by readers as they make sense of texts. Culler does not, as Frye effectively does, banish interpretation entirely; he merely subordinates it to poetics, thus making it 'an account of the ways in which the work complies with or undermines our procedures for making sense of things.' *Structuralist Poetics* is partly a critical survey of the European tradition of structuralist thinking on language and literature, but it doubles up as a kind of manifesto of renewal showing a way out of the repetitive dead-end of Anglo-American interpretative criticism, which Culler claims can no longer justify itself.

Culler's work represents the most important assimilation or, in his own terms, 'naturalization' of European structuralist principles into Anglo-American literary study at the level of more or less pure theory. Its most impressive counterpart in the field of applied textual analysis is David Lodge's work, particularly in *The Modes of Modern Writing*, but also in some of the essays found in *Working With Structuralism* (1981). Lodge's adaptation of structuralism is much more recognizably in the English tradition of 'close reading', and it expects theories of literature to be not just interesting in themselves but beneficial in 'practical' elucidation of texts. Lodge also has a more orthodox structuralist confidence in our ability to describe the objective characteristics of texts, whereas Culler (along with Stanley Fish and other theorists) abandons this project in favour of an account of operations performed by readers, so that there is no common feature of literary texts except that they happen to have been read according to literary reading-conventions such as fictionality, formal unity, and so forth. For Lodge, this reader-centred argument is one-sided, as it ignores the fact that most works of literature have been composed intentionally so as to oblige us to read them according to literary codes; their literary status, that is, has not been the result of readers' arbitrary whim.[3] Lodge and Culler are more closely aligned, however, in their healthy critical attitude to the structuralist tradition and its fruits: neither is willing to accept the implication found in 'high' French structuralism that the fundamental (and timeless) laws of human consciousness have at last been laid bare to the inspection of Science; and Lodge in particular is unwilling to accept the extreme anti-realist position of such structuralist and post-structuralist theorists as Roland Barthes. As Lodge observes truly, 'What is provocative overstatement in Barthes is apt to become intolerant dogma in his epigones'.[4] The dogmas of second-hand structuralist theory as they emerged in Britain and America in the 1970s tended to define literary realism as either (i) politically and morally wicked at any time; or (ii) excusable at one time, but now historically outdated, as a relic of nineteenth-century ideology with no purpose in the modern world. The valuable critical independence of Lodge's work derives from his conviction (not just as a reader but as a practising novelist) that realist devices have a valuable place in modern writing. Much of his writing, indeed, is an attempt to make peace between the modernist/

symbolist and the realist camps in modern literature, and to formulate the differences between them in terms more reliable than those of denunciation and anathema.

In *The Modes of Modern Writing*, Lodge adapts and develops for these purposes a distinction proposed in 1956 by the Russian Formalist linguist Roman Jakobson, who had classified two types of speech defect ('aphasia') according to the 'axis' of language that seemed to be blocked in each case. The 'horizontal' or syntagmatic axis of combination by which words (or other linguistic units) are joined into sentences is contrasted with the 'vertical' or paradigmatic axis of selection by which words may be substituted for one another (as synonyms or antonyms, for example) to occupy particular functional positions in a sentence. Thus an impairment of the first kind of association leads to a reliance upon the second, and vice versa: one kind of aphasia will result in inability to construct sequences, the other in an inability to substitute elements of the sequence one for the other. Jakobson also pointed to the resemblance between this distinction of aphasias and that between the rhetorical figures of metaphor (association by resemblance, along the 'vertical' axis) and metonymy (association by context, along the 'horizontal' axis), suggesting that entire literary forms and movements might be understood in these terms, poetry or Romanticism involving a bias towards metaphoric substitutions, while prose or realism emphasized metonymic connections based on context. *The Modes of Modern Writing* extends this kind of speculation to the tension between realist and symbolist principles in modern Anglophone literature, testing its usefulness in detailed examinations of texts by Joyce, Woolf, Lawrence, Auden, Orwell, Hemingway, Larkin, and others, showing how the reaction against high modernism in the 1930s and 40s manifested itself in a shift from the metaphoric mode to the metonymic. The opposition is by no means a simple *alternative*, but a matter of emphasis within a combination of two modes: in later writings, notably in the essay 'Analysis and Interpretation of the Realist Text' in *Working With Structuralism*, Lodge develops more sophisticated schemes for understanding the ways in which the two modes or figures work with or through one another.

Despite the note of caution sounded by Lodge and others on this point, the tendency of the more influential Cullerian version of structuralism was to reinforce a new theoretical emphasis on the importance of the reader as the active maker of meanings from textual data. Culler's argument – that literature could not be defined according to inherent properties of texts but only as the product of certain reading strategies – found support from another corner of the theoretical arena, in the body of work that came to be known as 'Reader-Response Criticism'. It is important to note that this is the name for a debate rather than for a distinct school, and that it embraces a spectrum of positions on the relative powers of text and reader: at the one end, the reader may be imagined as a submissive victim of the text, which takes over his or her mind like a parasite; at the other, s/he may be seen as the dominant partner in the process, using the text as a mirror in which to examine his or her own psyche. The swing of the pendulum in the United States in the 1970s was strongly towards the 'dominant' end of this spectrum, in such works as David Bleich's *Subjective Criticism* (1978), Norman Holland's *5 Readers Reading* and 'UNITY IDENTITY TEXT SELF' (both 1975). Holland's work is closer to experimental psychology – it reports on his work at the grandly-named Buffalo Center for the Psychological Study of the Arts – than to mainstream literary theory, and this betrays itself in the idiom of upbeat psychobabble in which it is couched ('. . . we can conceptualize sensing, knowing or remembering – indeed, the whole human mind – as a hierarchy of feedback networks, each set to a reference level from the loop above it.')[5] At its simplest, though, it puts forward the view that interpretation of a text will vary according to the person-ality-type of the reader, who will select and organize the details of the text so as to echo his or her 'identity-theme'. Thus (to resort to another vocabulary) if you are, say, a Pisces, your reading of *Hamlet* will differ in certain predictable ways from your neighbour's Sagittarian interpretation of the 'same' play. Apart from its narcissistic implications – the text as mirror, used to reaffirm our (stable, knowable) identities – a notable difficulty of this scheme is that it presupposes an ability to 'read' the personality-types of readers in a way that is not subject, in its turn, to the same subjective distortions.[6]

The liveliest figure in the reader-response debate has been Stanley Fish, whose second book, despite its apparently salacious title, *Surprised by Sin* (1967), comprises an account of the reader's expectations and hesitations in key passages of Milton's *Paradise Lost*. As Fish shows, the traps of Milton's syntax tempt the reader, like Eve and Adam, to 'fall' into error, thus replicating the central action of the poem in the reader's own experience of negotiating the text. For Fish, indeed, the meaning of a text *is* the experience of reading it, and so the analysis of the text resolves itself into a blow-by-blow description of the process by which the reader is 'surprised' by each successive word or punctuation mark. Fish insists, against the modernist tradition, that literature is experienced temporally as a series of shocks and adjustments rather than spatially as a single design. At this stage of his work, up to the mid-1970s, he assumes too that the reading experience, dictated by objective formal properties of the text, is essentially the same for all 'informed' readers of the same text, and that divergent readings arise only subsequently in the distorting language of critical evaluation. Some time before his 1976 essay 'Interpret-ing the *Variorum*', however, Fish seems to have undergone a Kantian conversion in which he abandoned the notion of an innocent reading experience. Now, it is not the text but the 'interpretive strategy' applied to it that counts in determining the reader's experience, because everything that is noticed in the text, right down to its grammar and punctuation, is made noticeable by the way in which we have been trained to read in our 'interpretive community'. Thus interpretation precedes and creates its objects. Against the influential work of the German reader-response theorist Wolfgang Iser, for whom any text is partly determinate and partly riddled with 'gaps' for the reader to fill in, Fish began to insist that every last element in the text is 'written' by the reader. His most startling illustration of this view is his account of an experiment in which he left a reading list comprising names of important stylisticians on a classroom blackboard, and told his next class, who had become familiar with the symbolic codes of seventeenth-century English religious poetry, that the list was a poem. Fish's students proceeded to discover in the 'poem' various layers of Christian typological meaning and a strong formal coherence, thus inadvertently demonstrating that, once armed with an interpretive scheme, they could 'write' a poem into existence.[7]

Fish's position might appear to threaten a potential babel of infinitely various interpretations. That prospect is precluded, though, by the fact that readers are creatures of the interpretive community in which they have been formed. It is a prominent irony of the reader-response debate that its implied promise of reader-liberation resulted in a series of deterministic models in which the reader's liberty of interpretation is constrained in advance either by her psychological constitution ('identity theme' in Holland' terminology) or by her education (learned 'competence' in Culler's scheme, 'interpretive strategy' in Fish's). Curiously, the possibility of breaking away from learned ways of reading and of discovering new or unorthodox strategies, seems to have been theorized away in this tradition. This may well be because the concept of 'the reader' has typically remained both unexamined and historically unspecified. On the other hand, numerous works of literary history since the 1970s, working in the somewhat distinct line of 'reception studies', have attempted to understand literary works in relation to specific readerships, reconstructing the changing expectations which condition the responses of successive generations, or of different subcultures at the same time.

Among the various fruits of European structuralism, the most startling, and for some observers the most dangerous new school of criticism in the 1970s was that of 'deconstruction'. This new trend took as one of its starting-points Saussure's principle of the arbitrariness of the linguistic sign, but it added a strong strain of philosophical scepticism derived from Nietzsche and Heidegger, with the result that the signifier was seen to run loose from the signified. In other words, texts could not be assigned a determinate meaning. One of the more alarming features of deconstruction was that it was not content to declare textual indeterminacy as a general principle, but insisted on conducting the most rigorous and exhaustive kinds of 'close reading' on particular texts in order to demonstrate it in practice. The close readings of the New Critics were shown to be not close enough, but inhibited by expectations of organic coherence. The deconstructionists – several of whom taught at Yale, a former stronghold of New Criticism – took the New Critics' ideas of ambiguity and irony at their word, and the word was shown to exceed any possibility of a single or stable 'meaning' in a text. They asserted 'the priority of language to meaning', in the words of Geoffrey Hartman's introduction to the collective Yale manifesto *Deconstruction and Criticism* (1979).[8] The point of criticism became, not to corral the text's various elements into a coherent meaning, but to demonstrate how the text *resists* meaning.

Deconstruction was imported into the United States in the late 1960s by the French philosopher Jacques Derrida, and established itself as an important force among teachers of literature at Johns Hopkins and Yale by the mid-1970s, later spreading to the declining British port cities of Southampton and Cardiff. As presented by Derrida, it undermined the scientific pretensions of high structuralism, exposing the covertly hierarchical nature of structuralism's binary oppositions (nature/culture, speech/writing, literature/criticism, male/female, etc.) and undermining them by showing the dependence of the privileged term upon its secondary term or 'supplement'. While struggling to formulate non-hierarchical oppositions, it tended in practice to privilege difference over identity, and absence over presence, showing that any apparently self-identical entity in fact differed from itself and was to some degree absent from itself. Where structuralism emphasized differences *between* things, deconstruction exposed differences *within* them, showing each term in a given opposition to be contaminated by the other. Derrida coupled the linguistic principle of differentiation with the logic of deferral, showing how each signifier refers us not directly to a signified but to another signifier and then another, along a potentially endless 'chain of signification' (as when one looks up a word in a dictionary, only to be given another word, and so on *ad infinitum*), which could never, in principle, lead us beyond the instabilities or 'play' of language or textuality to some stable guarantor of meanings. There is, as Derrida famously expressed it, nothing outside the text – which means not that nothing exists outside of books, but that language cannot take us outside itself. Nor can we ever reach, except in fantasy, a paradise of 'plenitude' or full presence in which sign and meaning could fully coincide. It follows that no 'metalanguage' such as philosophy, linguistics, or criticism can itself pretend to stand authoritatively above the indeterminacies of language.

It is a curious feature of modern intellectual history that these arguments found their most willing audience in America among critics and literary historians specializing in Romantic and post-Romantic poetry: to begin with, the so-called Yale school of Paul de Man, Geoffrey Hartman, J. Hillis Miller, and Harold Bloom. Romanticism thus became the favoured playground of American deconstruction, illustrating both a profound nostalgia for self-identical presence or for the fusion of subject and object, and an exemplary recognition – ironic or elegiac – of its impossibility. One of the tasks of the deconstructionist school was to make war upon the strong tradition of 'piety' in Romantic studies, in which the Romantics' desire for a reconciliation between mind and Nature, or for 'transcendence', had commonly been celebrated as if it had been fulfilled triumphantly. For de Man and his colleagues, though, the chief value of Romantic poetry lay, on the contrary, in its clear-sighted confession of failure and irreparable loss. The Yale critics' assimilation of Derrida to some degree protects imaginative writers from becoming victims of deconstructive subversion, because it finds that they have already deconstructed themselves, openly confessing their self-contradictions. As de Man declared in his first major work, *Blindness and Insight* (1971), literature is founded upon the awareness of the non-coincidence of sign and meaning: 'it is the only form of language free from the fallacy of unmediated expression.'[9] Setting aside much of the philosophical vocabulary of Derrida's own work, the Yale deconstructors adapted it in part for the purpose of defending literature's claims to superior, disillusioned insight. Other discourses – political, historical, or philosophical – might delude themselves that they had some reliable hold upon reality or truth, but literature at least knew, and owned up honestly, that its statements were figurative and fictional. From some quarters, de Man came under attack on this point, for re-instating the cult of canonized literature; but in principle at least, 'literature' in de Man's usage refers not just to authorized poems and plays but to any use of language that signals its own indeterminacy.

Deconstructive criticism proceeds not directly from Derrida so much as from the principle announced by his forerunner, Friedrich Nietzsche, that all language is fundamentally figurative or rhetorical. It is often assumed, both by over-zealous followers and by antagonists, that this means negating the mimetic and referential functions of language, although in fact all the leading deconstructors have explicitly affirmed that the referential is an ineradicable dimension of language and literature. It seems, though, that deconstruction takes this as read, showing no further interest in questions of reference, by comparison with which the problems of rhetoric appear all-absorbing. In any case, deconstructive criticism is noticeable for its revival of rhetorical terminology, much of it half forgotten since the eighteenth century: the deconstructors will invoke catachresis, synecdoche, and metalepsis, as casually as the New Critics before them referred to paradox or irony. One major difference in approach to tropes and figures is prominent, however: the practitioners of deconstruction are keen to resist what they see as the symbolist/ modernist privileging of metaphor above all other tropes. De Man especially is suspicious of metaphor and symbol, because they confuse language with nature, whereas metonymy and allegory self-consciously underline the gulf between them. This much could also be said of Frye

and of structuralists like Lodge; but de Man takes the issue beyond a
balancing of the claims of different tropes, and argues that the metaphor-
ical and metonymic modes are deeply in conflict, just as the literal and
the figurative are constantly interfering with one another. For de Man
and his colleagues, the goal of a deconstructive reading is to trace the
logic of the rhetorical tropes and figures employed in a text back to an
impasse or *aporia* at which it can be shown that the text is finally
'undecidable' or even plainly 'unreadable', because of an irreconcileable
clash between grammar (the literal sense) and rhetoric (the figurative). A
simple but striking example is given by de Man at the start of his book
Allegories of Reading (1979); and this, not coincidentally, is an overt case
of *aporia* or irresolution: the last line of Yeats's poem, 'Among School
Children',

How can we know the dancer from the dance?

We have a choice here between reading the line figuratively, as a rhetorical
question implying that dance and dancer are indistinguishable, and of
reading it literally, as an enquiry about making a distinction between
them. The usual reading is the first. De Man shows that there is a self-
contradiction in our act of reading this line in the rhetorical sense,
though, because we thus assert indivisibility only by acting upon a division
between the grammatical appearance of the line and its presumed rhetorical intention. So the meaning we derive from the line is fundamentally
at odds with the assumptions we must have employed in order to arrive
at that meaning.[10]

Deconstructive reading as practised by de Man and his followers is not,
as many objectors have assumed, a clever way of showing how poets
contradict themselves, but a method by which it can be shown that a
text's meanings will resist final incorporation into an interpretative frame.
It acts as a warning against critical ambitions to control texts, and against
critical self-belief in general. One of de Man's better-known propositions,
which gives *Blindness and Insight* its title, is that critics' best insights are
achieved by violating their declared principles and so saying what they
don't mean. At some stage, most deconstructive readings will become
metacritical: that is, they will move from the self-divisions of the text to
the impossibility of imposing coherent interpretations upon it. Among the
more lucid examples of this move is Barbara Johnson's reading of Melville's
tale *Billy Budd* in her book *The Critical Difference* (1980). In the Melville
story, the central, paradoxical incident is that in which the beautiful sailor
Billy is called upon by his ship's captain to answer a false accusation of
attempted mutiny, made by his enemy, Claggart; speechless, Billy strikes
Claggart dead on the spot. Two rival interpretations of Billy's murderous
blow have arisen: either that it is an accidental departure from Billy's
essentially innocent nature, or that it reveals the suppressed malevolence

(detected by Claggart) beneath the innocuous surface Billy has so far presented. The paradox is that Billy actually vindicates Claggart's view of him as a potentially violent troublemaker in the very act of denying it. More worryingly for critics, each of the contrary interpretations turns out to depend upon assumptions which seem to support the opposite view: if we support Billy, we have to endorse Claggart's view that there is a discrepancy between appearance and reality, while if we support Claggart, we must assume Billy's blow to be a consistent expression of his nature, thus denying Claggart's own argument.[11] As in de Man's example from Yeats, either interpretation is undermined by the assumptions employed in arriving at it. In each case, too, the literary text is seen to be 'about' the problem – the impossibility, indeed – of interpreting it. Deconstructive reading is very often commentary upon commentary, but instead of discriminating right from wrong interpretations it attributes the problems of commentators to the inherent duplicities of the text, which critics are condemned to re-enact. Thus Shoshana Felman's long essay on interpretations of Henry James's *The Turn of the Screw* (1977; reprinted in her *Writing and Madness*, 1985) shows how Edmund Wilson's attempted Freudian reading, in the very act of accusing the governess-narrator of being mad, actually reproduces the symptoms of her paranoid suspicion. The literary examples chosen by deconstructors are, as with other schools, specially selected for their purposes, but they help to emphasize the extent to which literature is already concerned with problems of interpretation and misreading, even before the professional critics arrive to decode it.

The inescapable entanglement of critical and creative texts constitutes one of the obsessions of deconstructive criticism, especially in the work of Geoffrey Hartman, whose most scandalous contribution to critical debate has been his suggestion that critical writing should release itself from its subordination to 'primary' texts and declare itself an autonomous literature. Deconstructing the hierarchy in which criticism merely serves literary texts, Hartman suggested in several essays in *The Fate of Reading* (1975) and *Criticism in the Wilderness* (1980) that criticism should be seen 'as a contaminated creative thinking'.[12] Hartman worries at length about how to get beyond the Arnoldian tradition in criticism, and how to accommodate the new principle of indeterminacy without jettisoning criticism's humane functions. The focus of many of these deliberations is the problem of the critic's 'style' – a problem to which Hartman himself responds by experimenting, more freely than the other deconstructors, with a 'creative' style of his own, dense with elaborate puns, conceits, and far-fetched etymological digressions. The title of his contribution to *Deconstruction and Criticism* – 'Words, Wish, Worth: Wordsworth' – suggests something of its flavour.

By the early 1980s, deconstruction had established itself as the critical school to which all others had to define a response, and against which all others had to measure themselves. As the most theoretically rigorous version of post-structuralist work on literature, it occupied a position something like that of New Criticism in the 1940s, colouring the attitudes and language even of those many critics who disputed its principles. The spirit of deconstruction extended into neighbouring discourses such as those of feminism and post-colonial discourse (through the work of Gayatri Spivak, among others), neo-Marxist cultural analysis, and psychoanalysis. In the psychoanalytic field, deconstruction had by now an ally in the school of Jacques Lacan, whose powerful revisions of Freud had emphasized the priority of language to identity, the 'split' subject riven by language, and the endless sliding of signifiers. Despite the fearsome accusation of 'phallogocentrism' levelled at the Lacanian camp by Derrida and some of his followers, deconstruction and Lacanian psychoanalysis clearly belong to the same intellectual movement of linguistic anti-humanism, although the latter school has tended to attract sectarian devotees at a greater rate. In terms of its consequences for literary study, Lacan's scheme has the great advantage of directing interpretation away from people (author, character, reader) and, in principle, towards the text itself, usually in terms of the ways in which the text negotiates the claims of the Imaginary (the fantasized condition of full self-presence and coherent selfhood) and the Symbolic (the realm of difference). Lacanian modes of interpretation have been practised more extensively in film studies – notably in the British film journal *Screen* – than in literary analysis, where Lacan's system has featured more often as part of the theoretical furniture among some Marxist and feminist critics than as a method of reading in itself.

The most surprising and innovative adaptation of psychoanalytic theory for purposes of literary criticism in this period came from the deconstructors' Yale colleague Harold Bloom, who derived a bizarre but strangely compelling theory of poetic influence from Freud, Nietzsche, Yeats, Emerson, and cabbalistic mystical writings. Bloom agreed with de Man on the Nietzschean principles that language is fundamentally figurative and that all reading is necessarily misreading; but beyond that, he refused to concede the predominance of language over human identity and will, and thus he stood outside the deconstructive camp proper. As he puts it in *Poetry and Repression* (1976), 'A poetic "text", as I interpret it, is not a gathering of signs on a page, but is a psychic battlefield upon which authentic forces struggle for the only victory worth winning, the divinating triumph over oblivion'.[13] Bloom's readings of poems are strongly focused upon rhetoric, but in a manner that ties tropes and figures to psychological defence-mechanisms. From the other side, his use of Freud is highly unorthodox in that it sets aside sexuality in favour of the aggressive impulses and their repression. The resulting theory of the 'anxiety of influence' proposes that poets struggle to define themselves against the crushing weight of their 'strong' predecessors, rather as children must combat the priority of their parents. The new poet suffers the agonies of 'belatedness', fearing that previous poets have already said all that can be said, leaving no room for latecomers. Poetry then becomes a process of 'misreading' or aggressively revising the precursor's poems, in which the new poem employs a range of rhetorical or 'revisionary' strategies to evade or deny the priority of the old. The English Romantic poets, for example, can be shown to be engaged in a desperate struggle with the father-figure of John Milton, against whom they cast themselves as reverent but envious sons.

The detailed working-out of Bloom's system is lavishly obscurantist, a series of conjuring tricks with a terminology full of abracadabras, but the principles upon which he works, in his cycle of books beginning with *The Anxiety of Influence* (1973) and *A Map of Misreading* (1975), are full of interest and potential development. For Bloom's view of poetry is fully intertextual: he clearly announces that 'there are *no* texts, but only relationships *between* texts'.[14] And if our attention is turned upon this 'intertext', we are released both from the tautologies of New Critical 'intrinsic' formalism, in which the poem 'means itself', and from the reductive tendency of 'extrinsic' explanations, in which the poem means something outside poetry; the perfect solution is that the meaning of a poem can only be *another* poem, which need not, Bloom adds perversely, be one that the poet has even read.[15] The proposition that poems (and indeed prose writings) are always defensive responses to, and misreadings of, previous poems has the attraction of showing us that there is something outside the text, even if it does turn out to be just one text the more.

Contextualisms: New-Left and Feminist Critiques

The rigorous textualism of the structuralist and deconstructive schools provoked, among other reactions, a persistent anxiety among teachers and critics for whom literature's value lay in its potential for social critique and emancipation. The rapidly growing body of literary amateurs and professionals who identified themselves after 1968 with the New Left or with social movements such as feminism and gay liberation was affronted by what appeared to be an attempt by a professional élite to deny the connections between texts and the world beyond them. The irrepressible liberal desire to identify literary creativity with 'progressive' social causes was not to be deflected by philosophical obfuscation about sliding signifiers; while more suspicious voices on the left regarded the new preoccupation with textuality as an invitation to political passivity or quietism. Such misgivings helped to turn the tide away from deconstruction and towards various kinds of politically-engaged criticism by the early 1980s. Polemics against textualism, such as Gerald Graff's *Literature Against Itself* (1979), Frank Lentricchia's *After the New Criticism* (1980), and Terry Eagleton's *Walter Benjamin* (1981) diagnosed the condition as a largely sterile variety of formalism equivalent to the New Criticism of the 1940s. The year 1983 saw Eagleton's *Literary Theory* (1983), with its call for a new 'political criticism', achieve the status of an academic best-seller, while Edward W. Said's volume of essays, *The World, the Text, and the Critic* (1983), won many readers to the cause of a 'worldly' criticism alive to social and historical questions. Both works favoured politically-guided eclecticism over the pursuit of pure theoretical rigour, and both indicated a shift of Parisian allegiances, from Derrida to the libertarian philosopher-historian Michel Foucault. Said's opening statement fairly summarizes the new mood:

> My position is that texts are worldly, to some degree they are events, and, even when they appear to deny it, they are nevertheless a part of the social world, human life, and of course the historical movements in which they are located and interpreted. Literary theory, whether of the Left or of the Right, has turned its back on these things.[16]

The broader rediscovery of contextual study or of 'cultural criticism' in the 1980s, owed much, however, to several developments in the previous decade, from the work of Raymond Williams to the emergence of a new feminist criticism.

The revolutionary excitements and disappointments of 1968 brought in their wake a renaissance of Marxist cultural theory, nourished by the rediscovery of the intellectual traditions of 'Western Marxism' – of the writings of Gramsci, Lukács, Benjamin, and more recent work by Sartre, Adorno, Marcuse, and Althusser. Whereas the British and American Marxist critics of the 1930s combined wayward improvisation with endorsement of the Party line, those of the 1970s had a far richer tradition behind them, and usually demonstrated the benefits of broader interests reaching beyond the confines of Marxism to embrace the insights of structuralism, post-structuralism, and psychoanalysis. They had also the incentive of new consumerist forms of capitalism, which threw into question the older 'economist' models of Marxism and demanded a stronger understanding of cultural domination and legitimacy ('hegemony') in the maintenance of the capitalist order. In the English-speaking world, the renaissance of Marxist criticism and literary theory was embodied in new journals like *Literature and History*, collaborative networks such as the Marxist-Feminist Literature Collective, and conferences such as those held in the 1970s at the University of Essex; its influence, however, has spread well beyond the ranks of self-declared Marxists. Its intellectual development has been associated with three principal champions: Raymond Williams and his former student Terry Eagleton in Britain, and Fredric Jameson in the United States. All three have combined an orthodox insistence on the role of class struggle and class domination in culture with a productive openness to non-Marxist influences.

The early work of Raymond Williams had maintained a careful distance from the old Marxist orthodoxies, but the flourishing of the New Left in the late 1960s drew him into much closer identification with a renewed Marxist tradition, notably in his books *The Country and the City* (1974), *Marxism and Literature* (1977), and *Problems in Materialism and Culture* (1980). His quarrel with the orthodox position revolved around the model of the economic 'base' which was held to determine the cultural 'superstructure', a scheme that Williams felt had only reinforced the notion of literature and other cultural products as immaterial shadows, his own insistence being, to the contrary, that culture was fully *material*. This kind of revisionism brought him into conflict with Eagleton – who, in *Criticism and Ideology* (1976), bemoaned Williams's incomplete divorce from left-Leavisite positions – and with the editors of *New Left Review* who engaged him in prolonged dialogue on these and other points in *Politics and Letters* (1979). Williams's emphasis on the materiality of cultural forms inspired him to describe his method as one of 'cultural materialism', the distinctive point of which is to examine culture not simply in terms of its products but in the context of its material conditions of production: as he put it in a 1973 essay, 'we should look not for the components of a product but for the conditions of a practice'.[17] He had already begun in the 1960s to mark out the extended territory of enquiry that we now call Cultural Studies; but in the 1970s he engaged in repeated assaults upon the category of 'Literature', arguing that it was an ideological fetish abstracted from the generality of writings. In a similar vein, he attacked the assumption, strongly rooted in Cambridge, that the centre of literary study should be occupied by literary criticism rather then by historical and linguistic investigation. His work as a whole, and more emphatically in the 1970s than before, pointed beyond the boundaries of 'Literature' to the wider interdisciplinary study of cultural forms and formations, including the technologies of writing, dramatic performance, and other kinds of communication. In so far as he still addressed questions of literature, it was to place literary texts back into their contexts of work and exploitation. His most impressive literary study in this phase is *The Country and the City*, which examines the long tradition of literary contrasts between rural and urban life in English writing since the fifteenth century, with devastating effects upon the Leavisian myth of the 'organic community': displacing the inadequate opposition between modern urban industrialization and traditional rustic integrity, Williams shows how capitalism had taken over the English countryside long before it evolved its industrial forms, and he shows how the traditions of pastoral and country-house writing masked and endorsed the exploitation of rural labour.

Whereas Williams's prolonged argument with the old Cambridge school of Richards and Leavis led him slowly towards a form of Marxist cultural analysis, Terry Eagleton attempted in the mid-1970s a more decisive break with that tradition, employing a more rigorously 'scientific' model of Marxist theory, derived in part from the structuralist Marxism of Louis Althusser and in part from the dramatic principles of Bertolt Brecht. His first major work of literary theory, *Criticism and Ideology* (1976), seeks a way out of the crude determinism of older Marxist criticism and especially of its assumption that literature 'reflects' social reality. Eagleton's crucial point of departure here was that the raw material of literary texts is not reality or even 'experience' but *ideology*, which in Althusser's sense is our imagined relation to reality. ('Ideology' is a difficult term, to which Eagleton has returned at various times, for example in *Ideology: An Introduction* (1991).) This means that literature stands at two removes from reality, to which it can gesture only obliquely by re-working the materials of ideology (or ideologies), which, again, it does not directly reflect or 'express', but which, in Eagleton's favoured metaphor, it 'produces', as a company of actors produces, and thereby reinterprets, a play. By putting an ideology to work in specific fictional cases, literary texts can expose – at least to the eye of a politically vigilant criticism – its contradictions or faultlines. As an attempt to define what Althusser called the 'relative autonomy' of the art-work from the economy or mode of production, *Criticism and Ideology* remains a substantial achievement, even though Eagleton himself soon abandoned some of the pretensions to scientific rigour that mark this work as a product of the structuralist phase in modern theory (one chapter, entitled 'Towards a Science of the Text', earned some notoriety for brandishing such new-minted categories as Authorial Ideology and Literary Mode of Production). It also includes a lively sequence of 'applied' studies in which several writers from Leavis's Great Tradition – from George Eliot to D. H. Lawrence – are read in terms of the relation between 'organic' literary form and an 'organicist' phase of British ideology in the later nineteenth century. It is an important feature of modern Marxist criticism, here and in the work of Jameson and Williams, that it refuses to confine its attention to the social or historical 'content' of literary works, looking rather for the political significance of literary *forms*.

Eagleton's numerous works of the 1980s, beginning with *Walter Benjamin, or Towards a Revolutionary Criticism* (1981), show him borrowing promiscuously from the new schools of feminist and post-structuralist interpretation to produce some dazzling performances, notably in *The Rape of Clarissa* (1982) and *William Shakespeare* (1986). He also re-estab-

lished his links with Williams's project, similarly undermining the category
of 'literature' in favour of a more extensive exploration of discourse and
rhetoric in all their forms. By this time, as he reveals in the conclusion
to *Literary Theory*, he had relaxed his earlier 'theoreticism', now viewing
the consistency of a theoretical system as less important than the political
demands of the given moment. One result is the cultivation of a mischievous sense of parodic humour in these works, which stands out especially
against the prevalent earnestness of Theory in general and of Raymond
William's leaden prose in particular. In *Literary Theory*, as in the later *The
Ideology of the Aesthetic* (1991), Eagleton summarizes the intellectual positions of several other critics and philosophers with such nonchalant dialectical agility that the dividing line between exposition and spoof often
vanishes. He is clearly a serious Marxist theoretician, remote from the
tendance Groucho, but more than ready to learn from Oscar Wilde (one
of his cultural heroes) or from the Monty Python team about the revolutionary potential of laughter.

Eagleton's American counterpart and precursor, Fredric Jameson, took
his intellectual bearings from the Hegelian strand of Marxism represented
by Lukács, Sartre, and Adorno, whose aesthetic principles he surveys in
Marxism and Form (1971), before attempting in the same work his first
ambitious sketch of a 'dialectical criticism'. Already in this early work
Jameson was drawing inventively upon recent examples of French structuralism, among numerous other influences, in attempting to elaborate a
passage from the analysis of the single text to the analysis of its position
in the history of class struggles. His next work, *The Prison-House of
Language* (1972), is a direct critique of the traditions of Formalism and
Structuralism: rather than simply reject these systems, Jameson aims to
work his way through to the other side of them, digesting them dialecti-
cally into a higher synthesis in which their static models of synchrony
and binary opposition can be re-historicized. This move becomes typical
of Jameson's subsequent work, in which non-Marxist concepts are hardly
ever refused but instead swept up into the all-forgiving embrace of the
Dialectic, where they can be reconnected to the ultimate horizon of
History. On a much larger scale, Jameson's *The Political Unconscious* (1981)
assimilates a range of other theories, including psychoanalysis, deconstruction, phenomenology, structuralist narratology, and myth criticism into a
grandly ambitious synthesis which deserves comparison with Frye's *Anatomy of Criticism*. Jameson's book achieves a number of improbable and
exciting connections between the systems from which it borrows: as its
title suggests, it looks for ways of discovering the repressed political or
historical dimensions of texts, and tries out on Conrad's *Lord Jim* an
elaborate exercise using the rectangular diagrams of the narratologist A.
J. Greimas to define that novel's unspoken secrets. The most important
idea running through *The Political Unconscious*, though, is the concept,
derived from Theodor Adorno and Paul Ricoeur, of the 'double her-

meneutic', according to which we are to interpret texts both negatively, by demystifying their ideological limits, and positively, by seeking the 'utopian' dimension in which they foreshadow human liberation.

Neo-Marxist criticism and theory had a distinct importance in this period, but in terms of its wider cultural repercussions it is a minor episode by comparison with the emergence of a new wave of feminist literary and cultural criticism in the 1970s and after. While Marxist theory found itself more or less marooned in the universities, the new women's movements developed extensive networks of communication and cultural expression, linking academic study with creative writing, journalism, political campaigning, and other activities. One result was that feminist work in literary criticism often took collaborative or collective forms, in the shape of conferences, symposia, publishing houses such as Virago, journals such as *Signs* (Chicago, 1975) and *m/f* (London, 1978), and joint- or multiple-authored books: many of the pioneering works were anthologies of essays and conference papers, including *Images of Women in Fiction* (ed. S. K. Cornillon, 1972), *Feminist Literary Criticism* (ed. J. Donovan, 1975), *Shakespeare's Sisters* (ed. M. Jacobus, 1979), and *The New Feminist Criticism* (ed. E. Showalter, 1985). Another consequence in terms of literary theory, overt or covert, was that the formalist conception of the self-contained art-work came under renewed assault from writers with an urgent sense of social and political engagement. In the academic context, literature was connected to work in sociology and history through cross-disciplinary Women's Studies courses. Literature, in its various accounts of sexual difference and of women's place in the social order, suddenly became 'relevant' in ways rarely discussed before, and merely formal analysis of novels or poems appeared not just insufficient but complicit in a conspiracy of silence on questions of sexual politics. The new feminist criticism that emerged rapidly in the United States in the 1970s was, at least to begin with, deeply anti-formalist, committed to the traditional notions of literature as an imitation of life and as an expression of authors' views and experiences.

Feminist criticism is one of the more self-conscious modern critical schools, much given to narrating its own relatively short history. The most commonly accepted of these narratives traces three phases of its emergence, at least in North America. The first two have been named by Elaine Showalter as 'feminist critique' (the exposure of sexism and stereotypes in literary and critical texts, usually texts by men, known as 'androtexts') and 'gynocritics' (the more sympathetic study of writings by women, or gynotexts); a third phase was given the name 'gynesis' by Alice Jardine, denoting a post-structuralist reconsideration of the 'feminine' as an indeterminate textual effect. This division is of course schematic, but it remains helpful so long as one avoids imagining each phase to have superseded the last; as often in the history of criticism, the older style persists alongside the newer.

The first phase of the new feminist criticism erupted quite suddenly in 1970. Two years earlier, Mary Ellmann's book *Thinking About Women* had exposed with devastating irony the absurd stereotypes of 'phallic criticism' with which male critics belittled women writers; but the more famous and influential founding work was Kate Millett's PhD thesis *Sexual Politics* (1970), which, as well as outlining a theory of patriarchy and establishing crucial distinctions between sex and gender, conducted a sustained assault upon the reputations of four modern writers – D. H. Lawrence, Norman Mailer, Henry Miller, and Jean Genet – who are denounced as misogynists, along with Sigmund Freud and others. Millett's crucial move here is to break simultaneously the customary code of reverence for literary genius and the unquestioned convention whereby readers are assumed to be male, by presenting herself consciously as a female reader affronted by violent phallicism. The appropriation of authority by Millett as reader leads to an exciting exercise in iconoclasm. Later feminist critics, however, notably Cora Kaplan and Toril Moi, have pointed out serious flaws in *Sexual Politics* and in its assumptions about literature: Millett tends to present literature as a simple form of indoctrination, and shows little care either to distinguish between fictional characters and real authors or to consider the difficult relation between fiction and social reality in general.[18] In *Sexual Politics* and in such later 'Images-of-Women' studies as Judith Fetterley's *The Resisting Reader* (1978), the indictment of 'false' depictions of women repeatedly implied that fiction should and could reflect the reality, and only the reality, of women's lives. Feminism was thus allied at this early stage with the simplest aesthetic principle of realistic 'reflection', allowing little room for fantasy or artifice. Moreover, Millett's concentration on writings by men offered no response to an apparently monolithic patriarchal culture other than readerly indignation.

It was this last difficulty that seemed to provoke a shift in feminist criticism in the mid-1970s from feminist critique of male-authored works to the 'gynocritical' study of women as writers and of writings by women. As defined by Elaine Showalter, the purpose of gynocritics is to rescue the lost traditions of women's literary work from the blindness of the male-dominated critical establishment, and to investigate the specific characteristics and contexts of that work. A sequence of influential works established this new direction: Ellen Moers's *Literary Women* (1976), Elaine Showalter's *A Literature of Their Own* (1977), and Sandra M. Gilbert and Susan Gubar's *The Madwoman in the Attic* (1979). For the most part, these books were devoted to women novelists of the nineteenth-century realist tradition, thus ratifying the alliance between feminist and mimetic principles. Moers's book commemorates the struggles and achievements of several women writers, approaching their work most often from a biographical angle that highlights uniquely female experience: thus *Frankenstein* is interpreted by Moers as a response to Mary Shelley's own experiences of miscarriage and childbirth. Nevertheless, Moers explicitly avoids the idea of a single or special 'female imagination'. The same is true of Showalter in her discussion of British women novelists from Charlotte Brontë to Doris Lessing in *A Literature of Their Own*: Showalter links women writers together not in biological or in psychological terms but as members of a subculture grounded in common experiences. Her aim is to recover the missing links in the 'female tradition' between the still-visible eminences of Brontë, Eliot, and Woolf; and the principal achievement of her book is indeed to open up the lost world of 'minor' women novelists. Showalter has been criticized for her anti-theoretical position and for her related tendency to equate literary texts with the 'experience' upon which they are supposed to be based, but there can be little doubt that the example of *A Literature of Their Own* has shifted the world of literary criticism away from male-centred assumptions, and inspired countless new investigations of women's writing.

The collaborative work of Sandra M. Gilbert and Susan Gubar in *The Madwoman in the Attic* is characterized by a much more adventurous adaptation of what many feminists anathematized as 'male theory'. For their extended study of Austen, the Brontës, Eliot, and Dickinson, Gilbert and Gubar rewrite Harold Bloom's notoriously masculine 'anxiety-of-influence' thesis in feminist terms so as to define the special basis of female creativity as an 'anxiety of authorship' in which women writers must combat the power of the literary Fathers, seeking out a 'foremother' who exemplifies successful revolt against the stereotypic roles of angelic selflessness expected of her. In a series of innovative and forceful interpretations, Gilbert and Gubar explore the ways in which their chosen novelists and poets employ the motifs of confinement and illness as part of their struggle against patriarchal definitions: each author engages in a duplicitous strategy in which her repressed rage against patriarchy is expressed obliquely through the figure of the madwoman or the monster. This may be convincing as an account of Charlotte Brontë and her use of Bertha Mason in *Jane Eyre*, but when applied to the very different fictional arts of Jane Austen the hypothesis of a constantly recurring covert female rage is less plausible. *The Madwoman in the Attic* is the most resourceful and sophisticated of these early feminist literary histories, but it shares some of the reductive shortcomings of archetypal criticism, discovering the same hidden truth behind very different textual surfaces, and ignoring differences of historical and cultural context.

The third, and most complex phase of feminist criticism emerges in the early 1980s with the importation of post-structuralist and psychoanalytic themes that unsettle the relatively stable concepts of author, experience, and mimesis upon which American feminist criticism had hitherto depended. The new wave of 'gynesis' replaced the former emphasis on knowable female identity with the radical indeterminacies of textual *difference*, and in its most thorough versions it dissolved 'woman' as a female person into 'woman' as a linguistic or textual construction. It became apparent at this stage that feminist criticism had become differentiated into at least two intellectual camps, schematically represented as the 'American' school of Showalter and other practitioners of gynocritics; the 'French' school of Julia Kristeva, Hélène Cixous, Luce Irigaray, and their various followers in the Anglophone world; and – in some accounts – a 'British' strand of feminism which retains closer ties to Marxism, to psychoanalysis, and to socialist historiography, distrusting the 'essentialism' into which the other two camps stray. A clear case of the new internal conflicts is seen in Toril Moi's *Sexual/Textual Politics* (1985), which, drawing on previous complaints from Cora Kaplan and Mary Jacobus against the deficiencies of American feminist theory, accuses Showalter, Gilbert, Gubar and others of complicity with patriarchal-humanist aesthetics in that they remain tied to realism and that they replicate simple binary oppositions between male and female realms. Where Showalter had rebuked Virginia Woolf's ideal of androgyny as an evasion of true femaleness, Moi wants to return to the project of an androgynous surpassing of sexed identities. Hence her recoil from American feminism, which *affirms* female creativity, and her preference for the French endeavour to question feminine identity or dissolve it into a free-floating principle of textual indeterminacy or openness. Like Jane Gallop and other theorists in the English-speaking world who have taken their directions from Jacques Lacan and from feminist revisions of his work, Moi is duly critical of certain aspects of 'French feminism' – notably the danger of 'biologism' in its attempts to found feminine creativity upon bodily rhythms and orgasmic pulsations – but she takes the deconstruction of binary oppositions of gender to be the most urgent theoretical goal, and in this she represents well the new currents of feminist thought in the 1980s.

As feminist critics and theorists variously adapted for their own uses the strategies of deconstructive or psychoanalytic or Marxist theory, or repudiated Theory in the name of History, these theoretical differentiations were overlaid by further political contests over the idea of 'identity'. Lesbian feminist critics, along with African-American and Hispanic feminists, repudiated the notion of 'woman' posited by white heterosexual feminists, regarding it as a universalizing of particular privileged interests. The idea of a single 'female tradition' unravelled still further in the work of the Bengali Marxist-feminist-deconstructionist Gayatri Chakravorty Spivak, whose writings also challenged the ethnocentrism of mainstream feminist criticism. Spivak's reading of *Jane Eyre*, for instance, invites us to approach it through Jean Rhys's rewriting and thus from a 'Third-World' perspective which shows that the feminist individualism of the novel is implicated in a cultural imperialism that enforces the silencing or exclusion of the colonial 'Other'.[19] A general theme of 1980s cultural theory, well illustrated by Spivak's work, is that apparently simple identities are not truly self-identical but composed of multiple and contradictory elements. Those theoretical approaches that became known as 'post-colonial' were especially concerned with emphasizing the unstable hybridity of the human 'subject' under conditions of imperialist subordination, and the intercontamination of language and cultures produced in colonial and post-colonial societies. Along with Spivak's essays and interviews, the densely abstruse essays of Homi K. Bhabha pursued these questions with deconstructive persistence. There are some parallels between these themes of post-colonial theory and those pursued by theorists of African-American literature, notably Henry Louis Gates. For Gates, black American culture had the status of a colonized zone, and similarly drew both upon the language of the dominant European power and on the distinctive vernacular language and folklore of black subcultures themselves. Drawing upon the rhetorical reading techniques of the Yale deconstructors, Gates outlined, in his edited collection *Black Literature and Literary Theory* (1984) and in his book *The Signifying Monkey* (1988), a theory of black writing that concentrated less on reflection or expression than on distinctive kinds of textuality, especially the characteristic figurative resources of the vernacular, such as its typically parodic style of 'signifying'.

The more widely influential founder of this post-colonial mode of critical theory was Edward Said, whose book *Orientalism* (1978) stands out as one of the key works of cultural analysis in this period. Said employs Frantz Fanon's concept of the colonized as an invented 'Other' projected by the colonizing power, and applies it at length to the history of Western (predominantly British and French) representation of the 'Orient' and of its supposedly eternal characteristics – 'feminine' indolence, deceit, sexual licence. As Said expounds it, Orientalism is a 'discourse' in Michel Foucault's sense; that is, an institutionalization of a special language which gives its users powers to define others. *Orientalism* is more disturbing than most accounts of racist ideology, though, in that it implicates respected European writers like Flaubert in the construction of imperialist culture, and further shows the ways in which Western scholarship and 'objective' academic discourses have taken part in the same project. A Palestinian by birth, Said saw this project as a timely exposé of Western prejudices that persist in American attitudes to his own people and to the monstrous 'Other' of Islam. Said's book has some similarities to Williams's *The Country and the City* (which it acknowledges as a precursor) and to the 'Images of Women' studies of that period, in that it explores the role of literary representations (in the widest sense, including historical and topographical writings) in the maintenance of oppressive forms of power. It helped to bring about in the next few years a swing from Derrida to Foucault, and thus from rhetorical analysis of textuality to cultural and historical modes of criticism.

It was evident in the 1980s that academic literary study was tending in various ways towards a concentration upon the interconnections between language and power, and towards what became known as a 'new historic-ism'. In its broadest sense, this last term refers to a general reaction against unhistorical approaches, and a fresh interest in the specific social and political contexts of literary works. It was noticeable in studies of English Romantic writing, for example, that scholars like Jerome McGann and Marilyn Butler were pursuing detailed contextual study in open oppo-sition to the formalist and deconstructive model of the self-contained Romantic poem. In a narrower sense, though, 'new historicism' was applied as a label for a particular new school of literary history deriving its principles from Michel Foucault's analysis of power, language, and discourse. Stephen Greenblatt, the central figure in this group, established a model for its work in his book *Renaissance Self-Fashioning* (1980), in which he studies the ways in which identities were formed within the contexts of institutions (Church, Court, Theatre, and so on) and their texts or discourses in the sixteenth century. The Renaissance or 'early modern' period soon became the favoured object of similar kinds of work. Greenblatt, with Jonathan Goldberg, Louis Montrose, and other collaborators in the American journal *Representations*, avoided declaring a doctrine or theory, but they had some important general principles, most importantly the insistence that literary texts should not be detached from the wider network of texts and other cultural activities or institutions from which they are generated: typically, a new-historicist reading of a literary text will involve reference to non-literary texts (legal documents, sermons, travelogues), demonstrating the presence of a similar governing discourse. New historicism also defined itself against older literary-histori-cal methods, of the kind represented by E. M. W. Tillyard, for whom literature was a reflection of a given age's shared 'world view'. An import-ant principle of new historicism was that no culture has a single homo-geneous world-view of this kind, but all are internally diverse. New historicism is perhaps best understood as a position intermediate between Marxism and post-structuralism, combining the idea of historical determi-nation (in weakened form) with that of textuality so that texts are recog-nized as being historical while histories are understood as textual. In this tension, it is the paranoid pessimism of Foucault that tends to prevail, especially in Greenblatt's work. Foucault had claimed that human desires are not repressed by 'power' — a notoriously abstract term in his work — but actually *produced* by it, since power requires some opposition against which to define and renew itself; thus every attempt at subversion or rebellion against power is in principle doomed to be recuperated by it, in an interminable cat-and-mouse game.

The implied pessimism of what Greenblatt called his 'cultural poetics' brought him and other American new historicists into collision with their British counterparts, who defined their own approach as 'cultural materialism', lifting a term from the writings of Raymond Williams. Although closely similar in other respects, the American and British wings

of new historicism divided on the crucial political question of containment and subversion. The cultural materialist view on this question,
which informs the work of such critics as Jonathan Dollimore, Alan
Sinfield, and Catherine Belsey, had been formulated by Williams in his
Marxism and Literature (1977): 'no dominant culture ever in reality includes
or exhausts all human practice, human energy, and human intention.'[20]
For Dollimore and his collaborators, it was an urgent political requirement
that the possibilities of subversion and resistance to the dominant power
should be seen to be open: human subjectivity was indeed constructed
by dominant ideologies and discourses (including those of literature and
drama), but the subject, and 'power' itself, both remained unstable or 'in
process', as Belsey, for example, affirmed in her *Critical Practice* (1980)
and *The Subject of Tragedy* (1985). More closely aligned with Marxist
theories of ideology and hegemony, the British cultural materialists thus
stressed the openness and multiplicity of literary and dramatic texts,
hoping to recover from them the marginalized voices of resistance. Coun-
tering Foucauldian pessimism, they often favoured Mikhail Bakhtin's concepts of 'carnival' and of 'heteroglossia', which revealed the degree to
which cultural products are 'sites' of contest between dominant and
subordinated voices. And since the meanings of literary texts remain
continuously open, the cultural materialists devoted a good deal of their
attention and their activist spirit to the later uses or 'appropriations' of
literature in the institutions of criticism, theatrical production, and education, 're-reading' its texts against the dominant conservative interpretations. The relevant context of, say, *Macbeth* was not just the social and
ideological conditions of its first performance, but now also the entire
later history of its theatrical and critical re-interpretations, including its
recent position in ideologies of 'great literature'. The British cultural
materialists, in their constant emphasis on subversion, transgression, and
fluid sexual identity, represented a generation of radical activists formed
in the wake of the 1968 uprisings and shaped by the sexual politics of
feminism and gay liberation. The underlying question at issue in their
refusal of Greenblattian resignation was, as Richard Wilson has observed
in a canny survey of this debate, nothing less than the fate of political
radicalism after its containment in 1968 and during its demoralization in
the Reagan/Thatcher period.[21]

Shakespearean Subversions

Amid the turmoil following the arrival of Theory in the 1970s, Shakespeare and the critical problems surrounding his work seemed to be

pushed to one side of the stage. Most of the new theoretical developments favoured the discussion of nineteenth- and twentieth-century literatures, thus leaving the once prestigious realm of Shakespearean studies strangely untouched, at least until the sudden explosion, in the mid-1980s, of post-structuralist, Marxist, feminist and new-historicist 'readings' and cultural histories. After a late start, then, by the end of the 1980s Shakespeare had been thoroughly overhauled, 'theorized', and 'historicized' by the irreverent new schools.

The quiescent early part of this period is marked by further explorations in genre study, archetypal criticism, and psychoanalytic interpretation. All three are combined in one of the more provocative works of the 1970s, Leslie Fiedler's *The Stranger in Shakespeare* (1972). This is a curiously transitional work, looking back to Carl Jung and to the modernists Wyndham Lewis and James Joyce in its speculative treatment of Shake-speare's supposed personal problems, and forward to the later literary politics of sex and race in its focus upon the fear of 'Others' in Shake-speare's works. Like any number of Shakespearean cranks, Fiedler starts by claiming to have found the 'key' to the whole oeuvre in the 'two loves' of Sonnet 144, but his account becomes more intriguing as he explores the various 'strangers' in Shakespeare – the woman-as-witch, the Jew, the Moor, the Indian – delving as he does so into the folkloric archetypes and psychological phobias from which these outsiders are made. The major theme holding all this together is Shakespeare's 'problem with women',[22] his queasiness about their sexuality, his rage at their treachery to their fathers, and his idealizing of male friendship. As in Fiedler's earlier studies of American fiction, the focus on male bonding and misogyny opens up exciting new angles on the plays, even though his presentation of Shakespeare and some of his characters as 'homosexual' may now be regarded as anachronistic. Fiedler reveals his usual gift for wading into taboo areas of discussion – here, father/daughter incest, cannibalism, transvestism, anti-semitism, pederasty, witch-burning, slavery, and other topics which before the 1970s would have been kept well away from the genteel discussion of England's National Poet, although fifteen years later they would become the most predictable subjects of Shake-spearean criticism. This sometimes iconoclastic daring gives us a startling new sense of the phobic violence and polymorphic perversity at work in *Othello, The Merchant of Venice, Henry VI Part One, The Tempest*, and other plays, but more significantly it shows Shakespeare's work to be continually fresh without being 'universal': in fact, precisely *because* it is so deeply marked by misogyny and racial xenophobia it touches the raw wounds of Western society in the 1970s.

Fiedler was not alone in directing new kinds of attention to the implied sexual politics and psychology of Shakespeare's works. The topic of 'Shakespeare's Women' had indeed been a favourite of nineteenth-century sentimentalists who enthused about the virtues of Cordelia or Portia. The new feminism of the 1970s, though, brought with it a different set of questions. Confronting the old enigma of Shakespeare's political standpoint, feminist critics saw a choice to be made between recruiting Shakespeare as a prestigious precursor of their cause, at the risk of anachronism, or castigating the misogynistic speeches found in his work, at the risk of confusing the poet with his characters. For the most part, they reserved their anti-sexist commentaries for those critics who had employed Cleopatra, Gertrude, or other characters as illustrations of the general failures of women, while they treated Shakespeare himself as some sort of prescient ally. Juliet Dusinberre, in *Shakespeare and the Nature of Women* (1975), views the playwrights of Elizabethan and Jacobean England as broadly progressive in that they endorsed the more egalitarian notions of women's place in marriage encouraged by English protestantism. Shakespeare in particular is applauded as virtually a feminist, since he regarded men and women as equals. The contributors to the collaborative feminist volume, *The Woman's Part: Feminist Criticism of Shakespeare* (ed. C. Lenz *et al.*, 1980) generally preferred to celebrate the strengths of particular female characters in the plays; likewise Germaine Greer in her later *Shakespeare* (1986) saw one of the playwright's merits as his rejection of the 'passive woman' stereotype. Somewhat more willing to find fault with Shakespeare were the psychological and archetypal approaches of Coppélia Kahn in *Man's Estate* (1981) and of Marilyn French in *Shakespeare's Division of Experience* (1982): Kahn tries to retrace Shakespeare's personal struggle for stable masculine identity, reading his characters' speeches in terms of male attempts to escape maternal power, while French sees Shakespeare's imagination as split between masculine and feminine 'principles' until he reconciled them in the late romances.

A second wave of feminist Shakespeare criticism, however, emerged in Britain in the early 1980s, complaining of serious inadequacies in the work of their American forerunners. Both Lisa Jardine and Kathleen McLuskie express irritation at the antiquated assumptions of Dusinberre, French, and others, especially the 'mimetic' belief that Shakespeare's characters are to be treated as real people and the 'essentialist' belief in unchanging male and female characteristics. These British feminists insist that there must be more productive ways of dealing with Shakespeare than just the cheerleading functions of speaking up for the female characters or approving the poet's 'feminine side'. In Jardine's *Still Harping on Daughters* (1983) and in McLuskie's article 'The Patriarchal Bard' (1985) the new feminist approach to Shakespeare is defined in terms of revealing the relation of his works to specific ideological systems of representation, rather than to the eternal tension between the masculine and the feminine. This means exploring in detail the codes of patriarchy and dramatic conventions by which sexual difference was represented. Both Jardine and McLuskie dissent from the positive, progressive picture of Shakespeare as a benign egalitarian: his plays seem rather to be voicing patriarchal anxieties about the dangers posed by scolds, shrews, and other unruly women. And Jardine points especially to the difficulty of referring to Shakespeare's 'women' in the context of the erotically ambiguous transvestism of the boy-actors for whom he wrote the parts.

The particular value of *Still Harping on Daughters* lay in its immersion in the minutiae of social history: it tells us not just of the theatre but of dowries, portraiture, and the cost of satin. Like the work of Stephen Greenblatt, with which it was soon compared under the label of 'new historicism', Jardine's book occupied a territory half-way between literary history and social anthropology. The fuller range of new theoretical engagements with Shakespeare's work became apparent in the next few years with the appearance of such works as Jonathan Dollimore's *Radical Tragedy* (1984), Francis Barker's *The Tremulous Private Body* (1984), Michael Bristol's *Carnival and Theater* (1985), *Political Shakespeare* (eds J. Dollimore and A. Sinfield, 1985), *Alternative Shakespeares* (ed. J. Drakakis, 1985), *Shakespeare and the Question of Theory* (eds P. Parker and G. Hartman, 1985), Terry Eagleton's *William Shakespeare* (1986), Leonard Tennenhouse's *Power on Display* (1986), Malcolm Evans's *Signifying Nothing* (1986), and Terence Hawkes's *That Shakespeherian Rag* (1986). Of this remarkable crop of innovative studies, the most influential has been the Dollimore-Sinfield collection, *Political Shakespeare*, which contains McLuskie's 'The Patriarchal Bard' along with an important pair of essays by Greenblatt and Dollimore illustrating the common interests of 'cultural poetics' and 'cultural materialism'.

Greenblatt's most celebrated Shakespearean essay, 'Invisible Bullets', works its way from Thomas Harriot's account of the native Algonquins in his *Brief and True Report* (1588) on the Virginia colony to *Henry V* and the two parts of *Henry IV*, outlining a Foucauldian theory of the dependence of power upon subversion in the Elizabethan period. As Tennenhouse also argued in *Power on Display*, there was a strong connection between the prevailing form of political authority, which rested on 'theatrical' display, and the theatre itself, which re-staged the processes of political legitimation. Greenblatt shows that 'Shakespeare's plays are centrally and repeatedly concerned with the production and containment of subversion and disorder'.[23] The Henry plays in particular reveal what appears to us to be a 'subversive' exposure of the deceitful basis of regal authority, as Prince Hal, later Henry V, betrays his commitments to Falstaff and others. But what appears simply subversive to us is revealed as part of a process of containment in which the fraudulence of the king actually adds to his authority, and the audience is drawn into its imaginative recreation. Dollimore's essay, 'Transgression and Surveillance in *Measure for Measure*' follows a similarly Foucauldian course, although it swerves (as Harold Bloom might put it) away from Greenblatt's gloomier conclusions. Dollimore notices how the 'subversion' attributed to the sexual deviants of the play is a construction placed upon them by people in authority, who exercise their control precisely by 'producing' such deviancy: power secretly incites desire, the better to contain it. Dollimore remembers, though, that power eventually comes up against resistance, although it is not possible to identify it in the play, as the exploited prostitutes are not given a voice of their own; so it is necessary to point outside or beyond the play itself if this resistance is to be invoked. Taken together, these two essays identify by their choice of Shakespearean texts a 'political' Shakespeare who stages the recuperative ruses of Power, just as a previous generation had identified for themselves a symbolist Shakespeare.

The ferment of new Shakespearean work in the mid-1980s was by no means exclusively Foucauldian: Keir Elam's *Shakespeare's Universe of Discourse* (1984) is grounded in semiotics, while Bristol's *Carnival and Theater* derives from Mikhail Bakhtin's ideas of 'carnivalesque' popular culture, and Francis Barker's *Tremulous Private Body*, while employing Foucault, makes stronger use of Lacan's concepts of desire and 'lack', showing Prince Hamlet to be a 'decentred' subject with no personal essence within him but only a void. Other works of this phase resort eclectically to various aspects of feminist, Marxist, psychoanalytic, deconstructive, and other post-structuralist theories in order to unravel the Bard. The one book that seems to combine them all, in a suitably unstable synthesis, is Terry Eagleton's short study, *William Shakespeare*, which at one level pursues a familiar Marxist argument that the tensions of Shakespeare's work are those of the agonizing transition from the feudal order to the emergent capitalist anarchy. Overlaid on this thesis, though, is a post-structuralist line of approach in which the principal Shakespearean contradiction is between the body and language, order and excess. As Eagleton announces on the first page, the contradiction presents itself to criticism in the following form: 'His [Shakespeare's] belief in social stability is jeopardized by the very language in which it is articulated.'[24] Shakespeare's astonishing rhetorical abundance is both his greatest strength and, Eagleton argues, his most haunting anxiety: repeatedly, the poet tries to find ways of reconciling signifier and signified, Language and Nature, but he always gloriously fails. This account is topped off with a feminist gesture of solidarity with what Dollimore and Sinfield would identify as the 'marginal' voices of the plays: in a perverse opening flourish, Eagleton declares that the three witches are the true heroines of *Macbeth*, although Shakespeare and just about every other reader has failed to notice the fact. As he explains, the witches function as the play's 'unconscious', a realm of linguistic instability that undermines binary oppositions and with them a violently oppressive social order. This kind of move to the 'margins' is a common strategy of radical Shakespeare criticism of this period, although the witches are less often its beneficiaries than are Caliban and the Roman crowd of *Coriolanus*.

In so far as these new approaches draw upon post-structuralist arguments, and most of them do, they conclude that Shakespeare's works have no fixed inherent meanings, but rather an open 'play' of signification from which different versions of 'Shakespeare' can be reconstructed. As a consequence, the focus of critical argument tends to be displaced from the 'true' meanings of the plays and poems to the history of the constructions placed upon them, and the cultural uses to which they have been put. A substantial section of *Political Shakespeare*, for example, is devoted to studies by Alan Sinfield and others of various 'reproductions' of Shakespeare in the educational system, in the theatre, and in cinematic or televisual forms, examining the political implications of attempts to 'fix' Shakespeare in place as an authority. Similar studies are collected in *The Shakespeare Myth* (ed. G. Holderness, 1988); and a full-length survey of the degree to which 'Shakespeare' has been transformed by successive generations of directors and critics was published by Gary Taylor as *Reinventing Shakespeare* (1990). The deconstructionist-Marxist treatment of Shakespeare offered by Malcolm Evans in *Signifying Nothing* includes some interpretative examination of *As You Like It* and other plays, but devotes more time to deploring the conservative ways in which modern critics (Frank Kermode, Marilyn French, and others) have resisted the openness of the texts. Within the same tradition, Terence Hawkes in *That Shakespeherian Rag* (1986) subjects an older generation of critics – including A. C. Bradley and John Dover Wilson – to ironic scrutiny, showing them to have recreated Shakespeare in their own conservative images. Hawkes announces clearly that 'beyond the various readings to which Shakespeare's plays may be subjected, there lies no final, authoritative or essential meaning to which we can ultimately turn. Our 'Shakespeare' is our invention: to read him is to write him.'[25] Similarly, Elaine Showalter's essay, 'Representing Ophelia' (1985) renounces any attempt to reclaim a 'true' Ophelia, and settles instead for an investigation of the changing ways in which the character has been used to link the ideas of women and madness.[26] This kind of work leads on to such interdisciplinary studies as Mary Hamer's *Signs of Cleopatra* (1993), which incorporates the Shakespearean text into larger accounts of history, art, film, psychology, and politics. Shakespearean criticism has thus transmuted from textual exegesis to the intertextual study of the cultural history of 'representations'.

The Novel Re-Opened

The theory of 'the novel' in this period tends to give way to a more extensive theory of 'narrative' in general, while critical engagement with novels veers sharply from defining their thematic unity to exposing their heterogeneity or plurality. One of the unmistakable benefits of the critical encounter with European structuralism in the 1960s and 70s was the learning of important lessons from the new science of 'narratology', in particular the crucial distinction made by the Russian Formalists between *fabula* (story-events) and *sjuzet* (arranged plot), and the numerous analytic distinctions developed from this foundation by Gérard Genette and other structuralist narratologists. The analytic clarity achieved by Wayne Booth's *The Rhetoric of Fiction* in 1961 was rapidly surpassed by Genette's more convincing discriminations between the different modes of narrative order and narrative point of view, ably summarized for English-speaking readers in such works as Shlomith Rimmon-Kenan's *Narrative Fiction* (1984). While these changes may be regarded as more or less technical adjustments, they reflect a deeper cultural shift within criticism, away from evaluative commentary and towards a 'scientific' account of the basic codes of intelligibility used by novels and their readers. Jonathan Culler's *Structuralist Poetics* devotes a substantial chapter to these questions, sifting the new models of narrative and often faulting them for their arbitrariness. Culler defines too the difference that structuralist principles could make to our view of the novel and its workings: 'In place of the novel as mimesis we have the novel as a structure which plays with different modes of ordering and enables the reader to understand how he makes sense of the world.'[27] By replacing our common notion of a novel as a direct imitation of the world, a slice of life, we might be able to see, that is, how it actually uses language and linguistic conventions.

A similar 'linguistic turn' had already been taken by J. Hillis Miller, who revised his former phenomenological emphasis on authorial 'consciousness' to take account of structuralist arguments in his short book *The Form of Victorian Fiction* (1968). Here he not only agrees with Kermode in rejecting the concept of 'spatial form' in favour of a temporal account of fiction, but also begins to question the assumption that a novel can have a 'centre' from which it can be grasped as a whole. At the same time he cuts away the mimetic 'ground' from under the novel, stressing its verbal artifice. Thus in Dickens's *Our Mutual Friend*, 'language constantly calls attention to the fact that it is language. Far from affirming the independent existence of what he describes, Dickens' narrator betrays in a number of ways the fact that fictional narrators and their world are made only of words.' More generally, any novel 'generates its own linguistic reality rather than bearing a one to one correspondence to some objective reality.'[28] In this work, Miller starts on the road to his later full-blown deconstructionist position, already moving from the 'vertical' connection between novel and world to the 'lateral' relations among the novel's own formal elements.

Even as he travelled this path from 'consciousness'-criticism to structuralism and beyond to deconstruction, Miller maintained a profound attachment to the value of nineteenth-century realist fiction. By contrast, several new theorists of the novel imbibed from the post-structuralism of Roland Barthes' *S/Z* (1970) an anti-mimetic doctrine that expressed itself not just as a critical preference for non-realistic modernist anti-novels (*Finnegans Wake*, the French *nouveau roman*) over such realist works as those of Balzac and George Eliot, but as a 'political' verdict upon the revolutionary potential of the former and the reactionary nature of the latter. Culler may have hoped that the new French influences would bring with them a neutrally scientific approach to the varieties of literary intelligibility, but he recognized that Barthes' discrimination between undemanding 'readerly' novels and challenging 'writerly' anti-novels threatened to put in place a false opposition, despite Barthes' own cautions and qualifications. In the English-speaking world, the problem appeared most starkly and controversially in Colin MacCabe's book *James Joyce and the Revolution of the Word* (1978), which begins by drawing a sharp contrast between the works of Joyce and the 'classic realist text' represented by George Eliot's *Middlemarch*. The apparently trivial fact that Joyce avoided using quotation marks whereas Eliot did use them leads into a larger accusation against the author of *Middlemarch*, that she suppresses the linguistic writtenness of her narrative discourse, setting up the bogus authority of a 'metalanguage' that looks down on the speeches of her characters, placing the reader in a comfortable position of dominance. MacCabe defines these general features of the classic realist text as follows:

> The meta-language within such a text refuses to acknowledge its own status as writing – as marks of material difference distributed through time and space. The text outside the area of inverted commas claims to be the product of no articulation, it claims to be unwritten. The unwritten text can then attempt to staunch the haemorrhage of interpretations threatened by the material of language. Whereas other discourses within the text are considered as materials which are open to reinterpretation, the narrative discourse functions simple as a window on reality. This relationship between discourses can be taken as the defining feature of the *classic realist text*.[29]

As he proceeds to apply these principles to *Middlemarch*, MacCabe argues that such realist novels use their supposed window on reality as part of their claim to represent the invariable features of humanity with unanswerable authority. By contrast with Eliot's hierarchy of discourses, Joyce's texts acknowledge their own linguistic construction and allow a free, egalitarian interplay of their various voices.

These provocative theses drew a number of responses, the most comprehensive of them from David Lodge in his essay '*Middlemarch* and the Idea of the Classic Realist Text' (1981). Lodge, who had already, in *The*

Modes of Modern Writing (1977), regretted the assaults on realism made by Barthes and his disciples, pointed out that nineteenth-century realism is distinguished not by authoritative narrative voices (which are found in all periods) separating themselves from the voices of their characters, but, on the contrary, by the mutual contamination of voices achieved by the complex ironies of free-indirect style (*style indirect libre*), in which narrator and character become impossible to disentangle. Moreover, Eliot does not disguise the writtenness of her narration, Lodge protests, but exposes it in her notorious direct addresses to the reader, who in turn is not made comfortable in this novel but implicated in the moral failures it describes.[30] Lodge's defence of the realist novel convinced some readers, but it could not quell all political suspicions about the 'authoritarian' qualities of the traditional omniscient narrator. Some years later, the American critic D. A. Miller produced an intriguing Foucauldian analysis of the nineteenth-century novel, *The Novel and the Police* (1988), which suggests that fiction played its part in maintaining a 'disciplinary culture' of surveillance and social control. Without reference to the MacCabe-Lodge dispute, Miller argues that free-indirect style is only one of the more subtle ruses of omniscient Power:

> The master-voice of monologism never simply soliloquizes. It continually needs to confirm its authority by qualifying, canceling, endorsing, subsuming all the other voices it lets speak. No doubt the need stands behind the great prominence the nineteenth-century novel gives to *style indirect libre*, in which, respeaking a character's thoughts or speeches, the narration simultaneously subverts their authority and secures its own.[31]

The term 'monologism' used here by Miller indicates the widespread influence of the Russian Formalist-Marxist critic Mikhail Bakhtin (1895–1975), whose most important works on the novel became available in English in the 1980s. Bakhtinian approaches to the novel have their own way of politicizing formal characteristics of narrative, contrasting the monological novel (Tolstoy's, in the original version of this case) in which all voices are subordinated to one dominant perspective, with the dialogical novel (Dostoevsky's, as Bakhtin argues) in which a variety of voices and discourses contend on equal terms. This kind of distinction has been used by numerous critics of different persuasions, even including Lodge.

The problems of Roland Barthes' distinction between readerly and writerly texts were encountered from a somewhat different angle by Frank Kermode, whose *Essays on Fiction, 1971–82* (1983) record a cautious and selective incorporation of continental Theory in the course of the 1970s. Kermode admires several aspects of Barthes' work, but accuses him of seeing value in nineteenth-century 'classic' novels only in so far as they foreshadow modernism, and maintains against him that supposedly 'read-erly' (*lisible*) novels are in fact much more self-aware than Barthes would acknowledge. Put to the test of Barthes' own methods, 'readerly' novels, Kermode shows, turn out not to be as 'closed' or 'naive' as we have been told to expect, and the reason for this is that 'plurality is in the nature of narrative'.[32] Kermode, in short, values plurality and openness as much as Barthes does, but he does not imagine that modernists have a monopoly on it. In his book *The Classic* (1975), Kermode argues that textual plurality, or openness to changing interpretations, is indeed the defining feature of the 'classic'. Taking as an example Emily Brontë's *Wuthering Heights*, he challenges a recent interpretation by Q. D. Leavis which had dismissed the Heathcliff episodes as not belonging to the 'true' and timeless novel; on his side, Kermode wants to accept the entire novel, acknowledging that its meanings will vary in time and will exceed any single interpretation. Drawing on reader-response theory and on main-stream French structuralism, Kermode speaks of 'responding creatively to indeterminacies of meaning inherent in the text' and of 'the text as a system of signifiers which always shows a surplus after meeting any particular restricted reading.'[33] On the way, he insists (implicitly against dismissive views of nineteenth-century monologism) that Emily Brontë invites the reader to collaborate in the making of meanings from the text's indeterminacies.

A related conception of plurality or 'heterogeneity' in the novel is expounded in Hillis Miller's major critical work, *Fiction and Repetition* (1982), which also takes *Wuthering Heights* as an occasion to announce an important general principle of interpretation. Miller lists a number of previous readings of the novel (including Kermode's), which he declares bluntly are wrong, not because they do not throw partial light on the text but because they assume it to have a unified, logically coherent meaning that can account for all its elements.

> My argument is that the best readings will be the ones which best account for the heterogeneity of the text, its presentation of a definite group of possible meanings which are systematically interconnected, determined by the text, but logically incompatible . . . The essays on *Wuthering Heights* I have cited seem to me insufficient, not because what they say is demonstrably mistaken, but rather because there is an error in the assumption that there *is* a single secret truth about *Wuthering Heights*. This secret truth would be something formulable as a univocal principle of explanation which would account for everything in the novel. The secret truth about *Wuthering Heights*, rather, is that there is no secret truth which criticism might formulate in this way. No hidden identifiable ordering principle which will account

for everything stands at the head of the chain or at the back of the back.[34]

This is far from being a claim that the novel is a random free-for-all that could mean anything. Rather, a specific impasse of meaning will be found in the novel (any novel, Miller implies), if one traces its metaphors back to the point at which they are revealed to be in fundamental contradiction with one another. Miller's treatment of classic novels, here and in his many scattered essays, tends to emphasize their 'ungrounded' status: his deconstructive studies of Dickens, for example, show how the readers and the fictional characters are led along unending metonymic 'chains' of signification, never arriving at a point at which these meanings could be stabilized, as fictional language rivals the postponements of the Circumlocution Office itself.

It is significant that Lodge, in his defence of *Middlemarch* against Mac-Cabe's strictures, appeals to Hillis Miller's earlier (1975) deconstructive reading of that novel, a reading that exposes the incompatibility of its primary metaphors of 'vision'. For Miller's approach reveals the impossibility of narrative 'mastery' while acknowledging George Eliot's own sophisticated awareness of rhetorical instability and of the slipperiness of language. As in the writings of his Yale colleague Paul de Man, the self-contradictory quality of the literary work is regarded as its chief glory, or at least its distinctive honesty. Unlike Barthes and MacCabe, Miller has no interest in constructing fundamental oppositions between the 'openness' of modernist texts and the 'closure' of nineteenth-century works, since in his view it was the writers of the nineteenth century who discovered the 'ungrounded' world of indeterminacy consequent upon the 'disappearance of God' – the major theme of his earlier critical writings. In combining a radically sceptical textualism with a traditionally humanist respect for the great realists, Miller formulated a critical stance that earned him a position as the most representative of the leading theorists of fiction in this period. With Kermode and others, he turned the discussion of the novel away from 'organic unity' and towards the discovery of internal heterogeneity and paradox. In Tony Tanner's *Adultery in the Novel* (1979), for example, the extended analysis of novels by Rousseau, Goethe, and Flaubert points at last to the breakdown of any stable opposition between marital contract and adulterous transgression, which are paradoxically implicated in one another; thus 'The bourgeois novel of adultery finally discovers its own impossibility, and as a result sexuality, narration, and society fall apart, never to be reintegrated in the same way – if, indeed, at all.'[35]

Beside the definitions of novelistic plurality offered by Kermode and Miller, one can identify in this period a range of other agendas for the discussion of novels. At one end of the spectrum, these include critical works that assume the centrality of classic English texts of the nineteenth century, like F. R. and Q. D. Leavis's *Dickens the Novelist* (1970) and Raymond Williams's *The English Novel from Dickens to Lawrence* (1970); somewhere in the middle one might place Lodge's *The Modes of Modern Writing* (1977), while at the other end could be placed a number of works that defend and define various kinds of non-realist or anti-realist fiction: Robert Scholes's *Fabulation and Metafiction* (1979), Linda Hutcheon's *Narcissistic Narrative* (1980), Rosemary Jackson's *Fantasy: The Literature of Subversion* (1981), Christine Brooke-Rose's *A Rhetoric of the Unreal* (1981), Patricia Waugh's *Metafiction* (1984), and Brian McHale's *Postmodernist Fiction* (1987). Related to this last class of avant-gardist works are some important theoretical studies which further undermine the traditional category of the fictional 'character' by dissolving it or fragmenting its illusory coherence: Leo Bersani's *A Future for Astyanax* (1978) and Thomas Docherty's *Reading (Absent) Character* (1983) are the principal cases. Meanwhile a momentous extension of narrative analysis to nonfictional works, foreshadowed in Frye's and Kermode's earlier writings, appeared in Hayden White's analyses of history books as 'fictions' or 'emplotments' in his *Tropics of Discourse* (1978). Gillian Beer's *Darwin's Plots* (1983) brought with it similar implications for scientific narratives, and Peter Brooks subjected several of Freud's case-histories to narratological scrutiny in his *Reading for the Plot* (1984), an ambitious work which attempts to synthesize formalist narratology with a psychoanalytic understanding of desire and its narrative dynamics. These diverse explorations either derive from or exploit the dominant theme of novel criticism in this period, the conflict – often enough presented in sentimental or melodramatic terms – between fiction 'closure' and 'openness'.

Canonicities in Question

The most visibly contentious area of critical dispute in this period – at least as digested in journalist summaries – has been that of 'the canon', or more precisely of the various canons of literature that have been taken to represent national cultures in the English-speaking world. In the United States, the conflicts about the canon have been at the centre of bitter 'Culture Wars' in which the very identity of the nation and its educational system has been symbolically contested. In England, and again in Scotland, Ireland, Australasia, and the English-speaking parts of Canada, Africa, and the Caribbean, the equivalent debates have followed different rhythms and directions according to local political circumstances. Despite these differences, it is fair to say that a similar pattern of controversy has emerged in various countries, in which an older kind of argument about the deserts of specific writers (Milton or Thoreau, say) has been displaced by more general conflict over the grounds of discrimination which project certain forms of social privilege into the cultural sphere. In short, the rankings of individual poets in a given national tradition have mattered less than the narrowness of the canon as a whole, and especially the canonical predominance of socially dominant groups: male writers, middle-class writers, white writers, heterosexual writers, metropolitan writers. The problem most often identified as a matter for remedy was the relative invisibility of other kinds of writers and writings, especially in the educational syllabus. In the canon wars since the late 1970s, the contending parties have often generated more heat than light in their rival claims: conservers of the inherited canons have complained of recent political interference in a question which has in fact always been political, and have treated the causes of black writing or women's writing as special-interest lobbies while assuming that white male writers are above particular interests; while on the other side it has been too often assumed that a literary canon or syllabus has the same functions as a democratic legislature in which proportional representation is owed to all constituent communities, and that the principal purpose of literature is to express or affirm the uncomplicated 'identity' of each author. Meanwhile, in another corner of the battlefield, each newly emerging school of Theory pulled the canon in a different direction, favouring such texts as confirmed its theses, and the older canon of plays, poems, and novels was occluded by a new canon of constantly-invoked theoretical scriptures.

The major debates on these questions were launched in the late 1970s, but there were some notable preliminary disturbances leading up to them. In England, the notoriously tight Leavisite canon of fiction had been unravelling slowly since its announcement in 1948. By 1970, F. R. and Q. D. Leavis had relented so far from their earlier dismissals of Dickens as to publish a joint volume of tributes to his genius in *Dickens the Novelist*. This belated rehabilitation was not greeted warmly by critics who had themselves been trying to uphold Dickens's reputation against Leavisite resistance, and the Leavises were rebuked for failing to account for their past injustice to the novelist. In the same year, Raymond Williams published his series of lectures on *The English Novel from Dickens to Lawrence*, a corrective response to Leavis's *The Great Tradition* which restores Hardy as well as Dickens to the list of the great English novelists. This book is unusual in Williams's writings in being the most traditionally 'canonical' in focus. His other works of this period either emphasize the importance of such neglected labouring writers as John Clare and Robert Tressell, or look well beyond the literary sphere into the worlds of journalism and television. While Williams attempted to revise the Leavisite canon as it disintegrated, Frank Kermode offered an important revisionist response to T. S. Eliot's 1945 lecture *What is a Classic?* in his series of lectures *The Classic* (1975). Designating Eliot's idea of the canon an 'imperialist' conception based upon belief in Virgil as the cultural father of the eternal Holy Roman Empire, Kermode offered a secular modern view of what is expected of a canonical or 'classic' text. Whereas the ancient classic was thought to provide definitive answers, the modern classic – like the modern way of reading the old classic – would raise a multitude of questions. Kermode argues that for a literary text to survive for a long time as a 'classic', it needs not a single positive quality such as 'maturity' but an openness to changing interpretations or, in stucturalist parlance, a 'surplus of signifier'. In this influential view, 'the only works we value enough to call classic are those which . . . are complex and indeterminate enough to allow us our necessary pluralities . . . It is in the nature of works of art to be open, in so far as they are "good"; though it is in the nature of authors, and of readers, to close them.'[36] These were important general reflections on the logic of 'canonicity', but they were soon overtaken by specific activist campaigns for major revision of the actually existing canons.

Of the various political challenges to 'the canon' – usually meaning the canons of British and American literature accepted in the anthologies and literary histories of the 1940s and 50s – the most successful and far-reaching has been that conducted by feminist scholars and publishers. Among the pioneering gynocritical studies, Ellen Moers's *Literary Women* (1976) included a catalogue of 250 women writers, and Elaine Showalter's *A Literature of Their Own* (1977) included brief accounts of many lost or forgotten figures awaiting rediscovery. They thus mapped out a pro-gramme of canonical reclamation, which was pursued into special literary periods by such critics as Nina Baym, who rescued American women novelists of the nineteenth century from Hawthorne's notorious dismissal in her *Woman's Fiction* (1978), and the Australian feminist Dale Spender, whose *Mothers of the Novel* (1986) showed how Ian Watt's and other standard accounts of the eighteenth-century 'rise of the novel' had pushed numerous women novelists into invisibility. A monument of feminist re-canonization was soon constructed as the compendious *Norton Anthology of Literature by Women* (ed. S. Gilbert and S. Gubar, 1985). At the same time the general anthologies and textbooks began to include recently rediscovered women writers. The difference can be felt in, for example, the difference between the first (1979) and second (1985) editions of the enormous two-volume *Norton Anthology of American Literature*, the most important such collection in the classrooms of the United States: for the second edition, the editors (who included Nina Baym) added Rebecca Harding Davis's *Life in the Iron Mills*, Charlotte Perkins Gilman's *The Yellow Wallpaper*, and works by Sarah Orne Jewett, Zora Neale Hurston, Ellen Glasgow, and Alice Walker. By this time, Kate Chopin's novel *The Awakening* (1899) had also reappeared from long neglect to become an American 'classic', with its own Norton Critical Edition (1976). The English canon too had, by the late 1980s, been overhauled to include

Aphra Behn and Mary Shelley, and to restore Elizabeth Barrett Browning and Christina Rossetti, while Virginia Woolf seemed to displace her male modernist contemporaries in critical attention. Specialist anthologies recovered a wealth of forgotten women's poetry from past centuries, as in Germaine Greer's *Kissing the Rod: An Anthology of Seventeenth-Century Women's Verse* (1988) and Roger Lonsdale's *Eighteenth-Century Women Poets* (1989). The important new market for reprints of works by redis-covered women writers, identified by feminist publishing houses and further exploited by others, established this major shift in the canon as a genuine remoulding of the reading public well beyond the confines of the academy.

A similar movement of canonical restoration has been conducted by and on behalf of African-American writers, helping to reshape the Ameri-can canon. A leading figure in this campaign has been Houston A. Baker Jr, who co-edited with Leslie Fiedler a collection of essays, *English Litera-ture: Opening Up the Canon* (1981), in which contributors complained of the canon's exclusion of black and other traditions. Baker's own contri-bution to the rediscovery of black writing has included an edition of the *Narrative of the Life of Frederick Douglass, an American Slave*, which has quickly become the most securely canonized of the many slave narratives rediscovered in this period. Another leading African-American literary scholar, Henry Louis Gates Jr, reprinted the first novel published by a black American, Harriet Wilson's *Our Nig* (1859, 1982), and went on to edit the 30–volume *Schomburg Library of 19th-Century Black Women Writers* (1988) and *The Classic Slave Narratives* (1987), while also organizing the rediscovery of countless stories, poems, and other pieces from black periodicals of the nineteenth and early twentieth centuries. In this period, the canon of twentieth-century African-American literature was rapidly 'feminized', as the formerly predominant figures of Hughes, Wright, Ellison, and Baldwin were overshadowed by the rediscovered Zora Neale Hurston and by more recent women writers, notably Alice Walker and Toni Morrison. Walker's *The Color Purple* (1982) and Morrison's *Beloved* (1987) were canonized almost as soon as they appeared.

A general insurgence of hitherto 'silenced' literary subcultures against the dominance of a restricted list of Englishmen and New Englanders had its repercussions across the Atlantic in the unusual conditions of Ireland, which had no recognized literary canon of its own until one was invented for it in the compendious three-volume *Field Day Anthology of Irish Writing* (1991), edited by Seamus Deane and a large team of collaborators. By-passing the exclusive approach beloved of the British, Deane's group went straight for an inclusive treatment, taking in a host of 'minor' writers under several categories, and embracing non-fictional genres including a section on the political prose and oratory of Ulster, edited by Tom Paulin. Despite its good intentions, the anthology failed to satisfy feminist critics, who lamented its meagre representation of Irish women's writing; and so a fourth, women-only volume was commissioned. Outside the anthology itself, the critical writings of Deane, Paulin, and others of their generation have been important in redefining the literary traditions of Ireland and their complicated relations with those of Britain.

The *Field Day Anthology* was not the only anthology of the 1990s to provoke canonical scandal. Jerome McGann's *New Oxford Book of Romantic Period Verse* (1993) represents a determined effort to display the poetry of its designated period (1785–1832) in a way that breaks up our inherited fascination with six or seven individual 'romantics' by dispersing their works among those of several long-forgotten poets, especially women poets such as Amelia Opie and Laetitia Landon. The poems selected are arranged not by author but by year of publication, allowing us to read major and minor figures alongside one another as their first readers would. The reputations prevailing in the period itself have some influence on the selections, so that Byron is restored to equal prominence with Wordsworth, whose *Prelude*, central to twentieth-century conceptions of Romantic poetry, of course disappears entirely as a work not published until 1850. British critics regretted the fact that John Clare was represented by only one poem, but otherwise recognized in McGann's anthology a refreshing new construction of the 'Romantic' age in English literature.

The principles applied by McGann in his anthology are essentially those of the 'new historicism'. Other schools of modern literary theory had their own ways of amending the canon, usually by highlighting particular works that proved amenable to their ideals or methods. In some cases, these works would be cited and reinterpreted repeatedly because they had been used as examples in key works of literary theory. Poe's tale 'The Purloined Letter' is an example, as it was used by Lacan himself, and so invoked in his psychoanalytic tradition evermore. Likewise, Balzac's novella *Sarrasine* would have remained utterly obscure had it not been treated to an exhaustive analysis by Roland Barthes. Post-structuralist theory also tended to favour the ludic self-referentiality of Sterne's *Tristram Shandy* to the more earnest line of English fiction, to prefer Woolf's *Orlando* to her *The Years*, and to revel in the equivocations of Melville's *The Confidence Man* or of Henry James's later works. Psychoanalytic critics and others found much to discover in previously uncanonized popular works of terror and fantasy, thus helping such works as *Frankenstein* and *Dracula* on to the academic syllabus. Deconstruction, as we have noticed, had a strong bias towards Romantic poetry, but it could perform its arts on realistic prose as well. Post-colonial theory and criticism had the curious effect of directing attention to novels such as *Kim* and *She*, which had been discarded as disreputable by liberal opinion. Marxist criticism, oddly, had far less impact on the canon than did structuralism, the 'scientific' neutrality of which helped to bring certain forms of popular fiction – especially the detective story and the women's romance – into the seminar room on what was in principle an equal basis with canonized works. Narratology proved to be, in this respect, a great leveller.

It was often noticed in the 1980s that the partisans of Theory objected in principle to the narrowness of the canon, or perhaps to the whole idea of canons, but then in practice usually proceeded to write about Shakespeare or Hawthorne all the same, 're-reading' them from yet another new angle. At the same time, a new pantheon of 'star' theorists emerged, the invocation of whose names alone would too often suffice in place of a substantiated argument. The translated writings of Barthes, Derrida, Kristeva, Lacan, Foucault, and Cixous, with numerous commentaries thereon, outsold the likes of Samuel Johnson or S. T. Coleridge, and were granted an equivalent authority as canonical texts. While chastely repudiating the hierarchical nature of canons, the culture of Theory inadvertently nourished a canon of its own.

Limits to Postcriticism

Some of the more important general trends we have noticed in the previous period can be seen to have asserted themselves with even greater force after 1968: the predominance of the still-expanding university system and of its professionalized protocols over the still-shrinking realm of public critical discussion, the theoretical and metacritical self-consciousness of the academic critics, and the related 'babel of interpretations'. The major new factors, already touched upon, have been the domestications of European intellectual influences, and the radicalizing ferment of various movements of social protest. In terms of the prevailing intellectual disposition of criticism and literary theory, the most significant effect of these trends has been the establishment of a pluralist 'bazaar' of critical approaches and theoretical schools, sustained by an ethos of 'openness', plurality or heterogeneity which governs attitudes to interpretative legitimacy, canonicity, and even aesthetic value. As each of these approaches has constructed self-confirming discourses which render it more or less deaf to critical challenge from its competitors, so the bazaar as a whole has tended to insulate itself from the corrective influences of a secular reading public outside the academy, thus exposing it instead to sudden vagaries of intellectual fashion and to the incrustations of jargon. At a superficial but symptomatic level, the effects can be registered in the forms of critical book-titles. Where a literary-critical work of the 1950s would usually be called something like *The Plangent Muse* or *The Indomitable Self*, its equivalent in the 1980s would appear under a title devised according to the Bracket/Slash/Buzzword formula sacred to the memory of Roland Barthes: *Discourse/Desire/(M)other*, for instance, or *Gendering/Bod(il)y/(Sub)versions*.

The pluralist bazaar of contemporary critical schools finds room for hitherto inconceivable kinds of argument and investigation. There have been full-length studies of brackets in English poetry, and even of cucumbers and pumpkins in literature.[37] Minor 'schools' of literary theory inspired by new political discourses have included eco-criticism, nuclear criticism, and feminist-vegetarian theory.[38] A more substantial new development in literary studies and in related fields of cultural analysis, and one that could not have appeared before 1968, is the emergence of Queer Theory among lesbian and gay academics, especially in the United States: there are now more new literary-theoretical works appearing on sodomy than on prosody. One of the leading Queer Theorists, Eve Kosofsky Sedgwick, presented a paper to the 1989 MLA convention entitled 'Jane Austen and the Masturbating Girl', of which the very title alone was sufficient to persuade some journalists that Western civilization had come to an end. In fact her essay as published is a thoughtful investigation of Marianne Dashwood's strange distraction in Austen's *Sense and Sensibility*. Like her later essay, 'Is the Rectum Straight?', on the 'anal erotics' of Henry James's *The Wings of the Dove*, it discovers sexual subtexts hitherto undetected by orthodox Freudians, and takes the canonical literary text as an occasion for questioning the ways in which sexualities have been defined and classified.[39] These may be provocatively 'deviant' readings, but they are in one sense orthodox, in their effort to 'open' the significances of a literary text and thereby to highlight the heterogeneity of sexual identities.

It is important to remember, though, that the same pluralism that harbours Queer Theory, deconstruction, and cultural materialism (all of them denounced in the public press as dangerous perversions) also tolerates the unfashionable survival of older humanist and formalist versions of criticism. This chapter has concentrated on the novelties in post-1968 criticism, but it should not finish without recalling the substantial numbers of critics who have not felt obliged to abandon their traditional conceptions of mimesis, aesthetic unity, and authorial intention, to learn the new language of fractured subject-positions and counter-hegemonic discursive formations, or to cast their every article on versification as a 'political' intervention into the crisis of patriarchal bourgeois subjectivity. Some of them, like M. H. Abrams, have engaged in direct debate with the practitioners of Theory, while most others have let Theory pass them by as a fad irrelevant to their essential literary interests. To take an example almost at random, the American critic Helen Vendler, a professor at Harvard who has also written regularly as poetry critic for the *New Yorker* magazine, still pursues sensitive 'close reading' of modern poetry according to New-Critical traditions, and sees little in the clamour of recent decades to distract her from this task. Her collection of essays, *The Music of What Happens* (1988), opens with a reaffirmation of her commitment to a distinctively 'aesthetic criticism':

> The aim of a properly aesthetic criticism . . . is not primarily to reveal the *meaning* of an art work or disclose (or argue for or against) the ideological *values* of an art work. The aim of an aesthetic criticism is to *describe* the art work in such a way that it cannot be confused with any other art work (not an easy task), and to *infer* from the art work the aesthetic that might generate this unique configuration.[40]

It is not that either interpretation or ideological analysis is, for Vendler, illegitimate: they may have a useful preparatory role. It is simply that they are insufficient: neither approach is finally able to respect the formal integrity and uniqueness of the art work. Likewise the deconstructive analysis of rhetorical self-contradictions leaves out the more complex aesthetic dimensions of the work. It is worth noting that Vendler cites the authority of the Marxist theorists Theodor Adorno and Walter Benjamin in defending the specifically aesthetic approach from hasty ideological 'decodings'.

The example of Helen Vendler – which may be taken as representative of many others – should be borne in mind when considering the directions that criticism might be taking after more than twenty years of debate about Theory. For there is an apocalyptic assumption, magnified by the discourses of 'postmodernism', that the successive Deaths of God, of the novel, of the Author and, needless to say, of Man have spelt also the deaths of literature and of criticism, which dissolve themselves into the undifferentiated randomness of signification. The kernel of truth in this overstated prognosis is that the commanding status within the academic realm of the humanities that was once claimed by literary criticism and is now silently assumed by literary theory has been undermined by various forms of interdisciplinary study – Women's Studies, Cultural Studies, and other formations which subsume literary study under the heading of cultural history. At the same time, within literary studies, the tradition of literary history, repudiated by a triumphant critical formalism in mid-century, has reasserted itself, not just in the form of the 'new historicism', but in various unaffiliated versions. The model of Lit. Crit. that reigned as New Criticism or in the form of the Leavisism has indeed succumbed to new assaults, but this does not put an end either to criticism or to its specifically literary applications. Wherever any culture produces texts, performances, or events that allow for diverse responses and disagreements, criticism will again break out spontaneously, as it regularly does outside every theatre, art gallery, concert hall, or cinema. As T. S. Eliot reminded us at the start of his most important essay, 'criticism is as inevitable as breathing'.[41]

Notes

1. Gerald Graff, *Literature against itself: Literary Ideas in Modern Society* (Chicago 1979), p. 28.
2. Jonathan Culler, *Structuralist Poetics: Structuralism, Linguistics and the Study of Literature* (1975), p. 130.
3. David Lodge, *The Modes of Modern Writing: Metaphor, Metonymy, and the Typology of Modern Literature* (1977), pp. 8–9.
4. Lodge, *Modes of Modern Writing*, p. 69.
5. Norman Holland, 'Reading and Identity: A Psychoanalytic Revolution', *Academy Forum* 23 (1979), p. 8.
6. See Elizabeth Freund, *The Return of the Reader: Reader-Response Criticism* (1987), pp. 124–9.
7. Stanley Fish, *Is There a Text in This Class? The Authority of Interpretive Communities* (Cambridge, MA, 1980), pp. 322–37.
8. Geoffrey H. Hartman, Preface to Harold Bloom, Paul de Man, Jacques Derrida, Geoffrey H. Hartman, and J. Hillis Miller, *Deconstruction and Criticism* (New York, 1979), p. vii.
9. Paul de Man, *Blindness and Insight: Essays in the Rhetoric of Contemporary Criticism* (2nd edn, Minneapolis, MN, 1983), p. 17.
10. Paul de Man, *Allegories of Reading: Figural Language in Rousseau, Nietzsche, Rilke, and Proust* (New Haven, 1979), pp. 11–12.
11. Barbara Johnson, *The Critical Difference: Essays in the Contemporary Rhetoric of Reading* (Baltimore, 1980), pp. 79–109.
12. Geoffrey H. Hartman, *Criticism in the Wilderness: The Study of Literature Today* (New Haven, 1980), p. 8.
13. Harold Bloom, *Poetry and Repression: Revisionism from Blake to Stevens* (New Haven, 1976), p. 2.
14. Harold Bloom, *A Map of Misreading* (New York, 1975), p. 3.
15. Harold Bloom, *The Anxiety of Influence: A Theory of Poetry* (New York, 1973), p. 70.
16. Edward Said, *The World, the Text, and the Critic* (Cambridge, MA, 1983), p. 4.
17. Raymond Williams, *Problems in Materialism and Culture* (1980), p. 48.
18. See Toril Moi, *Sexual/Textual Politics: Feminist Literary Theory* (1985), pp. 24–31; Cora Kaplan, 'Radical Feminism and Literature: Rethinking Millett's *Sexual Politics*', *Red Letters* 9 (1979), pp. 4–16.
19. Gayatri Chakravorty Spivak, 'Three Women's Texts and a Critique of Imperialism', *Critical Inquiry* 12 (1985), pp. 243–61.
20. Raymond Williams, *Marxism and Literature* (Oxford, 1977), p. 125.
21. Richard Wilson, Introduction to *New Historicism and Renaissance Drama* eds Richard Wilson and Richard Dutton (1992), pp. 1–18.
22. Leslie A. Fiedler, *The Stranger in Shakespeare* (1972; St Albans, 1974), p. 37.
23. Stephen Greenblatt, 'Invisible Bullets: Renaissance Authority and its Subversion, *Henry IV* and *Henry V*', in Jonathan Dollimore and Alan Sinfield (eds), *Political Shakespeare: New Essays in Cultural Materialism* (Manchester, 1985), p. 29. This

essay also appears in a revised form in Stephen Greenblatt, *Shakespearean Nego-tiations* (Oxford, 1988), pp. 21–65.

24. Terry Eagleton, *William Shakespeare* (Oxford, 1986), p. 1.
25. Terence Hawkes, *That Shakespeherian Rag: Essays on a Critical Process* (1986), p. 124.
26. Elaine Showalter, 'Representing Ophelia: women, madness, and the responsibilities of feminist criticism', in Patrica Parker and Geoffrey Hartman (eds), *Shakespeare and the Question of Theory* (1985), pp. 77–94.
27. Culler, *Structuralist Poetics*, p. 238.
28. J. Hillis Miller, *The Form of Victorian Fiction* (Notre Dame, IN, 1968), pp. 36, 72.
29. Colin MacCabe, *James Joyce and the Revolution of the Word* (1978), p. 15.
30. David Lodge, '*Middlemarch* and the Idea of the Classic Realist Text', in Arnold Kettle (ed.), *The Nineteenth Century Novel: Critical Essays and Documents* (1981), pp. 218–38.
31. D. A. Miller, *The Novel and the Police* (Berkeley, CA, 1988), p. 25.
32. Frank Kermode, *Essays on Fiction, 1971–82* (1983), p. 111; see also pp. 72–91.
33. Frank Kermode, *The Classic: Literary Images of Permanence and Change* (1975; revd edn, Cambridge, MA, 1983), pp. 134, 135.
34. J. Hillis Miller, *Fiction and Repetition: Seven English Novels* (Oxford, 1982), p. 51.
35. Tony Tanner, *Adultery in the Novel: Contract and Transgression* (Baltimore, MD, 1979), p. 14.
36. Kermode, *The Classic*, pp. 140, 121.
37. See John Lennard, *But I Digress: The Exploitation of Parentheses in English Printed Verse* (Oxford, 1991), and Ralf Norman and Jon Haarberg, *Nature and Language: A Semiotic Study of Cucurbits in Literature* (1980).
38. See Carol J. Adams, *The Sexual Politics of Meat: A Feminist-Vegetarian Critical Theory* (New York, 1990).
39. Both essays are reprinted in Eve Kosofsky Sedgwick, *Tendencies* (Durham, NC, 1993).
40. Helen Vendler, *The Music of What Happens: Poems, Poets, Critics* (Cambridge, MA, 1988), p. 2.
41. Eliot, *Sacred Wood*, p. 48 ('Tradition and the Individual Talent').

Chronology

DATE	WORKS OF CRITICISM, AND LITERARY PERIODICALS	OTHER WORKS	HISTORICAL/CULTURAL EVENTS
1890	Ellis *The New Spirit* Symonds *Essays Speculative and Suggestive* *Bookman* (London, to 1934) *Review of Reviews* (London, to 1953) *National Observer* (London, to 1897)	Morris *News from Nowhere* Frazer *The Golden Bough* Dickinson *Poems* Ibsen *Hedda Gabler*	Battle of Wounded Knee Fall of Parnell
1891	Wilde *Intentions* Shaw *Quintessence of Ibsenism* Howells *Criticism and Fiction* Moore *Impressions and Opinions* *Review of Reviews* (New York, to 1937)	Gissing *New Grub Street* Hardy *Tess of the D'Urbervilles* Wilde *Picture of Dorian Gray*	International Copyright Law
1892	Saintsbury *Miscellaneous Essays* *Sewanee Review* (Tennessee, to 1973) *Yale Review* (New Haven)	Wilde *Lady Windermere's Fan* Doyle *Adventures of Sherlock Holmes*	Death of Tennyson Death of Whitman

DATE	WORKS OF CRITICISM, AND LITERARY PERIODICALS	OTHER WORKS	HISTORICAL/CULTURAL EVENTS
1893	Symonds *Walt Whitman* James *Essays in London and Elsewhere* Gosse *Questions at Issue* *Pall Mall Magazine* (London, to 1914)	Crane *Maggie* Yeats *The Celtic Twilight* F. H. Bradley *Appearance and Reality*	Independent Labour Party
1894	Swinburne *Studies in Prose and Poetry* Garland *Crumbling Idols* Johnson *The Art of Thomas Hardy* *The Yellow Book* (London, to 1897) *New Age* (London, to 1938)	Moore *Esther Waters* Twain *Pudd'nhead Wilson* Shaw *Arms and the Man*	France: Dreyfus Trial Death of Pater Death of Christina Rossetti Death of Stevenson
1895	Howells *My Literary Passions* Shaw *A Degenerate's View of Nordau* Courthope *History of English Poetry* *Bookman* (New York, to 1933) *M'lle New York* (New York, to 1899)	Wilde *Importance of Being Earnest* Crane *The Red Badge of Courage* Hardy *Jude the Obscure* Wells *The Time Machine*	Wilde imprisoned for 2 years Lumière's Cinematograph X-rays discovered
1896	Saintsbury *History of Nineteenth Century Literature*	Housman *A Shropshire Lad* Jewett *Country of the Pointed Firs*	Edison film projector Nobel Prizes Olympic Games Puccini's *La Bohème* Death of William Morris

DATE	WORKS OF CRITICISM, AND LITERARY PERIODICALS	OTHER WORKS	HISTORICAL/CULTURAL EVENTS
	Savoy (London, 1896 only) *New York Times Saturday Review of Books* *Pageant* (London, to 1897) *Cosmopolis* (London, to 1898)		
1897	Raleigh *Style*	James *What Maisie Knew*	Klondike Gold Rush Vienna Secession artists
	Symons *Studies in Two Literatures*	Conrad *Nigger of the 'Narcissus'*	
	Dome (London, to 1900) *Literature* (London, to 1902) *Literary Review* (Boston, to 1901) *Journal of Germanic Philology* (Urbana)	Stoker *Dracula* Ellis *Sexual Inversion*	
1898	Saintsbury *Short History of English Literature* Gissing *Charles Dickens*	Wilde *Ballad of Reading Gaol* James *The Turn of the Screw* Hardy *Wessex Poems* Shaw *Plays Pleasant and Unpleasant*	Spanish-American War US annexes Hawaii British conquest of Sudan Radium discovered US acquires Philippines, Puerto Rico
1899	*Anglo-Saxon Review* (London, to 1901)	Yeats *The Wind Among the Reeds* Chopin *The Awakening*	Boer War, to 1902 Irish Literary Theatre
1900	Symons *Symbolist Movement in Literature*	Conrad *Lord Jim* Dreiser *Sister Carrie*	Labour Party founded China: Boxer Rebellion S. Africa: Relief of Mafeking

DATE	WORKS OF CRITICISM, AND LITERARY PERIODICALS	OTHER WORKS	HISTORICAL/CULTURAL EVENTS
	Saintsbury *History of Criticism* Santayana *Interpretations of Poetry &* *Religion* Raleigh *Milton* *Smart Set* (New York, to 1930) *Monthly Review* (London, to 1907)	Freud *Interpretation of Dreams* Quiller-Couch *Oxford Book of English* *Verse*	Death of Wilde Death of Nietzsche Planck's quantum theory Puccini's *Tosca*
1901	Howells *Heroines of Fiction* Collins *Ephemera Critica* Courthope *Life in Poetry, Law in Taste* *Samhain* (Dublin, to 1908)	Yeats *Poems* Washington *Up from Slavery* Chekhov *Three Sisters*	Death of Queen Victoria President McKinley assassinated T. Roosevelt President, to 1909 Transatlantic radio signal
1902	Howells *Literature and Life* Stephen *George Eliot* *Times Literary Supplement* (London) *South Atlantic Quarterly* (Durham, NC)	Conrad *Heart of Darkness* James *The Wings of the Dove* Bennett *Anna of the Five Towns*	First radio messages
1903	Yeats *Ideas of Good and Evil* Raleigh *Wordsworth* Norris *Responsibilities of a Novelist* *Modern Philology* (Chicago)	James *The Ambassadors* Butler *The Way of All Flesh* Shaw *Man and Superman*	Wright brothers' flight Ford Motor Company Pankhurst founds Women's Social and Political Union Bolshevik-Menshevik split Rhodes scholarships

DATE	WORKS OF CRITICISM, AND LITERARY PERIODICALS	OTHER WORKS	HISTORICAL/CULTURAL EVENTS
1904	Bradley *Shakespearean Tragedy* More *Shelburne Essays* (First Series) Stephen *English Literature & Society in the 18th Century* Symons *Studies in Prose and Verse*	Conrad *Nostromo* James *The Golden Bowl* Chekhov *The Cherry Orchard* Barrie *Peter Pan*	Abbey Theatre, Dublin Puccini's *Madame Butterfly* Russo–Japanese War
1905	Mencken *G. B. Shaw* Huneker *Iconoclasts* *Modern Language Review* (Cambridge) *The Dickensian* (London)	Wharton *The House of Mirth* Forster *Where Angels Fear to Tread* Shaw *Major Barbara* Freud *Three Essays on Sexuality*	Russian revolution Special theory of relativity Fauvist painting IWW founded Sinn Fein founded
1906	Saintsbury *History of English Prosody* Chesterton *Charles Dickens* *Studies in Philology* (Chapel Hill, NC)	Sinclair *The Jungle* Galsworthy *The Man of Property*	San Francisco earthquake Everyman's Library Death of Ibsen
1907	James Prefaces to Novels and Tales (to 1917) Raleigh *Shakespeare* Gosse *Ibsen*	Synge *Playboy of the Western World* Conrad *The Secret Agent* Adams *Education of Henry Adams*	Cubist painting Kipling wins Nobel Prize

DATE	WORKS OF CRITICISM, AND LITERARY PERIODICALS	OTHER WORKS	HISTORICAL/CULTURAL EVENTS
	Elton *Modern Studies* *English Association Bulletin* (London)	Gosse *Father and Son*	
1908	Babbitt *Literature and the American College* James *Views and Reviews* *English Review* (London, to 1937)	Forster *A Room With a View* Bennett *The Old Wives' Tale*	Suffragette rallies First nickelodeon Boy Scouts
1909	Bradley *Oxford Lectures on Poetry* Symons *Romantic Movement in English Poetry* Bennett *Literary Taste* *Friday Literary Review* (Chicago, to 1914)	Pound *Personae* Stein *Three Lives* Wells *Tono-Bungay*	NAACP founded Model T Ford Blériot's Channel flight Peary reaches North Pole Death of Swinburne Death of Meredith
1910	Babbitt *The New Laokoon* Santayana *Three Philosophical Poets* Pound *The Spirit of Romance*	Forster *Howard's End* Yeats *The Green Helmet* Wells *History of Mr Polly*	International Psychoanalytic Association Post-Impressionist Exhibition, London Deaths of Tolstoy, Edward VII Stravinsky's Firebird
1911	Hueffer *The Critical Attitude* Spingarn *The New Criticism* *Masses/Liberator* (New York, to 1924) *Rhythm* (London, to 1913)	Conrad *Under Western Eyes* Wharton *Ethan Frome* Pound *Canzoni*	Amundsen reaches South Pole House of Lords' powers reduced Mexican Revolution begins

DATE	WORKS OF CRITICISM, AND LITERARY PERIODICALS	OTHER WORKS	HISTORICAL/CULTURAL EVENTS
1912	Yeats *The Cutting of an Agate*	Marsh (ed.) *Georgian Poetry*	Sinking of the *Titanic* Scott reaches South Pole
	Babbitt *Masters of Modern French Criticism*	Dreiser *The Financier*	US invades Nicaragua Wave of strikes in Britain
	Saintsbury *History of English Prose Rhythm*	Mann *Death in Venice*	
	Elton *Survey of English Literature 1780–1830*		
	Ker *English Literature: Medieval*		
	Poetry (Chicago) *Poetry Review* (London)		
1913	Saintsbury *The English Novel*	Lawrence *Sons and Lovers*	W. Wilson President, to 1921 First assembly lines
	Hueffer *Henry James*	Proust *Du Côté de chez Swann*	Pankhurst imprisoned for riot English translation of
	Eastman *Enjoyment of Poetry*	Shaw *Pygmalion*	Freud's *Interpretation of Dreams* Stravinsky's *Rite of*
	Poetry and Drama (London, to 1914) *New Statesman* (London) *Reedy's Mirror* (St Louis, to 1920)	Conrad *Chance* Freud *Totem and Taboo*	*Spring*
1914	James *Notes on Novelists*	Joyce *Dubliners*	Great War begins Panama Canal opens US sends troops to
	Murray *Hamlet and Orestes*	Yeats *Responsibilities*	Mexico
	Little Review (Chicago/ New York, to 1928) *Blast* (London, to 1915) *Egoist* (London, to 1919)	Hardy *Satires of Circumstance* Bell *Art*	

DATE	WORKS OF CRITICISM, AND LITERARY PERIODICALS	OTHER WORKS	HISTORICAL/CULTURAL EVENTS
1915	Moulton *The Modern Study of Literature* V. W. Brooks *America's Coming of Age* *Texas Review/Southwest Review* (Austin)	Lawrence *The Rainbow* Hueffer *The Good Soldier* Lowell (ed.) *Some Imagist Poets* Griffith *Birth of a Nation* (cin.)	Sinking of the *Lusitania* Turkey and Italy enter war Gallipoli landings General theory of relativity
1916	Quiller-Couch *On the Art of Writing* Saintsbury *The Peace of the Augustans* Murry *Fyodor Dostoevsky* *Seven Arts* (New York, to 1917) *Dial* (New York; formerly Chicago, to 1929)	Joyce *A Portrait of the Artist* Pound *Lustra* Griffith *Intolerance* (cin.)	Easter Rising, Dublin Battle of Somme First use of tanks US invades Mexico Death of Henry James
1917	Mencken *Book of Prefaces* Spingarn *Creative Criticism* Sherman *Matthew Arnold* *Art and Letters* (London, to 1920) *To-Day* (London, to 1923)	Eliot *Prufrock* Yeats *The Wild Swans at Coole*	US enters war Russian revolutions Balfour Declaration
1918	Quiller-Couch *Studies in Literature* Beach *The Method of Henry James* Bridges *The Necessity of Poetry*	Hopkins *Poems* Strachey *Eminent Victorians* Cather *My Ántonia*	Brest-Litovsk Treaty German Republic Armistice ends Great War Limited female suffrage in Britain

DATE	WORKS OF CRITICISM, AND LITERARY PERIODICALS	OTHER WORKS	HISTORICAL/CULTURAL EVENTS
1919	Babbitt *Rousseau and Romanticism* Mencken *Prejudices* (1st Series) Aiken *Scepticisms* *London Mercury* (to 1939) *Voices* (London, to 1921) *Year's Work in English Studies* (London)	Woolf *Night and Day* Anderson *Winesburg, Ohio* Keynes *Economic Consequences of Peace*	Versailles Conference League of Nations Amritsar Massacre First transatlantic flight Bauhaus founded, Weimar
1920	Eliot *The Sacred Wood* Pound *Instigations* Murry *Aspects of Literature* Symons *Charles Baudelaire* V. W. Brooks *The Ordeal of Mark Twain* *Freeman* (New York, to 1924) *Saturday Review of Literature* (New York) *Time and Tide* (London, to 1979) *Frontier* (Missoula, MT, to 1939)	Lawrence *Women in Love* Yeats *Michael Robartes & the Dancer* Owen *Poems* Eliot *Poems* Pound *Hugh Selwyn Mauberley* Mansfield *Bliss & Other Stories* Weston *From Ritual to Romance*	Women's suffrage in USA Prohibition in USA Ireland partitioned
1921	Lubbock *The Craft of Fiction* James *Notes and Reviews* Mencken *Prejudices* (2nd Series)	Strachey *Queen Victoria* O'Neill *The Hairy Ape* Pirandello *Six Characters in Search of an Author*	BBC founded British-Irish Treaty Sacco-Vanzetti Trial New Economic Policy, Russia

DATE	WORKS OF CRITICISM, AND LITERARY PERIODICALS	OTHER WORKS	HISTORICAL/CULTURAL EVENTS
	Van Doren *The American Novel* *The Reviewer* (Richmond, VA, to 1925) *Double Dealer* (New Orleans, to 1926)		
1922	Murry *Problem of Style; Countries of the Mind* Sherman *Americans* Strachey *Books and Characters* *Criterion* (London, to 1939) *Fugitive* (Nashville, to 1925) *Secession* (New York, to 1924) *Golden Hind* (London, to 1924) *Philological Quarterly* (Iowa City)	Joyce *Ulysses* Eliot *The Waste Land* Yeats *Later Poems* Lewis *Babbitt* Mansfield *The Garden Party* Fitzgerald *The Beautiful and the Damned* Wittgenstein *Tractatus Logico-Philosophicus*	Irish Civil War Irish Free State First BBC radio broadcasts Mussolini dictatorship, Italy First use of insulin Tutankhamun's tomb opened Death of Proust
1923	Lawrence *Studies in Classic American Literature* Pound *Indiscretions* *Adelphi* (London, to 1955) *Modern Quarterly* (Baltimore, to 1938)	Stevens *Harmonium* O'Casey *Shadow of a Gunman* Cather *A Lost Lady* Freud *The Ego and the Id* Rilke *Duino Elegies*	France occupies Ruhr USSR proclaimed Failed Munich putsch Coolidge President (to 1929) Yeats wins Nobel Prize *Reader's Digest* launched
1924	Richards *Principles of Literary Criticism*	Dickinson *Complete Poems*	Death of Lenin First Labour government

DATE	WORKS OF CRITICISM, AND LITERARY PERIODICALS	OTHER WORKS	HISTORICAL/CULTURAL EVENTS
	Eliot *Homage to John Dryden* Woolf *Mr Bennett and Mrs Brown* Yeats *Essays* Hulme *Speculations* Murry *Discoveries; To The Unknown God* *Transatlantic Review* (Paris, 1924 only) *American Mercury* (New York)	Melville *Billy Budd* Forster *A Passage to India* O'Casey *Juno and the Paycock* Shaw *Saint Joan* Trotsky *Literature and Revolution* Ford *The Iron Horse* (cin.)	Death of Conrad Death of Kafka Gershwin's *Rhapsody in Blue*
1925	Woolf *The Common Reader* (1st Series) Murry *Keats and Shakespeare* Grierson *The Background of English Literature* *Calendar of Modern Letters* (London, to 1927) *New Yorker* *Review of English Studies* (London) *Virginia Quarterly Review* (Charlottesville)	Woolf *Mrs Dalloway* Fitzgerald *The Great Gatsby* Eliot *Poems 1909–25* Pound *Draft of XVI Cantos* Kafka *The Trial*	Baird develops television Scopes trial, Tennessee Hitler's *Mein Kampf* Charleston dance craze Surrealist exhibition, Paris Shaw wins Nobel Prize
1926	Richards *Science and Poetry* Read *Reason and Romanticism* Muir *Transition*	O'Casey *The Plough and the Stars* Hemingway *The Sun Also Rises* Hughes *The Weary Blues*	General Strike in Britain New York–London telephone link Book–of–the–Month Club

DATE	WORKS OF CRITICISM, AND LITERARY PERIODICALS	OTHER WORKS	HISTORICAL/CULTURAL EVENTS
	Sherman *Critical Woodcuts* *New Masses* (New York, to 1948)	Tawney *Religion and the Rise of* *Capitalism* Kafka *The Castle*	
1927	Forster *Aspects of the Novel* Riding/Graves *Survey of Modernist Poetry* Granville–Barker *Prefaces to Shakespeare* *Enemy* (London, to 1929) *Transition* (Paris, to 1938) *Hound & Horn* (Cambridge, MA, to 1934)	Woolf *To the Lighthouse* Hemingway *Men Without Women* Cather *Death Comes for the* *Archbishop* Lewis *Elmer Gantry*	'Talkies': *The Jazz* *Singer* Lindbergh's Atlantic flight Sacco and Vanzetti executed Trotsky expelled from CPSU US Marines in Nicaragua
1928	Eliot *For Lancelot Andrewes* Rickword (ed.) *Scrutinies* W. Lewis *Time and Western Man* Foerster *Reinterpretation of American* *Literature* Barfield *Poetic Diction* Muir *The Structure of the Novel* *English Journal* (Chicago, to 1939) *Life & Letters* (London, to 1950) *Experiment* (Cambridge, to 1931)	Yeats *The Tower* Lawrence *Lady Chatterley's Lover* Waugh *Decline and Fall* Huxley *Point Counter Point* Woolf *Orlando* Joyce *Anna Livia Plurabelle* Brecht/Weill *Threepenny Opera*	Extended female suffrage in Britain Penicillin discovered First television broadcasts Trotsky exiled First Mickey Mouse cartoons Death of Hardy

DATE	WORKS OF CRITICISM, AND LITERARY PERIODICALS	OTHER WORKS	HISTORICAL/CULTURAL EVENTS
1929	Richards *Practical Criticism* Woolf *A Room of One's Own* *Listener* (London, to 1992) *American Literature* (Durham, NC)	Faulkner *The Sound and the Fury* Yeats *The Winding Stair* Hemingway *A Farewell to Arms*	Hoover President (to 1933) Stock market crash Second Labour government Empire State Building Museum of Modern Art, New York
1930	Empson *Seven Types of Ambiguity* Knight *The Wheel of Fire* Leavis *Mass Civilisation and Minority Culture* Foerster *Towards Standards* Tillyard *Milton* Read *Wordsworth* *University of Toronto Quarterly*	Auden *Poems* Faulkner *As I Lay Dying* Crane *The Bridge* Eliot *Ash Wednesday* W. Lewis *Apes of God* Ransom, Tate, *et al.* *I'll Take My Stand*	Gandhi imprisoned Chrysler Building Death of Lawrence Sinclair Lewis wins Nobel Prize
1931	Wilson *Axel's Castle* Burke *Counter-Statement* Eastman *The Literary Mind* Knight *The Imperial Theme* Murry *Son of Woman*	Woolf *The Waves* Faulkner *Sanctuary* O'Neill *Mourning Becomes Electra*	National Government in Britain Spanish Republic

DATE	WORKS OF CRITICISM, AND LITERARY PERIODICALS	OTHER WORKS	HISTORICAL/CULTURAL EVENTS
1932	Eliot *Selected Essays 1917–32*	Auden *The Orators*	Indian National Congress banned
			First motorway (Autobahn)
	Woolf *The Common Reader* (2nd Series)	Faulkner *Light in August*	Galsworthy wins Nobel Prize
		Roberts (ed.) *New Signatures*	
	F. R. Leavis *New Bearings in English Poetry*	Huxley *Brave New World*	
	Q. D. Leavis *Fiction and the Reading Public*	MacDiarmid *First Hymn to Lenin*	
	Calverton *Liberation of American Literature*	Dos Passos *1919*	
		Yeats *Words for Music Perhaps*	
	Read *Form in Modern Poetry*	Onions *et al.* (eds) *Shorter Oxford English Dictionary*	
	Knight *The Shakespearian Tempest*		
	Scrutiny (Cambridge, to 1953) *American Scholar* (New York) *American Spectator* (New York, to 1937)		
1933	Eliot *The Use of Poetry & the Use of Criticism*	Stein *Autobiography of Alice B. Toklas*	F. D. Roosevelt President (to 1945)
			New Deal legislation
	Knights *How Many Children Had Lady Macbeth?*	Orwell *Down and Out in Paris & London*	Hitler becomes Chancellor
	Leavis *For Continuity*	West *Miss Lonelyhearts*	
	Hicks *The Great Tradition*	Murray *et al.* *Oxford English Dictionary*	

DATE	WORKS OF CRITICISM, AND LITERARY PERIODICALS	OTHER WORKS	HISTORICAL/CULTURAL EVENTS
	Housman *The Name and Nature of Poetry* *New Verse* (London, to 1939) *American Review* (New York, to 1937) *ELH* (Baltimore)	Cooper/Shoedsack *King Kong* (cin.)	
1934	Eliot *After Strange Gods* Bodkin *Archetypal Patterns in Poetry* Pound *ABC of Reading; Make It New* Richards *Coleridge on Imagination* W. Lewis *Men Without Art* Bateson *English Poetry and the English Language* Cecil *Early Victorian Novelists* *Partisan Review* (New York) *Left Review* (London, to 1938)	Fitzgerald *Tender is the Night* Williams *Collected Poems* Waugh *A Handful of Dust* Beckett *More Pricks Than Kicks* Roth *Call It Sleep* Graves *I, Claudius* Miller *Tropic of Cancer* Gibbon *Grey Granite*	Night of the Long Knives Catholic League of Decency Mao's Long March, China
1935	Empson *Some Versions of Pastoral* Spurgeon *Shakespeare's Imagery* Wilson *What Happens in Hamlet* Blackmur *The Double Agent*	Stevens *Ideas of Order* Odets *Waiting for Lefty* Moore *Selected Poems* Eliot *Murder in the Cathedral*	Popular Fronts Baldwin Prime Minister Nuremberg Decrees Left Book Club Penguin Books League of American Writers

DATE	WORKS OF CRITICISM, AND LITERARY PERIODICALS	OTHER WORKS	HISTORICAL/CULTURAL EVENTS
	Matthiessen *The Achievement of T. S. Eliot* *Southern Review* (Baton Rouge, to 1942)	MacNeice *Poems*	
1936	Leavis *Revaluation* Tate *Reactionary Essays* Lawrence *Phoenix* Forster *Abinger Harvest* Farrell *A Note on Literary Criticism* C. S. Lewis *Allegory of Love* Murry *Shakespeare* Read *In Defence of Shelley* *New Writing* (London, to 1942) *English* (London)	Auden *Look, Stranger* Faulkner *Absalom, Absalom!* Huxley *Eyeless in Gaza* Roberts (ed.) *Faber Book of Modern Verse* Yeats (ed.) *Oxford Book of Modern Verse* Mitchell *Gone With the Wind* Keynes *General Theory of Employment* Chaplin *Modern Times* (cin.)	Spanish Civil War (to 1939) Hitler occupies Rhineland Berlin Olympics Death of George V Abdication crisis Accession of George VI Battle of Cable Street, London Surrealist exhibition, London Death of Kipling O'Neill wins Nobel Prize
1937	Caudwell *Illusion and Reality* Winters *Primitivism and Decadence* Knights *Drama and Society*	Stevens *The Man With the Blue Guitar* Woolf *The Years* Orwell *The Road to Wigan Pier*	Japan invades China Moscow Trials Chamberlain Prime Minister First jet engine Picasso's *Guernica* Orff's *Carmina Burana*

DATE	WORKS OF CRITICISM, AND LITERARY PERIODICALS	OTHER WORKS	HISTORICAL/CULTURAL EVENTS
	West *Crisis and Criticism*	Blixen *Out of Africa*	
	Fox *The Novel and the People*	Hemingway *To Have and Have Not*	
	Pound *Polite Essays*	Auden/MacNeice *Letters from Iceland*	
1938	Ransom *The World's Body*	Isherwood *Goodbye to Berlin*	Germany annexes Austria
	Brooks/Warren *Understanding Poetry*	Yeats *New Poems*	Munich Conference Ball-point pen invented Committee on Un-American Activities
	Woolf *Three Guineas*	Beckett *Murphy*	Pearl Buck wins Nobel Prize
	Winters *Maule's Curse*	Greene *Brighton Rock*	
	Wilson *The Triple Thinkers*	Bowen *Death of the Heart*	
	Pound *Guide to Kulchur*	Dos Passos *U.S.A.*	
	Read *Collected Essays in Literary Criticism*	Sartre *La Nausée*	
	Rocky Mountain Review (Utah, to 1959)		
1939	Brooks *Modern Poetry and the Tradition*	Joyce *Finnegans Wake*	Germany invades Czechoslovakia German-Soviet Pact
	Trilling *Matthew Arnold*	O'Brien *At Swim-Two-Birds*	Germany and USSR invade Poland World War II begins
	Kitto *Greek Tragedy*	MacNeice *Autumn Journal*	'Phoney War' Conscription in Britain End of Spanish Civil War
	Lewis/Tillyard *The Personal Heresy*	Steinbeck *The Grapes of Wrath*	Nuclear fission discovered First helicopter Death of Yeats
		West *Day of the Locust*	

DATE	WORKS OF CRITICISM, AND LITERARY PERIODICALS	OTHER WORKS	HISTORICAL/CULTURAL EVENTS
	Daiches *The Novel and the Modern World*	Yeats *Last Poems*	Death of Freud
	Smith *Forces in American Criticism*	Ford *Stagecoach* (cin.)	
	Kenyon Review (Gambier, OH, to 1970) *Poetry (London)* (to 1951) *Poetry Quarterly* (London, to 1953) *American Imago* (Boston) *Medieval Studies* (Toronto)	Fleming *Gone With the Wind* (cin.)	
1940	Blackmur *The Expense of Greatness*	Hemingway *For Whom the Bell Tolls*	Germany occupies France Dunkirk evacuation
	Knight *This Sceptred Isle*	Wright *Native Son*	Axis alliance Churchill Prime Minister
	Horizon (London, to 1951) *Penguin New Writing* (Harmondsworth, to 1950) *Accent* (Urbana, to 1960)	Auden *Another Time* Eliot *East Coker*	Battle of Britain London Blitz Penicillin used medically Trotsky assassinated
1941	Ransom *The New Criticism*	Eliot *The Dry Salvages*	Germany invades USSR Hitler begins extermination of Jews
	Wilson *The Wound and the Bow*	Auden *New Year Letter*	Japan bombs Pearl Harbor
	Matthiessen *American Renaissance*	Woolf *Between the Acts*	USA enters World War II Manhattan Project
	Tate *Reason in Madness*	Warner *The Aerodrome*	National Gallery of Art, Washington, DC Death of Joyce Death of Woolf
	Burke *Philosophy of Literary Form*	Brecht *Mother Courage*	
	Antioch Review (Yellow Springs, OH) *Our Time* (London, to 1949)	Welles *Citizen Kane* (cin.) Huston *The Maltese Falcon* (cin.)	

DATE	WORKS OF CRITICISM, AND LITERARY PERIODICALS	OTHER WORKS	HISTORICAL/CULTURAL EVENTS
1942	Woolf *Death of the Moth* Lewis *Preface to Paradise Lost* Kazin *On Native Grounds* Knight *Chariot of Wrath* *Explicator* (Richmond, VA)	Stevens *Notes Toward a Supreme Fiction* Eliot *Little Gidding* Faulkner *Go Down, Moses* Curtiz *Casablanca* (cin.)	Fall of Singapore to Japan Battle of Midway Battle of El Alamein Battle of Stalingrad, to 1943 Beveridge Report proposes 'Welfare State' in Britain
1943	Winters *Anatomy of Nonsense* Brooks/Warren *Understanding Fiction* Tillyard *The Elizabethan World Picture* *Quarterly Review of Literature* (Princeton)	Eliot *Four Quartets* Sartre *Les Mouches* Brecht *Good Woman of Setzuan; Life of Galileo*	Race riots in USA Fall of Mussolini Teheran Conference
1944	Tillyard *Shakespeare's History Plays* Matthiessen *Henry James* *Windmill* (London, to 1948)	Auden *For the Time Being* Bellow *Dangling Man* Olivier *Henry V* (cin.)	D-Day Normandy landings V1 and V2 rockets on London Butler Education Act, Britain Bretton Woods Conference: IMF, World Bank
1945	Burke *A Grammar of Motives* Eliot *What is a Classic?* Hoffmann *Freudianism and the Literary Mind*	Orwell *Animal Farm* Waugh *Brideshead Revisited* Williams *The Glass Menagerie*	Truman President (to 1953) German surrender Atomic bombs on Hiroshima and Nagasaki Japanese surrender Yalta and Potsdam Conferences

DATE	WORKS OF CRITICISM, AND LITERARY PERIODICALS	OTHER WORKS	HISTORICAL/CULTURAL EVENTS
	Connolly *The Condemned Playground* *Commentary* (New York) *Nineteenth-Century Fiction* (Los Angeles)	Larkin *The North Ship*	Concentration camps opened Nuremberg Trials, to 1946 Labour government under Attlee United Nations founded
1946	Knights *Explorations* Pritchett *The Living Novel* Grierson *Critical History of English Poetry* *Chicago Review*	Thomas *Deaths and Entrances* Hershey *Hiroshima* Spock *Baby and Child Care*	TV broadcasts in USA National Health Act and Coal Nationalization in Britain Bikini atomic tests Churchill 'Iron Curtain' speech Start of 'Baby Boom' French war in Vietnam (to 1954)
1947	Brooks *The Well Wrought Urn* Frye *Fearful Symmetry* Winters *In Defense of Reason* Knight *The Crown of Life* Waldock *Paradise Lost and Its Critics* *Cambridge Journal* (to 1954) *Perspective* (St Louis, to 1975) *Georgia Review* (Athens) *Epoch* (Ithaca, NY)	Miller *All My Sons* Lowry *Under the Volcano* Williams *A Streetcar Named Desire* Stevens *Transport to Summer* Camus *La Peste* Sartre *Qu'est-ce que la littérature?* Capra *It's a Wonderful Life* (cin.)	Truman Doctrine Cold War; CIA established Marshall Aid programme Indian partition and Independence Rail nationalization, Britain First supersonic flight Dead Sea Scrolls discovered UN partition of Palestine
1948	Leavis *The Great Tradition*	Auden *The Age of Anxiety*	Berlin blockade and airlift

DATE	WORKS OF CRITICISM, AND LITERARY PERIODICALS	OTHER WORKS	HISTORICAL/CULTURAL EVENTS
	Tate *On the Limits of Poetry* Graves *The White Goddess* *Hudson Review* (New York) *Shakespeare Survey* (Cambridge) *Yale French Studies* (New Haven)	Pound *Pisan Cantos* Mailer *The Naked and the Dead* Eliot *Notes Towards the Definition of Culture* Kinsey *Sexual Behavior in the Human Male*	State of Israel proclaimed Gandhi assassinated Guerrilla war in Malaya Eliot wins Nobel Prize
1949	Wellek/Warren *Theory of Literature* Rahv *Image and Idea* Chase *Quest for Myth* Fergusson *The Idea of a Theater* *Comparative Literature* (Eugene, OR) *Tulane Studies in English* (New Orleans)	Orwell *Nineteen Eighty-Four* Miller *Death of a Salesman* de Beauvoir *Le Deuxième sexe* Brecht *Mother Courage* Reed *The Third Man* (cin.)	Chinese Revolution NATO founded Germany divided Soviet atomic bomb developed Eire leaves British Empire Apartheid in S. Africa Jerusalem partitioned Faulkner wins Nobel Prize
1950	Trilling *The Liberal Imagination* Wilson *Classics and Commercials* Burke *A Rhetoric of Motives* Auden *The Enchafèd Flood* *Shenandoah* (Lexington, VA)	Lessing *The Grass is Singing* Riesman *The Lonely Crowd* Wilder *Sunset Boulevard* (cin.)	Korean war (to 1953) McCarthyism (to 1954) Steel nationalization, Britain Death of Shaw Death of Orwell

DATE	WORKS OF CRITICISM, AND LITERARY PERIODICALS	OTHER WORKS	HISTORICAL/CULTURAL EVENTS
1951	Empson *The Structure of Complex Words* Kettle *Introduction to the English Novel* *Shakespeare Quarterly* (Washington, DC) *Essays in Criticism* (Oxford) *American Quarterly* (Philadelphia) *Keats-Shelley Journal* (Cambridge, MA)	Beckett *Molloy; Malone meurt* Salinger *The Catcher in the Rye* Auden *Nones* Faulkner *Requiem for a Nun* Mills *White Collar*	Churchill Prime Minister (to 1955) Burgess and Maclean defect Festival of Britain Death of Wittgenstein
1952	Crane (ed.) *Critics and Criticism* Leavis *The Common Pursuit* Blackmur *Language as Gesture* Davie *Purity of Diction in English Verse* Williams *Drama from Ibsen to Eliot* *Stand* (London/Newcastle)	Hemingway *The Old Man and the Sea* Ellison *Invisible Man* O'Connor *Wise Blood* Lessing *Martha Quest* Zinnemann *High Noon* (cin.)	Death of George VI; accession of Elizabeth II Contraceptive pill developed American H-bomb Guerrilla war in Kenya
1953	Auerbach *Mimesis* Abrams *The Mirror and the Lamp* Crane *The Languages of Criticism* Tate *The Forlorn Demon*	Miller *The Crucible* Beckett *Watt; En attendant Godot* Bellow *Adventures of Augie March* Williams *Camino Real*	Eisenhower President (to 1961) Coronation of Elizabeth II Soviet H-bomb East Berlin uprising Death of Stalin Rosenbergs executed for spying DNA structure discovered Everest ascended Cinemascope and 3–D movies

DATE	WORKS OF CRITICISM, AND LITERARY PERIODICALS	OTHER WORKS	HISTORICAL/CULTURAL EVENTS
	Van Ghent *The English Novel: Form and Function* *Encounter* (London) *Paris Review* (Paris/New York)	Fleming *Casino Royale* Baldwin *Go Tell It on the Mountain*	Winston Churchill wins Nobel Prize
1954	Wimsatt *The Verbal Icon* Pound *Literary Essays* Ford (ed.) *Pelican Guide to English Literature* Hartman *The Unmediated Vision* *Black Mountain Review* (N. Carolina, to 1957) *Encore* (London, to 1965) *London Magazine*	Stevens *Collected Poems* Thomas *Under Milk Wood* Amis *Lucky Jim* Golding *Lord of the Flies* Hitchcock *Rear Window* (cin.) Kazan *On the Waterfront* (cin.)	Food rationing ends in Britain Battle of Dien Bien Phu Communist Party banned in USA Four-minute mile Hemingway wins Nobel Prize
1955	Tate *The Man of Letters in the Modern World* Leavis *D. H. Lawrence, Novelist* Blackmur *The Lion and the Honeycomb* Trilling *The Opposing Self* Davie *Articulate Energy* *Modern Fiction Studies* (Lafayette, IN) *Twentieth-Century Literature* (Hempstead, NY)	Auden *The Shield of Achilles* Nabokov *Lolita* Miller *A View from the Bridge* Golding *The Inheritors* Larkin *The Less Deceived* Ray *Rebel Without a Cause* (cin.)	Churchill retires; Eden Prime Minister (to 1957) Warsaw Pact Anti-polio vaccine Commercial TV in Britain Death of Einstein

DATE	WORKS OF CRITICISM, AND LITERARY PERIODICALS	OTHER WORKS	HISTORICAL/CULTURAL EVENTS
1956	Trilling *A Gathering of Fugitives* Kreiger *New Apologists for Poetry* *Critique* (Atlanta, GA) *Tennessee Studies in Literature* (Knoxville)	Ginsberg *Howl* Osborne *Look Back in Anger* Berryman *Homage to Mistress Bradstreet*	USSR suppresses Hungarian revolt Suez crisis Aldermarston March by Campaign for Nuclear Disarmament Presley leads Rock 'n' Roll craze
1957	Frye *Anatomy of Criticism* Kermode *Romantic Image* Wimsatt/Brooks *Literary Criticism* Eliot *On Poetry and Poets* Winters *The Function of Criticism* Chase *The American Novel and Its Tradition* Watt *The Rise of the Novel* Langbaum *The Poetry of Experience* *Victorian Studies* (Bloomington, IN) *English Literature in Transition* (Tempe, AZ) *Evergreen Review* (New York, to 1973)	Kerouac *On the Road* Gunn *The Sense of Movement* White *Voss* Malamud *The Assistant* Hughes *The Hawk in the Rain* Osborne *The Entertainer* Braine *Room at the Top* Durrell *Justine* Barthes *Mythologies*	Macmillan Prime Minister (to 1963) Civil rights protests in USA Ghana and Malaya independent Treaty of Rome founds European Community Sputnik launched Bernstein's *West Side Story*
1958	Williams *Culture and Society* Miller *Charles Dickens*	Beckett *Endgame; Krapp's Last Tape* Achebe *Things Fall Apart*	Algerian war De Gaulle President of France Notting Hill race riots Parking meters Stereo records

DATE	WORKS OF CRITICISM, AND LITERARY PERIODICALS	OTHER WORKS	HISTORICAL/CULTURAL EVENTS
	R. P. Warren *Selected Essays* *Tri-Quarterly* (Evanston, IL)	Pinter *The Birthday Party* Hitchcock *Vertigo* (cin.)	High-rise housing blocks
1959	Tate *Collected Essays* Knights *Some Shakespearean Themes* Bloom *Shelley's Mythmaking* Kenner *The Invisible Poet* *Critical Quarterly* (Hull/ London/Manchester) *Criticism* (Detroit) *X.* (London, to 1962) *Agenda* (London) *Canadian Literature* (Vancouver) *Texas Studies in Literature and Language* (Austin)	Lowell *Life Studies* Burroughs *The Naked Lunch* Arden *Serjeant Musgrave's Dance* Roth *Goodbye, Columbus* Grass *The Tin Drum* Ellmann *James Joyce* Wilder *Some Like It Hot* (cin.)	Cuban revolution Hawaii joins USA as 50th state First motorway in Britain
1960	Fiedler *Love and Death in the American Novel* Hough *Image and Experience* Kermode *Wallace Stevens* Bayley *The Characters of Love* *Studies in English Literature* (Houston) *Review of English Literature* (London, to 1967)	Pinter *The Caretaker* Plath *The Colossus* Lee *To Kill a Mockingbird* Updike *Rabbit Run* Hitchcock *Psycho* (cin.)	Sharpeville massacre Nigerian independence Congo civil war Contraceptive pill in use Polaris submarines in Scotland Penguin Books win *Chatterley* obscenity trial First weather satellite *New Left Review*

DATE	WORKS OF CRITICISM, AND LITERARY PERIODICALS	OTHER WORKS	HISTORICAL/CULTURAL EVENTS
1961	Booth *The Rhetoric of Fiction*	Heller *Catch-22*	Kennedy President Berlin Wall built Gagarin, first man in space
	Steiner *The Death of Tragedy*	Spark *Prime of Miss Jean Brodie*	First US space flights Invasion of Cuba fails
	Williams *The Long Revolution*	Murdoch *A Severed Head*	Kennedy sends troops to Vietnam British university expansion
	Empson *Milton's God*	Naipaul *A House for Mr Biswas*	
	Bloom *The Visionary Company*	Gunn *My Sad Captains*	
	Studies in Romanticism (Boston)	Foucault *Histoire de la folie*	
1962	Wilson *Patriotic Gore*	Lessing *The Golden Notebook*	Cuban missile crisis Algerian independence Second Vatican Council
	Leavis *Two Cultures?*	Nabokov *Pale Fire*	National Service ends in UK First TV satellite
	Kenner *Samuel Beckett*	Alvarez (ed.) *The New Poetry*	Pop Art *Private Eye* launched Death of Marilyn
	Auden *The Dyer's Hand*	Lévi-Strauss *La Pensée sauvage*	Monroe Steinbeck wins Nobel Prize
	Kermode *Puzzles and Epiphanies*	Friedan *The Feminine Mystique*	
	The Review/New Review (London, to 1978) *Victorian Poetry* (W. Virginia)	Kuhn *Structure of Scientific Revolutions*	
1963	Frye *Fables of Identity*	Pynchon *V*	Kennedy assassinated; Johnson President (to 1969)
	Miller *The Disappearance of God*	Plath *The Bell Jar*	Profumo scandal: Douglas-Home Prime Minister (to 1964)
	Wellek *Concepts of Criticism*	McCarthy *The Group*	Philby defects to USSR Martin Luther King 'I have a dream' speech

DATE	WORKS OF CRITICISM, AND LITERARY PERIODICALS	OTHER WORKS	HISTORICAL/CULTURAL EVENTS
	Levin *The Gates of Horn*	Spark *Girls of Slender Means*	Organization of African Unity Beatles' first LP
	Frank *The Widening Gyre*	Ginsberg *Reality Sandwiches*	Death of Plath
	New York Review of Books *Southern Review* (Adelaide) *Australian Literary Studies* (Hobart) *English Language Notes* (Boulder, CO) *James Joyce Quarterly* (Tulsa, OK)	Thompson *Making of the English Working Class* Dylan *The Freewheelin' Bob Dylan*	
1964	Stead *The New Poetic*	Lowell *For the Union Dead*	Labour government: Wilson Prime Minister (to 1970)
	Allen *Tradition and Dream*	Larkin *The Whitsun Weddings*	Civil Rights Act in USA Vietnam War escalates
	Hardy *The Appropriate Form*	Bellow *Herzog*	Khrushchev ousted by Brezhnev Death penalty abolished
	Hartman *Wordsworth's Poetry*	McLuhan *Understanding Media*	in Britain Beatlemania
	Papers on Language and Literature (Illinois)	Kubrick *Dr Strangelove* (cin.)	
1965	Trilling *Beyond Culture*	Plath *Ariel*	US bombs North Vietnam Watts riots
	Eliot *To Criticize the Critic*	Mailer *An American Dream*	Johnson's 'Great Society' reforms Malcolm X assassinated
	Rahv *The Myth and the Powerhouse*	Bond *Saved* Pinter	Rhodesia declares independence Race Relations Act in Britain
	Miller *Poets of Reality*	*The Homecoming*	Death of Churchill Death of Eliot
	Frye *A Natural Perspective*	Haley *Autobiography of Malcolm X*	

DATE	WORKS OF CRITICISM, AND LITERARY PERIODICALS	OTHER WORKS	HISTORICAL/CULTURAL EVENTS
	Shakespeare Studies (S. Carolina) *Salmagundi* (Saratoga Springs, NY) *Cambridge Quarterly* *Journal of Commonwealth Literature* (Leeds)	Dylan *Bringing It All Back Home*	
1966	Woolf *Collected Essays* Lodge *Language of Fiction* Sontag *Against Interpretation* Williams *Modern Tragedy* Burke *Language as Symbolic Action* *Chaucer Review* (Pennsylvania) *Denver Quarterly* *Mosaic* (Winnipeg)	Pynchon *The Crying of Lot 49* Achebe *A Man of the People* Heaney *Death of a Naturalist* Fowles *The Magus* Rhys *Wide Sargasso Sea* Orton *Loot* Foucault *Les Mots et les choses*	Chinese 'Cultural Revolution' (to 1972) NOW founded 'Swinging London' fad
1967	Kermode *The Sense of an Ending* Frye *Fools of Time* Hirsch *Validity in Interpretation* Steiner *Language and Silence* Fish *Surprised by Sin*	Naipaul *The Mimic Men* O'Brien *The Third Policeman* Ashbery *Selected Poems* Stoppard *Rosencrantz and Guildenstern*	Six-Day War in Middle East Biafran War Demonstrations against Vietnam War Military coup in Greece Homosexual acts and abortion legalized in Britain First heart transplant Beatles' *Sergeant Pepper* album

DATE	WORKS OF CRITICISM, AND LITERARY PERIODICALS	OTHER WORKS	HISTORICAL/CULTURAL EVENTS
		Ngugi *A Grain of Wheat*	
	Blackmur *Primer of Ignorance*	Styron *Confessions of Nat Turner*	
	Leavis *Anna Karenina and Other Essays*	Marquez *One Hundred Years of Solitude*	
	Eighteenth-Century Studies (Davis, CA) *Novel* (Providence, RI)	Derrida *L'Ecriture et la différence*	
1968	Frye *Study of English Romanticism* Miller *The Form of Victorian Fiction* Ellmann *Thinking About Women* Holland *Dynamics of Literary Response* *Milton Studies* (Pittsburgh) *Genre* (Chicago)	Mailer *Armies of the Night* Updike *Couples* Didion *Slouching Toward Bethlehem* Dylan *John Wesley Harding* Althusser *Lénine et la philosophie* Kubrick *2001: A Space Odyssey* (cin.)	USSR invades Czechoslovakia Student revolt and general strike in France Tet Offensive, Vietnam Anti-war protests escalate Martin Luther King assassinated Robert Kennedy assassinated Civil Rights marches in N. Ireland US astronauts orbit moon Theatre censorship abolished in Britain
1969	Millett *Sexual Politics* Rahv *Literature & the Sixth Sense* Leavis *English Literature in Our Time* *New Literary History* (Charlottesville, VA) *Studies in the Novel* (Denton, TX)	Fowles *The French Lieutenant's Woman* Vonnegut *Slaughterhouse-Five* Roth *Portnoy's Complaint* Atwood *The Edible Woman*	Nixon President (to 1974) First man on moon British troops in N. Ireland Woodstock festival Concorde flies Open University founded Beckett wins Nobel Prize

DATE	WORKS OF CRITICISM, AND LITERARY PERIODICALS	OTHER WORKS	HISTORICAL/CULTURAL EVENTS
1970	Frye *The Stubborn Structure* Hartman *Beyond Formalism* Leavises *Dickens the Novelist* Bloom *Yeats* Williams *The English Novel*	Farrell *Troubles* Hughes *Crow*	Heath Prime Minister (to 1974) Internment in N. Ireland Kent State University shootings USA attacks Cambodia Beatles disband Death of Forster
1971	de Man *Blindness and Insight* Jameson *Marxism and Form* Bloom *The Ringers in the Tower* *Diacritics* (Ithaca, NY) *English Literary Renaissance* (Amherst, Ma)	Pinter *Old Times* Gunn *Moly*	Bangladesh secedes China joins UN Decimal currency in UK
1972	Trilling *Sincerity and Authenticity* Fish *Self-Consuming Artifacts* Jameson *The Prison-House of Language* Fiedler *The Stranger in Shakespeare* *Boundary 2* (Binghampton, NY) *Feminist Studies* (New York)	Atwood *Surfacing* Heaney *Wintering Out* Stoppard *Jumpers* Coppola *The Godfather* (cin.)	Britain joins EEC Nixon re-elected Equal Rights Amendment 'Bloody Sunday' in N. Ireland Death of Pound Death of Edmund Wilson

DATE	WORKS OF CRITICISM, AND LITERARY PERIODICALS	OTHER WORKS	HISTORICAL/CULTURAL EVENTS
1973	Bloom *The Anxiety of Influence* Williams *The Country and the City* Bradbury *Possibilities*	Pynchon *Gravity's Rainbow* Vonnegut *Breakfast of Champions* Shaffer *Equus*	USA ends role in Vietnam war Military coup in Chile Watergate hearings Middle East war: oil crisis Three-day week in Britain Death of Auden Death of Picasso
1974	Ricks *Keats and Embarrassment* *Critical Inquiry* (Chicago)	Lessing *Memoirs of a Survivor* Larkin *High Windows* Stoppard *Travesties*	Wilson Prime Minister (to 1976) Watergate scandal: Nixon resigns Ford President (to 1977) Turkey invades Cyprus Pub bombings in Britain Death of Ransom
1975	Culler *Structuralist Poetics* Bloom *A Map of Misreading* Said *Beginnings* Donovan (ed.) *Feminist Literary Criticism* Kermode *The Classic* Eagleton *Myths of Power* *Literature and History* (London)	Heaney *North* Griffiths *Comedians* Naipaul *Guerrillas* McEwan *First Love, Last Rites* Jhabvala *Heat and Dust* Mahon *The Snow Party*	Fall of Saigon Death of Trilling
1976	Eagleton *Criticism and Ideology*	Ashbery *Self-Portrait in a Convex Mirror*	Wilson resigns: Callaghan Prime Minister (to 1979)

DATE	WORKS OF CRITICISM, AND LITERARY PERIODICALS	OTHER WORKS	HISTORICAL/CULTURAL EVENTS
	Hirsch *The Aims of Interpretation* Bloom *Poetry and Repression* *Glyph* (Baltimore)	Gunn *Jack Straw's Castle* Scorsese *Taxi Driver* (cin.)	Civil war in Beirut Death of Mao Bellow wins Nobel Prize
1977	Showalter *A Literature of Their Own* Williams *Marxism and Literature* Lodge *The Modes of Modern Writing*	Morrison *Song of Solomon* Coover *The Public Burning* Ngugi *Petals of Blood*	Carter President (to 1981) Military coup in Pakistan Punk rock Death of Chaplin Death of Nabokov
1978	Said *Orientalism* MacCabe *James Joyce and the Revolution of the Word* *Oxford Literary Review* (Oxford/Southampton)	Hare *Plenty* Harrison *The School of Eloquence*	First test-tube baby born
1979	Gilbert & Gubar *The Madwoman in the Attic* Bloom *et al.* *Deconstruction and Criticism* Harari (ed.) *Textual Strategies* de Man *Allegories of Reading* Jacobus (ed.) *Women Writing & Writing About Women* Kermode *The Genesis of Secrecy* Williams *Politics and Letters*	Heaney *Field Work* Barth *Letters* Mailer *The Executioner's Song* Golding *Darkness Visible* Carter *The Bloody Chamber* Shaffer *Amadeus* Raine *A Martian Sends a Postcard Home*	Thatcher Prime Minister (to 1990) Iranian Revolution Three-Mile Island leak Bhutto executed in Pakistan Nicaraguan Revolution Tehran hostage crisis USSR invades Afghanistan

DATE	WORKS OF CRITICISM, AND LITERARY PERIODICALS	OTHER WORKS	HISTORICAL/CULTURAL EVENTS
	London Review of Books *Feminist Review* (London)	Coppola *Apocalypse Now* (cin.)	
1980	Johnson *The Critical Difference*	Golding *Rites of Passage*	Zimbabwean independence
	Greenblatt *Renaissance Self-Fashioning*	Brenton *The Romans in Britain*	Strike wave in Poland Iran-Iraq war begins Lennon assassinated
	Hartman *Criticism in the Wilderness*	Cimino *Heaven's Gate* (cin.)	Eradication of smallpox announced Death of Sartre
	Fish *Is There a Text in This Class?*		Death of Barthes Death of Hitchcock
	Belsey *Critical Practice*		
	Steiner *On Difficulty*		
	Lentricchia *After the New Criticism*		
	Raritan (New Brunswick, NJ)		
1981	Jameson *The Political Unconscious*	Rushdie *Midnight's Children*	Reagan President (to 1989)
	Culler *The Pursuit of Signs*	Gordimer *July's People*	Irish hunger strikes: 9 dead Labour Party split
	Eagleton *Walter Benjamin*	Morrison *Tar Baby*	Riots in British cities Sadat assassinated Martial law in Poland
	Brooke-Rose *A Rhetoric of the Unreal*	M. Amis *Other People*	(to 1983)
	Hartman *Saving the Text*	Gray *Lanark*	
	Q. D. Leavis *Collected Essays*		

DATE	WORKS OF CRITICISM, AND LITERARY PERIODICALS	OTHER WORKS	HISTORICAL/CULTURAL EVENTS
	Tulsa Studies in Women's Literature		
1982	Culler *On Deconstruction* Frye *The Great Code* Miller *Fiction and Repetition* Eagleton *The Rape of Clarissa* Bloom *Agon*	Mahon *The Hunt by Night* Mo *Sour Sweet* Churchill *Top Girls*	Falklands/Malvinas war Israel invades Lebanon Death of Brezhnev: Andropov leads USSR
1983	Said *The World, the Text & the Critic* McGann *The Romantic Ideology* Eagleton *Literary Theory* Jardine *Still Harping on Daughters* Kermode *Essays on Fiction* *Representations* (Berkeley, CA)	Swift *Waterland* Coetzee *Life and Times of Michael X* Rushdie *Shame*	Thatcher re-elected US cruise missiles in Europe US invades Grenada Reagan proposes 'Star Wars' US Marine base bombed in Beirut
1984	de Man *The Rhetoric of Romanticism* Empson *Using Biography* Eagleton *The Function of Criticism*	Carter *Nights at the Circus* M. Amis *Money* Barnes *Flaubert's Parrot*	Miners' strike in Britain Reagan re-elected Chernenko succeeds Andropov Indira Gandhi assassinated IRA bombs Tory conference

DATE	WORKS OF CRITICISM, AND LITERARY PERIODICALS	OTHER WORKS	HISTORICAL/CULTURAL EVENTS
	Gates (ed.) *Black Literature and Literary Theory*	Heaney *Station Island*	Death of Foucault
	Dollimore *Radical Tragedy*	Ginsberg *Collected Poems*	
	Brooks *Reading for the Plot*	Gray *1982, Janine*	
	Williams *Writing in Society*	Ballard *Empire of the Sun*	
1985	Showalter (ed.) *The New Feminist Criticism*	Dunn *Elegies*	Gorbachev succeeds Chernenko
	Belsey *The Subject of Tragedy*	Brenton & Hare *Pravda*	British miners' strike defeated Heysel football stadium disaster
	Sedgwick *Between Men*	Ackroyd *Hawksmoor*	Death of Orson Welles Death of Robert Graves
	Kermode *Forms of Attention*	Winterson *Oranges Are Not the Only Fruit*	
	Dollimore & Sinfield *Political Shakespeare*		
	Hertz *The End of the Line*		
	McGann *The Beauty of Inflections*		
1986	de Man *The Resistance to Theory*	Boland *The Journey*	Chernobyl nuclear accident USA bombs Libya Fall of Marcos in Philippines
	Eagleton *William Shakespeare*		
	Evans *Signifying Nothing*		
	Textual Practice (Cardiff)		
1987	Johnson *A World of Difference*	Morrison *Beloved*	Stock market crash Thatcher re-elected again

DATE	WORKS OF CRITICISM, AND LITERARY PERIODICALS	OTHER WORKS	HISTORICAL/CULTURAL EVENTS
	Spivak *In Other Worlds*	Winterson *The Passion*	Death of Warhol
	Bowie *Freud, Proust and Lacan*	Heaney *The Haw Lantern*	
	Miller *The Ethics of Reading*	Wolfe *Bonfire of the Vanities*	
1988	Greenblatt *Shakespearean Negotiations*	Rushdie *The Satanic Verses*	
	Gates *The Signifying Monkey*	Lodge *Nice Work*	
	Culler *Framing the Sign*		
	Barrell *Poetry, Language and Politics*		
	Gilbert & Gubar *No Man's Land*		
	Genders (Austin, TX)		
1989	Fish *Doing What Comes Naturally*	Reading *Perduta Gente*	Bush President (to 1993) Berlin wall comes down *Fatwa* against Rushdie
	Kermode *An Appetite for Poetry*		Tienanmen Square demonstrations Death of Beckett
	McGann *Towards a Literature of Knowledge*		
	Abrams *Doing Things With Texts*		
1990	Eagleton *Ideology of the Aesthetic*	Byatt *Possession*	Germany re-unified Fall of Thatcher Major Prime Minister
	Spivak *The Post-Colonial Critic*	Boland *Outside History*	

DATE	WORKS OF CRITICISM, AND LITERARY PERIODICALS	OTHER WORKS	HISTORICAL/CULTURAL EVENTS
	Showalter *Sexual Anarchy*		
	Sedgwick *Epistemology of the Closet*		
	Bersani *Culture of Redemption*		
1991	Kermode *The Uses of Error*	Heaney *Seeing Things*	Gulf War Soviet Union dissolved
	Greenblatt *Learning to Curse*	Amis *Time's Arrow*	
	Jameson *Postmodernism*	Brodkey *The Runaway Soul*	
	Miller *Theory Now and Then*		
1992	Paulin *Minotaur*	Morrison *Jazz*	
1993	Said *Culture and Imperialism*	Seth *A Suitable Boy*	Clinton President
	Sedgwick *Tendencies*		
	Eliot *Varieties of Metaphysical Poetry*		
1994	Bloom *The Western Canon*	Hollinghurst *The Folding Star*	S. Africa: Mandela President Channel Tunnel IRA ceasefire

General Bibliography

Note: Each section is arranged alphabetically. Place of publication is London unless otherwise stated.

(i) Reference Books

Borklund, E.	*Contemporary Literary Critics* (2nd edn, 1982). (Essays on 120 modern critics, with useful bibliographies.)
Brier, P. A. and Arthur, A.	*American Prose and Criticism 1900–1950: A Guide to Information Sources* (Detroit, MI, 1981).
Champion, L. S.	*The Essential Shakespeare: an annotated bibliography of major modern studies* (Boston, MA, 1986).
Chielens, E. E.	*The Literary Journal in America, 1900–1950* (Detroit, MI, 1977).
Chielens, E. E., ed.	*American Literary Magazines: The Twentieth Century* (Westport, CT, 1992).
Groden, M. and Kreiswirth, M., eds	*The Johns Hopkins Guide to Literary Theory and Criticism* (Baltimore, MD, 1994). (Encyclopaedic in bulk, but rather selective in coverage; some good entries on critical schools and individuals.)
Humm, M.	*An Annotated Critical Bibliography of Feminist Criticism* (1987).
Jay, Gregory S., ed.	*Dictionary of Literary Biography, Volume 63: Modern American Critics, 1920–1955* (Detroit, MI, 1988).
Jay, Gregory, S., ed.	*Dictionary of Literary Biography, Volume 67: Modern American Critics Since 1955* (Detroit, MI, 1988). (Extensive articles on 27 leading figures; bibliographies.)
Makaryk, I. R., ed.	*Encyclopedia of Contemporary Literary Theory* (Toronto, 1993). (Good coverage of numerous schools, critics, terms.)
Marshall, D. G.	*Contemporary Critical Theory: A Selective Bibliography* (New York, 1993).

Sullivan, A. ed.   *British Literary Magazines: The Victorian and Edwardian Era* (Westport, CT, 1984).

Sullivan, A. ed.   *British Literary Magazines: The Modern Age, 1914–1984* (Westport, CT, 1986).

(ii) General Histories and Surveys

Bradbury, M. and Palmer, D. eds   *Contemporary Criticism* (1970). (Various accounts of the state of play in the 1960s.)

Cassedy, S.   *Flight From Eden: The Origins of Modern Literary Criticism and Theory* (Berkeley, CA, 1991).

Dickstein, M.   *Double Agent: The Critic and Society* (New York, 1992). (On 'public' critics since Arnold.)

Eagleton, T.   *The Function of Criticism: From the 'Spectator' to Post-Structuralism* (1984). (Brief essay on the contradictions of the modern critical endeavour.)

Fekete, J.   *The Critical Twilight* (1978). (Forceful critique of Eliot's followers.)

Krieger, M.   *The New Apologists for Poetry* (Minneapolis, 1956). (On Eliot, Richards, and the New Critics.)

Parrinder, P.   *Authors and Authority: English and American Criticism, 1750–1990* (1991). (Has incisive chapters on modern developments.)

Schwarz, D. R.   *The Humanistic Heritage: Critical Theories of the English Novel from James to Hillis Miller* (1986). (Uninspired.)

Todd, J.   *Feminist Literary History* (Cambridge, 1988).

Wellek, R.   *A History of Modern Criticism, 1750–1950* (8 vols, 1955–92). (See especially the fifth and sixth volumes. Magisterial verdicts on most major critics; little interest in cultural context.)

(iii) Studies in British and Irish Criticism

Baldick, C.   *The Social Mission of English Criticism, 1848–1932* (Oxford, 1983). (Chapters on Eliot, Richards, the Leavises.)

Bergonzi, B.	*Exploding English: Criticism, Theory, Culture* (Oxford, 1990). (On the Theory wars and their background.)
Day, Gary, ed.	*The British Critical Tradition* (1993). (Short essays, of varying quality, on the major critics.)
Gross, J.	*The Rise and Fall of the Man of Letters: Aspects of English Literary Life Since 1800* (1969). (Richly anecdotal.)
Kermode, F.	*Romantic Image* (1957). (Major reassessment of the Symbolist inheritance.)
Mulhern, F.	*The Moment of 'Scrutiny'* (1981). (Painstaking Marxist critique of the Leavis group.)

(iv) Studies in American Criticism

Arac, Jonathan *et al.*, eds	*The Yale Critics: Deconstruction in America* (Minneapolis, 1983).
Bagwell, J. T.	*American Formalism and the Problem of Interpretation* (Houston, TX, 1986).
Cooney, T.	*The Rise of the New York Intellectuals:* Partisan Review *and Its Circle* (Madison, WI, 1986). (Careful group portrait; ends at 1945.)
Cowan, L.	*The Southern Critics* (Irving, TX, 1971). (On Ransom and the 'Fugitive' group.)
Fraiberg, L.	*Psychoanalysis and American Literary Criticism* (Detroit, MI, 1960). (On six critics, including Wilson and Trilling.)
Gallop, J.	*Around 1981: Academic Feminist Literary Theory* (New York, 1992). (Unorthodox history of feminist criticism since the 1970s.)
Graff, G.	*Poetic Statement and Critical Dogma* (Evanston, IL, 1970). (Critique of New Criticism.)
Graff, G.	*Literature Against Itself: Literary Ideas in Modern Society* (Chicago, 1979). (Lively arguments: New Critics to post-modernists.)
Graff, G.	*Professing Literature: An Institutional History* (Chicago, 1987). (Vivid account of academic literary study.)
Greenblatt, S. and Gunn, G. eds	*Redrawing the Boundaries: The Transformation of English and American Literary Studies* (New York, 1993). (Compendious guide to the various schools and period specialisms since the 1960s.)
Jancovitch, M.	*The Cultural Politics of the New Criticism* (Cambridge, 1993).

Jumonville, N.   *Critical Crossings: The New York Intellectuals in Postwar
                     America* (Berkeley, CA, 1991). (Good study of this
                     group's attempts to define a role for the intellectual.)

Leitch, V. B.   *American Criticism from the Thirties to the Eighties* (New
                     York, 1988). (Useful survey of several critical
                     schools.)

Lentricchia, F.   *After the New Criticism* (Chicago, 1980). (Forceful
                     account of developments in the 1960s and 70s.)

Ruland, R.   *The Rediscovery of American Literature: Premises of Literary
                     Taste, 1900–1940* (Cambridge, MA, 1967).

Stovall, F., ed.   *The Development of American Literary Criticism* (Chapel
                     Hill, NC, 1955).

Sutton, W.   *Modern American Criticism* (Englewood Cliffs, NJ,
                     1963). (A handy round-up of the contending schools,
                     from Babbitt to Frye.)

Webster, G.   *The Republic of Letters: A History of Postwar American
                     Literary Opinion* (Baltimore, MD, 1979). (On the
                     New Critics and New York Intellectuals.)

Individual Authors

Notes on biography, major works and criticism

Each entry is divided into three sections:

(a) *Outline of author's life and literary career.*

(b) *Selected biographies and letters.* Place of publication is London unless otherwise stated.

(c) *Selected critical works, etc.* Listed alphabetically by author. Place of publication is London unless otherwise stated.

BABBITT, Irving (1865–1933), born in Dayton, Ohio, the son of an eccentric spiritualist publisher and faith-healer; raised in Cincinatti. Worked briefly as a cowboy on uncle's Wyoming farm. Graduated from Harvard in 1889, then taught at College of Montana before further study at Sorbonne. Returned to Harvard for a master's degree in Oriental Studies (1893), and stayed on there to teach French and Comparative Literature, becoming Assistant Professor (1902) and Professor (1912–33). Married Dora Drew, 1900; two children. His lectures on European Romanticism attracted an important following (students included T. S. Eliot, Stuart Sherman, Norman Foerster, Van Wyck Brooks, Harry Levin, and Walter Lippmann). His consistent anti-Romantic position is expounded in *Literature and the American College* (1908), *The New Laokoon* (1910), *The Masters of Modern French Criticism* (1912), and *Rousseau and Romanticism* (1919). Later works of a more general character are *Democracy and Leadership* (1924), which prefers Mussolini over Lenin, *On Being Creative* (1932), and the posthumous collection *Spanish Character* (1940). With his friend Paul Elmer More, he was embroiled in public controversy in 1929–30 about their shared 'New Humanist' stance, clashing with Santayana, Eliot, and an assortment of realist, modernist, and liberal critics. Some uncollected essays were later gathered in *Representative Writings* (ed. G. A. Panichas, Lincoln, NE, 1981).

> Manchester, F. and O. Shephard, eds, *Irving Babbitt, Man and Teacher* (New York, 1941). (Tributes and reminiscences.)
> Warren, A., *New England Saints* (Ann Arbor, MI, 1956), 143–64.

> See: Brennan, S. C., and S. R. Yarborough, *Irving Babbitt* (Boston, 1987).
> Davis, R. C. and R. Schleifer, *Criticism and Culture* (1991), 57–72.
> Levin, H., *Irving Babbitt and the Teaching of Literature* (Cambridge, MA, 1961).

Nevin, T. R., *Irving Babbitt: An Intellectual Study* (Chapel Hill, NC, 1984). (The best account.)

Panichas, G. A., Introduction to Babbitt, *Representative Writings* (Lincoln, NE, 1981).

BLACKMUR, Richard Palmer (1904–65), born in Springfield, Massachusetts; his father was a failed stockbroker, his mother a physical therapist who conducted his early education privately. Spent boyhood in New York City and Cambridge, Massachusetts; expelled from Cambridge High and Latin School (1918), receiving no further formal education. Worked for ten years in various bookstores and libraries. Edited the 'little magazine' *Hound and Horn* (1928–30), writing numerous critical essays and attempting novels without success. Married Helen Dickson, a painter, 1930; divorced 1951, settling in Boston. Began major studies of Henry Adams and Henry James, neither of which was completed. Edited James's Prefaces as *The Art of Fiction* (1934). Published early essays as *The Double Agent* (1935), and a volume of poems, *From Jordan's Delight* (1937). Held Guggenheim fellowship (1936–38). Published further essays as *The Expense of Greatness* (1940). Began teaching at Princeton University as Allen Tate's assistant (1940), eventually securing tenured professorship (1951–65). Published further poems in *The Second World* (1942) and *The Good European* (1947); and critical essays in *Language as Gesture* (1952), and *The Lion and the Honeycomb* (1955). Lectured in Japan (1956) and Cambridge, England (1961–62). Published *Form and Value in Modern Poetry* (1957), *New Criticism in the United States* (1959), and *Eleven Essays in the European Novel* (1964). Posthumous works are *A Primer of Ignorance* (ed. J. Frank, 1967), *Poems* (1977), *Henry Adams* (ed. V. Makowsky, 1980), and *Studies in Henry James* (ed. V. Makowsky, 1983).

Fraser, R., *A Mingled Yarn: The Life of R. P. Blackmur* (New York, 1981).

See: Boyers, R., *R. P. Blackmur: Poet-Critic* (Columbia, MO, 1980).

Cone, E. T. *et al.*, eds, *The Legacy of R. P. Blackmur: Essays, Memoirs, Texts* (New York, 1987).

Frank, J., *The Widening Gyre* (New Brunswick, NJ, 1963), 229–51.

Hyman, S. E., *The Armed Vision: A Study in the Methods of Modern Literary Criticism* (New York, 1948), 239–71.

Jones, J. T., *Wayward Skeptic: The Theories of R. P. Blackmur* (Urbana, IL, 1986).

Pannick, G. J., *Richard Palmer Blackmur* (1981).

Wellek, R., *A History of Modern Criticism 1750–1959, Volume 6: American Criticism 1900–1950* (1986), 218–34.

BLOOM, Harold (1930–), born in New York City; educated at Cornell University (BA, 1951). Went to Yale University for postgraduate study, also spending a year in Cambridge, England (1954–55), as Fulbright Fellow. In 1955, took his PhD and started teaching at Yale, becoming full professor in 1965. Reviewed Frye's *Anatomy of Criticism* for the *Yale Review* (1957). Married Jeanne Gould, 1958; two children. Published *Shelley's Myth-making* (1959), *The Visionary Company* (1961), and *Blake's Apocalypse* (1963), followed by *Yeats* (1970), and *The Ringers in the Tower* (1971). Began his sequence of studies in the theory of influence with *The Anxiety of Influence* (1973), continuing it with *A Map of Misreading* (1975), *Kabbalah and Criticism* (1975), and *Poetry and Repression* (1976). Published *Figures of Capable Imagination* (1976), *Wallace Stevens: The Poems of Our Climate* (1977), and a novel, *The Flight to Lucifer* (1980).

Contributed an essay to the 'Yale School' collection *Deconstruction and Criticism* (1979). Published *Agon* (1982) and *The Breaking of the Vessels* (1982). Began from 1984 to edit and write introductions to collections of critical essays in several series published by Chelsea House, running to more than 400 volumes. Published a volume of essays, *Poetics of Influence* (1988), and *Ruin the Sacred Truths* (1989), followed by *The Western Canon* (1994).

> Moynihan, T., *A Recent Imagining* (Hamden, CT, 1986), 1–50. (Interview.)
> Salusinszky, I., *Criticism in Society* (1987), 44–73. (Interview.)

> See: Allen, G., *Harold Bloom: A Poetics of Conflict* (Hemel Hempstead, 1994). (Well-balanced introduction.)
> Bruss, E. W., *Beautiful Theories* (Baltimore, MD, 1982), 283–362.
> de Bolla, P., *Harold Bloom: Towards Historical Rhetorics* (1988).
> de Man, P., *Blindness and Insight* (2nd edn, 1983), 267–76. (Review of *The Anxiety of Influence*.)
> Fite, D., *Harold Bloom: The Rhetoric of Romantic Vision* (Amherst, MA, 1985).
> Handelman, S. A., *The Slayers of Moses: The Emergence of Rabbinic Interpretation in Modern Literary Theory* (Albany, NY, 1982).
> Leitch, V. B., *Deconstructive Criticism* (New York, 1983), 129–42.
> Lentricchia, F., *After the New Criticism* (Chicago, 1980), 318–46.
> Mileur, J.-P., *Literary Revisionism and the Burden of Modernity* (Berkeley, CA, 1985).
> O'Hara, D. T., *The Romance of Interpretation: Visionary Criticism from Pater to de Man* (New York, 1985), 55–92.

BOOTH, Wayne Clayson (1921–), born in American Fork, Utah, of a Mormon family; educated in Salt Lake City at Brigham Young University, where he converted from chemistry to English, graduating in 1944. Served in US Army, 1944–46. Married Phyllis Barnes, a clinical psychologist, 1946; three children. Studied at University of Chicago under R. S. Crane, taking his PhD in 1950. Taught at Chicago (1947–50), then at Haverford College, Pennsylvania (1950–53), and as chair of the English department at Earlham College, Indiana (1953–62). Published his most important work, *The Rhetoric of Fiction* (1961). Moved to University of Chicago as Professor of English (1962–86). Published *Now Don't Try To Reason With Me* (1970), *Modern Dogma and the Rhetoric of Assent* (1974) and *A Rhetoric of Irony* (1974). Served as co-editor of the journal *Critical Inquiry* (1974–85). Published *Critical Understanding: The Powers and Limits of Pluralism* (1979). After retirement, published *The Company We Keep: An Ethics of Fiction* (1988), and *The Vocation of a Teacher* (1989).

> See: Antczack, F. J., ed., *Keeping Company: Rhetoric, Pluralism and Wayne Booth* (Ohio, 1994).
> Richter, D., 'The Second Flight of the Phoenix: Neo-Aristotelianism since Crane', *Eighteenth Century*, 23 (1982), 27–48.
> Schwarz, D. R., *The Humanistic Heritage* (1986), 151–69.

BRADLEY, Andrew Cecil (1851–1935) born in Cheltenham, son of a vicar. Graduated from Balliol College, Oxford (1873). Took up Balliol fellowship, then lectureship in English (1876) and later in philosophy (1881). Came under strong influence of Hegelian philosopher T. H. Green; published an edition of Green's *Prolegomena to Ethics* (1883). Became first Professor of Literature and History at University College, Liverpool (1882–89), involving himself in adult education. Moved to Glasgow University as Professor of English Language and Literature (1889–1900), publishing inaugural lecture, *Poetry and Life* (1899). Retired early to London; published *A Commentary on Tennyson's In Memoriam* (1901), based on his Liverpool classes. Came out of retirement upon election as Professor of Poetry at Oxford (1901–6); began lectures there with *Poetry for Poetry's Sake* (1901), and proceeded to famous series of Shakespeare lectures, published as *Shakespearean Tragedy* (1904); others collected in *Oxford Lectures on Poetry* (1909). Retired to London again; declined the offer of a new chair at Cambridge, but helped establish the English Association, becoming its President in 1911. Collected various lectures and essays in *A Miscellany* (1929); died, unmarried, in London.

Mackail, J. W., 'Andrew Cecil Bradley', *Proceedings of the British Academy* XXI (1935), 385–92.

See: Cooke, K., *A. C. Bradley and his Influence on Twentieth Century Shakespearean Criticism* (Oxford, 1972).
Hawkes, T., *That Shakespeherian Rag: Essays on a Critical Process* (1986), 27–50.
Hunter, G. K., 'A. C. Bradley's *Shakespearean Tragedy*', *Essays and Studies* 21 (1968), 101–17.

BROOKS, Cleanth (1906–94) born in Murray, Kentucky, son of an Episcopalian minister. Studied at Vanderbilt University, Nashville, and at Tulane University, New Orleans, before going on to Oxford, England, as a Rhodes Scholar (1929–32). Taught at Louisiana State University, Baton Rouge, as Professor of English (1932–47). Married Edith Blanchard, 1934. Published a monograph on the Alabama-Georgia dialect, and co-edited the *Southern Review* (1935–41) with Robert Penn Warren. Collaborated with Warren on the college textbook *Understanding Poetry* (1938). Published his first independent critical work, *Modern Poetry and the Tradition* (1939), and a further textbook with Warren, *Understanding Fiction* (1943). Moved to Yale University (1947–75), and published his best-known work, *The Well Wrought Urn* (1947), followed by two further textbooks with Warren: *Modern Rhetoric* (1949) and *Fundamentals of Good Writing* (1950). Collaborated with W. K. Wimsatt on *Literary Criticism: A Short History* (1957), contributing chiefly to its section on modern criticism. Published studies in modern literature as *The Hidden God* (1963), along with *William Faulkner: The Yoknapatawpha Country* (1963). Spent two years in England as Cultural Attaché to the US Embassy in London (1964–66). Published later essays in *A Shaping Joy* (1971), followed by *William Faulkner: Toward Yoknapatawpha and Beyond* (1978). Returned to his earlier linguistic studies with *The Language of the American South* (1985).

Cutrer, T. W., *Parnassus on the Mississippi: The 'Southern Review' and the Baton Rouge Literary Community, 1935–1942* (Baton Rouge, LA, 1984).
Walsh, J. M., *Cleanth Brooks: An Annotated Bibliography* (New York, 1990).

See: Bové, P., 'Cleanth Brooks and Modern Irony: A Kierkegaardian Perspective', *Boundary 2*, 4 (1976), 727–59.
Crane, R. S., 'The Critical Monism of Cleanth Brooks', in *Critics and Criticism, Ancient and Modern*, ed. R. S. Crane (Chicago, 1952), 83–107.
Graff, G., *Poetic Statement and Critical Dogma* (Evanston, IL, 1970), 87–111.

Shankar, D. A., *Cleanth Brooks: An Assessment* (Bangalore, 1981). (The
most extensive account.)

Simpson, L. P., ed., *The Possibilities of Order: Cleanth Brooks and His
Work* (Baton Rouge, LA, 1976). (Includes long interview, and
tributes by colleagues.)

Taylor, G., *Re-Inventing Shakespeare* (1990), 285–94.

Wellek, R., *A History of Modern Criticism 1750–1950, Volume 6:
American Criticism 1900–1950*, 188–213.

Wilde, A., 'Modernism and the Aesthetics of Crisis', *Contemporary
Literature* 20 (1979), 13–50.

BURKE, Kenneth Duva (1897–1986) born in Pittsburgh; educated at Ohio State
University, Columbus, and at Columbia University, New York. Moved among
avant-garde groups in Greenwich Village. Married Lily Batterham, 1919; three
children. Published *The White Oxen and Other Stories* (1924), and translated
Mann's *Death in Venice* (1925). Settled in Andover, New Jersey, growing fruit
and working in New York as music critic for the *Dial* (1927–29). Published
his first critical book, *Counter-Statement* (1931), and a novel, *Towards a Better
Life* (1931). Divorced Lily, and married her sister Elizabeth, 1933; two
children. Worked as music critic for the *Nation* (1934–35). Published the
philosophical works *Permanence and Change* (1935) and *Attitudes Toward
History* (1937). Taught briefly at University of Chicago before publishing *The
Philosophy of Literary Form* (1941). Taught part-time at Bennington College,
Vermont (1943–61); also took visiting fellowships at Princeton (1949) and
other universities. Published *A Grammar of Motives* (1945), *A Rhetoric of
Motives* (1950), and *A Rhetoric of Religion* (1961). Subsequently taught and
researched at several American universities including the University of
California at Santa Barbara (1964–65) and Harvard (1967–68). Published
Perspectives by Incongruity and *Terms for Order* (both 1964), *Language as Symbolic
Action* (1966), and *Collected Poems* (1968). He contributed several essays to
Critical Inquiry in the 1970s.

> *Selected Correspondence of Kenneth Burke and Malcolm Cowley,* ed. P. Jay
> (New York, 1988).

See: Bygrave, S., *Kenneth Burke: Rhetoric and Ideology* (1993).

Frank, A. P., *Kenneth Burke* (New York, 1969).

Heath, R. L., *Realism and Relativism: A Perspective on Kenneth Burke*
(Macon, GA, 1986).

Henderson, G., *Kenneth Burke: Literature and Language as Symbolic Action*
(Athens, GA, 1988).

Hyman, S. E., *The Armed Vision: A Study in the Methods of Modern
Literary Criticism* (New York, 1948), 347–94.

Knox, G., *Critical Moments: Kenneth Burke's Categories and Critiques*
(Seattle, 1957).

Lentricchia, F., *Criticism and Social Change* (Chicago, 1983).

Pretext 6 (Fall/Winter 1986). (Special Burke issue.)

Rueckert, W. H., *Kenneth Burke and the Drama of Human Relations*
(Minneapolis, MN, 1963).

Rueckert, W. H., ed., *Critical Responses to Kenneth Burke: 1924–1966*
(Minneapolis, MN, 1969).

Simons, H. W. and T. Melia, eds, *The Legacy of Kenneth Burke* (Madison,
WI, 1989).

Wellek, R., *A History of Modern Criticism 1750–1950, Volume 6:
American Criticism 1900–1960* (1986), 235–56.

White, H., and M. Brose, eds, *Representing Kenneth Burke* (Baltimore, 1982).

CAUDWELL, Christopher (pseudonym of Christopher St John SPRIGG) (1907–37) born in Putney, son of William Sprigg, a journalist, and Jessica Caudwell, an artist. Educated at Roman Catholic schools in Bognor Regis and Ealing. Left school at 15 to join his father on the *Yorkshire Observer* in Bradford. Returned to London in 1926 and formed with his brother Theodore a press agency specializing in aviation. Began writing technical books and manuals on aviation, including *The Airship* (1931) and *Fly With Me* (1932). Suffered business failure in 1933, turning to hack aviation journalism and writing detective thrillers including *Crime in Kensington* (1933). Discovered Marxism; spent summer of 1935 in Cornwall writing *Illusion and Reality* and other works; settled in Poplar, joining Communist Party, and writing *Studies in a Dying Culture*. Published the novel *This My Hand* (1936) under Caudwell name. Having sent *Illusion and Reality* (1937) to the press, travelled to Spain in December 1936 as volunteer driver in the International Brigade; became machine-gun instructor. Died in battle for Madrid, leaving behind numerous manuscripts, posthumously published as *Studies in a Dying Culture* (1938), *Poems* (1939), *The Crisis in Physics* (1939), and *Further Studies in a Dying Culture* (1949). Much later, further writings were collected, including *Romance and Realism* (ed. S. Hynes, Princeton, 1970) and *Scenes and Actions* (ed. J. Duparc and D. Margolies, 1986).

See: Draper, M., 'Christopher Caudwell's Illusions', in J. Lucas, ed., *The 1930s: A Challenge to Orthodoxy* (Brighton, 1978), 78–102.

Hyman, S. E., *The Armed Vision: A Study in the Methods of Modern Literary Criticism* (New York, 1948), 168–208.

Margolies, D., *The Function of Literature: A Study of Christopher Caudwell's Aesthetics* (New York, 1969).

Mulhern, F., 'The Marxist Aesthetics of Christopher Caudwell', *New Left Review* 85 (May/June 1974), 37–58.

Pawling, C., *Christopher Caudwell: Towards a Dialectical Theory of Literature* (New York, 1989).

Sullivan, R., *Christopher Caudwell* (1987). (The fullest account.)

Thompson, E. P., 'Caudwell', *Socialist Register* (1977), 228–76.

CULLER, Jonathan Dwight (1944–) born in Cleveland, Ohio, son of A. Dwight Culler, a professor of literature; brought up in New Haven, Connecticut. Studied literature and history at Harvard (BA, 1966). Went to Oxford as Rhodes scholar reading modern languages (1966–69; BPhil, 1968), then to Cambridge as fellow of Selwyn College (1969–74). Married Veronica Forrest-Thompson, 1971; shortly divorced. Completed his DPhil thesis on French structuralism (1972). Returned to Oxford as lecturer in French at Brasenose College (1974–77). Published *Flaubert: The Uses of Uncertainty* (1974), *Structuralist Poetics* (1975), and *Saussure* (1976). Married Cynthia Chase, 1976. Returned to USA as Professor of English and Comparative Literature at Cornell (1977–). Published *The Pursuit of Signs* (1981), *On Deconstruction* (1982), *Barthes* (1983), *Framing the Sign* (1988); and edited *On Puns* (1988).

See: Freund, E., *The Return of the Reader* (1987), 69–89.

Lentricchia, F., *After the New Criticism* (Chicago, 1980), 103–24.

Ray, W., *Literary Meaning: From Phenomenology to Deconstruction* (Oxford, 1984), 110–23.

DE MAN, Paul (1919–83) born in Antwerp, son of a manufacturer and nephew of Hendrik de Man, a leading Belgian socialist theorist and political figure. Studied engineering at Université Libre de Bruxelles (1939–42). Contributed articles to collaborationist newspaper *Le Soir* (1941–42) during German occupation. Became attached – possibly married – to Anaide Baraghian, who had three children by him. Worked in publishing, and translated *Moby Dick* into Dutch. Failing as a publisher, he emigrated to New York (1948), working in bookselling, while Anaide settled in Argentina. Taught at Bard College (1949–51). Married Patricia Woods, 1950; two children. Moved to Boston, teaching French and doing some translation. Joined the Harvard Society of Fellows (1952), undertaking postgraduate research (MA, 1958; PhD, 1960). Taught at Cornell (1960–67) and Johns Hopkins (1967–70) before settling at Yale (1970–83). Published *Blindness and Insight* (1971) and *Allegories of Reading* (1979). First posthumous collections were *The Rhetoric of Romanticism* (1984) and *The Resistance to Theory* (ed. W. Godzich, 1986). His youthful involvement with collaborationist journals was revealed in 1987, and charges of anti-semitism were laid against one article. Further posthumous works include *Critical Writings, 1953–1978* (ed. L. Waters, 1989), *Wartime Journalism, 1939–1943* (ed. W. Hamacher *et al.*, 1989), and *Romanticism and Contemporary Criticism* (ed. E. S. Burt *et al.*, 1993).

> De Graef, O., *Serenity in Crisis: A Preface to Paul de Man 1939–1960* (Lincoln, NE, 1993). (Defence of his early life.)
> Hamacher, W., *et al.*, eds, *Responses: On Paul de Man's Wartime Journalism* (Lincoln, NE, 1989).
> Lehman, D., *Signs of the Times: Deconstruction and the Fall of Paul de Man* (New York, 1991).

> See: Brooks, P. *et al.*, eds, *The Lesson of Paul de Man* (New Haven, CT, 1985). (Special issue of *Yale French Studies*.)
> Corngold, S., 'Error in Paul de Man', in J. Arac, W. Godzich, and W. Martin, eds, *The Yale Critics: Deconstruction in America* (Minneapolis, MN, 1983), 90–108.
> Culler, J., *On Deconstruction* (Ithaca, NY, 1982), 227–80.
> Culler, J., *Framing the Sign: Criticism and Its Institutions* (Oxford, 1988), 107–35. (Brief, lucid account.)
> Derrida, J., *Mémoires: For Paul de Man* (New York, 1986).
> Godzich, W. and L. Waters, eds, *Reading de Man Reading* (Minneapolis, MN, 1988).
> Lentricchia, F., *After the New Criticism* (Chicago, 1980), 282–317.
> Loesberg, J., *Aestheticism and Deconstruction: Pater, Derrida, and de Man* (Princeton, 1991).
> Norris, C., *Paul de Man: Deconstruction and the Critique of Aesthetic Ideology* (1988).
> Rosiek, J., *Figures of Failure: Paul de Man's Criticism, 1953–1970* (Aarhus, 1992).

EAGLETON, Terence Francis (1943–) born in Salford, Lancashire; educated at De La Salle College, Salford, and Trinity College, Cambridge, graduating in 1964. Studied for PhD on Edward Carpenter as Fellow of Jesus College, Cambridge (1964–69). Married Rosemary Galpin, 1966; two children; later divorced. Published *The New Left Church* (1966) and *Shakespeare and Society* (1967). Began regular reviews of new poetry for *Stand* magazine (1967). Moved to Oxford as Fellow of Wadham College (1969–89), establishing a seminar on Marxist criticism there. Published another theological work, *The Body as Language* (1970), and the critical works *Exiles and Emigrés* (1970) and

Myths of Power: A Marxist Study of the Brontës (1975). Published the ambitious work *Criticism and Ideology* and the brief guide, *Marxism and Literary Criticism* (both 1976), followed by *Walter Benjamin, or Towards a Revolutionary Criticism* (1981) and *The Rape of Clarissa* (1982). Published his most popular work, *Literary Theory* (1983), followed by *The Function of Criticism* (1984), *William Shakespeare* (1986), a volume of essays, *Against the Grain* (1986), and a comic novel, *Saints and Scholars* (1987). Took up new post at Oxford as Lecturer in Critical Theory (1989–92), and published *Ideology: An Introduction* (1991) and *The Ideology of the Aesthetic* (1990), as well as a play about Wilde, *Saint Oscar* (1989). Accepted new post as Warton Professor of English Literature at Oxford (1992). Published *Heathcliff and the Great Hunger* (1995).

> Eagleton, T., *The Significance of Theory* (Oxford, 1990). (Interview, bibliography, and introductory essay by Michael Payne and M. A. R. Habib.)

> See: Bennett, T., *Outside Literature* (1990), 221–43.
> Frow, J., *Marxism and Literary History* (Cambridge, MA, 1986), 18–50.
> Smallwood, P., *Modern Critics in Practice* (1990), 7–40.

ELIOT, Thomas Stearns (1888–1965) born in St Louis, Missouri, to a Unitarian family. Studied at Harvard, under Santayana and Babbitt among others, writing doctoral thesis on F. H. Bradley. Left for Europe in 1914, settling in London in 1915, when he married Vivien Haigh-Wood (d. 1947). Worked as schoolteacher and as bank clerk at Lloyd's; worked on editorial team of the *Egoist*, collaborating with Pound, and began writing for *Athenaeum* and *Times Literary Supplement*. Early poems appeared in *Prufrock and Other Observations* (1917) and *Poems* (1920). Highly influential essays published as *The Sacred Wood* (1920) and *Homage to John Dryden* (1924). Founded *The Criterion*, publishing his major poem 'The Waste Land' in first issue (1922); edited the journal until 1939. Joined Faber publishing house as editor (1926), later becoming Director. Disappointing some admirers, became an Anglican and a British subject (1927), now describing himself as a classicist, royalist Anglo-Catholic in the essays of *For Lancelot Andrewes* (1928). Subsequent critical writings, from *The Use of Poetry and the Use of Criticism* (1933) and *After Strange Gods* (1934; never reprinted after objections to its anti-semitism) show broad cultural concern for order and hierarchy, leading to *Notes Towards the Definition of Culture* (1948). Poetry became predominantly religious from 'The Hollow Men' (1925) and 'Ash Wednesday' (1930) to the extended philosophical sequence *Four Quartets* (1943). Attempted to revive verse drama in several plays, notably *Murder in the Cathedral* (1935). Received Order of Merit and Nobel Prize (1948). Second marriage, to Valerie Fletcher, 1957. Critical essays gathered in successive collections, culminating in third edition (1951) of *Selected Essays*. Further uncollected critical writings appeared in *On Poetry and Poets* (1957) and *To Criticize the Critic* (1965); and in *Selected Prose* (ed. John Hayward, 1953) and *Selected Prose* (ed. Frank Kermode, 1975). His 1926 Clark lectures have appeared as *The Varieties of Metaphysical Poetry* (ed. Ronald Schuchard, 1993).

> Ackroyd, P., *T. S. Eliot* (1984).
> Gordon, L., *Eliot's Early Years* (Oxford, 1977).
> Gordon, L., *Eliot's New Life* (Oxford, 1988).
> *The Letters of T. S. Eliot, Volume 1: 1898–1922*, ed. Valerie Eliot (1988).

> See: Austin, A., *T. S. Eliot: The Literary and Social Criticism* (1974).
> Craig, C., *Yeats, Pound, Eliot and the Politics of Poetry* (1982).

Ellmann, M., *The Poetics of Impersonality: T. S. Eliot and Ezra Pound* (Brighton, 1987).

Fekete, J., *The Critical Twilight* (1978).

Lobb, E., *T. S. Eliot and the Romantic Critical Tradition* (1981).

Margolis, J. D., *T. S. Eliot's Intellectual Development 1922–1939* (1971).

Martin, G., ed., *Eliot in Perspective* (1970).

Newton-De Molina, D., ed., *The Literary Criticism of T. S. Eliot: New Essays* (1977).

Shusterman, R., *T. S. Eliot and the Philosophy of Criticism* (1988).

Stead, C. K., *The New Poetic: Yeats to Eliot* (1964).

Svarny, E., *'The Men of 1914': T. S. Eliot and Early Modernism* (Milton Keynes, 1988).

EMPSON, Sir William (1906–84), born into the landed gentry in Yokefleet, Yorkshire; educated at Winchester College. Studied mathematics at Magdalene College, Cambridge, then English under I. A. Richards. Founded and briefly edited the modernist magazine *Experiment* (1928–29). Developed his undergraduate essays on poetic ambiguity into book form; was elected to research fellowship at Magdalene, but expelled from the college (1929) upon discovery of condoms in his rooms. Published *Seven Types of Ambiguity* (1930). Taught English at Tokyo National University (1931–34). Published *Poems* and *Some Versions of Pastoral* (both 1935). Taught at the National University, Peking (1937–39). Worked in London for the BBC's Far Eastern Section during the Second World War. Married Hester Crouse, 1941; two children. Returned to Peking (1947–52), spending occasional summers at Kenyon College, Ohio and contributing to the *Kenyon Review*. Published *Collected Poems* (1949) and *The Structure of Complex Words* (1951). Took up post as Professor of English Literature at Sheffield University (1953–71). Published *Milton's God* (1961). Retired to Hampstead; received knighthood in 1979. Posthumous works include *Using Biography* (1984), *Essays on Shakespeare* (ed. David B. Pirie, Cambridge, 1986), *Argufying: Essays on Literature and Culture* (ed. John Haffenden, 1987), and *Essays on Renaissance Literature* (ed. John Haffenden, 2 vols, Cambridge, 1993–94).

Gill, R., ed., *William Empson: The Man and His Work* (1974). (Numerous tributes, memoirs, and a bibliography.)

See: Culler, J., *Framing the Sign* (Oxford, 1988), 69–95. (Two important chapters.)

Eagleton, T., 'The Critic as Clown' in *Against the Grain* (1986), 149–65.

Fry, P. H., *William Empson: Prophet Against Sacrifice* (1991).

Hyman, S. E., *The Armed Vision: A Study in the Methods of Modern Literary Criticism* (New York, 1948), 272–306.

Jensen, J., 'The Construction of Seven Types of Ambiguity' *Modern Language Quarterly* 27 (1966), 243–59.

Norris, C., *William Empson and the Philosophy of Literary Criticism* (1978). (Thorough and stimulating; includes postscript by Empson himself.)

Norris, C., and N. Mapp, eds, *William Empson: The Critical Achievement* (Cambridge, 1993). (Some substantial essays.)

Norris, C., 'William Empson and the Claims of Theory', in B. McGuirk, ed., *Redirections in Critical Theory* (1994), 1–109.

Olson, E., 'William Empson, Contemporary Criticism and Poetic Diction', in R. S. Crane, ed., *Critics and Criticism, Ancient and Modern* (Chicago, 1952), 45–82.

Willis, J. H., *William Empson* (New York, 1969).

FIEDLER, Leslie Aaron (1917–), born in Newark, New Jersey, the son of a Jewish pharmacist. Studied at New York University (BA, 1938), then at the University of Wisconsin (MA, 1939; PhD, 1941). Married Margaret Ann Shipley, 1939; six children; divorced 1972. Taught at University of Montana, Missoula (1941–42). Served in US Naval Reserve as Japanese translator and interrogator (1942–46). After a year's research fellowship at Harvard (1946–47), returned to teach at University of Montana (1947–51; 1953–64), spending two intervening years studying in Italy (1951–53). Published *The Jew in the American Novel* (1959), and two volumes of essays, *An End to Innocence* (1955) and *No! in Thunder* (1960). Began a trilogy of works on interracial male bonding in American literature with his most celebrated work, *Love and Death in the American Novel* (1960); continued this with *Waiting for the End* (1964) and *The Return of the Vanishing American* (1968), meanwhile publishing two novels and three volumes of stories. Moved to a new post as Professor of English at the State University of New York at Buffalo (1964–). Appealed successfully against conviction on charges of marijuana possession (1967); enjoyed some celebrity, and published an account of this episode, *Being Busted* (1969). Published *The Stranger in Shakespeare* (1972), and five volumes of essays: *Collected Essays* (2 vols, 1971), *Unfinished Business* (1972), *To the Gentiles* (1972), and *Cross the Border – Close the Gap* (1972). Married Sally Andersen (1973). Later works are *Freaks* (1978), *The Inadvertent Epic* (1979), *What Was Literature?* (1982), and *Olaf Stapledon* (1983).

> See: Winchell, M. R., *Leslie Fiedler* (Boston, 1985).
>> Reising, R., *The Unusable Past: Theory and the Study of American Literature* (New York, 1986), 129–40.

FISH, Stanley Eugene (1938–), born in Providence, Rhode Island to Jewish parents; grew up in Philadelphia. Studied at University of Pennsylvania (BA, 1959). Married Adrienne A. Aaron, 1959; one child; divorced 1980. Studied under E. T. Donaldson at Yale (MA, 1960; PhD, 1962) Taught at University of California, Berkeley (1962–74). Published his doctoral thesis as *John Skelton's Poetry* (1965). Published *Surprised by Sin: The Reader in 'Paradise Lost'* (1967), and *Self-Consuming Artifacts* (1972). Moved to Johns Hopkins University, Baltimore (1974–85); published *The Living Temple* (1978) and a collection of essays, *Is There a Text in This Class?* (1980). Married Jane. P. Tompkins, 1982. Moved to Duke University, North Carolina (1985–). Published *Doing What Comes Naturally* (1989) and *There's No Such Thing as Free Speech* (1994).

> See: Cain, W. E., *The Crisis in Criticism* (Baltimore, MD, 1984), 51–64.
> Culler, J., *The Pursuit of Signs* (Ithaca, NY, 1981), 119–31.
> de Man P., *Blindness and Insight* (2nd edn, 1983), 277–89.
> Freund, E., *The Return of the Reader* (1987), 90–111.
> Goodheart, E., *The Skeptic Disposition* (Princeton, NJ, 1984), 88–110.
> Holland, N., 'Stanley Fish, Stanley Fish', *Genre* 10 (1977), 433–41.
> Horton, S. R., 'The Experience of Stanley Fish's Prose, or The Critic as Self-Creating, Self-Consuming Artificer', *Genre* 10 (1977), 443–53.
> Mailloux, S. J., 'Evaluation and Reader Response Criticism: Values Implicit in Affective Stylistics', *Style* 10 (1976), 329–43.
> Ray, W., *Literary Meaning: From Phenomenology to Deconstruction* (Oxford, 1984), 152–69.

FORD, Ford Madox, *see* HUEFFER, Ford Madox

FRYE, Herman Northrop (1912–91), born in Sherbrooke, Quebec, the son of a Methodist hardware salesman; moved to Moncton, New Brunswick and attended Aberdeen High School. Studied English and Philosophy at Victoria College, University of Toronto (1929–33), under E. J. Pratt and G. Wilson Knight, among others. Studied for second BA degree in theology at Emmanuel College, University of Toronto (1933–36). Was ordained as minister in United Church of Canada (1936), but without assuming pastoral duties. Studied in England at Merton College, Oxford (1936–37; 1938–39), with an intervening year teaching back in Victoria College. Married Helen Kemp, 1937. Returned to Victoria College in 1939 as Lecturer in English, later becoming full professor (1947) and college principal (1957–67). Published *Fearful Symmetry: A Study of William Blake* (1947), followed by his most important book, *Anatomy of Criticism* (1957). Published *The Educated Imagination, Fables of Identity, T. S. Eliot,* and *The Well-Tempered Critic* (all 1963). Later works include *The Return of Eden: Five Essays on Milton's Epics* (1965), three books on Shakespeare – *A Natural Perspective* (1965), *Fools of Time* (1967), and *The Myth of Deliverance* (1983) – along with such influential works as *The Secular Scripture: A Study of the Structure of Romance* (1976), *The Great Code: The Bible and Literature* (1982), and the latter work's sequel, *Words With Power* (1990). Frye also published two collections of essays on Canadian literature and culture, *The Bush Garden* (1971) and *Divisions on a Ground* (1982), and several general collections of essays including *The Stubborn Structure* (1970) and *Spiritus Mundi* (1977), besides numerous minor works.

> Adamson, J., *Northrop Frye: A Visionary Life* (Toronto, 1993). (Brief biography.)
> Ayre, J., *Northrop Frye: A Biography* (Toronto, 1989).
> Cayley, D., *Northrop Frye in Conversation* (Toronto, 1992).
> Denham, R. D., ed., *A World in a Grain of Sand: Twenty-Two Interviews with Northrop Frye* (New York, 1991).
> Salusinszky, I., *Criticism in Society* (1987), 26–42. (Interview.)

> See: Balfour, I., *Northrop Frye* (Boston, 1989).
> Bates, R., *Northrop Frye* (Toronto, 1971).
> Berry, R., 'Shakespearean Comedy and Northrop Frye', *Essays in Criticism* 22 (1972), 33–40.
> Cook, D., *Northrop Frye: A Vision of the New World* (Montreal, 1985). (On Frye's cultural politics.)
> Cook, E. *et al.,* eds, *Centre and Labyrinth: Essays in Honour of Northrop Frye* (Toronto, 1983.)
> Denham, R. D., *Northrop Frye and Critical Method* (University Park, PA, 1978). (Oddly focused; numerous diagrams.)
> Denham, R. D. and T. Willard, eds, *Visionary Poetics: Essays on Northrop Frye's Poetics* (New York, 1991).
> Fekete, J., *The Critical Twilight* (1978), 107–31. (Marxist critique of Frye.)
> Fletcher, A., 'Northrop Frye: The Critical Passion', *Critical Inquiry* 1 (1975), 741–56. (Defence of Frye.)
> Hamilton, A. C., *Northrop Frye: Anatomy of His Criticism* (Toronto, 1990). (Commendable full-length study.)
> Hart, J., *Northrop Frye: The Theoretical Imagination* (1994). (Thorough survey.)
> Krieger, M., ed., *Northrop Frye in Modern Criticism* (New York, 1966). (Several distinguished contributions.)
> Lentricchia, F., *After the New Criticism* (Chicago, 1980), 2–26. (Astute.)

Mackey, L., 'Anatomical Curiosities: Northrop Frye's Theory of Criticism', *Texas Studies in Language and Literature* 23 (1981), 442–69.

O'Hara, D. T., *The Romance of Interpretation: Visionary Criticism from Pater to de Man* (New York, 1985), 147–204.

Riccomini, D. R., 'Northrop Frye and Structuralism: Identity and Difference', *University of Toronto Quarterly* 49 (1979), 33–47.

HARTMAN, Geoffrey H. (1929–), born in Frankfurt, Germany, to Jewish parents. Left Germany in 1939, and continued schooling in Aylesbury, England. Joined his mother in New York in 1946, studying at Queens College of City University (BA, 1949); moved to Yale University for postgraduate study under René Wellek, during which he spent a year in France at the University of Dijon as Fulbright Fellow (1951–52); took his PhD in 1953. Served in public information division of US Army (1953–55). Published his thesis as *The Unmediated Vision* (1954). Returned to Yale to teach (1955–62). Married Renee Gross, 1956; two children. Moved to University of Iowa (1962–65); published *Wordsworth's Poetry, 1787–1814* (1964). Taught at Cornell University (1965–67), then returned to Yale (1967–). Collected his essays as *Beyond Formalism* (1970) and *The Fate of Reading* (1975), and published a book of verse, *Akiba's Children* (1978). Contributed a chapter to the 'Yale School' collection *Deconstruction and Criticism* (1979). Published *Criticism in the Wilderness* (1980), followed by *Saving the Text: Literature/Derrida/Philosophy* (1981) and the essays collected in *Easy Pieces* (1985). Published *The Unremarkable Wordsworth* (1987), and a collection of essays, *Minor Prophecies* (1991).

Moynihan, R., *A Recent Imagining* (Hamden, CT, 1986), 51–96. (Interview.)

Salusinszky, I., *Criticism in Society* (1987), 74–96. (Interview.)

See: Atkins, G. D., *Geoffrey Hartman: Criticism as Answerable Style* (1990).

Atkins, G. D., *Reading Deconstruction/Deconstructive Reading* (Lexington, KY, 1983).

Handelman, S. A., *The Slayers of Moses: The Emergence of Rabbinic Interpretation in Modern Literary Theory* (Albany, NY, 1982).

O'Hara, D. T., *The Romance of Interpretation: Visionary Criticism from Pater to de Man* (New York, 1985), 93–145.

Sprinker, M., 'Aesthetic Criticism: Geoffrey Hartman' in Arac, J. *et al.*, eds, *The Yale Critics: Deconstruction in America* (Minneapolis, MN, 1983), 43–65.

HOWELLS, William Dean (1837–1920), born in Martin's Ferry, Ohio, the son of a journalist; raised without formal education. Worked as compositor and journalist on Ohio papers. Campaign biography of Abraham Lincoln (1860) earned him US consulship in Venice (1861–65). Settled in Boston as assistant editor (1866–71) then editor (1871–81) of *Atlantic Monthly*, establishing that journal's reputation. Resigned to concentrate on his novels: the most important are *A Modern Instance* (1882), *The Rise of Silas Lapham* (1885), and *A Hazard of New Fortunes* (1890). Established his critical position with regular 'Editor's Study' column (1886–92) in *Harper's Monthly*, and moved to New York. Briefly edited *Cosmopolitan* (1892), then wrote freelance for various journals. Returned to *Harper's Monthly* for regular 'Editor's Easy Chair' column (1900–20). Founder Member, NAACP (1909). Principal critical books are *Criticism and Fiction* (1891) and *My Literary Passions* (1895); lesser works are *Modern Italian Poets* (1887), *Heroines of Fiction* (1901), and *Literature and*

Life (1902). The most important magazine articles are collected in *W. D. Howells as Critic* (ed. E. H. Cady, 1973) and in the more compendious *Selected Literary Criticism* (ed. D. J. Norloh, *et al.*, 3 vols, Bloomington, IN, 1992). Howells also published travel books and memoirs, including *Years of My Youth* (1916).

> Cady, E. H., *The Road to Realism: The Early Years, 1837–1885, of William Dean Howells* (Syracuse, NY, 1956).
> Cady E. H., *The Realist at War: The Mature Years, 1885–1920, of William Dean Howells* (Syracuse, NY, 1958).
> Howells, W. D., *Selected Letters*, ed. G. Arms *et al.* (6 vols, Boston, MA, 1979–83).
> Lynn, K. S., *William Dean Howells: An American Life* (New York, 1971).

> See: Bennett, G. N., *The Realism of William Dean Howells, 1889–1920* (Nashville, TN, 1973).
> Carter, E., *Howells and the Age of Realism* (Philadelphia, PA, 1954).
> McMurray, W., *The Literary Realism of William Dean Howells* (Carbondale, IL, 1967).
> Vanderbilt, K., *The Achievement of William Dean Howells* (Princeton, NJ, 1968).

HUEFFER (FORD), Ford Madox (1873–1939); born Ford Hermann Hueffer, renamed himself Ford Madox Hueffer, then (from 1919) Ford Madox Ford. Born in Merton, Surrey, son of a German music critic, grandson of the Pre-Raphaelite painter Ford Madox Brown (on whom he published a book in 1896), and nephew to W. M. Rossetti. Marriage to Elsie Martindale (1894) broke up after fifteen years. Collaborated with Joseph Conrad in *The Inheritors* (1901), *Romance* (1903), and *Nostromo* (1904). Trilogy of historical novels began with *The Fifth Queen* (1906). Founded *English Review* in 1908, but had to give up editorship a year later. Early critical works: *The Critical Attitude* (1911), *Henry James* (1913). Contributed some poems to Imagist anthologies. Finest of many novels is *The Good Soldier* (1915). Active service in war, in which he was victim of gas attack, formed basis of fictional war tetralogy *Parade's End* (1924–28). Settled in Paris in 1923, founding *Transatlantic Review* there in 1924; published work by Pound, Hemingway and others. Later works include *Joseph Conrad* (1924), *The English Novel* (1930), *The March of Literature* (1938), and various memoirs. Some critical articles later collected in *Critical Writings* (ed. F. MacShane, Lincoln, NE, 1964).

> Ford, F. M., *Your Mirror to My Times: Selected Autobiographies and Impressions*, ed. M. Killigrew (New York, 1971; reprinted as *Memoirs and Impressions*, Harmondsworth, 1979).
> *Letters of Ford Madox Ford*, ed. R. M. Ludwig (Princeton, NJ, 1965).
> Judd, A., *Ford Madox Ford* (1990).
> Lindberg-Seyersted, B., *Pound/Ford: The Story of a Literary Friendship* (1982). (Includes their correspondence.)
> MacShane, F., *The Life and Work of Ford Madox Ford* (1965).
> Mizener, A., *The Saddest Story* (Cleveland, OH, 1971).

> See: Cassell, R., ed., *Ford Madox Ford: Modern Critical Judgments* (1972).
> Stang, S. J., ed., *The Presence of Ford Madox Ford* (Philadelphia, PA, 1981). (Includes some essays on Ford as critic and editor, with various reminiscences.)

JAMES, Henry (1843–1916), born in New York City to a wealthy family, younger
brother to the philosopher William James. Educated privately, taken by his
father on extensive European travels. Studied briefly at Harvard Law School
(1862), but turned to writing, contributing critical articles to *The Nation* in
late 1860s. Lived in Paris in early 1870s, met Turgenev, Flaubert, and other
literary leaders: settled in London in 1876. Career in fiction launched with
the novel *Roderick Hudson* and the stories in *A Passionate Pilgrim* (both 1875).
Daisy Miller (1879) brought him fame; similar studies of conflict between
American and European manners in this early phase include *The Europeans*
(1878) and *The Portrait of a Lady* (1881). Early critical books: *French Poets
and Novelists* (1878), *Hawthorne* (1879), *Partial Portraits* (1888) – which includes
'The Art of Fiction' (1884) – and *Essays in London and Elsewhere* (1893).
Failed attempts at writing for theatre in early 1890s. Fictions of the 'middle
period' include the technical *tour de force, What Maisie Knew* (1897), and
the uncanny tale 'The Turn of the Screw' (1899). Last three completed
novels, *The Wings of the Dove* (1902), *The Ambassadors* (1903), and *The
Golden Bowl* (1904) show elaborate analytic subtlety. As a wartime gesture
(partly against US isolationism) James became a British subject in 1915.
Later miscellaneous critical writings appear in *Notes on Novelists* (1914) and
in the posthumous collections *Within the Rim and Other Essays* (1918)
and *Notes and Reviews* (1921). Most influential are the Prefaces written
between 1907 and 1909 for the New York edition of his *Novels and Tales*
(1907–17); these were later collected as *The Art of the Novel* (ed. R. P.
Blackmur, New York, 1934). Other collections of his critical writings have
appeared as *Literary Reviews and Essays* (ed. A. Mordell, New York, 1957),
Selected Literary Criticism (ed. M. Shapira, 1963), *Literary Criticism* (ed. L.
Edel, 2 vols, 1984) and *The Critical Muse* (ed. R. Gard, 1987).

> Edel, L., *Henry James* (5 vols, 1953–72; reprinted in 2 vols as *The Life
> of Henry James*, Harmondsworth, 1977; revd and condensed as
> *Henry James: A Life*, New York, 1985).
> Moore, H. T., *Henry James* (New York, 1974).
> *Henry James: Letters*, ed. L. Edel (4 vols, 1974–84).
> *Selected Letters*, ed. L. Edel (1987).
> *The Complete Notebooks of Henry James*, ed. L. Edel and L. H. Powers
> (New York, 1987).

> See: Daugherty, S. B., *The Literary Criticism of Henry James* (Athens, OH,
> 1981).
> Jones, V., *James the Critic* (1984). (Perceptive account.)
> Roberts, M., *Henry James's Criticism* (New York, 1929). (Still useful.)

JAMESON, Fredric R. (1934–), born in Cleveland, Ohio; brought up in New
Jersey. Studied at Haverford College (BA, 1954), then under Erich Auerbach
at Yale (MA, 1956; PhD, 1960). Taught at Harvard University (1959–67);
published a version of his doctoral thesis as *Sartre: The Origins of a Style*
(1961). Moved to University of California at San Diego (1967–76); published
Marxism and Form (1971) and *The Prison-House of Language* (1972). Moved
to Yale (1976–83); published *Fables of Aggression: Wyndham Lewis, the Modernist
as Fascist* (1979), and *The Political Unconscious* (1981). Co-founded the journal
Social Text (1979). After two years at the University of California, Santa Cruz,
moved to Duke University (1986). Published a collection of essays as *The
Ideologies of Theory* (1988), then the ambitious work of cultural analysis,
Postmodernism (1991), along with *Late Marxism: Adorno* (1990) and two
books on cinema: *Signatures of the Visible* (1990) and *The Geopolitical Aesthetic*
(1992).

See: Darius, S., 'In Search of Totality: On Narrative and History in Fredric
    Jameson's *The Political Unconscious*,' in B. McGuirk, ed., *Redirections*
    in Critical Theory (1994), 197–263.
    Diacritics 12 (Fall 1982). (Special Jameson number.)
    Dowling, W. C., *Jameson, Althusser, Marx: An Introduction to 'The*
    Political Unconscious' (Ithaca, NY, 1984).
    Eagleton, T., *Against the Grain* (1986), 65–78.
    Frow, J., *Marxism and Literary History* (Cambridge, MA, 1986), 30–41.
    Kellner, D., ed., *Postmodernism/Jameson/Critique* (Washington, DC,
    1989).
    LaCapra, D., *Rethinking Intellectual History* (1983), 234–67.
    Weber, S., *Institution and Interpretation* (Minneapolis, MN, 1987), 40–58.
    White, H., *The Content of the Form* (Baltimore, MD, 1987), 142–68.

KERMODE, Sir John Frank (1919–), born in Douglas, Isle of Man, son of a grocer;
educated at Douglas High School and University of Liverpool. Served in
Royal Navy (1940–46); married Maureen Eccles, 1947; two children,
divorced 1970. Taught at King's College, Newcastle (1947–49), then
University of Reading (1949–58). Published Arden edition of *The Tempest*
(1954), and his first major work, *Romantic Image* (1957). Moved to
Manchester University as Professor of English Literature (1958–65); published
Wallace Stevens (1960) and *Puzzles and Epiphanies* (1962). Moved to another
chair at Bristol (1965–67); published *The Sense of an Ending* (1967), and acted
briefly as co-editor of *Encounter* (1966–67). Moved to third professorial post at
University College, London (1967–74); published *Continuities* (1968), two
volumes of essays: *Shakespeare, Spenser, Donne* and *Modern Essays* (both 1971),
and *D. H. Lawrence* (1973); edited the Fontana Modern Masters series and
co-edited the *Oxford Anthology of English Literature* (1973). Took up
appointment as King Edward VII Professor of English at the University of
Cambridge (1974–82); published *The Classic* (1975). Married Anita Van Vactor
(1976). Published *The Genesis of Secrecy* (1979). Resigned from Cambridge
chair (1982), following the acrimonious 'MacCabe Affair'; subsequently taught
as occasional visiting professor at Columbia University. Published *Essays on*
Fiction, 1971–82 (1983), *Forms of Attention* (1985), *History and Value* (1988),
An Appetite for Poetry (1989), and *Uses of Error* (1991). Received knighthood,
1991.

    Kermode, F., *Poetry, Narrative, History* (Oxford, 1990), 68–121.
    (Includes interview and bibliography.)
    Salusinszky, I., *Criticism in Society* (1987), 99–121. (Interview.)

See: Arac, J., *Critical Genealogies* (New York, 1987), 217–37.
    Gardner, H., *In Defence of the Imagination* (Oxford, 1982), 112–37.
    Gorak, J., *Critic of Crisis: A Study of Frank Kermode* (Columbia, MO,
    1987).
    Gorak, J., *The Making of the Modern Canon* (1991), 153–85. (Chapter
    on Kermode and canons.)
    Lentricchia, F., *After the New Criticism* (Chicago, 1980), 29–60. (On
    Kermode's 'conservative fictionalism'.)
    Payne, M., and H. Schweizer, Introduction to F. Kermode, *Poetry,*
    Narrative, History (Oxford, 1990), 1–28.
    Schwarz, D. R., *The Humanistic Heritage* (1986), 170–86. (Chapter on
    The Sense of an Ending.)
    Tudeau-Clayton, M. and M. Warner, eds, *Addressing Frank Kermode*

(1991). (Includes five essays on Kermode's work, with his own response; inadequate bibliography.).

KNIGHT, George Wilson (1897–1985), born in Sutton, Surrey; educated at Dulwich College. Served in Royal Engineers, 1916–20, as a motor-cycle dispatch rider in Iraq and India. Studied English at St Edmund Hall, Oxford. Worked as mathematics and English teacher in Kent and Cheltenham. Published articles in *Adelphi* and his two most influential studies of Shakespeare, *The Wheel of Fire* (1930), and *The Imperial Theme* (1931). Moved to University of Toronto as Professor of English (1931–40), also producing Shakespeare plays there. Published *The Shakespearean Tempest* (1932), *The Christian Renaissance* (1933), *Principles of Shakespearean Production* (1936), and *The Burning Oracle* (1939), along with an autobiographical novel, *Atlantic Crossing* (1936). Taught at Stowe School, Buckinghamshire (1941–46), turning literature into war propaganda in *This Sceptred Isle* (1940), *Chariot of Wrath* (1942), and other works. Taught at University of Leeds (1946–62; as Professor from 1956), continuing to produce Shakespeare plays. Published further works on Shakespeare including *The Crown of Life* (1947) and *The Mutual Flame* (1955), as well as various books on Byron, Pope, Ibsen, and Nietzsche. Became a Spiritualist in 1950, later holding high office in the Spiritualist Association. Gave numerous Shakespearean recitals, usually from *Timon of Athens*, either naked or in a small loincloth: these were later photographically illustrated in *Symbol of Man* (1979). Retired to Exeter in 1962. Published essays on modern literature in *Neglected Powers* (1971); a biography of his brother Jackson Knight, a classical scholar; a volume of verse, *Gold-Dust, with Other Poetry* (1968); and *Shakespearean Negotiations* (1984).

> Jefferson, D. W., ed., *The Morality of Art: Essays Presented to G. Wilson Knight by his Colleagues and Friends* (1969). (Includes two brief tributes, and a bibliography.)
>
> Van Domelen, J. E., *Tarzan of Athens: A Biographical Study of G. Wilson Knight* (Bristol, 1987). (Poorly produced, with no bibliography; still intriguing.)

> See: Grady, H., *The Modernist Shakespeare* (Oxford, 1991), 74–112.
>
> Sale, R. 'G. Wilson Knight', *Modern Language Quarterly* 29 (1968), 77–83.
>
> Viswanathan, S., *The Shakespeare Play as Poem: A Critical Tradition in Perspective* (Cambridge, 1980).
>
> Wellek, R., *A History of Modern Criticism 1750–1950, Volume 5: English Criticism 1900–1950* (1986), 128–38.

KNIGHTS, Lionel Charles (1906–), born in Grantham, Lincolnshire; studied at Selwyn College and Christ's College, Cambridge, graduating in 1928. Founded the quarterly journal *Scrutiny* and remained a co-editor throughout its existence (1932–53). Published the pamphlet *How Many Children Had Lady Macbeth?* (1933). Taught English Literature at University of Manchester (1933–47), completed PhD on Renaissance drama (1936), publishing it as *Drama and Society in the Age of Jonson* (1937). Married Elizabeth Mary Barnes, 1936; two children. Published his early essays as *Explorations* (1946). Moved to University of Sheffield as Professor of English Literature (1947–52), then to second chair at University of Bristol (1953–64). Published a lecture, *Shakespeare's Politics* (1957), then *Some Shakespearean Themes* (1959) and *An Approach to Hamlet* (1960). Moved to Cambridge as King Edward VII Professor of English Literature and fellow of Queen's College (1965–73).

Published *Further Explorations* (1965) and his Clark lectures, *Public Voices* (1971). After retirement, published *Explorations 3* (1976), *Hamlet and Other Shakespearean Essays* (1979), and *Selected Essays in Criticism* (1981).

See: Grover, P. R., 'The Ghost of Dr Johnson: L. C. Knights and D. A. Traversi on *Hamlet*', *Essays in Criticism* 17 (1967), 143–57.

Newton, J. M., '*Scrutiny*'s Failure with Shakespeare', *Cambridge Quarterly* 1 (1965), 144–77.

Nuttall, A. D., 'The Argument About Shakespeare's Characters', *Critical Quarterly* 7 (1965), 107–20.

Viswanathan, S., *The Shakespeare Play as Poem: A Critical Tradition in Perspective* (Cambridge, 1980), 122–55.

LAWRENCE, David Herbert (1885–1930) born in Eastwood, Nottinghamshire, son of a coalminer. Worked as clerk, then as pupil teacher, training at University College, Nottingham before teaching in Croydon. Published poems and stories in *English Review*, then first novel, *The White Peacock* (1911). Eloped in 1912 with Frieda von Richthofen, wife of his former tutor Ernest Weekley; married her in 1914. Published *Sons and Lovers* (1913) followed by numerous volumes of stories, poems, plays, essays, travel writings, and the major novels *The Rainbow* (1915; banned by censors, reissued 1924) and *Women in Love* (1920). After the Great War, left England forever, living in Italy, Australia, New Mexico, and Italy again. Published *Studies in Classic American Literature* (1923) and important essays on the novel including 'Morality and the Novel' (1925). His last novel, *Lady Chatterley's Lover* (1928) was banned in England until 1960. Died in Vence, France, after prolonged struggles with tuberculosis. Unpublished critical essays including 'Why the Novel Matters' and 'Study of Thomas Hardy' appeared posthumously in *Phoenix* (1936); and further essays and stories in *Phoenix II* (1968). Other posthumous collections include *Selected Literary Criticism* (ed. Anthony Beal, 1956), *A Selection from Phoenix* (ed. A. A. H. Inglis, 1971), and *Study of Thomas Hardy and Other Essays* (ed. Brian Steele, Cambridge, 1985). An earlier version of the essays on American literature appeared as *The Symbolic Meaning* (ed. Armin Arnold, 1964).

Boulton, J. T. *et al.*, eds, *The Letters of D. H. Lawrence* (7 vols, Cambridge, 1979–93). (Richly annotated.)

Worthen, J., *D. H. Lawrence: A Literary Life* (1989).

See: Fernihough, A., *D. H. Lawrence: Aesthetics and Ideology* (Oxford, 1993). (Places Lawrence in context of Bloomsbury group.)

Gordon, D. J., *D. H. Lawrence as Literary Critic* (1966).

Klingopulos, G. D., 'Lawrence's Criticism', *Essays in Criticism* 7 (1957), 294–303.

Rahv, P., *Literature and the Sixth Sense* (New York, 1969; London, 1970), 289–306.

Sharma, K. K., *Modern Fictional Theorists: Virginia Woolf and D. H. Lawrence* (Atlantic Heights, NJ, 1982).

Swigg, R., *Lawrence, Hardy and American Literature* (1972).

Wellek, R., *A History of Modern Criticism 1750–1950, Volume 5: English Criticism 1900–1950* (1986), 116–28. (Scathing.)

Zytaruk, G. J., *D. H. Lawrence's Response to Russian Literature* (1971).

LEAVIS, Frank Raymond (1895–1978) born in Cambridge, son of a music-shop proprietor. Educated in Cambridge at the Perse School and Emmanuel College. As a conscientious objector, served as stretcher-bearer for Quaker ambulance unit in Great War; later insomnia and poor digestion possibly attributable to wartime gassing and shell-shock. Wrote PhD thesis on journalism and literature (1924). Taught at Cambridge for several years before finding secure employment at Downing College (1936) and with the University – which never awarded him a Professorship. Married his former student Queenie Dorothy Roth, 1929; three children. She was a powerful influence on his writings and a significant critic in her own right. Published cultural manifestos – *Mass Civilization and Minority Culture* (1930), *For Continuity* (1933), and *Culture and Environment* (with Denys Thompson, 1933) – on behalf of the discriminating minority against 'mass' culture. Became leading light of the influential journal *Scrutiny* (1932–53), as co-editor with L. C. Knights and others. Revised the canon of English poetry in *New Bearings in English Poetry* (1932) and *Revaluation* (1936); then of the novel in *The Great Tradition* (1948). Later critical works concentrate on a 'romantic' anti-industrial tradition in English fiction, notably in *D. H. Lawrence, Novelist* (1955) and *Dickens the Novelist* (with Q. D. Leavis, 1970). Engaged in bitter debate with C. P. Snow about scientific and literary culture, publishing *Two Cultures?* (1962) Retired from Cambridge teaching (1962), becoming Visiting Professor at York and Bristol; but continued living in Cambridge and wearing open-necked shirts. Principal collections of critical essays are *The Common Pursuit* (1952) and *Anna Karenina and Other Essays* (1967), and the posthumous volumes *The Critic as Anti-Philosopher* (ed. G. Singh, 1982) and *Valuation in Criticism and Other Essays* (ed. G. Singh, Cambridge, 1986).

> McKillop, I., *F. R. Leavis: A Life in Criticism* (1995)
> Leavis, F. R., *Letters in Criticism*, ed. J. Tasker (1974). (Collects many angry letters to the press.)
> Thompson, D., ed., *The Leavises: Recollections and Impressions* (Cambridge, 1984). (Some thoughtful assessments).

> See: Baldick, C., *The Social Mission of English Criticism* (Oxford, 1983), 161–95.
> Bell, M., *F. R. Leavis* (1988). (Defends Leavis's attitude to language.)
> Bilan, R. P., *The Literary Criticism of F. R. Leavis* (Cambridge, 1979). (Rather pedestrian.)
> Casey, J., *The Language of Criticism* (1966), 153–78. (Subjects Leavis's terms to 'close reading'.)
> Mulhern, F., *The Moment of 'Scrutiny'* (1979). (Acute, detailed study of the Leavis circle.)
> Robertson, P. J. M., *The Leavises on Fiction* (1981).
> Samson, A., *F. R. Leavis* (Hemel Hempstead, 1992). (Thoughtful, duly critical survey.)
> Walsh, W., *F. R. Leavis* (1980). (Uncritical.)

LUBBOCK, Percy (1879–1965), born in London, the son of a merchant banker; educated at Eton and King's College, Cambridge, where he gained a First in the Classical Tripos (1901). Worked briefly in journalism, and published *Elizabeth Barrett Browning in her Letters* (1906). Worked as Pepys librarian at Magdalene College, Cambridge (1906–8), publishing an introductory guide, *Samuel Pepys* (1909). Wrote frequently for the *Times Literary Supplement*; came to know Henry James. Served in Red Cross during Great War. Following James's death in 1916, edited his unfinished works *The Ivory Tower, The Middle Years*, and *The Sense of the Past* (all 1917); then edited *The Letters of Henry James* (2 vols, 1920), and a 35–volume edition of James's *Novels and Stories* (1921–23). Published his most important work, *The Craft of Fiction*

(1921), followed by a childhood memoir, *Earlham* (1922), a comic novel, *Roman Pictures* (1923) and a second novel, *The Region Cloud* (1925). Married Lady Sybil Scott (1926), and emigrated to Italy, at which point his literary career virtually ends, but for the further memoirs in *Shades of Eton* (1929) and the literary study *Portrait of Edith Wharton* (1947).

> See: Liddell, R., 'Percy Lubbock', *Kenyon Review* 29 (1967), 493–511.
> Schorer, M., Foreword to Lubbock, *The Craft of Fiction* (New York, 1957).
> Schwarz, D. R., *The Humanistic Heritage* (1986), 28–40. (Ungainly.)

MILLER, Joseph Hillis (1928–), born in Newport News, Virginia, son of a Baptist minister turned college administrator. Studied at Oberlin College, Ohio, graduating in 1948; then at Harvard (PhD, 1952). Married Marian Dorothy James, 1949; three children; contracted polio, suffering partial paralysis. After a year teaching at Williams College, taught English at Johns Hopkins University, Baltimore (1953–72). Edited the journal *Modern Language Notes* (1953–61). Revised his doctoral thesis under influence of Georges Poulet, publishing it as *Charles Dickens: The World of His Novels* (1958). Followed this with *The Disappearance of God: Five Nineteenth-Century Writers* (1963), *Poets of Reality: Six Twentieth-Century Writers* (1965), *The Form of Victorian Fiction* (1968), and *Thomas Hardy: Distance and Desire* (1970). By now under the growing influence of Derrida, moved to Yale (1972–86), and published numerous articles of a 'deconstructionist' character, contributing a chapter to the collection *Deconstruction and Criticism* (1979). Published *Fiction and Repetition* (1982) and *The Linguistic Moment* (1985). Moved to the University of California at Irvine (1986). Published *The Ethics of Reading* (1987) and *Versions of Pygmalion*, and collected his essays as *Tropes, Parables, Performatives, Victorian Subjects* (both 1990) and *Theory Now and Then*. Published *Ariadne's Thread* (1992).

> Moynihan, R., *A Recent Imagining* (Hamden, CT, 1986), 97–131. (Interview.)
> Salusinsky, I., *Criticism in Society* (1987), 208–40. (Interview.)

> See: Cain, W. E., *The Crisis in Criticism* (Baltimore, MD, 1984), 31–50.
> Heusser, M., and H. Schweizer, Introduction and 'The Authority of Reading: An Interview with J. Hillis Miller' in J. H. Miller, *Hawthorne and History* (1991), 1–45; 133–71. (Followed by full bibliography to 1989.)
> Leitch, V. B., *Deconstructive Criticism* (1983), 190–97.
> Pease, D., 'J. Hillis Miller: The Other Victorian at Yale', in J. Arac, *et al.*, eds, *The Yale Critics: Deconstruction in America* (Minneapolis, MN, 1983), 66–89.
> Schwarz, D. R., *The Humanistic Heritage* (1986), 222–66. (On Miller's theory of fiction.)

MURRY, John Middleton (1889–1957), born in Peckham, London, son of an Inland Revenue clerk. Educated at Christ's Hospital and at Brasenose College, Oxford. As a student, visited Paris and founded the journal *Rhythm* (1911–13; succeeded by *Blue Review*, 1913), promoting post-Impressionist art and modernist writing. Lived with his co-editor Katherine Mansfield from 1912 (later as her husband from 1918 until her death in 1923). Began turbulent association with D. H. Lawrence (partly reflected in the latter's *Women in Love*), jointly producing the short-lived journal *Signature* (1915). Worked in political intelligence department of War Office (1916–19), becoming Chief

Censor; received OBE (1920) for this work. Published *Fyodor Dostoevsky* and the novel *Still Life* (both 1916), and became regular reviewer for *Times Literary Supplement*. Edited the *Athenaeum* (1919–21). Published critical essays as *Aspects of Literature, Evolution of an Intellectual* (both 1920), and *Countries of the Mind* (1922); gave lectures at Oxford published as *The Problem of Style* (1922); published *Poems* (1921) and the novel *The Things We Are* (1922). Founded and edited the *Adelphi* (1923–32) as a vehicle for the work of his late wife and of Lawrence. Married Violet le Maistre, 1924; three children; dressed her up to resemble Mansfield. Published further critical and mystical writings as *Discoveries, To the Unknown God* (both 1924), *Keats and Shakespeare* (Clark Lectures, 1925), *The Life of Jesus* (1926), *Things to Come* (1928), and *Studies in Keats* (1930); edited Mansfield's journals and letters (1927, 1928). Became a widower for second time, had affair with Frieda Lawrence, then married Violet's nurse Betty Cockbayne 1931; separated 1941. Published *Son of Woman: The Story of D. H. Lawrence* (1931), *The Life of Katherine Mansfield, William Blake* (both 1933), and *Shakespeare* (1936), and minor works reflecting successive conversions to Marxism (1931–34) and Pacifism (1936–46). Became editor of *Peace News* (1940–46); founded a community farm in Norfolk with Mary Gamble (later his wife, 1954–7). Published various collections of essays, and a biography of Swift (1954). Posthumous collections are *Selected Criticism 1916–1957* (ed. R. Rees, 1960), *Poets, Critics, Mystics* (ed. R. Rees, 1970), and *Defending Romanticism* (ed. M. Woodfield, Bristol, 1989).

Carswell, J., *Lives and Letters* (New York, 1978).

Lea, F. A., *John Middleton Murry* (New York, 1960). (Standard biography.)

Murry, J. M., *Between Two Worlds* (1935). (Autobiography; covers period to 1918.)

Murry, J. M., *God: An Introduction to the Science of Metabiology* (1929). (Includes some autobiographical chapters.)

Murry, K. F., *Beloved Quixote: The Unknown Life of John Middleton Murry* (1986).

The Letters of John Middleton Murry to Katherine Mansfield, ed. C. A. Hankin (1983).

See: Casey, J., *The Language of Criticism* (1966), 105–19.

Cassavant, S. G., *John Middleton Murry: The Critic as Moralist* (Alabama, 1982).

Griffin, E. G., *John Middleton Murry* (New York, 1969).

Heath, W. W., 'The Literary Criticism of John Middleton Murry', *PMLA* 70 (1958), 41–57.

Sharma, L. R., *In Defence of J. Middleton Murry* (Allahabad, 1986).

Sharma, L. R., *The T. S. Eliot-Middleton Murry Debate* (Allahabad, 1994).

Stanford, D., 'Middleton Murry as Literary Critic', *Essays in Criticism* 8 (1958), 60–67.

Wellek, R., *A History of Modern Criticism 1750–1950, Volume 5: English Criticism 1900–1950* (1986), 92–116.

Woodfield, M., Introduction to *Defending Romanticism: Selected Criticism of John Middleton Murry* (Bristol, 1989), 1–52. (Best introduction to the criticism.)

POUND, Ezra Weston Loomis (1885–1972) born in Hailey, Idaho, raised near Philadelphia. Studied Romance Philology at University of Pennsylvania and Hamilton College; took MA degree (1907), but abandoned PhD after failing course in history of criticism. Dismissed from teaching post at Wabash

College, Indiana for alleged sexual misconduct. Travelled to Italy, where he published first book, *A Lume Spento* (1908). Settled in London (1908–20), producing six volumes of poems and translations in four years. Wrote for several 'little magazines', and formed his critical position through successive encounters with Yeats, Hueffer, Hulme, the Imagist group of Richard Aldington and Hilda Doolittle (he edited the anthology *Des Imagistes*, 1914), then Wyndham Lewis (in the 'Vorticist' journal *Blast*), and T. S. Eliot. Married Dorothy Shakespear, 1913. Promoted the new talents of Eliot and James Joyce; edited Eliot's long manuscript to produce published version of 'The Waste Land' (1922). Published his own verse collection *Hugh Selwyn Mauberley* (1920), and the first of his Cantos in 1919. Early critical books: *The Spirit of Romance* (1910), *Pavannes and Divisions* (1918), *Instigations* (1920), *Indiscretions* (1923). Moved to Paris (1921–24), where he met his lifelong mistress, Olga Rudge (1 child); then settled in Rapallo, Italy (1924–45), producing successive instalments of the Cantos (final collection 1970). Later critical works include the misleadingly titled *Make It New* (1934) which is in fact a collection of old essays, *ABC of Reading* (1934), and *Guide to Kulchur* (1938). Broadcast Fascist propaganda on Rome radio in Second World War. Arrested by US forces in Pisa and imprisoned in small cage; extradited to US to face treason charges, but adjudged to be of unsound mind and placed in Washington sanatorium (1946). Awarded Bollingen Prize for the *Pisan Cantos* (1948), amid great controversy. Permitted to return to Italy (1958); last years largely silent; died in Venice. Critical writings collected by T. S. Eliot in *Literary Essays of Ezra Pound* (1954) and by William Cookson in *Selected Prose 1909–1965* (1973).

> Ackroyd, P., *Ezra Pound* (1981). (Short but lavishly illustrated life.)
> Carpenter, H., *A Serious Character: The Life of Ezra Pound* (1988).
>   (Standard biography.)
> *Letters of Ezra Pound, 1907–1941*, ed. D. D. Paige (1950).
> Stock, N., *Life of Ezra Pound* (1970).
> Tytell, J., *Ezra Pound: The Solitary Volcano* (1987).

> See: Bell, I. F., *Critic as Scientist: The Modernist Poetics of Ezra Pound* (1981).
> De Nagy, N. C., *Ezra Pound's Poetics and Literary Tradition* (Bern, 1966).
> Gugelberger, G. M., *Ezra Pound's Medievalism* (Frankfurt, 1978).
> Kayman, M. A., *The Modernism of Ezra Pound: The Science of Poetry*
>   (1986).
> Kenner, H., *The Pound Era* (Berkeley, CA, 1971).
> Lindberg, K. V., *Reading Pound Reading* (New York, 1987).
> Ruthven, K. K., *Ezra Pound as Literary Critic* (1990).
> Singh, G., *Ezra Pound as Critic* (Basingstoke, 1994).

RALEIGH, Sir Walter Alexander (1861–1922) born in London, son of a Congregationalist minister. Schooled in Edinburgh and London. Studied at University College, London, and King's College, Cambridge, where he briefly edited the *Cambridge Review* and published a paper given to the Browning Society (1884). Graduated in History (1885); took up post as Professor of English Literature at Anglo-Oriental College, Aligarh (1885–87); returned from India for medical reasons. Lectured at Victoria University, Manchester. Married Lucie Jackson, 1890; five children. Succeeded A. C. Bradley as Professor of Modern Literature and History at Liverpool (1890–1900). Published *The English Novel* (1894), *Robert Louis Stevenson* (1895), and the widely-ridiculed *Style* (1897). Gave lectures at Cambridge, published as *Milton* (1900). Succeeded Bradley again as Professor of English at Glasgow (1900–04); published *Wordsworth* (1903) and prefatory essays on Hakluyt and

Blake. Became first holder of new chair in English Literature at Oxford (1904–22). Wrote *Shakespeare* (1907); lectured in South Africa; edited *Johnson on Shakespeare* (1908); published *Six Essays on Johnson* (1910). Received knighthood in 1911. Gave up criticism for war propaganda from 1914: wrote patriotic introduction to *Shakespeare's England* (1916), and several lectures collected as *England and the War* (1918). Accepted invitation to write official history of Royal Air Force; completed only the first volume (1922) of *The War in the Air*. Contracted typhoid fever during flight to Baghdad while researching second volume; died in Oxford. Various lectures posthumously collected as *Some Authors* (Oxford, 1923); lecture-notes and other fragments collected as *On Writing and Writers* (ed. G. Gordon, 1926).

> Crum, V., *Sir Walter Alexander Raleigh* (1923).
>
> Jones, H. A., *Sir Walter Raleigh and the Air History: A Personal Recollection* (1922).
>
> *The Letters of Sir Walter Raleigh, 1874–1922*, ed. Lady Raleigh (2 vols, 1926).

> See: Baldick, C., *The Social Mission of English Criticism 1848–1932* (Oxford, 1983), 75–80.
>
> Hawkes, T., *That Shakespeherian Rag: Essays on a Critical Process* (1986), 51–72.
>
> Woolf, V., 'Walter Raleigh', *Collected Essays 1*, ed. L. Woolf (1966), 314–18.

RANSOM, John Crowe (1888–1974) born in Pulaski, Tennessee, son of a Methodist minister. Spent two years teaching in schools before graduating from Vanderbilt University, Nashville in 1909. Studied in Oxford, England, as Rhodes Scholar (1910–13), returning to Vanderbilt as lecturer (1914); teaching interrupted by service in US Army in France (1917–19). Published *Poems About God* (1919). Married Robb Reavill, 1920; three children. Founded *The Fugitive* with his student Allen Tate (1922). Published his most important verse collections *Chills and Fevers* (1924) and *Two Gentlemen in Bonds* (1927). Published the religious tract *God Without Thunder* (1930), and contributed to the Agrarian manifesto *I'll Take My Stand* (1930). Published his first critical book, *The World's Body* (1938), having now moved to Kenyon College, Ohio, as Professor of Poetry (1937–58). Here he founded and edited the distinguished *Kenyon Review* (1939–59), and published *The New Criticism* (1941), *Selected Poems* (1945), and *Poems and Essays* (1955). He won the Bollingen Prize in 1951. After retirement, he published expanded versions of the *Selected Poems* (1963, 1969), along with *Beating the Bushes: Selected Essays 1941–70* (1972).

> Young, T. D., *Gentlemen in a Dustcoat: A Biography of John Crowe Ransom* (Baton Rouge, LA, 1976).
>
> *Selected Letters of John Crowe Ransom*, ed. T. D. Young and G. Core (Baton Rouge, LA, 1985).

> See: Fekete, J., *The Critical Twilight* (1978), 41–103. (Extended Marxist critique.)
>
> Jancovitch, M., *The Cultural Politics of the New Criticism* (Cambridge, 1993).
>
> Magner, J. E., *John Crowe Ransom: Critical Principles and Preoccupations* (The Hague, 1971).
>
> Parsons, T. H., *John Crowe Ransom* (New York, 1969).

Wellek, R., *A History of Modern Criticism 1750–1950, Volume 6: American Criticism 1900–1950* (1986), 159–73.

Young, T. D., ed., *John Crowe Ransom: Critical Essays and a Bibliography* (Baton Rouge, LA, 1968).

RICHARDS, Ivor Armstrong (1893–1979) born in Sandbach, Cheshire, son of a Welsh factory manager. After his father's death (1902), moved to Bristol, studying at Clifton College. Suffered intermittently from tuberculosis and associated lung complaints. Studied Moral Sciences at Magdalene College, Cambridge (1911–15), and pursued passion for mountaineering. Lectured in English at Cambridge from 1919, collaborating with C. K. Ogden in *The Foundations of Aesthetics* (1922) and *The Meaning of Meaning* (1923). Published his major works of literary theory: *Principles of Literary Criticism* (1924), *Science and Poetry* (1926), and *Practical Criticism* (1929), the last based on experiments with his students and colleagues. Married Dorothy Pilley, 1926. Supervised the undergraduate work of William Empson published as *Seven Types of Ambiguity* (1930). Developed, with Ogden, the simplified language-learning system Basic English, spending much of his later life promoting it, partly on visits to China (1929–30; 1936–38) and in numerous textbooks. After *Coleridge on Imagination* (1934), devoted later writings mostly to general issues of language, education, and communication. Settled in Cambridge, Massachusetts, teaching at Harvard (1939–63); served on Harvard Committee, drafting important sections of its influential report, *General Education in a Free Society* (1945). Published *Goodbye Earth* (1959) and three further volumes of poetry. Retired to Cambridge, England (1973). Uncollected essays later appeared as *Complementarities* (ed. J. P. Russo, Cambridge, MA, 1976); a more representative selection has appeared as *Richards on Rhetoric* (ed. Ann E. Berthoff, New York, 1991).

> 'Beginnings and Transitions: I. A. Richards Interviewed by Reuben Brower', in Berthoff, ed., *Richards on Rhetoric* (New York, 1991), 3–22.
>
> 'An Interview Conducted with B. A. Boucher and J. P. Russo', in Richards, *Complementarities* (ed. J. P. Russo, Cambridge, MA, 1976), 254–69.
>
> Russo, J. P., *I. A. Richards: His Life and Work* (Baltimore, MD, 1989).
>
> *Selected Letters of I. A. Richards*, ed. John Constable (Oxford, 1990).

> See: Baldick, C., *The Social Mission of English Criticism 1848–1932* (Oxford, 1983).
>
> Bové, P. A., *Intellectuals in Power* (New York, 1986), 39–77.
>
> Brower, R., *et al.* (eds), *I. A. Richards: Essays in His Honor* (New York, 1973).
>
> Hotopf, W. H. N., *Language, Thought, and Comprehension: A Case Study in the Writings of I. A. Richards* (1965).
>
> Hyman, S. E., *The Armed Vision: A Study in the Methods of Modern Literary Criticism* (New York, 1948), 307–46.
>
> McCallum, P., *Literature and Method: Towards a Critique of I. A. Richards, T. S. Eliot and F. R. Leavis* (Dublin, 1983).
>
> Needham, J., *The Completest Mode: I. A. Richards and the Continuity of English Literary Criticism* (Edinburgh, 1982).
>
> Schiller, J. P., *I. A. Richards' Theory of Literature* (New Haven, CT, 1969).

SAID, Edward W. (1935–), born in Jerusalem, the son of an Anglican Palestinian businessman. Followed his family into exile in 1947; studied at Victoria College, a British school in Cairo; then at a boarding school in rural New York. Studied at Princeton, graduating in 1957; took his PhD at Harvard (1964). Taught English and Comparative Literature at Columbia University (1963–). Published his PhD thesis as *Joseph Conrad and the Fiction of Autobiography* (1966). Married Mariam Cortas, 1970; two children. Published *Beginnings* (1975), and his most influential work, *Orientalism* (1978), followed by *The Question of Palestine* (1979). Served as a member of the Palestine National Council (1977–91). Collected his essays as *The World, the Text and the Critic* (1983). Published *Culture and Imperialism* (1993) and *The Politics of Dispossession* (1994).

> Salusinszky, I., *Criticism in Society* (1987), 122–48. (Interview.)

> See: Bové, P., *In the Wake of Theory* (Middletown, CT, 1992).
> Sprinker, M., ed., *Edward Said: A Critical Reader* (Cambridge, MA, 1992). (Several essays, and an interview.)

SAINTSBURY, George Edward Bateman (1845–1933) born in Southampton, son of a dock administrator. Graduated from Merton College, Oxford (1866). Married Emily Fenn, 1868; two sons. Taught in various schools and contributed articles on French literature to the *Fortnightly Review*. Became full-time literary journalist (1876), associated with the circle of Lang, Henley, and Stevenson. Published more articles and anthologies, and *A Short History of French Literature* (1882). Edited Dryden's works (18 vols, 1882–93), and wrote *Dryden* (1881), *A History of Elizabethan Literature* (1887), and many articles for *Macmillan's Magazine*. Wrote numerous introductions to Balzac's novels and to selected editions of English authors. Meanwhile worked as assistant editor (1883–94) of the *Saturday Review*, upholding Tory opposition to Gladstone's Irish policy. Became Regius Professor of Rhetoric and English Literature at Edinburgh (1895–1915). Produced yet more books: *A History of Nineteenth Century Literature* (1896), *A Short History of English Literature* (1898), and his major work, the *History of Criticism and Literary Taste in Europe* (3 vols, 1900–4). Followed these with his *History of English Prosody* (3 vols, 1906–10) and *History of English Prose Rhythm* (1912); later works include *The English Novel* (1913), *The Peace of the Augustans* (1916), and *A History of the French Novel* (2 vols, 1917–19). Retired to Bath, continuing to write reviews. Also published *Notes on A Cellar-Book* (1920) – a connoisseur's guide to wines – and his fragmentary memoirs and reflections as *Scrap-Books* (3 vols, 1922–24).

> Jones, D. R., *'King of Critics': George Saintsbury, 1845–1933* (Ann Arbor, MI, 1992). (Definitive biography.)
> *George Saintsbury: The Memorial Volume*, ed. J. W. Oliver *et al.* (1945). (Tributes, etc.)
> Saintsbury, G., *A Last Vintage*, ed. J. W. Oliver *et al.* (1950). (Includes further memoirs.)

> See: Leuba, W., *George Saintsbury* (New York, 1967).
> Orel, H., *Victorian Literary Critics* (1984), 151–76.
> Potter, S., *The Muse in Chains* (1937), 126–39. (Jocular account.)
> Richardson, D., 'George Saintsbury and Art for Art's Sake in England', *PMLA* 59 (1944), 243–60.

SANTAYANA, George (1863–1952) born in Madrid as Jorge Ruiz de Santayana y Borrais; retained Spanish nationality. Shortly after birth, his mother took children from previous marriage (to an American) to Boston; he joined her there at the age of eight. Graduated from Harvard (1886), studied at Berlin, returned to Harvard. After PhD (1889), taught philosophy there, becoming Professor in 1907; students included Wallace Stevens, T. S. Eliot, Gertrude Stein. Published two volumes of poems (*Sonnets*, 1894, *A Hermit of Carmel*, 1901), and a verse tragedy, *Lucifer* (1899). Aesthetic and literary matters treated in *The Sense of Beauty* (1896), *Interpretations of Poetry and Religion* (1900), and *Three Philosophical Poets* (1910). Major philosophical work, on rational quest for harmony, is *The Life of Reason* (5 vols, 1905–6). Retired early from Harvard (1912), lived in London and Paris; settled in Rome from 1925. Later philosophical works are *Scepticism and Animal Faith* (1923) and four-volume *Realms of Being* series (1927–40). Portrayed American intellectual life in *Character and Opinion in the United States* (1920), *The Genteel Tradition at Bay* (1931), and in his novel *The Last Puritan* (1935). Published his *Works* in 14 volumes (1936–37), and his memoirs, *Persons and Places* (3 vols, 1944–53). In Second World War, took refuge in English nunnery in Rome. Died after falling down steps of Spanish consulate. Literary writings later collected by Irving Singer as *Essays in Literary Criticism* (New York, 1956); also *Selected Critical Writings*, ed. Norman Henfrey (2 vols, Cambridge, 1968).

> Cory, D. (ed.), *Letters of George Santayana* (New York, 1955).
> McCormick, J., *George Santayana* (New York, 1988). (Standard biography.)

> See: Arnett, W. E., *George Santayana* (New York, 1968). (General introduction to his thought.)
> Singer, I., *Santayana's Aesthetics: A Critical Introduction* (Cambridge, MA, 1957).
> Singer, I., Introduction to Santayana, *Essays in Literary Criticism* (New York, 1956).
> Stallknecht, N. P., *George Santayana* (Minneapolis, MN, 1971). (Brief; some treatment of the critical writing.)

SHAW, George Bernard (1856–1950) born and raised in Dublin, son of an impoverished lawyer. Worked in an estate agent's office, then left Dublin (1876) for London. Wrote five unsuccessful novels, studied Marx and Wagner, and joined Fabian Society (1884). Threw himself into journalism from 1885 as prolific book reviewer, music and drama critic. Edited *Fabian Essays in Socialism* (1889); wrote *The Quintessence of Ibsenism* (1891) and 'A Degenerate's View of Nordau' (1895; later revised as *The Sanity of Art*, 1908). Married Charlotte Payne-Townshend, 1898. Staged his first play, *The Widowers' Houses* (1892); other early plays failed until 1905 productions of *Man and Superman* and *Major Barbara*. Published his plays with long, opinionated prefaces (later reprinted as *Prefaces*, 1934); often protested against 'bardolatry' (i.e. Shakespeare-worship). Founded the weekly *New Statesman* (1913) and achieved lasting success with *Pygmalion* (1913). Ostracized for his wartime pamphlet *Common Sense About the War* (1914) – perceived as anti-British. Major post-war plays were *Heartbreak House* (1919) and *Saint Joan* (1924). Won Nobel Prize (1925). Resumed political writing with *The Intelligent Woman's Guide to Socialism and Capitalism* (1928). Collaborated in film versions of his plays. Reprinted three early works as *Major Critical Essays* (1931). Theatre reviews later collected as *Shaw's Dramatic Criticism, 1895–1898* (ed. J. F. Matthews, New York, 1959). Further posthumous collections include *Shaw on Shakespeare* (ed. E. Wilson, 1962) and *Shaw on Dickens* (ed. D. H. Laurence and M. Quinn, New York, 1985).

> Holroyd, M., *Bernard Shaw* (4 vols, 1988–92).

Collected Letters, 1874–1950, ed. D. H. Laurence (4 vols, 1965–88).

See: Adams, E. B., *Bernard Shaw and the Aesthetes* (Columbus, OH, 1971).
Fromm, H., *Bernard Shaw and the Theater in the Nineties: A Study of Shaw's Dramatic Criticism* (Lawrence, KS, 1967).

SHOWALTER, Elaine, *née* Cottler (1941–), born in Cambridge, Massachusetts, of Jewish immigrant parents. Graduated in English from Bryn Mawr in 1962; studied at Brandeis University (MA, 1964). Against parental veto, married English Showalter, a scholar of French literature, 1963; two children, moving with him to the University of California, Davis, where she began her doctoral research. Moved again to Princeton upon her husband's appointment there (1965), and became active in NOW. Taught English and Women's Studies at Rutgers University (1967–84). Completed her PhD on the double standard in Victorian criticism of women's fiction (1970). Edited an anthology, *Women's Liberation and Literature* (1971). Published *A Literature of Their Own* (1977), followed by important essays on feminist criticism, including 'Toward a Feminist Poetics' (1979). Moved to Princeton University as Professor of English (1984–). Published *The Female Malady* (1985), and edited a collection of feminist critical essays, *The New Feminist Criticism* (1985). Published *Sister's Choice* (1989), and *Sexual Anarchy: Gender and Culture at the Fin de Siècle* (1990), and edited an anthology of late-Victorian feminist stories, *Daughters of Decadence* (1993).

See: Moi, T., *Sexual/Textual Politics* (1985), 75–80.
Todd, J., *Feminist Literary History* (1988), 34–50.

SONTAG, Susan (1933–), born Susan Rosenblatt in New York City, the daughter of Jewish fur-traders. After her father's death (1938), she developed asthma, and was moved for the desert air to Tucson, Arizona. Her mother's second marriage (1945) took her to the Los Angeles suburbs under the Sontag name. Enrolled at the University of California at Berkeley at the age of 15 (1948), then transferred to University of Chicago, where she studied under Kenneth Burke and suddenly married the social theorist Philip Rieff, 1950; one child; divorced 1958. After graduation (1951), moved to Boston and took master's degrees at Harvard in English and philosophy (1954–55); then began teaching there as a doctoral student. Studied at Oxford and the Sorbonne (1957–58). After divorce, moved to New York as freelance writer, also teaching at City College and at Columbia. Published two novels, *The Benefactor* (1963), and *Death Kit* (1967), and two books of essays, *Against Interpretation* (1966), and *Styles of Radical Will* (1969). Travelled to Hanoi, Cuba, and Sweden; began writing and directing films. Discovered she had breast cancer (1975), and underwent prolonged treatment. Published the celebrated essays *On Photography* (1977) and *Illness as Metaphor* (1978), along with a volume of stories, *I, Etcetera* (1978), and a third collection of essays, *Under the Sign of Saturn* (1980). Published the essay *AIDS and its Metaphors* (1989), and a historical romance, *The Volcano Lover* (1992). A selection of her writings has appeared as *A Susan Sontag Reader* (1981).

Sontag, S., 'Pilgrimage', *New Yorker*, 21 December 1987, 38–54. (Autobiographical essay.)

See: Brookeman, C., *American Culture and Society Since the 1930s* (New York, 1984), 203–14.
Bruss, E. W., *Beautiful Theories: The Spectacle of Discourse in Contemporary Criticism* (Baltimore, MD, 1982), 203–80.

Nelson, C., 'Soliciting Self-Knowledge: The Rhetoric of Susan
Sontag', *Critical Inquiry* 7 (1980), 707–29.
Sayres, S., *Susan Sontag: The Elegiac Modernist* (1990).

SYMONS, Arthur William (1865–1945) born in Milford Haven, son of a Methodist
minister of Cornish origin; brought up in Devon. Edited Shakespeare plays.
First critical work, *Introduction to the Study of Browning* (1886), followed by
verse collections: *Days and Nights* (1889), *Silhouettes* (1892), and *London
Nights* (1895). On frequent visits to Paris, met Verlaine, Mallarmé, and other
Symbolist writers; translated Verlaine's poems and Zola's *L'Assommoir*;
became active connoisseur of female dancers in Paris and London. Wrote
critical articles for several London journals; befriended Yeats and other writers
of the Rhymers' Club; founded and edited the 'decadent' journal *The Savoy*
(1896). Wrote more decadent verses in *Amoris Victima* (1897) and *Images of
Good and Evil* (1899); published *Studies in Two Literatures* (1897), followed by
most influential book, *The Symbolist Movement in Literature* (1900). Married
Rhoda Bowser, 1901; translated novels of d'Annunzio. Collected further
critical essays in *Studies in Prose and Verse* (1904); also published *Spiritual
Adventures* (short stories, 1905), and *William Blake* (1907). Suffered mental
breakdown in 1908; confined to hospitals for two years, never recovering
fully. *The Romantic Movement in English Poetry*, written earlier, appeared in
1909. Later volumes mainly reprint earlier essays, as in *Figures of Several
Centuries* (1916) and *Dramatis Personae* (1923); the nine-volume *Collected Works*
remained incomplete. The memoir *Confessions* (1930) recalls his period of
derangement. Also published *Charles Baudelaire: A Study* (1920), and translated
selected poems and prose of Baudelaire. Died at his home in Wittersham, Kent.

> Beckson, K., *Arthur Symons: A Life* (Oxford, 1987). (Standard
>   biography.)
> Lhombreaud, R., *Arthur Symons: A Critical Biography* (1963).
>   (Substantial but often careless.)
> *Memoirs of Arthur Symons: Life and Art in the 1890s*, ed. K. Beckson
>   (University Park, PA, 1977). (Fragmentary but fascinating.)
> *Letters to W. B. Yeats, 1892–1902*, ed. B. Morris (Edinburgh, 1989).

> See: Ellmann, R., *Golden Codgers* (1973). (Good chapter on *The Symbolist
>   Movement*.)
> Gibbons, T., *Rooms in the Darwin Hotel: Studies in English Literary
>   Criticism and Ideas 1880–1920* (Nedlands, W. A., 1973).
> Markert, L. W., *Arthur Symons: Critic of the Seven Arts* (Ann Arbor,
>   MI, 1988).
> Munro, J. M., *Arthur Symons* (New York, 1969). (Superficial on
>   criticism.)
> Temple, R. Z., *The Critic's Alchemy: A Study of the Introduction of French
>   Symbolism into England* (1953).

TATE, John Orley Allen (1899–1979) born in Winchester, Kentucky, the son of a
failed businessman. Studied at Vanderbilt University, Nashville (1918–23).
Co-founded *The Fugitive* with his teacher J. C. Ransom in 1922. Married
Caroline Gordon, 1924; divorced 1959, and moved to New York as a
freelance writer. Published *Mr Pope and Other Poems* (1928), and biographies
of Stonewall Jackson and Jefferson Davis, also co-editing *Fugitives: An
Anthology of Verse* (1928). Visited France on study scholarship (1928–30).
Contributed to the Agrarian manifesto *I'll Take My Stand* (1930). Published
Poems (1932); made second visit to France (1932–33). Began lecturing in
English at Southwestern College, Memphis (1934–36) and at The Woman's

College, Greensboro, N. Carolina (1938–39). Published *Reactionary Essays on Poetry and Ideas* (1936), *The Mediterranean and Other Poems* (1936), and *Selected Poems* (1937), along with his only novel, *The Fathers* (1938). Moved to Princeton as Poet in Residence (1939–42). Published *Reason in Madness* and *Sonnets at Christmas* (both 1941). Worked in Washington, DC, as poetry consultant to Library of Congress (1943–44). Moved to Tennessee to edit the *Sewanee Review* (1944–46); published more poems in *The Winter Sea* (1944). Worked as publisher's editor in New York (1946–48); then lectured at New York University (1948–51), publishing two further collections of essays, *On the Limits of Poetry* and *The Hovering Fly* (both 1948). Converted to Roman Catholicism (1950). Became Professor at University of Minnesota (1951–68), lecturing widely in Europe in the 1950s. Published more essays in *The Forlorn Demon* (1953) and in *The Man of Letters in the Modern World* (1955), followed by the *Collected Essays* (1959). Married the poet Isabella Gardner, 1959; divorced 1966; then his student Helen Heinz, 1966; three children. Retired to Sewanee. Collected his *Essays of Four Decades* (1969), and later his *Collected Poems* (1977). Posthumously collected were *The Poetry Reviews of Allen Tate, 1924–1944* (ed. A. Brown and F. N. Cheney, Baton Rouge, LA, 1983).

Squires, R., *Allen Tate: A Literary Biography* (Indianapolis, IN, 1971).

Sullivan, W., *Allen Tate: A Recollection* (Baton Rouge, LA, 1988).

Tate, A., *Memoirs and Opinions 1926–1974* (Chicago, 1975); also published as *Memories and Essays: Old and New, 1926–1974* (Manchester, 1976).

The Literary Correspondence of Donald Davidson and Allen Tate, ed. J. T. Fain and T. D. Young (Athens, GA, 1974).

The Republic of Letters in America: The Correspondence of John Peale Bishop and Allen Tate, ed. T. D. Young and J. J. Hindle (Lexington, KY, 1981).

See: Bishop, F., *Allen Tate* (New York, 1967). (Concentrates on the poetry; but some attention to critical writing.)

Hemphill, G., *Allen Tate* (Minneapolis, 1964).

Jancovitch, M., *The Cultural Politics of the New Criticism* (Cambridge, 1993).

Meiners, R. K., *The Last Alternatives: A Study of the Works of Allen Tate* (Denver, 1962).

Squires, R., ed., *Allen Tate and His Work: Critical Evaluations* (Minneapolis, 1972). (Collects several significant responses to Tate's work.)

TRILLING, Lionel (1905–75), born to immigrant Jewish parents in New York City, where he spent all his life; studied at De Witt Clinton High School and Columbia University, graduating in 1925. Worked in temporary teaching posts at University of Wisconsin (1926–27) and Hunter College, New York (1927–30), and wrote for the *Menorah Journal* (1925–31). Married Diana Rubin, 1929, who, as Diana Trilling, became a noted essayist; one child. Settled in Greenwich Village, and began long teaching career from 1932 in English department at Columbia, resisting anti-semitic hostility to become full professor (1948–75). Completed his long-delayed PhD thesis (1938), and published it as *Matthew Arnold* (1939). Published *E. M. Forster* (1943), and a novel, *The Middle of the Journey* (1947). Followed these with his best-known book, *The Liberal Imagination* (1950), a collection of essays that established him as the most important heir to Edmund Wilson among American liberal critics. Further essays were collected as *The Opposing Self* (1955), *A Gathering of*

Fugitives (1956), and *Beyond Culture* (1965). His last substantial work was
Sincerity and Authenticity (1972). Later essays appeared posthumously in *The
Last Decade* (ed. D. Trilling, 1979), and early essays were gathered in *Speaking
of Literature and Society* (ed. D. Trilling, 1980), as part of the 12–volume
Works of Lionel Trilling (1977–80).

> Anderson, Q., *Art, Politics, and Will: Essays in Honor of Lionel Trilling*
> (New York, 1977). (Includes some biographical material.)
> Tanner, S. L., *Lionel Trilling* (Boston, 1988).
> Trilling, D., 'Lionel Trilling: A Jew at Columbia', in L. Trilling,
> *Speaking of Literature and Society*, ed. D. Trilling (New York, 1980),
> 411–29.
> Trilling, L., 'Some Notes for an Autobiographical Lecture', in D.
> Trilling, ed., *The Last Decade* (New York, 1979), 226–41.

> See: Boyers, R., *Lionel Trilling: Negative Capability and the Wisdom of
> Avoidance* (Columbia, MO, 1977).
> Chace, W. M., *Lionel Trilling: Criticism and Politics* (Stanford, CA, 1980).
> Frank, J., *The Widening Gyre* (New Brunswick, NJ, 1963), 253–74.
> (On the conservative bias of Trilling's 'liberal' stance.)
> Krupnick, M., *Lionel Trilling and the Fate of Cultural Criticism* (Evanston,
> IL, 1986). (The most substantial study.)
> O'Hara, D. T., *Lionel Trilling: The Work of Liberation* (Madison, WI,
> 1988).
> *Salmagundi* 41 (Spring 1978). (Special Trilling issue.)
> Scott, N. A., *Three American Moralists: Mailer, Bellow, Trilling* (Notre
> Dame, IN, 1973).
> Shoben, E. J., *Lionel Trilling* (New York, 1981).
> Wellek, R., *A History of Modern Criticism 1750–1950, Volume 6:
> American Criticism 1900–1950* (1986), 123–43.

WELLEK, René (1903–), born in Vienna to a Czech father – a government lawyer
– and Italian mother. Moved to Prague in 1918; studied Germanic Philology
and English at Charles University from 1922, taking his PhD in 1926. Studied
at Princeton University (1927–8), also teaching German there. Returned
to Prague in 1930 and presented his *Habilitation* thesis, later published as
Immanuel Kant in England (1931). Taught at Charles University, and joined
the Prague Linguistic Circle (1930–35). Married Olga Brodská, a
schoolteacher, 1932; one child. Moved to London as lecturer in Czech
Language and Literature at the School of Slavonic Studies (1935–39);
contributed to *Scrutiny*. Moved to University of Iowa (1939–41), where he
met Austin Warren. Published *The Rise of English Literary History* (1941). Held
various fellowships, and trained US Army interpreters in the War. Became
a naturalized US citizen (1946) and accepted appointment as Professor of
Slavic and Comparative Literature at Yale University (1946–72). Published
(with Warren) *Theory of Literature* (1949). Published first two volumes (1955)
of his planned four-volume *History of Modern Criticism, 1750–1950*, which
eventually came to eight volumes (1955–92). Published *Concepts of Criticism*
and *Essays on Czech Literature* (both 1963), followed by third and fourth
volumes of the *History* (1965). After his first wife's death (1967), married
Nonna Shaw, a Professor of Russian Literature (1968). Published
Discriminations (1970) and *The Attack on Literature and Other Essays* (1982),
followed by fifth and sixth volumes of the *History* (1986). Injured in an
accidental fall, dictated the last two volumes (1991–92) from his sickbed.

> Bucco, M., *René Wellek* (Boston, 1981).

Wellek, R., 'Prospect and Retrospect', in Wellek, *The Attack on Literature and Other Essays* (Chapel Hill, NC, 1982), 146–58. (Brief survey of his career.)

See: Creed, W. G., 'René Wellek and Karl Popper on the Mode of Existence of Ideas in Literature and Science', *Journal of the History of Ideas* 44 (1983), 639–56.

Lawall, S., 'René Wellek: Phenomenological Literary Historian', in J. Strelka, ed., *Literary Theory and Criticism: Festschrift in Honor of René Wellek* (Bern, 1984), 393–416.

Lawall, S., 'René Wellek and Modern Literary Criticism', *Comparative Literature* 40 (1988), 3–24.

Webster, G., *The Republic of Letters: A History of Postwar American Literary Opinion* (Baltimore, MD, 1979), 177–89.

WILDE, Oscar Fingal O'Flahertie Wills (1854–1900), born in Dublin, son of an eminent eye surgeon and of the writer Jane 'Speranza' Wilde. Studied at Trinity College, Dublin, and Magdalen College, Oxford (1874–88) – where he met Ruskin and Pater, flirted with Catholicism and freemasonry, won the Newdigate poetry prize, acquired a reputation as an idle wit, and graduated with a double first. Moved to London; his aesthetic flamboyance caricatured in *Punch* and in the Gilbert & Sullivan comic opera *Patience* (1881). Published *Poems* (1881). Extensive lecture tour of USA (1882); met Whitman. Married Constance Lloyd (1884), read Huysmans' *A Rebours* on Paris honeymoon, and had two sons. Further lectures in Britain (1884–85), and occasional book reviews in *Pall Mall Gazette* (1885–89). Began homosexual affairs with Robert Ross, John Gray and others from 1886. Edited *Woman's World* (1887–89), and published 'The Portrait of Mr W. H.' (1889) and 'The Soul of Man Under Socialism' (1891). Published *The Happy Prince and Other Tales* (1888), *The Picture of Dorian Gray* (1890), and essays collected in *Intentions* (1891). Wrote the play *Salomé* in French; performance in England forbidden, but produced in Paris (1896). Found theatrical success with *Lady Windermere's Fan* (1892) and *A Woman of No Importance* (1893). Began turbulent affair from 1892 with Lord Alfred Douglas ('Bosie'), who introduced him to numerous rent-boys. Further success of *An Ideal Husband* and *The Importance of Being Earnest* (both 1895) shattered by Bosie's father, Marquess of Queensberry, who provoked libel case leading to further trials on indecency and sodomy charges. Convicted and sentenced to two years' hard labour, served at Pentonville and Reading (1895–97). Wrote *The Ballad of Reading Gaol* (1898) and *De Profundis* (posthumously published 1905). Spent last years in Paris, dying in a hotel room. Body transferred from Bagneux to Père Lachaise cemetery (1909). Critical writings collected as *The Artist as Critic* (ed. R. Ellmann, New York, 1969).

Ellmann, R., *Oscar Wilde* (1987). (Best of many lives.)
The Letters of Oscar Wilde, ed. R. Hart-Davis (1962).
More Letters of Oscar Wilde, ed. R. Hart-Davis (1985).

See: Ellmann, R., Introduction to Wilde, *The Artist as Critic* (New York, 1969).

Small, I., *Conditions for Criticism* (Oxford, 1991).

WILLIAMS, Raymond (1921–88), born near Abergavenny, Wales, the son of a railway signalman. Studied at Abergavenny Grammar School; won scholarship to study at Trinity College, Cambridge (1939–46). Married Joy

Dalling, 1942; three children. Served in anti-tank regiment in the war
(1942–45). Worked in adult education (1946–60), teaching in Sussex. Co-
edited the journal *Politics and Letters* (1947–48). Published *Drama from Ibsen
to Eliot* (1952), and his major early works *Culture and Society, 1780–1950*
(1958) and *The Long Revolution* (1961), along with a novel, *Border Country*
(1960). Moved to Cambridge as University Lecturer in English and fellow of
Jesus College (1961–83). Published *Communications* (1962) and *Modern
Tragedy* (1966). Left the Labour Party (1966), to become important figure of
the British 'New Left'. Published *The English Novel from Dickens to Lawrence*
(1970), *Orwell* (1971), and his major late work, *The Country and the City*
(1974). Published *Keywords* (1976) and *Marxism and Literature* (1977);
collected his essays in *Problems in Materialism and Culture* (1981) and *Writing
in Society* (1984). Posthumous collections include *What I Came to Say* (1989)
and *The Politics of Modernism* (ed. T. Pinkney, 1989).

Inglis, F., *Raymond Williams* (1995). (Biography).

Williams, R., *Politics and Letters* (1979). (Fascinating sequence of
interviews.)

See: Eagleton, T., *Criticism and Ideology* (1976), 21–43. (Questions Williams's
'culturalism'.)

Eagleton, T., ed., *Raymond Williams: Critical Perspectives* (Oxford, 1989).

Morgan, W. J. and P. Preston, eds, *Raymond Williams: Politics, Education,
Letters* (Basingstoke, 1993).

O'Connor, A., *Raymond Williams: Writing, Culture, Politics* (Oxford,
1989). (Uninspired; extensive bibliography.)

Taylor, J. B., 'Raymond Williams: Gender and Generation', in T.
Lovell, ed., *British Feminist Thought: A Reader* (Oxford, 1990),
296–308.

Watkins, E., 'Raymond Williams and Marxist Criticism', *Boundary 2*,
4 (1976), 933–46; rpt. in Watkins, *The Critical Act: Criticism and
Community* (New Haven, CT, 1978).

WILSON, Edmund (1895–1972) born in Red Bank, New Jersey, son of an attorney.
Graduated from Princeton (1916); worked briefly as reporter on *New York
Evening Sun*. Served in US Army in France during Great War, as wound-
dresser, then in Intelligence Corps (1917–19). Worked as Managing Editor
of *Vanity Fair* (1922–23). Married an actress, Mary Blair, 1923; divorced 1929;
pursued numerous sexual affairs. Joined editorial staff of *New Republic*
(1923–31). Had nervous breakdown (1929). Published poems and essays in
Poets, Farewell! (1929), and a novel, *I Thought of Daisy* (1929); published major
study of modern literature as *Axel's Castle* (1931). Married Margaret Canby,
1930; who died 1932. Visited Russia (1935). Married Mary McCarthy,
1938; one child; divorced 1945. Published various books of essays, notably
The Triple Thinkers (1938) and *The Wound and the Bow* (1942), and an
historical work on Marxism, *To the Finland Station* (1940). Travelled in Europe
(1945). Married Elena Thornton (1946). Published short stories as *Memoirs
of Hecate County* (1946), and articles against the Cold War. Collected numerous
essays and reviews for the *New Yorker* and other journals in *Classics and
Commercials* (1950), *The Shores of Light* (1952), and *The Bit Between My Teeth*
(1965). Published various works on the Dead Sea Scrolls; on American
Indians; and a study of literature and the Civil War, *Patriotic Gore* (1962);
then an attack on pedantic scholarship in *The Fruits of the MLA* (1968).
Posthumous works include notebooks and journals (ed. L. Edel) published as
The Twenties (1975), *The Thirties* (1980), *The Forties* (1983), *The Fifties*

(1986), and *The Sixties* (1993). A Selection has appeared as *The Portable Edmund Wilson* (ed. L. Dabney, 1983).

Costa, E. H., *Edmund Wilson* (Syracuse, NY, 1980).
Edel, L., 'A Portrait of Edmund Wilson', in Wilson, *The Twenties* (New York, 1975), xvii–xlvi.
Meyers, J., *Edmund Wilson* (1995).
Wilson, E., *A Prelude* (New York, 1967), (Memoirs.)
Wilson, E., *Letters on Literature and Politics 1912–1972*, ed., Elena Wilson (New York, 1977).
The Nabokov-Wilson Letters: Correspondence Between Vladimir Nabokov and Edmund Wilson, 1940–1971, ed. Simon Karlinsky (New York, 1979).

See Castronovo, D., *Edmund Wilson* (New York, 1984).
Frank, C. P., *Edmund Wilson* (New York, 1970).
Groth, J., *Edmund Wilson: A Critic for Our Time* (Athens, OH, 1989).
Hyman, S. E., *The Armed Vision: A Study in the Methods of Modern Literary Criticism* (New York, 1948), 19–48. (Hostile; chapter omitted from later editions.)
Kermode, F., *Modern Essays* (1971), 119–36.
Kriegel, L., *Edmund Wilson* (Carbondale, IL, 1971).
Paul, S., *Edmund Wilson: A Study of the Literary Vocation in Our Time* (Urbana, IL, 1965).
Wain, J., ed., *An Edmund Wilson Celebration* (Oxford, 1978). (Several short studies, tributes, memoirs.)
Wellek, R., *A History of Modern Criticism 1750–1950, Volume 6: American Criticism 1900–1950* (1986), 99–122.

WIMSATT, William Kurtz, Jr (1907–75), born in Washington, DC, the son of a lumber merchant; studied there at Georgetown University, (BA, 1928; MA, 1929). Taught English and Latin at Portsmouth Priory School, Rhode Island (1930–35); studied at Catholic University of America (1935–36). Studied at Yale University towards his PhD (1939), later published as *The Prose Style of Samuel Johnson* (1941). Began teaching at Yale as instructor (1939), later becoming full professor (1955–75). Married Margaret Elizabeth Hecht, 1944; two children. Published two influential essays with Monroe C. Beardsley: 'The Intentional Fallacy' (1946), and 'The Affective Fallacy' (1949), and a further study of Johnson, *Philosophic Words* (1948). Published his early essays, including the collaborations with Beardsley, in *The Verbal Icon* (1954). Collaborated with Cleanth Brooks in writing *Literary Criticism: A Short History* (1957), contributing the greater part of this work. Published further essays as *Hateful Contraries* (1965) and, posthumously, as *The Day of the Leopards* (1976).

Brady, F. *et al.*, eds, *Literary Theory and Structure: Essays in Honor of William K. Wimsatt* (New Haven, CT, 1973).

See: Wellek, R., *A History of Modern Criticism 1750–1950, Volume 6: American Criticism 1900–1950* (1986), 281–92.

WINTERS, Arthur Yvor (1900–68) born in Chicago, but brought up near Pasadena, California; studied at University of Chicago (1917–18). Suffered from tuberculosis, spending two years in sanatorium at Santa Fé, New Mexico. Published *The Immobile Wind* (1921) and several further volumes of verse. Taught in New Mexico schools (1921–23); studied at University of Colorado

(1923–25). Taught French and Spanish at University of Idaho (1925–27). Married the poet and novelist Jane Lewis, 1926; two children. Joined English Department at Stanford University (1927–66; as full professor from 1949). Edited *The Gyroscope* (1929–31). While acting as Western editor of *Hound and Horn* (1932–34), completed his PhD (1934). Published his three most influential works: *Primitivism and Decadence* (1937), *Maule's Curse* (1938), and *The Anatomy of Nonsense* (1943). Collected these writings in *In Defense of Reason* (1947), after publishing *Edward Arlington Robinson* (1946). Published his *Collected Poems* (1952; revised 1960). Later books include *The Function of Criticism* (1957), *On Modern Poets* (1959), *The Poetry of W. B. Yeats* (1960), and *Forms of Discovery* (1967). Other critical writings appeared posthumously in *Uncollected Essays and Reviews* (ed. F. Murphy, Chicago, 1976).

> Levin, D., 'Yvor Winters at Stanford', *Virginia Quarterly Review* 54 (1978), 454–73.
> *Hart Crane and Yvor Winters: Their Literary Correspondence*, ed. T. F. Parkinson (Berkeley, CA, 1978).

See: Comito, T., *In Defense of Winters* (Madison, WI, 1986).
> Davis, D., *Wisdom and Wilderness: The Achievements of Yvor Winters* (Athens, GA, 1983).
> Holloway, J., 'The Critical Theory of Yvor Winters', *Critical Quarterly* 7 (1965), 54–68.
> Hyman, S. E., *The Armed Vision: A Study in the Methods of Modern Literary Criticism* (New York, 1948), 49–72.
> McLean, K. F., *The Moral Measure of Literature* (Denver, 1961).
> Sexton, R., *The Complex of Yvor Winters' Criticism* (The Hague, 1974).
> Wellek, R., *A History of Modern Criticism 1750–1950, Volume 6: American Criticism 1900–1950* (1986), 257–80.

WOOLF, Adeline Virginia, *née* Stephen (1882–1941), born in London, daughter of the man of letters Sir Leslie Stephen (editor of the *Dictionary of National Biography*) and his second wife Julia Duckworth; educated privately. Her mother's death (1895) was followed by the first of several bouts of mental disturbance. After her father's death (1904), settled in Bloomsbury with her two brothers and her sister Vanessa (who married Clive Bell in 1907); the Stephen and Bell households were the first centres of the Bloomsbury Group. Began regular series of anonymous reviews for *Times Literary Supplement* (1905). Married the political journalist Leonard Woolf (1912). Published her first novel, *The Voyage Out* (1915). With Leonard, established the Hogarth Press (1917), publishing works by Mansfield, Eliot, Freud, Woolf, and others. Published further novels: *Night and Day* (1919) and *Jacob's Room* (1922), and short stories in *Monday or Tuesday* (1921). Wrote reviews and essays for the *Nation and Athenaeum* and other journals; published the critical pamphlet *Mr Bennett and Mrs Brown* (1924), followed by selected essays and reviews in two volumes of *The Common Reader* (1925, 1932). Published major novels *Mrs Dalloway* (1925) and *To the Lighthouse* (1927). Lesbian affair with the writer Vita Sackville-West, inspired the novel *Orlando* (1928). Published lectures on women and literature in *A Room of One's Own* (1929), and later feminist reflections in *Three Guineas* (1938). Published further novels: *The Waves* (1931), *The Years* (1937), and *Between the Acts* (1941); along with *Flush* (1933) – a life of Elizabeth Barrett Browning's spaniel – and *Roger Fry* (1940), a more orthodox biography. Fearing the onset of madness, drowned herself. Posthumous volumes of her essays were edited by Leonard Woolf as *The Death of the Moth* (1942), *The Moment* (1947), *The Captain's Death Bed*

(1950), *Granite and Rainbow* (1958), and *Collected Essays* (4 vols, 1966–67). Numerous other selections have appeared, including *Women and Writing* (ed. M. Barrett, 1979) and *A Woman's Essays* (ed. R. Bowlby, 1992); the most comprehensive collection is the scholarly annotated edition *The Essays of Virginia Woolf* (ed. Andrew McNeillie, 6 vols projected, 1986–).

> Bell, Q., *Virginia Woolf: A Biography* (2 vols, 1972; one-volume edition, 1982).
>
> Gordon, L., *Virginia Woolf: A Writer's Life* (1984).
>
> *The Diary of Virginia Woolf*, ed. Anne Olivier Bell and Andrew McNeillie (5 vols, 1977–84).
>
> *The Letters of Virginia Woolf*, ed. Nigel Nicolson and Joanne Trautmann (6 vols, 1975–80).

> See: Bell, B. C. and Ohmann, C., 'Virginia Woolf's Criticism: A Polemical Preface', *Critical Inquiry* 1 (1974), 361–71.
>
> Brewster, D., *Virginia Woolf* (New York, 1962). (Chapter on the critical essays.)
>
> Caughie, P., *Virginia Woolf and Postmodernism* (Urbana, IL, 1991). (Chapter devoted to the criticism.)
>
> Da Silva, N. T., *Modernism and Virginia Woolf* (Windsor, 1990).
>
> Fox, A., *Virginia Woolf and the Literature of the English Renaissance* (Oxford, 1990).
>
> Goldman, M., *The Reader's Art: Virginia Woolf as Literary Critic* (The Hague, 1974).
>
> Guiget, J., *Virginia Woolf and Her Works* (1965).
>
> Humm, M., *Feminist Criticism: Women as Contemporary Critics* (Brighton, 1986), 123–54.
>
> Marcus, J., *Art and Anger: Reading Like a Woman* (Columbus, OH, 1988).
>
> Meisel, P., *The Absent Father: Virginia Woolf and Walter Pater* (New Haven, 1980). (Good study of the essays.)
>
> Rosenberg, B. C., *Virginia Woolf and Samuel Johnson: Common Readers* (Basingstoke, 1994).
>
> Sharma, K. K., *Modern Fictional Theorists: Virginia Woolf and D. H. Lawrence* (Atlantic Heights, NJ, 1982).
>
> Wellek, R., *A History of Modern Criticism 1750–1950, Volume 5: English Criticism 1900–1950* (1986), 65–84.
>
> Zwerdling, A., *Virginia Woolf and the Real World* (Berkeley, CA, 1986).

YEATS, William Butler (1865–1939) born in Dublin, son of portrait-painter Jack Yeats; schooled in London and Dublin. Came under influence of spiritualists; studied Blake. First notable works were folktales of *The Celtic Twilight* (1893), and *Poems* (1895); several verse collections followed. Associated both with Irish nationalists in Dublin – including Maud Gonne, by whose beauty he became obsessed – and with the London aesthetes of the Rhymers' Club, notably Symons. With Lady Gregory, founded the Irish Literary Theatre; staged his verse play *The Countess Cathleen* in 1899, followed by *Cathleen ni Houlihan* (1902). Established small journals to promote Irish theatre: *Beltaine* (1899–1900), *Samhain* (1901–08), *The Arrow* (1906–09). Published critical essays as *Ideas of Good and Evil* (1903). Co-founded (1904) and managed Abbey Theatre, Dublin, and defended Synge's plays. Developed mature verse style in *The Green Helmet* (1910), *Responsibilities* (1914) and *The Wild Swans at Coole* (1917). Collected more critical essays in *The Cutting of an Agate* (1912), combined with mystical speculation in *Per Amica Silentia Lunae*

(1918). Married Georgie Hyde-Lees (1917), using her dreams and 'automatic writing' as basis for schematic symbology of *A Vision* (1925). Spent part of Irish Civil War (1922–23) in old tower near Lady Gregory's Coole Park estate. Became senator (1922–28) of new Irish Free State; won Nobel Prize (1923); collected his *Essays* (1924). Published many of his greatest poems in *Michael Robartes and the Dancer* (1921), *The Tower* (1928), and *The Winding Stair* (1929). Published his *Collected Poems* (1933), *Collected Plays* (1934), and edited the *Oxford Book of Modern Verse* (1936). Underwent vasectomy (1934) in failed attempt to restore sexual vigour. Published further verse collections: *Words for Music Perhaps* (1932), *A Full Moon in March* (1935), and *Last Poems* (1939). Died outside Monaco, inspiring memorable elegy by Auden. Critical writings later collected in *Essays and Introductions* (1961) and in *Selected Criticsm* (ed. A. N. Jeffares, 1964).

> Ellmann, R., *Yeats: The Man and the Masks* (New York, 1949; revd, Oxford, 1979).
> Jeffares, A. N., *W. B. Yeats: A New Biography* (1988).
> Yeats, W. B., *Autobiographies* (1926; revd 1938).
> *The Letters of W. B. Yeats*, ed. A. Wade (1954).
> *Collected Letters of W. B. Yeats*, ed. J. Kelly (12 vols projected, Oxford, 1986–).

> See: Ellmann, R., *Eminent Domain: Yeats Among Wilde, Joyce, Pound, Eliot and Auden* (New York, 1967).
> Engelberg, E., *The Vast Design: Pattern in W. B. Yeats's Aesthetic* (Toronto, 1964; revd Washington, DC, 1988).
> Lentricchia, F., *The Gaiety of Language: An Essay on the Radical Poetics of W. B. Yeats and Wallace Stevens* (Berkeley, CA, 1968).
> Sena, V., *W. B. Yeats: The Poet as Critic* (1980).
> Temple, R. Z., *The Critic's Alchemy: A Study of the Introduction of French Symbolism into England* (New York, 1953).

Index